The Psychobiology of Sex Differences and Sex Roles

Edited by
Jacquelynne E. Parsons
University of Michigan

○ HEMISPHERE PUBLISHING CORPORATION
Washington   New York   London

McGRAW-HILL BOOK COMPANY
*New York   St. Louis   San Francisco   Auckland   Bogotá
Hamburg   Johannesburg   London   Madrid   Mexico
Montreal   New Delhi   Panama   Paris   São Paulo
Singapore   Sydney   Tokyo   Toronto*

THE PSYCHOBIOLOGY OF SEX DIFFERENCES AND SEX ROLES

1 2 3 4 5 6 7 8 9 0   E B E B   7 8 3 2 1 0 9

This book was set in Press Roman by Hemisphere Publishing
Corporation. The editors were Cindy De Moss and Rolfe W.
Larson; the production supervisor was Rebekah McKinney;
and the typesetter was Shirley J. McNett.
Edwards Brothers, Inc. was printer and binder.

Library of Congress Cataloging in Publication Data

Main entry under title:

The Psychobiology of sex differences and sex roles.

    Includes bibliographies and indexes.
    1. Sex difference (Psychology) 2. Sex differences.
3. Sex role. I. Parsons, Jacquelynne E.
BF692.2.P75   1980   155.3'3   79-22030
ISBN 0-07-048540-2

*To Christopher and Amy Parsons
and the children of today, in hope that
gender-role research will help to create
a more egalitarian world for them*

Contents

Contributors

JEANNE BROOKS-GUNN received her Ph.D. in educational psychology from University of Pennsylvania in 1975. She is currently at Educational Testing Service, Princeton, New Jersey, where she is doing work on infant social development.

DONALD M. BROVERMAN received his Ph.D. in clinical psychology from Clark University in 1958. Since then he has been at Worcester State Hospital where he is the director of the Psychology Department.

ANNE CLARKE is currently in the Psychology Department at Princeton University, doing research with Diane Ruble in the area of social development.

TONI FALBO received her Ph.D. in social psychology at UCLA. She is currently in the department of Educational Psychology at the University of Texas, Austin working on issues related to only children and to power strategies.

SUSAN REED HAHN is a graduate student in sociology at the University of California at Berkeley. She worked as a registered nurse for four years prior to reentering the University of California at Davis, where she graduated with highest honors in psychology. Hahn is a coeditor (with Karen Paige, Elizabeth Magnus, and Cher Carrie) of *The Female Reproductive Cycle: An Annotated Bibliography.* to be published by G. K. Hall. She has recently completed research on class and sex differences in rates of mental disorders over the life cycle. Her other major research interests are the sociology of the family and reproductive events and rituals.

ALEXANDRA G. KAPLAN received her Ph.D. in clinical psychology at Columbia University in 1968. She currently teaches at the University of Massachusetts, Amherst. She has coedited *Beyond Sex-Role Stereotypes* with J. Bean and has edited a special issue on androgyny for the *Psychology of Women Quarterly.*

EDWARD L. KLAIBER received his M.D. in 1956 and completed a research fellowship in endocrinology in 1962, both at Syracuse University. He has had a joint appointment to the Worcester Foundation for Experimental Biology and Worcester State Hospital since 1962.

FLORENCE LEDWITZ-RIGBY received a Ph.D. in endocrinology–reproductive physiology from the University of Wisconsin, Madison in 1972. She was an NIH postdoctoral fellow at the University of Pittsburgh School of Medicine from 1972 to 1974, visiting assistant professor in the University of Pittsburgh Department of Biology from 1974 to 1975, and has been assistant professor of biological sciences at Northern Illinois University since 1975. She has published several papers on cellular and molecular aspects of the control of ovarian function.

ELISABETH M. MAGNUS is currently at the University of California, Davis working with Karen Paige on issues related to female reproductive functioning. She is a coeditor of *The Female Reproductive Cycle: An Annotated Bibliography.*

HEINO F. L. MEYER-BAHLBURG is associate clinical professor of medical psychology in the Department of Psychiatry at the College of Physicians and Surgeons of Columbia University, New York City, and a research scientist at the New York State Psychiatric Institute, where he studies hormones, sex, and gender. From 1970 to 1977 he taught in the Department of Psychiatry and Pediatrics at the State University of New York at Buffalo and codirected a research program, similar to his current one at the Children's Hospital of Buffalo.

MALKAH NOTMAN attended the University of Chicago, (Ph.D. 1946, B.S. 1937) and the Boston University School of Medicine (1952). She trained in psychiatry at Boston State Hospital and Beth Israel Hospital and in psychoanalysis at the Boston Psychoanalytic Institute. She is currently associate clinical professor at Harvard Medical School and psychiatrist at the Beth Israel Hospital, where she teaches and also administers psychiatric consultations to obstetrics and gynecology. She is also on the faculty of the Boston Psychoanalytic Institute. She has been interested in the psychological development of women and in the relationship between life cycle concerns and development.

KAREN ERICKSEN PAIGE is an associate professor of psychology at the University of California at Davis. She received her Ph.D. in 1969 at the University of Michigan, where she began research on both the physiological and social causes of women's psychological responses to reproductive events such as menstruation. She and Jeffery M. Paige have recently completed a cross-cultural analysis of reproductive rituals of both sexes, *Politics and Reproductive Rituals,* to be published by University of California Press, and is a coeditor of the *Female Reproductive Cycle: An Annotated Bibliography.*

JACQUELYNNE E. PARSONS received her Ph.D. in developmental psychology at UCLA in 1974. She taught for $3\frac{1}{2}$ years at Smith College and is now at the University of Michigan, Ann Arbor. She has coauthored two other books—*Women and Sex Roles* (with I. Frieze, P. Johnson, D. Ruble, and G. Zellman) and *Sex Roles: Persistence and Change* (a special issue of the *Journal of Social Issues* coedited with I. Frieze and D. Ruble)—and published several articles on various achievement-related and career behaviors.

ANNE C. PETERSEN received her Ph.D. in system methods and issues at the University of Chicago in 1973. She is currently the director of the Laboratory for the Study of Adolescents and teaches in the Department of Psychiatry at the University of Chicago. She has published several articles on the interactions of biological and social events in adolescent development.

ALICE S. and *PETER E. ROSSI* are currently professors of sociology at the University of Massachusetts, Amherst. Alice's work on female roles and on biopsychological influences on parenting and Peter's work on program evaluation have appeared in a variety of journals and books.

DIANE N. RUBLE received her Ph.D. from the University of California at Los Angeles in 1973 and is currently assistant professor of psychology at Princeton University. She has coedited a special issue on sex roles for the *Journal of Social Issues* and has coauthored a textbook entitled *Women and Sex Roles: A Social Psychological Perspective*. In addition to her work on sex roles and attitudes toward menstruation, she is interested in social developmental processes, especially in the area of achievement and self-evaluation.

CAROLYN WOOD SHERIF received her Ph.D. in social psychology at the University of Texas, Austin in 1961. She is currently at Pennsylvania State University. Her work in the social psychology of groups and attitudes has appeared in a variety of journals and has served as the basis for several books that she has authored or coauthored.

WILLIAM VOGEL received his Ph.D. in clinical psychology from Clark University in 1959. He has been chief of service of a Research Depression Ward at Worcester State Hospital since 1962.

Preface

The question of the existence and origin of sex differences has been debated by philosophers and scientists for centuries. Much of the debate has centered around the relative importance of biological-versus-experiential influences. At one extreme it has been argued that men and women are destined by biology to play quite different roles in society and to have quite distinct personalities (e.g., Freud). At the other extreme it has been argued that sex roles in modern society result totally from markedly different socialization experiences for boys and girls; biology is assumed to play a minimal role in the maintenance of sex roles. Most scientific investigators today do not take a simple either–or position concerning the determinants of sex differences. Instead, human development is seen as the result of the dynamic interaction between an individual's biological makeup and experiences with the environment. The crux of the debate today lies in the relative role that biology plays in creating sex-role differences and in the specific nature of its influence.

Despite the progress in scientific thinking, public debate often reverts to the more simplistic issue of whether sex roles are primarily the result of biology or socialization. Advocates of the socialization view argue quite vehemently that biology ought not be considered important unless the evidence overwhelmingly indicates that it creates a universal difference, making virtually every woman different from every man on important traits and behaviors other than reproduction. These advocates of social change fear that the political pressure for new social roles will decrease to the extent that people believe that biological processes are implicated in sex-role behaviors. Based on this fear, there has been a bias against biological evidence coupled with a preference for socialization explanations of sex differences if the biological data leave any room for doubt. Since most behavior is multiply determined and since it is extremely difficult to separate the effects of biology and socialization, it is fairly easy to let this bias lead to an underplaying of the importance of biology.

While sympathetic with these political concerns, it is our view that both the socialization and biological evidence ought to be evaluated carefully and that real progress in sex-role change depends on an accurate understanding of the factors underlying current sex-role behavior. Only by fully understanding the bases of sex-role dimorphism can we set up an efficient strategy for change. As Raynor Reiter so aptly stated, "before a structure of inequality can be dismantled, we must first know the base on which it rests. Thus our [feminists inside and outside the academic field] common search for origins is implicitly a search for a strategy with a politicized goal" (1976, p. 1).

This book represents our attempt at evaluating the evidence relevant to biological explanations of sex-role dimorphism. Research on these subjects is difficult and still very much in the preliminary stages. Therefore much of what is discussed throughout the book is tentative at present.

The book grew out of a conference sponsored jointly by Smith College, the Five College Women's Studies Committee, and each of the following affiliated institutions: Mt. Holyoke, Hampshire College, Amherst College, and the University of Massachusetts, Amherst. The conference was designed to meet what we judged to be a growing need in the Five College Women's Studies Program. It was clear that there was an expanding empirical literature on biological processes that might increase our understanding of the origins and maintenance of sex roles. Yet most of us were not trained in the biological or biochemical sciences and were having difficulty evaluating this body of work. As a consequence, it was not having the impact on our own thinking or on our teaching that it might otherwise have had. The conference was designed to provide professionals concerned with women's studies in several separate academic disciplines with a critical overview and evaluation of the current status of biological theories of sex-role dimorphism and women's life cycles.

Experts who could integrate and evaluate the biological and experiential viewpoints on several important topics were brought together to present their critiques of the various subareas. The participants were also asked to meet together to share ideas. The chapters in this book are the outcome of that conference. Most of the participants wrote up their talks taking into account both the discussions at the conference and subsequent empirical research. As the need became apparent, other individuals were asked to contribute additional chapters.

As editor of the book and coordinator of the conference I would like to thank all the participants of both projects. Everyone was cooperative, prompt, and extremely helpful throughout both the planning and implementation stages. In addition I would like to thank President Jill Conway, who opened the doors of Smith College for the conference; the psychology departments at Smith College and the University of Michigan for providing me with the necessary secretarial and emotional support; the students at Smith College who helped throughout the project; the members of the Five College Women's Studies Program, especially Jackie Pritzen, who supported me emotionally and the projects financially; and finally my many friends and colleagues without whose support I would have collapsed under the responsibility and pressure. In producing this book the helpful suggestions of Robert Bannon, Carol Jacklin, Helen Lambert, and Daniel Offer, and the proofing and indexing of Carol Wallace are gratefully acknowledged.

Jacquelynne E. Parsons

I

PSYCHOSEXUAL
NEUTRALITY

1

Psychosexual Neutrality: Is Anatomy Destiny?

Jacquelynne E. Parsons
University of Michigan

In considering the possible role of biological processes in the origin and persistence of sex-role dimorphism, five issues need careful examination: (1) What is included under the rubric of biological influences? That is, how do we or even can we distinguish between biological and experiential influence? (2) How do biological processes interact with other behavioral determinants and socialization forces? (3) How does one determine if biological processes might be influential? (4) What are the specific mechanisms through which biology exerts its influence? (5) How modifiable are each of the various biological processes found to have important effects on gender-role dimorphism? Each chapter in this book addresses these issues: The chapters in the first two sections focus on gender-role dimorphism, those in the last two sections focus on patterns of fluctuations in female behavior that have been linked theoretically or empirically to biological processes. This chapter will focus primarily on the first three issues but will touch on the last issues in passing.

DELINEATING BIOLOGICAL INFLUENCES

The distinction between biological and experiential causes is rarely a clear issue. The empirical data are generally ambiguous enough to allow room for interpretations based more on the scientist's theoretical perspective than on the data itself. Key to these interpretations are the individual scientist's assumptions regarding the behavioral phenomena to be explained, the presumed mechanisms of the biological effect, and the malleability of this effect. Take the impact of anatomical differences on development as an example. In deeming anatomy to be destiny, Freud suggested that a child's anatomical structure, which is biologically determined, has an inevitable and irreversible effect on the child's personality development that is independent of any differential treatment from socialization agents. This stance has been classified

3

within the domain of biological influences on behavioral development prob-ably because it stresses an inevitable effect of anatomical features that originate inside the individual. In contrast, a number of investigators have focused on the effect of the child's anatomical sex on the caregivers' behavior. While these studies also place the causal source of the behavioral sequence in the child's anatomy, this work is generally cited as evidence supporting an experiential explanation of the origin of gender-role dimorphism. The link of anatomy to behavioral development is not assumed to be direct, internally generated, or inevitable. It is assumed that the caregiver's responses could be changed if the meaning of anatomical differences were changed and that the impact of caregivers responses can be modified by subsequent experiences.

The issue is further complicated by the range of effects that might reflect biological processes. For example, hormones have a direct effect on prenatal morphological development leading to anatomical gender dimorphism. Hor-mones also have a direct effect on the development of the brain such that exposure to prenatal androgens in sufficient dosages produces adult acyclic gonadal control. Both of these examples illustrate a direct link between a biological process and a gender-related consequence.

At a more indirect level, boys and girls may differ not because of gender dimorphism itself but because of interactions between gender and other bio-logical processes that have a direct effect on behavior and experience. For example, maturational rates, presumably a biological process, influence both behavior and experiences. Girls on the average mature more rapidly than boys. They are born more neurologically mature, pass many of the developmental milestones earlier, and reach sexual maturity sooner than boys (Frieze, Par-sons, Johnson, Ruble, & Zellman, 1978). Because boys and girls differ in their maturational rates, they may develop different skills thus eliciting different responses from their social environment. Thus some behavioral and socializa-tion differences may be mediated by the interaction of gender and some other biological process (e.g., maturation rate) rather than by biological processes linked more directly to gender (e.g., hormonal effects).

Even more indirectly, biological processes may affect some factor that is correlated with gender and is assumed to be related to other factors eliciting differential socialization experiences. For example, males are born larger and remain larger than females. Size and muscle mass may be linked phenomeno-logically to perceived fragility, which may in turn be related to the treatment of the individual. Thus boys, because they are assumed to be tough and because they are in fact born bigger and may have stronger neck muscles (see later section), may be treated less gingerly than girls (Maccoby & Jacklin, 1974).

Finally, if cognitive developmentalists like Parsons, Kohlberg, and Ullian (see Frieze et al., 1978) are correct, maturation influences cognitive processes, which in turn affect children's interpretations of the world and the nature of the stereotypes and personal goals that they develop. While only indirectly related to behavior and individual differences, maturational influences on cognitive processing represent an additional biological process that might influence gender-role dimorphism.

It can be seen from these examples that determination of what constitutes a biological effect is a complex issue. Biological processes can impinge on gender-role dimorphism directly (e.g., females have babies while males do not, males have penises while females do not) or indirectly (e.g., through maturational rates, body size, or morbidity rates). Further, no matter how the biological processes are manifest, their influence on behavior is mediated by their interaction with experiential forces. Finally, the interpretation of a specific cause as biological, experiential, interactional, or dialectical is dependent upon a variety of extraneous factors, such as the theoretical orientation of the interpreter, and the assumed inevitability and permanence of the effect.

Interaction between Biology and Experience: A Dialectical Approach

As stressed in the preceding section, it is impossible to delineate biological effects independent of a consideration of experiential effects. Biological processes do not unfold in a cultural, experiential vacuum. Likewise the delineation of experiential effects independent from a consideration of biological processes is futile, if not impossible. Experience does not accumulate in a biologically neutral organism. In addition, neither of these processes (biological or experiential) take place in a sociohistorically neutral context. Chapter 2 presents a thorough discussion of a dialectical model of the interactive effects of biology and experience. Let me note briefly here the important points of this model. First, it is assumed that individuals continue to grow and change throughout their life-spans. Second, this growth is determined by the interplay of biological, psychological, sociocultural, and historical processes. Third, the interactive nature of development is itself not static but shifting and accumulating across time. Thus not only the relative importance of each of these processes but the form of the interaction between them changes as an individual grows and develops. Consequently there will be no easy answer to the question of the origin of gender-role dimorphism. One will need to specify the particular behavior being considered, the developmental age of individuals being considered, and the sociocultural environment in which these individuals are developing. Such an analysis may help us describe the interaction of biological and experiential forces at one point in time. But even more interestingly, such an analysis may lead us to an investigation of the nature of the interactive processes themselves rather than to a static analysis of the differential causes of temporally fixed behavioral events.

Sources of Evidence Suggesting Biological Mediators

Several sources of evidence have been used to generate hypotheses regarding possible biological influences. Classically these sources fall into four basic clusters: (1) studies of hormonal variations, either naturally or experimentally induced; (2) studies of gender differences in infants and very young children; (3) cross-cultural studies of gender-role dimorphism, and (4) cross-primate studies of gender-role dimorphism. Evidence of consistent gender-related effects from each of these clusters have formed the empirical foundation for innumerable biological hypotheses. Evidence from each will be discussed in the following sections.

STUDIES OF HORMONAL VARIATIONS

Genetic and Hormonal Influences on the Developing Anatomical Structure

Though biology's influence on sex differences in behavior remains a debatable issue, its impact on anatomical gender dimorphism is reasonably clear. An embryo's genetic sex (XX or XY) determines whether its gonadal cells become ovaries or testes. If the human embryo carries a Y chromosome, testes are formed approximately 6 weeks after fertilization has taken place. These embryonic testes then begin producing androgens. If the embryo carries two X chromosomes, the gonadal differentiation begins later and by the 6th month of gestation two ovaries have formed. Further differentiation of reproductive structures is primarily dependent on the presence or absence of androgens. Thus for about 6 weeks the fetus retains the potential to develop into either a male or female. Complete anatomical differentiation as a male requires the presence of both androgen and a Y chromosome. Differentiation as a fertile female depends on the *absence* of androgen and the presence of two X chromosomes (Money & Ehrhardt, 1972).

In addition to controlling the morphological development of a fetus, a number of studies indicate that prenatal hormones also have some influence on the development of an animal's brain (e.g., Gorski, 1968; Goy, Bridson, & Young, 1964). Prenatal hormones have been implicated in the brain's control over the release of gonadal hormones following puberty, which is indirectly controlled by the hypothalamus. More specifically, the hypothalamus controls the hormonal secretions of the pituitary gland, which in turn regulate the release of the gonadal hormones after puberty. Evidence from animal research indicates that the presence of fetal androgens at a critical period in development causes a gender-related differentiation of the hypothalamus producing the acyclic pattern of gonadal hormone control characteristic of males.

Hormonal Influence on Behavior

Experimental Studies with Animals

If prenatal androgens have such a powerful influence on the differentiation of the reproductive system and on at least certain areas of the brain, early exposure to androgens may also have psychological and behavioral consequences for the developing fetus. The results of animal studies investigating the behavioral effects of early hormones are quite complex and often depend on the particular technique and species used. In general, however, the findings indicate that the levels of hormones, especially androgens, present during critical periods early in development affect the behavior patterns of most laboratory animals (e.g., rats, mice, hamsters, rabbits, and monkeys), in two ways. First, the levels of hormones present during early development affect some kinds of behaviors in the young animal, such as activity level and rough-and-tumble play. Both genetic male and female animals exposed to prenatal androgens exhibit mating and nonmating behavior (such as fighting) characteristic of the males of the particular species being studied. For example, prenatally androgenized female rhesus monkeys exhibit a high incidence of rough-and-tumble play and a leg-clasp sexual mount—behaviors characteristic of male rhesus monkeys (Money & Ehrhardt, 1972; Young, Goy, & Phoenix, 1964). However, it should be noted that such effects are not necessarily specific to the early administration of androgen. Injections of either estrogen or androgen into newborn female rats produced increased fighting behavior in adulthood (Bronson & Desjardins, 1968).

Second, early hormone levels mediate the sensitivity of the mature animal to gonadal hormones. The sexual behavior of most subprimate mammals is heavily dependent on circulating levels of hormones; female mating behavior is generally elicited by the presence of appropriate stimulus when the female has been exposed to female hormones. The presence of female hormones does not elicit female sexual behavior in genetic adult female rats who have been exposed neonatally to androgen. Instead these females are responsive only to injections of androgen, which elicit the standard masculine sexual behavior such as increased mounting and sometimes simulated copulation.

In sum, experimental studies with animals demonstrate a relationship between hormones and behavior. However, the implications of such findings for gender-role dimorphism in humans are unclear. It is difficult to generalize findings from one species of rodent to another, much less from rodents to humans. In addition, the effects of hormones on behaviors become less dramatic, the cortex exerts increasing control, and thus the role of learning and experience becomes more important as the evolutionary ladder is ascended.

Correlational Studies with Humans

Comparable experimentation with humans is out of the question, but there are naturally occurring variations in prenatal hormonal exposure. Money, Ehrhardt, and their associates have used these naturally occurring deviations from the normal pattern of sexual differentiation to assess the possible impact of prenatal hormones on human gender-role dimorphism. However, a word of caution is necessary before beginning this review. Since prenatal hormonal experimentation with humans is ethically and practically out of the question, the studies reported in this section are based on a small number of clinical cases. The subjects differed from a normal sample in several important ways, for example, prenatal hormonal history, appearance of genitalia at birth, and membership in a clinical population. Given the uniqueness of these individuals, generalizations must be made with extreme caution. In addition, the causal origins of their behavioral patterns are unclear. The patterns could have resulted from their exposure to the prenatal hormones, their familiarity with the clinical setting, their awareness of their own uniqueness, the reactions of others who know about their unique status, or from some interaction of two or more of these.

Androgenized Genetic Females   The best clinical evidence for the effects of prenatal androgens on human behavior comes from the studies of genetic females born with masculinized external genitalia as a result of prenatal exposure to androgens. In two such studies, extensive interviews were given to 25 fetally androgenized genetic females ranging in age from 4 to 16 who had been receiving cortisone since birth and/or had undergone surgical feminization early in life and a control group matched on age, socioeconomic status, race, and IQ (see Money & Ehrhardt, 1972). In a more recent study Ehrhardt and Baker (Note 1) used the siblings of the patients as the control group and used both male and female patient groups. Unfortunately, the data in all three studies come primarily from the reports of the mothers, who are not unbiased observers. Thus the results of all three studies must be interpreted cautiously.

In general the fetally androgenized female subjects showed a higher incidence of interest in masculine-associated clothing and toy preference than the control subjects and relatively less interest in infant care and feminine-associated clothing and toys. They considered themselves tomboys and were considered as such by their mothers; they reported a greater interest in careers but not to the exclusion of eventual romance, marriage, and motherhood.

These data suggest that fetal exposure to androgens is associated with a higher incidence of "masculine" sex-typed behaviors and attitudes. But, as noted earlier, these androgenized girls differed from the control populations in several ways, only one of which was the prenatal exposure to androgens. Most importantly, they were more familiar as a group with the clinical setting and were aware of their unique status. Finally, because of their parents' knowledge, it seems very likely that they were exposed to very different socialization experiences than were the control children. Thus it is possible that the results reflect a greater willingness of the clinical sample to mention cross-sex-typed attitudes and behaviors rather than a true behavioral difference between the patient group and the control group. This alternative interpretation seems even more plausible after examining the responses of the control group. It is unusual that such a high proportion of the control sample preferred dresses, wearing slacks or shorts only occasionally, and played only with dolls and that none expressed any ambivalence about their female sex role. Data from other sources (Brown, 1956, 1957; Hartup & Zook, 1960; Kagan, 1964) suggest a much higher incidence in most young girls of ambivalence about their sex role, of wearing slacks, and of playing with toys other than dolls.

It is interesting to note that while the androgenized females did evidence higher acitivity levels, they were not more physically aggressive. A higher incidence of physically aggressive behavior in males is one of the few sex differences in children and animals that finds repeated support in experimental studies (Maccoby & Jacklin, 1974). The lack of significant differences in these studies suggests that socialization dictates the expression, if not the emergence, of any potential for greater aggressive behavior that might be created by prenatal androgens. Perhaps instead of physical agressiveness per se, prenatal androgens predispose the developing organism to a higher level of physical activity, the exact manifestation of which is dependent on socialization (Frieze et al., 1978). Alternatively, prenatal androgens may create a potential for aggressiveness that requires postnatal androgens for its expression. Since these females are being treated and therefore are not being exposed to postnatal androgens, it would not be expected that they would exhibit the typically high level of aggression displayed by males (Frieze et al., 1978).

Turners' Syndrome and Androgen-insensitive Syndrome What happens when a fetus that is not a genetic female (XX) is not exposed to androgen? There are two clinical syndromes relevant to this question: Turner's syndrome (XO) females and androgen-insensitive (XY) males. Since members of these groups are not exposed to androgens prenatally, they develop female external genitals and are generally reared as females. But because they do not have two X chromosomes, neither group has ovaries. If individuals with either syndrome develop normal feminine behavior patterns, then it can be concluded that the feminine behavior patterns are not dependent on the possession of either two X chromosomes or ovaries.

Using a methodology comparable to that used in the study of the adrenogenital syndrome population, Ehrhardt, Greenberg, and Money (1970) interviewed 15 girls with Turner's syndrome, 10 XY androgen-insensitive females, and 15 matched controls. In general both patient groups were as feminine in their behavior and interest patterns as the control group and more so than the andrenogenital syndrome populations. Thus the development of a normal female gender-role behavior pattern is not dependent on the presence of ovaries or two X chromosomes.

What does seem to be important for the development of gender-role identity is the assigned sex of rearing (Money & Ehrhardt, 1972). In each of these three clinical populations the children were labeled and reared as females, and in each population the children developed a normal female gender identity despite wide variations in their genetic and prenatal hormonal sex.

Hormonal Fluctuation in Adults   Normally occurring hormonal fluctuation in adult women has provided another natural "experiment" of hormonal effects on human behavior. There is a long tradition of correlating behavioral rhythms with women's hormonal fluctuations. Since this is the topic of Part III of this book, I will not discuss it further here.

There has also been some recent work on hormonal fluctuation in men. Perskey and his colleagues (e.g., Persky, Smith, & Basu, 1971) have demonstrated a positive link between testosterone production rates and responses to self-report measures of hostility. Goldberg (1973) used this evidence to support his conclusion that men are biologically more aggressive than women. This conclusion is unwarranted for several reasons. First, while testosterone may be related to some specific behaviors like hostility, it is an overgeneralization of these results to assume a causal relation with the broad array of loosely defined behaviors commonly associated with the concept of aggression. Second, it is unclear as yet what these specific testosterone-linked behaviors might be. Hostility and sexual libido are possible candidates, but the evidence even for these is still equivocal (Archer, 1976; Rogers, 1976). Third, the causal direction of the relationship is also unclear at present. Several studies have demonstrated the responsiveness of testosterone production systems to environmental fluctuations. For example, Rose and his colleagues (e.g., Kreuz, Rose, & Jennings, 1972; Rose, Holaday, & Bernstein, 1971) have shown that human males and other higher primates "respond to stress with the suppression of androgens" (Kreuz et al., 1972, p. 479). Levels of androgen production have also been shown to be responsive to anticipated sexual activity ("Effects of," 1970).

Fourth, the generalization of hormonal effects found in men to the broader issue of gender differences is unfounded. Higher levels of androgens may foster hostility or sexual libido in men; but men are not necessarily naturally hostile or more sexual than women because they have higher levels of androgens than women. The body has an amazing ability to develop tolerance levels for commonly present chemicals. Males and females may have different tolerance levels for gonadal hormones with the result that low levels of androgens may have as marked effects in females as high levels have in males. Evidence suggests that this is the case (Rossi, 1977). Similarly, we know that prenatal exposure to androgens alters the responsiveness of the central nervous system to gonadal hormones in some very specific ways. The full extent of these influences are not yet known, but it seems likely that the biological consequences of various levels of both male and female hormones are not equivalent in men and women. Finally, even if a link is clearly established between androgens and some components of aggressiveness and sexuality, the behavioral expression of this relationship is undoubtedly subject to environmental forces. Recall that adrenogenital females were not any more aggressive than their female controls. Cross-cultural variations also attest to the malleability of this relationship, if it exists, and to the ability of females to learn aggressive or sexual behaviors even in the absence of male levels of androgens.

Conclusions

What then can be concluded from studies of hormonal variations in humans? Exposure to prenatal androgens probably has some behavioral effects, especially with regard to activity level and "tomboyism," but the nature of these effects and their interaction with experience is not clear. As pointed out in Chapter 4, the heightened androgen exposure may result in more androgynous behavior, especially for females. These effects could be indirect consequences of the girls' increased activity level. Because they have higher activity levels, they may play more outdoor, "masculine" games, which brings them into more contact with males and consequently with male concerns. Thus, because these girls are around boys more, they may be exposed to a wider range of models than most girls and may develop more androgynous styles and aspirations. The evidence for this interpretation or any other is quite weak at present.

The effects of adult hormonal fluctuations are even harder to interpret. By adulthood, socialization and culture have had a major impact on the individual. Consequently, the separation of biological and experiential factors at this time is extremely difficult if not impossible.

INFANT SEX DIFFERENCES

Investigations of gender dimorphism in infancy and early childhood are another source of biological hypotheses. Assuming that the effects of culture accumulate with age, the effects of culture should be at a minimum in infants. Sex differences found at or near birth may be constitutional. It is less clear whether differences emerging later in life result from biological processes, experience, or an interaction between the two. However, it is important to note that, no matter how close to birth sex differences appear, cultural training and experience may already have had an effect and that, no matter how old the child is, biological effects can still emerge.

The task of examining sex differences in very young infants and attempting to relate them to later behaviors is not easy. First, the methodological problems of testing young infants are enormous. One must control for the state of the infant; a crying or hungry infant is likely to respond quite differently than a sleeping or peaceful one. One also must select characteristics that are stable over time. In a recent study of newborns, only 12 out of 31 behaviors proved to be stable enough for use in longitudinal analysis (Bell, Weller, & Waldrop, 1971).

Determining how to relate the kinds of things that infants do to characteristics of older children and adults poses another set of problems. For example, Bell et al. (1971) found only one stable behavior that revealed a sex difference: males were able to lift their chins higher than females when placed on their stomachs. It is difficult to intuit the kinds of later characteristics this difference would produce. Nevertheless, some infant responses have been related to later behavior patterns (see Bell et al., 1971; Kagan, 1970). Tactile sensitivity, for instance, is related to vigor, assertiveness, and persistence in the later preschool years (Bell et al., 1971). Thus it is of interest to know whether infant sex differences are found in such behaviors.

Possible differences in rate of maturation between boys and girls present another obstacle to the study of sex differences in infants. If, for example, a particular function develops earlier in girls than in boys, then a sex difference in that function may represent a developmental difference rather than a true sex difference. In other words, equating the sexes on age may not provide an adequate comparison.

There are some indications that the sexes do differ in rate of maturation. Based on evidence such as rate of bone ossification (Roche, 1968) and pattern of electroencephalographic (EEG) recordings (Engel & Benson, 1968), Garai and Scheinfeld (1968) concluded that females are 1-6 weeks more mature than males at birth. However, the girls' skeletal advantage disappears by the 2d year (Maccoby & Jacklin, 1974), and the difference does not always generalize to other systems. For example, the functions of the orbital cortex may develop earlier in males than in females (Goldman, Crawford, Stokes, Galkin, & Rosvold, 1974). While Hindley (1967) reported that girls walk earlier than boys, other studies (Hindley, Filliozat, Klackenberg, Nicolet-Meister, & Sand, 1966; Peatman & Higgins, 1940; Scott, Ferguson, Jenkins, & Cutter, 1955) have failed to demonstrate significant sex differences. Similar inconsistencies have been reported in studies using various infant developmental scales, such as the Bayley Developmental Scales, the Gesell Developmental Schedule, and the California Infant Scale (Bayley, 1933, 1965; Frankenburg & Dodds, 1967; Gardner & Swiger, 1958; Hindley, 1965; Rosenblith, 1961; Singer, Westphal, & Niswander, 1968). Thus while there may be maturational differences in some areas, one gender is not consistently ahead of the other; nevertheless, when there are significant gender effects, it is generally the female who is the more mature. Thus one should be cautious in interpreting gender differences found in young children, since they may be reflective of a temporary maturational difference as much as of a more permanent gender difference.

It should be noted, however, that early maturational differences could produce effects that are still evident long after the maturational differences have disappeared. These early differences could set into motion a chain of interaction patterns between children and both their parents and their broader social environment that reinforce and maintain certain behavior patterns, coping strategies, or cognitive styles (Bell, 1968). For example, a less colicky baby may be more easily soothed by words of comfort, which in turn reinforces the mother's talking. Consequently, because the baby is exposed to more verbal stimulation, she or he may learn to speak earlier, which in turn should elicit even more verbal stimulation from her or his parents and further language development.

Infant Behaviors Related to Aggression

Activity Level

Activity level in infancy is one possible precursor of later aggressive-assertive behaviors. Exposure to prenatal androgens is related to both the activity level and aggressive behaviors of animals and possibly humans. Since human infants cannot be aggressive in the strictest sense of the term, the effects of prenatal androgen might be manifest in some measure of the general level of their gross motor activity. And, if both activity level and aggression are affected by exposure to prenatal androgens, males should be both more active throughout their lives and more aggressive in a variety of situations.

Another argument linking infant activity level to later aggression suggests that aggression may be the result of parent-child interactions that are directly influenced by the infant's activity level (Bell, 1968). An infant who is very active and awake much of the time may create extra work for caretakers and elicit certain interactions with caretakers, which in turn directly affect the development of aggression-related behavior.

Both of these arguments assume a link between aggressiveness in children and activity levels in infants. If male children are indeed more aggressive than female children, then male infants should be more active than female infants. Moss (1967) provided initial support for this hypothesis. More recent studies, however, have not yielded consistent sex differences in the general level of infant activity (e.g., Bell et al., 1971; Clarke-Stewart, 1973; Kagan, 1970), at least during the first year (Korner, 1974; Maccoby & Jacklin, 1974). Nor have they revealed any consistent sex difference in the response of infants to caretakers that would support Bell's hypothesis (Korner, 1974).

Irritability

Some evidence suggests that male infants are fussier or more irritable than female infants (e.g., Moss, 1967). The results depend, however, on a variety of other factors, such as specific age at testing, prenatal and delivery complications, and birth order. Nevertheless, when differences are found, male infants are generally the more irritable.

These early sex differences may be a function of the greater immaturity of male infants at birth and of the higher incidence of pregnancy and birth complications for male infants (Bell et al., 1971). There is an association between complications during pregnancy and delivery and infant irritability; infants who experience complications are more irritable. Parmalee and Stern

(1972) concluded that the higher incidence of irritability in male infants might be related to this higher incidence of prenatal and birth complications among males. In support of their hypothesis, the likelihood of finding sex differences in irritability decreases when experimental samples consist only of children born in normal deliveries.

Whatever the cause of this early difference in irritability, gender-related differences in neonatal irritability could set in motion a social interaction pattern that would result in boys being more negative, resistive, and aggressive than girls. Circular interactive processes between the parent and child thus could turn the irritable baby into the aggressive child (Bell, 1968).

Infant Behaviors Related to Nurturance and Social Orientation

The popular stereotype and some empirical data suggest that females are more nurturant and oriented toward the social environment than are males. Early response patterns to human faces might shed light on the origin of such differences. Sex differences in these infant behaviors would suggest the possibility of biological influences on sociability. Unfortunately, the relevant data are equivocal. While some studies support a gender difference in response to faces and humans (e.g., Beckwith, 1972; Clarke-Stewart, 1973; Kagan, Henker, Hen-Tov, Levine, & Lewis, 1966), other results are not consistent with the hypothesis (e.g., Clarke-Stewart, 1973; Kagan et al., 1966; Lewis, 1969). For example, while infant girls vocalize more to faces than infant boys, they do not smile at faces any more than do boys (Lewis, 1969).

Studies of gender differences in the nurturing behaviors of preschoolers exhibit the same inconsistent pattern. On the one hand, Goodenough (1957) reported that preschool-age girls draw and talk more about people; Hutt (1973) found that girls were more nurturing in the preschools; and Hoffman and Levine (1976) found preschool-age girls to be more empathic than boys. On the other hand, Bell et al. (1971) reported no sex differences in friendliness with peers, positive interactions with adults or smiling among 27–33-month-old children; and Eisenberg (Note 2) found that preschool boys and girls were equally likely to reinforce the behaviors of their peers. Thus the question of whether females are naturally more nurturant or socially oriented must remain open.

Infant Behaviors Related to Independence–Dependence

Attachment Behaviors

Both separation anxiety and fear of strangers (as evidenced by distress or crying when the child's caretaker is leaving or out of the room, unwillingness to play when the caretaker is gone, or clinging to the caretaker either in a novel environment or in the presence of strangers) could be early precursors to dependency. In general, studies investigating these behavior patterns do not yield consistent gender differences. Goldberg and Lewis (1969) found that 11-month-old females stand and cry while boys try to remove the barrier in response to a separation from their mothers and that girls sit and play quietly with their toys and spend more time closer to their mothers than boys. Other studies, however, have not revealed comparable gender differences (Coates, Anderson, & Hartup, 1972; Jacklin, Maccoby, & Dick, 1973). After reviewing the results of many of these types of studies, Maccoby and Jacklin (1974) concluded that attachment-related behaviors in early childhood are not gender dimorphic.

Exploratory Behavior

Exploratory behavior is another infant behavior that might relate to later independence. Goldberg and Lewis (1969) found boy toddlers (11 months old) to be more exploratory than girls. However, the majority of other relevant studies fail to support this conclusion (Maccoby & Jacklin, 1974). It appears that under the age of 3 boys and girls are equally exploratory and curious about their environment.

Infant Behaviors Related to Intellectual and Perceptual Capabilities

The recent development of a number of sophisticated techniques and a rapid accumulation of data with regard to visual perception and infant memory has led Cohen and Gelber (1975) to describe the field of infant attention, perception, and memory as follows: "No topic is more confusing, no evidence more contradictory, than that on sex differences in infant attention and memory" (p. 381). With respect to other perceptual systems, the picture is not quite so confused. Researchers are now able to assess quite accurately the degree to which even very young infants are able to perceive and discriminate among stimuli representing the different senses, smell, touch, and so on. Since most of these studies automatically analyze for sex differences, there is a substantial data base relevant to the concerns of this chapter. According to these data, there do not appear to be any gender differences in auditory perception or sensitivity. In contrast, females do appear to be more sensitive and/or more variable than males in their responses to touch, taste, and smell (Korner, 1974; Maccoby & Jacklin, 1974). There is also some evidence suggesting that female infants exhibit more oral behaviors than males. They are more likely than males to evidence reflective smiling, rhythmical mouthing, clonus of the tongue, and a variety of mouth-searching behaviors.

The implications of these differences are not clear. One possibility is that they might elicit differential responses from infant caretakers. For example, the rhythmical and smilelike oral and facial behaviors might sooth and reward caretakers or might elicit more warm interactive social responses from the caretaker.

Conclusion

There are few behavioral gender differences detectable during the early years of life. Gender similarities are far more common than differences. In addition, the majority of the differences that do exist may reflect maturational rate differences rather than differences more directly linked to gender or sex-linked genetic or hormonal effects.

However, a few consistent differences do exist. Neonatally, girls are more responsive to tactile and oral stimulation; boys have stronger neck muscles, are larger, and in some instances are more irritable. But boys are not consistently more active, independent, dependent, or exploratory.

During the preschool years, there are more consistent gender differences. Girls develop language skills sooner than boys (Frieze et al., 1978; Harris, 1978; Maccoby & Jacklin, 1974) and may exhibit more empathic behavior (Hoffman & Levine, 1976); boys exhibit more aggressive and physically active behavior and are more resistant to both adult and peer control (Frieze et al., 1978; Hetherington, Note 3; Maccoby & Jacklin, 1974; Rosenblatt & Cunningham, 1976). The origin of these differences, however, is not certain.

ANTHROPOLOGICAL FINDINGS

The current state of knowledge of infant characteristics leaves open the question of biological determinants of sex differences. However, a given sex difference need not show up as a difference in infancy to have a biological basis. It is not uncommon for biologically based systems to emerge and develop at points in the life cycle other than infancy. For example, the genital system does not reach functional maturity until puberty. Consequently we would not necessarily expect the sex differences in the many behavioral systems (e.g., aggression, nurturance, and sexuality) that might be influenced by the gonadal hormones (estrogens, progesterones, and androgens) to emerge prior to the onset of puberty. Separating the influence of socialization from the influence of biology at this point in a person's development, however, is extremely difficult. For along with the biological changes, cultural expectations of sex-appropriate behavior patterns also undergo a marked shift at puberty.

Correlating the effects of experimentally induced hormonal changes with behavioral patterns has been one technique used to investigate this issue. As discussed earlier, some behavioral changes can be induced this way. But the magnitude of the effect depends on the particular hormones used, the species involved, the prenatal hormonal environment of the particular animal, and a wide variety of environmental stimuli. Various hormonal therapies have also been used with humans and apparently have some effect on behavior. For example, doses of testosterone have been reported to increase both sexual drive and behavior in both men and women (Rogers, 1976). But placebos given to men expecting testosterone also produce some increases in sexual behaviors. Similarly, estrogen replacement therapy at menopause has been widely endorsed as a means of altering the physical and psychological side effects of aging. It is undoubtedly true that some of this effect is biological, but again it is not completely clear how much results from the expectation of the patient. Thus even using these refined experimental techniques, it is difficult to disentangle the effects of biology and socialization on behavior patterns that emerge beyond infancy and to pinpoint the important biological mechanism that might be involved.

Cultural Universals

Anthropologists have developed another approach to this whole issue: the search for cultural universals. If one or more behavioral differences express themselves consistently across most cultures, despite varying cultural patterns, then it is argued that there is reason to believe these differences may result from basic biological realities of the human race (Goldberg, 1973). To give an extreme example, if only women bear children, then it is reasonable to suspect that men are biologically incapable of this function. Of course, we know this is true and understand the mediating biological mechanisms, but the argument can be extended to other more subtle behavioral patterns that represent near cultural universals. Although we do not yet understand the biological mechanisms that might be involved, we should nevertheless begin to consider the likelihood that such mechanisms do indeed exist and will be understood more fully at some future time.

In considering cross-cultural patterns, however, it must be noted that there is considerable overlap in socialization patterns and in the ecological realities to which cultures must adapt. For example, women are the child raisers in most cultures, but at the same time, in most cultures, girls are differentially socialized into this role (Barry, Bacon, & Child, 1957), and mothers are the primary protein food source for infants. Similarly, while it is true that men in general fulfill the public leadership, high-status roles, it is also true that self-reliance and achievement are major socialization goals for males but not females in 85–87% of the cultures sampled by Barry et al. (1957) and that females, by necessity in many cultures, are generally relegated to the home or nonpublic domain (Rosaldo & Lamphere, 1974). Thus it is difficult to know whether this division of roles was selected according to evolutionary factors or whether it reflects a common solution to a common survival problem (Archer, 1976).

Such overlaps in socialization patterns, ecological demands, and cultural universals make evaluation of the relative importance of socialization and biology very difficult. Socialization could be producing the differences, it could be exaggerating a small biologically based difference, or it could be mirroring a powerful biologically determined behavioral system (Archer, 1976; Goldberg, 1974; Maccoby & Jacklin, 1974; Reiter, 1975, 1976; Rosaldo & Lamphere, 1974). Because these distinctions between relative weighting are crucial in our conceptualization of sex-role malleability, they have important implications for social change. Unfortunately, for most behaviors it is not yet possible to decide this issue, and much of what is being debated today is primarily speculative.

To complicate the issue further there is a problem in deciding what constitutes a cultural universal. Advocates of the socialization perspective cite exceptions to cultural universals as evidence against a biological argument (McClelland, 1976; Mead, 1935). In response, protagonists of the biological view argue that varying environmental factors could result in diverging evolutionary paths that might alter the relevant biological mechanisms in some cultural groups. As a result they do not agree that a few notable exceptions rule out the possibility of biological precursors. At present what constitutes a few exceptions is a value judgment rather than a scientific decision.

Furthermore, it is difficult to assess the presence or absence of a particular construct when the manifestation of that construct varies cross-culturally. For example, it was concluded in the early 1970s that women are universally less powerful and of lower status than men, but anthropologists have recently begun to question this conclusion. They argue that the assigning of status to various tasks and traits was based on the Western values of the ethnographers rather than on the values of the cultures being described (Quinn, 1977; Reiter, 1975, 1976; Rosenblatt & Cunningham, 1976). Quinn (1977) enumerated several other examples of the influence of Western male bias on currently available ethnographic material. In addition to the interpretative bias outlined above, she noted that male informants and male researchers have reported and gathered data that largely reflect the interests and attitudes of males. Thus as in the case of other social science disciplines, the prevalence of male scientists and collaborators has served to limit the body of "scientific" knowledge in anthropology.

Behavioral Differences

Aggression   Adult males (both humans and other primates) generally exhibit more intraspecies physical aggression (Archer, 1976; Rosenblatt & Cunningham, 1976). They are far more likely than females to be involved in combat and in various other forms of antisocial aggression. Younger males exhibit more rough-and-tumble play and more verbal and physical aggression (Whiting & Edwards, 1973). In addition, males have body characteristics that may suit them better for physical aggression: they are bigger, have more muscle mass, have higher metabolism rates, more androgens, and a higher proportion of red blood corpuscles (Scheinfeld, 1958).

Cross-cultural evidence does imply some biological basis for gender dimorphism in aggression. But as noted earlier, the concept of aggression is too amorphous, and the biological substrates for various behaviors related to the aggression may vary. Males may exhibit more of a physical assaulting type of aggression; females may exhibit more of other forms of aggression that have not been studied intensively. In addition the extent and form of male and female aggression varies markedly across cultures (Mead, 1935). Thus until more detailed ethnographic descriptions are available on a wider range of aggressive behaviors, the extent of biological influences on gender-dimorphic aggression cannot be fully understood.

Spatial Skills Gender differences in the use of spatial information have emerged with great regularity. In most cultures tested (the Eskimo culture being the primary exception, Berry, 1967) males on the average do better than females on a wide variety of tasks requiring spatial skills (Harris, 1978). Thus it seems likely that biological processes mediate to some extent this gender-dimorphic behavior. The gender difference, however, can be overcome with appropriate training (Sherman, Note 4). The biological process thus may predispose males to the acquisition of spatial skills but does not predestine females to inferior performance.

Division of Labor

Overview All cultures use gender as a major criterion for assigning roles and have gender distinctions built into their language (Rosaldo & Lamphere, 1974; Rosenblatt & Cunningham, 1976). In addition, they all expect certain inevitable temperamental differences to exist between the sexes that suit each sex for its assigned role. But while role differentiation is universal, the magnitude of gender-role dimorphism varies as a function of the economic, political, and familial structure of the societies. Economies based on hunting and fishing and on a reliance on male strength have the most marked gender differentiation in roles and socialization patterns. In contrast, societies based on animal husbandry and food storage have less marked gender differentiation in roles and socialization (Barry et al., 1957).

Using status differential as the criterion, Reiter (1976) argued that gender-role status dimorphism also varies with political structure. She concluded that sexual hierarchies are most marked in capitalistic states and much less marked in communal kinship systems. As major support for her contention, she cited evidence of the structural changes occurring in Third World cultures in response to Western capitalistic imperialism. Quinn (1977) reiterated this argument and offered additional evidence of the impact of Western colonialism on women's status in third world culture.

In terms of familial structure, societies with elaborate extended family systems and within-group cooperation tend to have the most marked sex-role differentiation. In contrast, societies with small nuclear family groupings that are independent of each other tend to have less marked sex-role differentiation and socialization patterns (Barry et al., 1957). This distinction probably reflects practical necessities arising from group size. That is, if the living group is quite small, then everyone must be able to fulfill several roles and fit into every role if the need arises. In contrast, if the living group is large, subgroups can specialize in one or two roles and can fill in for each other within the subgroups.

The specifics of the role divisions vary considerably from culture to culture. For example, in many West African cultures, women market and distribute goods while in most of western Europe and the U.S., men take responsibility for marketing and distribution. Nonetheless, two roles are fairly universally linked to one sex or the other: child raiser and warrior–hunter. There are exceptions, but in most cultures women raise the children and men fight the battles. While biological predispositions other than reproduction functions may have influenced this role differentiation, the necessities of survival were undoubtedly also important. Since women were needed to nurse the infants they bore and since contraceptives were not readily available, women had to spend most of their adult years around the children. It made practical sense, then, to assign them the role of raising the children. And since the women were occupied, only the men were available to play the warrior and hunter roles.

Parenting Parenting in both humans and other primates is generally the females' job. But whether this role assignment is biologically based is an extremely difficult question. As noted above, having women do the major parenting is adaptive from both a cultural and an evolutionary perspective. Thus it is plausible that both biosocial and socialization forces could be pushing women to fulfill this role. The role of socialization has been demonstrated time and again, but the role of biosocial forces is much harder to assess.

In one of the most persuasive discussions of this issue, Rossi (1977) aruged that evolutionary forces have selected for heightened maternal investment in children, greater propensity for acquiring parenting skills in females, and reciprocal physiologically based bonding systems in both infants and mothers. The evidence she cited speaks most directly to the last of these three: namely, the physiologically based bonding system. There are physiological events associated with early attachment. For example, an infant's cry stimulates the mother's secretion of oxytocin, which prepares her breasts for nursing. The hormone oxytocin is also involved in sexual responsiveness. Thus there is a link between the sexual response and the lactation system such that nursing can produce enjoyable sexual sensations. On a more behavioral level,

Rossi cited several studies indicating that there may be a biosocial component in early attachment. For example, mothers regularly exhibit a fixed sequence of behaviors when they first explore their new infants. In addition, disruption of the early contact between mothers and infants may have long-range effects on mother–child attachments evidenced by such behaviors as child abuse and neglect (see chapter 9 for a more complete discussion of this issue). Thus it does seem that biosocial forces may be involved in mother–child bonding, but the nature of these forces and the extent to which they operate differentially in men and women are unknown.

Because childrearing is assumed to be the domain of women, these biosocial processes have not been studied systematically in men. Further, in many cultures, fathers are systematically excluded from the birth process and from early contact with infants. If bonding is affected by early contact (a debatable hypothesis), then cultures effectively block the natural attachment between fathers and their infants. Some evidence does in fact suggest that early contact between father and infant affects subsequent measures of attachment in the predicted direction (see chapter 9). Thus, it is not yet possible to assess the extent to which biosocial forces foster parent–child bonding as opposed to mother–child bonding. An examination of cross-cultural and cross-species fathering can at least provide some insights into the potential for and range of expression of father–child attachment. And by showing the range of potential father–child involvement, we can at least speculate on the possible malleability of parenting role assignments.

The degree of paternal involvement in the parenting of higher primates is quite variable. In some species (e.g., rhesus monkeys, baboons, and chimpanzees) males play little if any direct role in parenting; in other species (e.g., Barbary macaque and most new world monkeys) males play a very active parenting role (Redican, 1976). Further, there have been instances in which the males of a low-paternal species exhibited a high degree of involvement when the situation warranted these behaviors.

The range of parenting behaviors is also quite broad. According to Redican (1976), males exhibit, albeit with lower frequency, the full range of parental behaviors commonly exhibited by females. For example, they prepare the infants' food by premasticating it; they transport, sleep with, groom, play with, and teach the young; and they provide refuge at critical times. In addition, they exhibit the behaviors commonly associated with the male protector role. Thus it seems that paternal involvement is clearly within the repertoire of behaviors available to higher primate species.

Are there factors that influence the extent of paternal involvement of primates? Redican (1976) suggested that the following factors increase the involvement of subhuman primate fathers in raising offspring: (1) monogamous social organization, (2) availability of stable food supply, (3) low levels of between-group competition and hostility, and (4) relaxed, permissive maternal-infant interactions. These facilitative structural characteristics suggest that paternal involvement will be high when paternity is readily identifiable, when males are not needed for the warrior-hunter role, and when females tolerate and encourage male parenting.

Can one generalize the findings concerning subhuman primate parenting to humans? With results similar to those of Redican, West, and Konner (1976) argued that plasticity in the extent and form of paternal behavior is also characteristic of human males. Like other primates, human males are universally less involved in parenting than females, but they too exhibit a wide range of parenting behaviors when necessary. West and Konner (1976) suggested the following structural arrangements as facilitative of human paternal involvements: (1) monogamy, (2) nuclear family units, (3) low levels of local warfare, (4) maternal employment, and (5) a gathering and/or agricultural economy. As is the case with the lower primates, human paternal involvement is increased by easily identifiable paternity, low demand for the warrior-hunter role, and high opportunity and need for father-child interaction. Men take care of their children if they are sure they are the father, if they are not needed as warriors and hunters, if the mother contributes to family resources, and if their parenting is functionally essential and encouraged.

But even when all of these conditions are present, men still play a less active role than women in childrearing. Is this difference biologically based? And does it reflect differential investment in children? We do not know. In response to the first question the data are mixed. On the one hand, there is some evidence that testosterone lowers maternal behavior in lower animals (West & Konner, 1976). On the other hand, neither socialization pressures nor birthing practices encourage paternal involvement. For example, Ember (1973) found that helping to take care of younger children increases nurturant, communion (Bakan, 1966) behaviors in boys. Whether these boys will exhibit more paternal behaviors as adults is yet to be seen. But if they do, then early involvement with childcare may be another of those precursors of maternal caring that is generally denied to males. In a study aimed at separating the natural, unlearned psychophysiologically based responses from the more overt, learned behavioral responses, Frodi and Lamb (in press) also reported findings that run counter to the theme of a biologically based sex difference in parenting. While the males and females in their study did differ in their overt behavioral response to infants, they did not differ in their psychophysiologically based responses.

In response to the question of differential investment relevant data are hard to come by. Most studies have defined investment in terms of typical maternal behaviors. Few studies have attempted to assess investment in terms of male values or male behaviors. Can we conclude that males are less invested in their children if they are not actively involved in day-to-day childcare? Men may express investment in their children through their provider-protector role rather than through a nurturing parent role. Hoffman and Hoffman (1973) reported that children serve many different needs for adults, some needs being more typical of women and others more typical of men. Assessing the differential subjective importance of these various values will be an extremely difficult task.

In conclusion it appears that adaptability in parenting styles for both males and females is as much a part of our biosocial heritage as is heightened maternal investment in children. In addition it is clear that investment can be expressed in a variety of ways and more research is needed on the whole range of relevant behaviors.

Patriarchy and Male Dominance

Males generally have power over females of equal age and status (Goldberg, 1974; Mead, 1935; Rosaldo & Lamphere, 1974). On the individual level a particular woman, because of either her age, her status, or her unique personality style, may have authority over a particular subset of males, but she will not as a rule have authority over her male counterpart. Women also occasionally occupy powerful political positions. But these cases are very rare and are usually the result of a personal tie with a powerful male or the absence of an appropriate male to fill the role. In addition, women in specific cultures sometimes exhibit authority in certain private domains. For example, American women have the authority in some areas of family decision making (Blood & Wolfe, 1960). Goldberg (1974) argued, however, that women's power in the private domain reflects the delegation of authority by men to women and that in the event of a dispute or conflict the male's authority will generally reemerge.

Further examples of this power and status differential include the predominance of male occupancy of positions of power, greater male access to valued resources (e.g., sexual partners and education), husbands' legal rights over wives and their property, and the cultural and legal tolerance of aggression against wives (Rosenblatt & Cunningham, 1976). More indirectly, patriarchy finds expression in the very definition of success and status and in the supportive institutions that are available (Frieze et al., 1978). For example, in the United States guaranteed seniority is generally provided for leaves of absence for military duty but not for leaves for maternity.

The universal denigration of women's reproductive functions has been cited as another example of patriarchy. Paige (1977) noted that 63.1% of a sample of world societies practice a pregnancy sex taboo, 73.2% a menstrual sex taboo, and 93.5% a postpartum taboo. In many of the cultures studied, women's reproductive functions are considered polluting enough to warrant restrictions of women's social activities "by such means as the segregation of menstruating and pregnant women in specially built huts, the construction of men's clubs where husbands may reside during a wife's menstruation or birth process, and the institution of a host of special avoidance of foods, animals or individuals" (Paige, 1977, p. 145). But as was the case with status differential, the meaning of menstrual restrictions have not been fully assessed; most ethnographic accounts rely on the males' perspective. Few investigators have measured the affective consequences of menstrual taboos upon women. Until these data are gathered, it is not clear whether both males and females denigrate women's reproductive functions or whether the females also denigrate some aspect of males' reproductive functions.

The predominant preference for male infants over female infants is another common example of female undervaluing. Male children are both preferred and given greater access to a wide range of valued and essential commodities, for example, protein, education, and inheritance (Hoffman & Hoffman, 1973). In some cultures this preferential treatment reflects the parents' accurate belief that sons will take care of them in the future while daughters will become a part of their future husbands' families. Consequently, the parents may conclude that it is better to invest love and resources in sons than in daughters. For these cultures, then, the more basic question is why patrilineage and patrilocal residence is the norm.

These examples on the surface seem to provide fairly strong support for the contention that females and their roles are of lower status. But as noted throughout, there has been growing concern that the status differential may have been overemphasized, reflecting male biasing in data gathering and interpretation as much as "truth." Women's autonomy, power, and status are relatively greater in matrilineal societies in which more than one male or no male is dominant in the family unit, warfare is unimportant, and women produce goods of high market value (Rosenblatt & Cunningham, 1976) and in cultures that have not been influenced by Western colonialism (Quinn, 1977). Thus differential status does vary and seems to be influenced as much by economic and political structures as by biosocial factors. Quinn (1977) went so far in fact, as to conclude that the apparent cross-cultural universal differential in status could be explained almost entirely by a consideration of "the bias of male informants in reporting, ethnographers in describing, and cross cultural workers in interpreting various disparate customs as evidence of women's universally low status, and the depressive effects of colonialism on many aspects of women's lives" (p. 186). Thus at present both the issue of patriarchy itself and the question of its origins are still contested.

But to the extent that the status differential has some biosocial origin, it could reflect the impact of at least two quite different phenomena, each requiring a different biological mechanism. On the one hand, it is possible that maleness, or characteristics associated with males such as height or strength, are inherently valued more than femaleness, or characteristics associated with females such as childbearing or nurturance, and consequently whatever is associated with males comes to be valued more and acquires more status than whatever is associated with females. If this is the case, then we need to explore the differences between males and females that lead people in general to ascribe greater value to males or maleness. On the other hand, males may seek out high prestige and status more than females and therefore select themselves into those roles that are valued by their society. If this is the case, then we should be looking for a different type of biological mechanism, namely one that accounts for greater male competitiveness and/or the need for power and status.

Culturally Relative Behaviors

Many aspects of the gender role patterns are not universal. The specific roles played by men and women are quite diverse; the nature of the relationships between men and women and between men and women and children take many forms; and the personality dispositions associated with masculinity and feminity vary markedly. For example, in her comparison of the Arapesh, the Mundugamore, and the Tchambuli, Mead demonstrated the flexibility of human personality. Among the Arapesh both men and women are expected to be and are gentle, nurturant, responsive, cooperative, and willing to be subordinate to others. In contrast, among the Mundugamore everyone is hostile, suspicious, and extremely aggressive. "Mother love" as we know it is virtually nonexistent. Finally, among the Tchambuli, men take on "feminine" behaviors and personality characteristics while females exhibit "masculine" traits and behaviors.

Conclusion

Cross-cultural and cross-species evidence has not yielded many unequivocal answers. Some near unviersals (e.g., spatial skills and aggressiveness) do reflect a major component of biological differentiation. But even these behaviors are highly malleable. Other roles, like childcare or defense, are consistently assigned to one gender or the other. But on inspection it is not clear what biological processes might be mediating this role assignment, and more importantly it is not yet clear how malleable these role structures are. On an even more global level the issues of differential power and status and differential investments in roles were discussed. Methodological problems have left these areas in such a confused state that few definitive conclusions can be made.

While it has been noted that the degree of gender dimorphism varies markedly across cultures, the degree to which gender dimorphism is expected or prescribed has not been investigated systematically. In addition, variations in the penalities for deviance have received little attention. These are important issues, given the current interest in androgyny and gender-role transcendence. Analysis of the conditions fostering gender-role transcendence would provide invaluable insights into both the theoretical issues and the social policy implications growing out of this area of interest.

SUMMARY

Based on what we have learned from studies of hormonal manipulations, gender differences in infancy and early childhood, and cross-cultural and cross-species similarities, it can be concluded that gender-role malleability and diversity are the norm rather than the exception. Humans acquire culturally prescribed roles that are usually well adapted to ecological realities. Nonetheless, a few biosocial conclusions can be made. Biological processes are implicated most clearly in aggressiveness and cognitive processes requiring spatial and verbal skills. But even for these two areas, the specific biological mechanisms and the interaction of various biological forces are not yet understood. The role of biosocial processes are less clear in the more global areas such as male dominance, division of parenting responsibilities, and behavioral cyclicity. Little is known about either the relative magnitude or the nature of the biological influences on these gender-role behaviors.

Across the board, gender dimorphism reflects the coinfluence of biological, historical, psychological, and sociological forces. The dialectical perspective implied in this statement is outlined more fully in the next chapter. An evaluation of the specific dialectical processes associated with each of the behavioral domains suggested as important in this chapter are provided in subsequent chapters.

REFERENCE NOTES

1. Ehrhardt, A. A., & Baker, S. W. *Hormonal aberrations and their implications for the understanding of normal sex differentiation.* Paper presented at the meeting of the Society for Research in Child Development, Philadelphia, 1973.
2. Eisenberg, S. *The sex-typed play behavior of children in two cultural settings: A kibbutz Gan and an American pre-school.* Unpublished manuscript, Smith College, 1974.
3. Heatherington, M. Personal communication, 1978.
4. Sherman, J. A. *Effects of biological factors on sex-related differences in mathematical achievement.* Unpublished report to the National Institute of Education, 1977.

REFERENCES

Archer, J. Biological explanations of psychological sex differences. In B. Lloyd & J. Archer (Eds.), *Exploring sex differences.* London: Academic Press, 1976.

Bakan, D. *The duality of human existence.* Chicago: Rand McNally, 1966.

Barry, H. III, Bacon, M. K., & Child, I. L. A cross-cultural survey of some sex differences in socialization. *Journal of Abnormal and Social Psychology*, 1957, *55*, 327–332.

Bayley, N. Mental growth during the first three years: A developmental study of sixty-one children by repeated tests. *Genetic Psychology Monographs*, 1933, *14*, 1–92.

Bayley, N. Comparisons of mental and motor test scores for ages 1–15 months by sex, birth order, race, geographical location, and education of parents. *Child Development*, 1965, *36*, 379–411.

Beckwith, L. Relationships between infants' social behavior and their mothers' behavior. *Child Development*, 1972, *43*(2), 397–411.

Bell, R. Q. A reinterpretation of the direction of effects in studies of socialization. *Psychological Review*, 1968, *75*(2), 81–95.

Bell, R. Q., Weller, G. M., & Waldrop, M. F. Newborn and preschooler: Organization of behavior and relations between periods. *Monographs of the Society for Research in Child Development*, 1971, *36*(1-2, Serial No. 142).

Berry, J. W. Temne and Eskimo perceptual skills. *International Journal of Psychology*, 1966, *1*, 207-229.

Berry, J. W. Ecological and cultural factors in spatial perceptual development. *Canadian Journal of Behavioural Science*, 1971, *3*(4), 324-336.

Blood, R. O., Jr., & Wolfe, D. M. *Husbands and wives: The dynamics of married living.* Glencoe, IL: Free Press, 1960.

Bronson, F. H., & Desjardins, C. Aggression in adult mice: Modification by neonatal injections of gonadal hormones. *Science*, 1968, *161*(3842), 705-706.

Brown, D. G. Sex-role preference in young children. *Psychological Monographs*, 1956, *70*(14, Whole No. 421).

Brown, D. G. Masculinity-femininity development in children. *Journal of Consulting Psychology*, 1957, *21*(3), 197-202.

Clarke-Stewart, K. A. Interactions between mothers and their young children: Characteristics and consequences. *Monographs of the Society for Research in Child Development*, 1973, *38*(6-7, Serial No. 153).

Coates, B., Anderson, E. P., & Hartup, W. W. Interrelations in the attachment behavior of human infants. *Developmental Psychology*, 1972, *6*(2), 218-230.

Cohen, L. B., & Gelber, E. R. Infant visual memory. In L. Cohen & P. Salapatek (Eds.), *Infant perception: From sensation to cognition* (Vol. 1). New York: Academic Press, 1975.

Effects of sexual activity on beard growth in man. *Nature*, 1970, *226*, 869-870.

Ehrhardt, A. A., Greenberg, N., & Money, J. Female gender identity and absence of fetal gonadal hormones: Turner's syndrome. *Johns Hopkins Medical Journal*, 1970, *126*, 237-248.

Ember, C. R. The effects of feminine task assignment on the social behavior of boys. *Ethos*, 1973, *1*, 424-439.

Engel, R. & Benson, R. C. Estimate of conceptional age by evoked response activity. *Biologia Neonatorum*, 1968, *12*, 201-213.

Frankenburg, W. K., & Dodds, J. B. The Denver developmental screening test. *The Journal of Pediatrics*, 1967, *71*, 181-191.

Frieze, I. H., Parsons, J. E., Johnson, P. I., Ruble, D. N., & Zellman, G. *Women and sex roles: A social psychological perspective.* New York: Norton, 1978.

Frodi, A. M., & Lamb, M. E. Sex differences in responses to infants: A developmental study of psychophysiological and behavioral responses. *Child Development*, in press.

Garai, J. E., & Scheinfeld, S. Sex differences in mental and behavioral traits. *Genetic Psychology Monographs*, 1968, *77*(2), 169-299.

Gardner, D. B., & Swiger, M. K. Developmental status of two groups of infants released for adoption. *Child Development*, 1958, *29*(4), 521-530.

Goldberg, S. *The inevitability of patriarchy.* New York: Morrow, 1973.

Goldberg, S., & Lewis, M. Play behavior in the year-old infant: Early sex differences. *Child Development*, 1969, *40*(1), 21-31.

Goldman, P. S., Crawford, H. T., Stokes, L. P., Galkin, T. W., & Rosvold, H. E. Sex-dependent behavioral effects of cerebral cortical lesions in the developing rhesus monkey. *Science*, 1974, *186*(4163), 540-542.

Goodenough, E. W. Interest in persons as an aspect of sex difference in the early years. *Genetic Psychology Monographs*, 1957, *55*(2), 287-323.

Gorski, R. A. Influence of age on the response to perinatal administration of a low dose of androgen. *Endocrinology*, 1968, *82*(5), 1001-1004.

Goy, R. W., Bridson, W. E., & Young, W. C. Period of maximal susceptibility of the prenatal female guinea pig to masculinizing actions of testosterone propionate. *Journal of Comparative and Physiological Psychology*, 1964, *57*(2), 166-174.

Harris, L. J. Sex differences in spatial ability: Possible environmental, genetic, and neurological factors. In M. Kinsbourne (Ed.) *Asymmetrical functions of the brain.* Cambridge, England: Cambridge University Press, 1978.

Hartup, W. W., & Zook, E. A. Sex-role preferences in three- and four-year-old children. *Journal of Consulting Psychology,* 1960, *24*(5), 420–426.

Hindley, C. B. Stability and change in abilities up to five years: Group trends. *Journal of Child Psychology and Psychiatry,* 1965, *6,* 85–99.

Hindley, C. B. Racial and sexual differences in age of walking: A reanalysis of Smith et al. (1930) data. *Journal of Genetic Psychology,* 1967, *111,* 161–167.

Hindley, C. B., Filliozat, A. M., Klackenberg, G. Nicolet-Meister, D., & Sand, E. A. Differences in age of walking in five European longitudinal samples. *Human Biology,* 1966, *38*(4), 364–379.

Hoffman, L. W., & Hoffman, M. L. The value of children. In J. T. Fawcett (Ed.), *Psychological perspectives on population.* New York: Basic Books, 1973.

Hoffman, M. L., & Levine, L. Early sex differences in empathy. *Developmental Psychology,* 1976, *12,* 557–558.

Hutt, C. J. *Males and females.* London: Penguin, 1973.

Jacklin, C. N., Maccoby, E. E., & Dick, A. E. Barrier behavior and toy preference: Sex differences (and their absence) in the year-old child. *Child Development,* 1973, *44*(1), 196–200.

Kagan, J. Acquisition and significance of sex typing and sex role identity. In M. L. Hoffman & L. W. Hoffman (Eds.), *Review of child development research* (Vol. 1). New York: Russell Sage Foundation, 1964.

Kagan, J. The determinants of attention in the infant. *American Scientist,* 1970, *58,* 298–306.

Kagan, J., Henker, B. A., Hen-Tov, A., Levine, J., & Lewis, M. Infant's differential reactions to familiar and distorted faces. *Child Development,* 1966, *37,* 519–532.

Korner, A. F. The effect of the infant state, level of arousal, sex, and ontogenetic stage on the caregiver. In M. Lewis & L. A. Rosenbaum (Eds.), *The effect of the infant on the caregiver.* New York: Wiley, 1974.

Kreuz, L. E., Rose, R., & Jennings, I. R. Suppression of plasma testosterone levels and psychological stress. *Archives of General Psychiatry,* 1972, *26,* 479–482.

Lewis, M. Infants' responses to facial stimuli during the first year of life. *Developmental Psychology,* 1969, *1*(2), 75–86.

McClelland, D. C. *Power: The inner experience.* New York: Halsted Press, 1976.

Maccoby, E. E., & Jacklin, C. N. *The psychology of sex differences.* Stanford, CA: Stanford University Press, 1974.

Mead, M. *Sex and temperament in three primitive societies.* New York: Morrow, 1935.

Money, J., & Ehrhardt, A. A. *Man and woman, boy and girl: The differentiation and dimorphism of gender identity from conception to maturity.* Baltimore: Johns Hopkins University Press, 1972.

Moss, H. A. Sex, age, and state as determinants of mother-infant interaction. *Merrill-Palmer Quarterly,* 1967, *13,* 19–36.

Paige, K. E. Sexual pollution: Reproductive taboos in American society. *Journal of Social Issues,* 1977, *33*(2), 144–165.

Parmalee, A. H., Jr., & Stern, E. Development of states in infants. In C. D. Clemente, D. P. Purpura, & F. E. Mayer (Eds.), *Sleep and the maturing nervous system.* New York: Academic Press, 1972.

Peatman, J. G., & Higgins, R. A. Development of sitting, standing and walking of children reared with optimal pediatric care. *American Journal of Orthopsychiatry,* 1940, *10,* 88–110.

Persky, H., Smith, K. D., & Basu, G. K. Relation of psychologic measures of aggression and hostility to testosterone production in man. *Psychosomatic Medicine,* 1971, *33*(3), 265–277.

Quinn, N. Anthropological studies on women's status. *Annual Review of Anthropology,* 1977, *6,* 181–225.

Redican, W. K. Adult male-infant interactions in non-human primates. In M. E. Lamb (Ed.), *The role of the father in child development.* New York: Wiley, 1976.

Reiter, R. R. (Ed.) *Toward an anthropology of women.* New York: Monthly Review Press, 1975.

Reiter, R. R. Unraveling the problem of origins: An anthropological search for feminist theory. In *The scholar and the feminist III: Proceedings.* New York: Barnard College, 1976.

Roche, A. F. Sex-associated differences in skeletal maturity. *Acta Anatomica,* 1968, *71,* 321–340.

Rogers, L. Male hormones and behaviour. In B. B. Lloyd and J. Archer (Eds.), *Exploring sex differences.* London: Academic Press, 1976.

Rosaldo, M. Z. & Lamphere, L. (Eds.), *Women, culture and society.* Stanford, CA: Stanford University Press, 1974.

Rose, R. M., Holaday, J. W., & Bernstein, I. S. Plasma testosterone, dominance rank and aggressive behavior in male rhesus monkeys. *Nature,* 1971, *231,* 366–368.

Rosenblatt, P., & Cunningham, M. R. Sex differences in cross-cultural perspective. In B. B. Lloyd & J. Archer (Eds.), *Exploring sex differences.* London: Academic Press, 1976.

Rosenblith, J. F. Imitative color choices in kindergarten children. *Child Development,* 1961, *32,* 211–223.

Rossi, A. S. A biosocial perspective on parenting. *Daedalus,* 1977, *106*(2), 1–32.

Scheinfeld, A. The mortality of men and women. *Scientific American,* 1958, *198,* 22–27.

Scott, R. B., Ferguson, A. D., Jenkins, M. E., & Cutter, F. F. Growth and development of negro infants: V. Neuromuscular patterns of behavior during the first year of life. *Pediatrics,* 1955, *16,* 24–30.

Singer, J. E., Westphal, M., & Niswander, K. R. Sex differences in the incidence of neonatal abnormalities and abnormal performance in early childhood. *Child Development,* 1968, *39,* 103–112.

West, M. M., & Konner, M. L. The role of the father: An anthropological perspective. In M. E. Lamb (Ed.), *The role of the father in child development.* New York: Wiley, 1976.

Whiting, B., & Edwards, C. P. A cross-cultural analysis of sex differences in the behavior of children aged three through 11. *Journal of Social Psychology,* 1973, *91,* 171–188.

Young, W. C., Goy, R. W., & Phoenix, C. H. Hormones and sexual behavior. *Science,* 1964, *143*(3603), 212–218.

2

Biopsychosocial Processes in the Development of Sex-related Differences

Anne C. Petersen
Michael Reese Hospital and Medical Center
The University of Chicago

This chapter has three components: (1) a review of the current state of the knowledge about which psychological characteristics differentiate the sexes: (2) the presentation of a general model for the development of sex-related differences, which will then be used to organize the existing evidence; and (3) an evaluation of the nature of the current knowledge about sex-related differences and their development, with recommendations about future research directions.

SEX-RELATED DIFFERENCES

Before we can discuss the development of sex-related differences we must first determine what these differences appear to be. Maccoby and Jacklin (1974) have provided the most thorough and careful review of the sex difference literature to date. Their refusal to accept unsubstantiated claims and their willingness to ask new, intriguing questions has made their volume an invaluable source.

Maccoby and Jacklin conclude that there is only clear evidence for sex-related differences with four traits: aggression and three cognitive abilities, quantitative, spatial visualization, and verbal skills. The cognitive differences do not appear consistently until adolescence. Maccoby and Jacklin labeled as myths sex differences in sociability, suggestibility, self-esteem, rote learning and simple repetitive tasks versus tasks that require higher level cognitive processing and the inhibition of previously learned responses, analytic cognitive style, influence by heredity versus environment, achievement motivation, and auditory-versus-visual responsivity. Traits for which there is currently insufficient information include tactile sensitivity; fear, timidity, and anxiety; activity level; competitiveness; dominance; compliance; and nurturance or maternal behaviors.

Maccoby and Jacklin pointed out the limitations of their conclusions, due in part to the nature of the research surveyed and the necessarily arbitrary nature of many of their decision rules. For example, which constructs are similar enough to be grouped and which need to be considered alone? Should all studies be weighted equally or should those with better methodology or larger samples be given greater weight? Also, once the results from the various studies are combined and totalled in some fashion, what are our criteria for determining when some number of significantly different results in fact provide evidence for a sex-related difference? And, while Maccoby and Jacklin did document their procedures and decision rules, they have been criticized for some of their decisions (Block, 1976a, 1976b).

Maccoby and Jacklin also pointed out the pitfalls of the "primacy effect": some initial results become enshrined as truth even when subsequent research produces new and different conclusions. In addition to their examples we may also point to Horner's (1972) research on fear of success. Important as her research was conceptually, the results have never been replicated, and many methodological problems have been noted (e.g., Tresemer, 1976). Nevertheless it is popularly believed that women fear success. Hence it is important to remain open to new research results that may support or refute current conclusions regarding sex-related differences.

Each of the reviewers (Block, 1976a; Dwyer, 1975; Emmerich, 1975; Sherman, 1975) in some way suggested that the Maccoby and Jacklin volume should be considered a starting point for further research on sex differences rather than a definitive conclusion. I agree. Furthermore, I hope that the social changes effected by the women's movement will begin to produce some different results in sex differences research. With the Maccoby and Jacklin summary as a starting point I shall summarize more recent research and literature reviews.

With regard to the cognitive differences, subsequent studies of spatial ability generally support the conclusion of a male advantage (Goldberg & Meredith, 1975; Hyde, Geiringer, & Yen, 1975; Mitchelmore, 1974; Sherman, 1974; Yen, 1975; McDaniel & Guay, Note 1) with one study finding sex differences in only two of four schools studied (Fennema & Sherman, 1977).

When one considers mathematics, the results are less clear. In a study in which all subjects had taken the same advanced mathematics courses appropriate for each grade, Fennema and Sherman (1977) found sex-related differences in only two of the four schools tested. They note that previous studies have not used such controls in their sample selection and hence were comparing groups unequal in course preparation, which would be expected to differ in achievement shown. Fennema (1977) has argued that the sex-related difference in mathematics achievement results from differential course taking rather than from significant differences between abilities of the two sexes. The possibility exists, of course, that girls drop out of mathematics courses because they lack the ability. Current evidence does not, however, support this conclusion.

The sex-related differences with verbal ability are at least as problematic as those with mathematical ability but have not been as rigorously examined in recent years. Maccoby and Jacklin (1974) considered tests of both receptive and productive language and of higher level as well as lower level skills. I found only one study more recent than those reviewed by Maccoby and Jacklin (1974). Coltheart, Hull, and Slater (1975) attempted to separate visual from verbal processing and found support for greater female superiority in verbal processing (as well as greater male superiority in visual processing). Clearly, more research is needed to clarify the tasks at which females excel.

With regard to social behavior, Maccoby and Jacklin (1974) concluded that only aggression differentiates the sexes. A more recent review of aggression (Frodi, Macaulay, & Thorne, 1977) basically agreed with the conclusion of Maccoby and Jacklin regarding sex-related differences in aggression but qualified and elaborated the differences. As for other behaviors, Sherman (1975), Block (1976a), and L. W. Hoffman (1977) have pointed out that the focus on early childhood taken by Maccoby and Jacklin may have biased their conclusions regarding differences in social behavior. Of the studies reviewed by Maccoby and Jacklin, 75% used subjects age 12 or younger and 40% used preschool children. Block (1976b) argued, using the Maccoby and Jacklin data, that sex differences increase with age. Only 37% of comparisons show sex differences among children 4 years old or less, but 55% show differences in persons 13 or older. Further, Block (1976a) noted that sex differences on two other traits, compliance (females higher) and self-esteem (males higher), emerge from the studies reviewed by Maccoby and Jacklin, using their criteria. If, in addition, studies included in the bibliography but not the tables are counted, the list also includes activity, dominance, and curiosity (males higher in all three).

L. W. Hoffman (1977) concluded that females have less confidence in their ability to perform many tasks and are more likely to seek the help and reassurance of others. Lenney (1977), however, demonstrated that situational variables are very important to the existence of the sex-related difference in self-confidence. The (occasional) lower self-confidence of females may be related to their lower self-esteem. Further support for a lower self-image in females is found in the research of Davis (1962); Gove and Herb (1974); Gove and Tudor (1973); Gurin, Veroff, and Feld, (1960); Offer, Ostrov, and Howard (1972); Rosenberg and Simmons (1972); Rosenkrantz, Vogel, Bee, Broverman, and Broverman (1968); and Simmons and Rosenberg (1975).

Empathy is another trait that M. L. Hoffman (1977) claimed is more characteristic of females than males. In his review of research on empathy, M. L. Hoffman (1977) differentiated two types of empathy: (1) cognitive awareness of the feelings of others and (2) the vicarious affective response to another's feelings. He concluded that females are more likely than males to exhibit the latter type of empathy in all studies reviewed (though only 3 of the 16 studies attain the conventional .05 level of significance). Neither cognitive awareness (16 studies) nor perspective taking (21 studies) differentiated the sexes.

It is not likely that a definitive list of the "real" sex-related differences will ever be compiled. No researcher can ever review all the evidence pertaining to an issue. Also, the variations in construct definitions and measurement procedures as well as age and other sample characteristics make it virtually impossible to consider most studies as true replications. Finally, there may be real changes occurring in values and behaviors pertaining to sex-related differences. The increased awareness in our society of sex roles, sex stereotyping, and sex discrimination are likely to influence our feelings. Over time, some sex-related differences may disappear and others emerge.

Despite the ambiguities of any review of the sex difference literature, it is possible to extract some generalizations. Following Maccoby and Jacklin, let us consider differences in two broad areas: cognitive abilities and social behaviors, or personality traits. On the average, males currently seem to be better at spatial and quantitative skills while females excel at verbal skills. Males seem to be more aggressive and perhaps more active, dominant, and curious and seem to have higher self-esteem, while females are more empathic and compliant. Most of these sex-related differences appear at adolescence. Taking these statements as approximations of the truth, let us now consider how these differences may develop.

BIOPSYCHOSOCIAL MODEL FOR DEVELOPMENT

It is likely that we will only understand the development of a psychological phenomenon when we have integrated our knowledge from several perspectives, biological, psychological, and sociocultural. We function, after all, in an open system and are influenced by factors from within and without. Furthermore, we interact with and influence our internal and external environments. Only by evaluating the total system of human functioning can we fully understand any single aspect of functioning.

I shall describe a model in which biological, psychological, and sociocultural factors are all considered as influences on psychological phenomena. To some extent this comprehensive systems view of development cannot produce a model at all. Or, at best, it is what statisticians call an overidentified model, in which there is too much information relative to the number of parameters to be estimated. On the other hand, models are useful for structuring our concepts. The function of the model is to reflect some generalized reality. It is quite simple in implementing or testing a model to attach limiting assumptions that render it more manageable, both conceptually and statistically. For example, we may wish to study biological influences on aggressive behavior. Our focus on biological influences would say nothing about influences from other sources. For the purposes of our study, however, we would be ignoring such effects in order to limit the number of factors being considered.

A major purpose in presenting this model of biopsychosocial development is to provide a framework within which to evaluate the current evidence for the development of sex-related differences. This task is somewhat complicated by the fact that most studies are similar to the hypothetical one investigating biological influences on aggression in that they limit the number of influences (and outcomes) investigated. Hence we know little about any interactions among different influences. I shall return to this issue later.

The process of development is best considered as a transaction between the individual and the environment (e.g., Sameroff, 1977). While interactive models are those generally proposed to account for both the individual and environment and the relation between them (e.g., Archer & Lloyd, 1974), these modes are static in time. Development, however, assumes a process, and neither the individual nor the environment are likely to remain constant over time. Since these two aspects change, the interaction between them changes over time. The individual and the environment exert reciprocal influences. The term *transaction* has been used to describe this changing interaction between a changing individual and a changing environment over time.

Transactional theory has primarily been discussed in relation to child development (e.g., Sameroff, 1977; Scarr-Salapatek, 1975) but is readily generalizable to the total life-span. Dialectic psychology provides a model of development over the life cycle considering continual change in both the individual and the environment (e.g., Riegel, 1976).

The transactional process of development begins at conception. We are each born with genetic potentials that influence our biological as well as our psychological characteristics. The genetic influences on behavior, however, are always indirect; they must be expressed through biochemical and physiological mechanisms and generally are extensively influenced by various environmental factors.

In a clear discussion of genetic mechanisms in development, Scarr-Salapatek (1975) presents the concepts *canalization* and *reaction range,* which are associated with all characteristics. Canalization is the process by which phenotypes are restricted to one, a few, or many outcomes. The degree of canalization varies inversely with the possible effects of the environment. For example, Scarr-Salapatek (1975) compares the strong canalization of infant intellectual development with the greater modifiability of later intelligence. Similarly, infant babbling seems to be strongly canalized since even deaf infants babble.

Reaction range is the particular range of quantitatively different phenotypes possible from the same genotype under varying environmental conditions. For example, Scarr-Salapatek (1975) concludes that most genotypes for IQ include phenotypes in a 25-point IQ range.

The transaction between the genotype and environment, influenced by degree of canalization and reaction range, continues constantly throughout development. Thus genetic influences are not fixed once and for all at conception.

In addition to genetic factors operating prior to birth, there is also evidence that prenatal endocrine levels influence later behavior (Money & Ehrhardt, 1972; Reinisch, 1976). A critical period for sexually differential behavior was first noted in primates and other mammals (Harris, 1964; Young, Goy, & Phoenix, 1964). More recently, researchers have found sex differences in testosterone levels in human fetuses, with the prenatal level in males reaching that of adult males (Abramovich, 1974; Reyes, Boroditsky, Winter, & Faiman, 1974). While we cannot experimentally manipulate prenatal hormone levels in humans, we can observe outcomes in two groups of individuals: (1) those with "accidental" or anomalous endocrine status and (2) those with drug-induced endocrine status. The evidence from studies of these individuals suggests that prenatal hormone levels do influence some aspects of psychosexual development.

Most of the human studies of prenatal hormone influence to date have been of masculinized girls, with testosterone the presumed active agent. The precise mechanism for hormonal influence on the brain during the prenatal period is not yet known, however, and the current evidence is complicated and controversial. Furthermore, these subjects and their parents were fully aware of the unusual endocrine status and may have subtly biased socialization.

Social and psychological factors also begin to operate at conception. For example, adequate nutrition, which is related to economic and educational level, is essential for optimal prenatal development. There is also some evidence from the animal literature that stress on the mother during the prenatal period may influence the psychosexual development of the individual.

Once birth occurs, the developing individual is confronted with a broader array of environmental influences. Parental socioeconomic status, psychological characteristics, and attitudes increase in importance as influences. As a child grows and broadens his or her world, the range of influences expands to include attitudes and characteristics of friends, relatives, neighbors, teachers, and classmates, and the broader sociocultural values of society become increasingly relevant. All these factors interact with the individual in a particular way depending upon the individual's biological, psychological, and social characteristics, as well as prior experiences and the immediate circumstances and situation. One of the most critical individual characteristics for responses as well as stimuli appears to be sex.

Socialization as a male or female is reinforced in a myriad of ways. Not only do we hold stereotypes as models for what boys and girls should be like, we also sex-type tasks, skills, and other behaviors as being appropriate for one sex or the other. For example, higher mathematics and, until recently, physical activity are strongly sex typed as male behaviors. Verbal skill and maternal behavior (e.g., doll play, playing house) are equally strongly sex typed as female.

But how might socialization throughout childhood lead to the observed sex-related differences? Maccoby and Jacklin (1974) could not find evidence for sexually differential socialization practices. At the same time, we feel certain that socialization effects are strong and influential. Nash (1979) has outlined a hypothesis by which socialization throughout childhood serves to engender and support sex-related differences. Her analysis was specifically focused on cognitive differences but applies equally well to other areas. Sex typing of behaviors and sociocultural stereotypes for females versus males necessarily coexists with such differences. There must be some mechanism by which these societal pressures become internalized; this mechanism is probably gender (or sex role) identity. A girl who identifies with the stereotype of a feminine person would have feminine identity. But not all females or males conform to the stereotypes for appropriate feminine or masculine behavior. Bem's (1974) identification of androgynous individuals provides an alternative category. / An androgynous person is less influenced by the sociocultural stereotypes and, by manifesting both masculine and feminine attributes, behaves in ways that are deviant from the stereotypes. /

The next task then is to explain how gender identity influences behavior. Nash (1979) suggests that cognitive consistency is an important construct linking gender identity to behavior. We behave in ways that are consistent with our identities. A masculine or feminine individual might be more likely than an androgynous individual to behave in ways expected from the observed sex-related differences. In addition, perhaps those with weak identities or poor self-confidence more readily adopt the societal sterotype. Finally, the cognitive consistency hypothesis is easily integrated with the evidence that gender identity is related to cognitive developmental stages (e.g., Kohlberg, 1966; Ullian, 1976).

In summary, this hypothesis for how sex-related differences are influenced by socialization posits that sex-typed behaviors are performed by individuals in ways that are cognitively consistent with their gender identities. Sex-related differences would increase at adolescence, then, because of the increased salience of gender resulting from the emergence of more obviously male or female bodies and the associated social and psychological attributions and expectations at adolescence. While this socialization hypothesis has logical merit, more direct evidence is needed.

The onset of puberty marks the beginning of a period in which both biological and sociocultural factors converge on sex-role development. In fact, puberty has been called the most significant biological event in postnatal development (Grave, 1974), considered by some (e.g., Tiefer, Note 2) as the time of activation for events programmed earlier in the organizational period of development. But adolescence, particularly in our society, has developmental importance far exceeding that which can be attributed to the biological events of puberty. Petersen (in press-a, in press-b, in press-c) has described some of the ways in which puberty does and does not influence psychosocial development at adolescence. But while biological changes are dramatic and cannot be denied, many aspects of adolescent behavior have been attributed to "hormones" with no clear evidence.

We have already discussed how sexually differential socialization at adolescence might produce the observed sex-related differences. The biological changes at puberty clearly play a role in this socialization process by transforming boys and girls into men and women. But we have little evidence of any direct, internal influence of pubertal hormones on psychological processes, though it is possible that they might have such direct effects. Aspects of puberty, in addition to maturation itself, that influence psychosocial development in an indirect way include the timing of maturation (especially quite early or late relative to peers) and the effect of experiencing such a dramatic biological change with a cohort at various stages of puberty. Current evidence does not, however, enable us to separate biological from sociocultural processes at adolescence. Indeed it seems likely that they are totally confounded and unseparable.

Biological factors become particularly important at several other points in the life cycle after puberty. Menstruation, pregnancy, menopause, and the general decline in bodily functions with aging all remind us of our biological selves. These biological processes, however, all have social significance, and the social beliefs about biological events may be stronger than biological influences alone in determining effects. For example, Ruble and Brooks (see chapter 11), have presented evidence for the strong social beliefs about changes in moods and symptoms over the menstrual cycle that may override any hormonal influences.

Just as there are critical biological events in the lives of males and females, there are critical social events of significance in human development, many operating differentially for each sex. The obvious factors among these are marriage (and divorce), births of children, deaths of parents and other loved ones, and children leaving home. These critical events are all embedded within an array of other significant influences on socialization and development. Such effects on adult development are just beginning to be investigated.

Guttman (1975) has argued that sex differences decrease or even reverse with aging. We could attribute this to declining hormonal levels with masculinizing effects in women and feminizing effects in men (Marcus & Korenman, 1976). Alternatively, we might suspect a decrease in the sociocultural pressures maintaining sex differentiation. The need for role differentiation clearly decreases as children become independent and the wife returns to paid employment.

In summary, there is a broadening field of influences on the developmental process. Figure 1 portrays these influences and the developmental process. Prenatally, there is a minor peak of genetic and hormonal influences

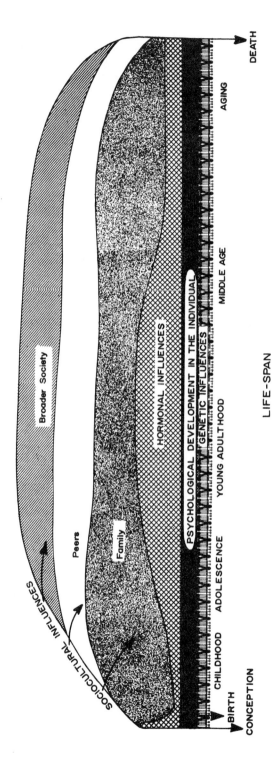

Figure 1   Hypothetical influences on the psychological development of the individual over the life-span.

with a small sociocultural contribution (e.g., nutrition). The shape broadens by maturity to a complex interactive open system of influences. The two-dimensional picture unfortunately cannot show the transactions between kinds of influences.

Because this author's research has been biologically oriented, biologic influences are perhaps more adequately reviewed. But social factors are clearly at least as important. They cannot be neglected in any discussion of influences on sex-related differences. And no trait is solely influenced by biology or environment. The nature-versus-nurture controversy perpetuates this false dichotomy. Let me discuss one other myth as well. Social and behavioral scientists tend to believe that our variables are extremely imprecise and subjective relative to biological variables. Biological factors are no more real or objective than psychosocial ones. Furthermore, they are not necessarily' more easily measured. There are validity and reliability problems with biological measures just as with psychosocial measures. With both we generally must infer the status of a characteristic based on a measurement that includes error.

Further, social influences do not just affect the psychological aspects of the individuals; physiological factors can be influenced as well. Stress affects hormone levels (Kreuz, Rose, & Jennings, 1972); fear of or belief in pregnancy can produce its hormonal concomitants (Yen, Rebar, & Quesenberry, 1976); and environment influences the phenotype of the genotype (Scarr-Salapatek, 1975), to mention a few examples. Thus the total system is open to influence, not just the psychological system. I shall elaborate on this point later in discussing hypotheses for sex-related differences.

Finally, as suggested in the examples above, the interactions are not just between the external environment and the individual but also between physiological and psychological aspects of the same individual. The interactions occur on all levels.

I recognize that this model of biopsychosocial development is somewhat abstract and general. But it is especially useful in planning or evaluating research on the development of sex-related differences. By operating from a model that includes the spectrum of influences, from biological to sociocultural, we increase the likelihood that our research designs or evaluations will include or at least consider the variety of influences on development. After all the question is not whether sex-related differences are biologically based or socioculturally determined. Both are likely involved, at least to some extent. Rather we should investigate their relative influences.

In addition, it is likely that the relative influence of biological-versus-sociocultural factors will vary for individuals and groups. It is known, for example, that when environmental conditions are optimal their variability is restricted, and genetic factors will contribute relatively more to the resulting variance in measures of the trait under investigation. Similarly, if some influence is uniform for all members of a sex, it is totally confounded with sex itself and its contribution cannot be independently assessed. While such a situation is unlikely to occur in such an extreme way, it is possible, for example, that there could be great socialization pressure on girls to avoid mathematics or engineering. Similarly, strong societal pressure on males to avoid childcare tasks would produce little variance in the effect of socialization for males; nevertheless, the effect could be very strong but simply totally confounded with sex.

An excellent example of an integrated biopsychosocial approach to a phenomenon, in this case behavior rather than development, has been provided by Koeske (in press). She has proposed a new theoretical perspective on premenstrual emotionality based on an attributional approach. Her arousability-labeling hypothesis predicts that experienced emotion results only from the simultaneous presence of a state of arousal and an emotional label derived from the immediate situation, which could explain or interpret it. Preliminary data support her hypothesis. We cannot do justice to Koeske's theory here. We have presented it for its significance in integrating what is known about both biological and sociocultural influences on a particular phenomenon, in this case premenstrual tension. Her focus is on explaining the phenomenon rather than demonstrating particular kinds of influences. The theory serves as an exemplar for research on the development of sex-related differences.

EVIDENCE FOR DEVELOPMENTAL INFLUENCES ON SEX–RELATED DIFFERENCES

Using this model for biopsychosocial development to examine the evidence for both biological and sociocultural influences on sex-related differences, it becomes clear that more evidence exists for biological influence with cognitive traits. Personality differences seem to be influenced more by social factors. This conclusion, however, is strongly affected by the nature of the studies conducted. You cannot find social influences while examining a biological factor or vice versa; and there appears to be a bias in the type of influence investigated. There is evidence of biological influences on cognitive functioning because the bulk of the research effort has focused on the investigation of biological factors. The role of socialization or related learning factors in sex differentiation of cognitive functioning has not been studied to nearly the same extent as the role of the various biological influences.

Cognitive Differences

As stated earlier, girls are better at verbal tasks while boys are better at spatial visualization and quantitative tasks, with none of these differences appearing consistently until adolescence. It has been suggested that the quantitative difference is related to spatial ability (Fennema, 1974; Sherman, 1967; Aiken, Note 3). While mathematics is not totally based on spatial ability, sex differences generally are found on math tests requiring spatial visualization such as geometry. When the problem can be solved verbally, as in algebra, no consistent sex differences are found (Fennema, Note 4). More importantly, there is evidence that the sex differences in mathematics decrease when the number and kind of courses taken in math are controlled (Fennema & Sherman, 1977).

Until recently it was believed that spatial ability might be inherited by an X-borne (i.e., X-linked or sex-linked) recessive major gene (Bock & Kolakowski, 1973; Yen, 1975). More recent studies (Bouchard, Note 5; Defries, Ashton, Johnson, Kuse, McClearn, Mi, Rashad, Vandenberg, & Wilson, 1976; Bouchard, Note 5; Sherman & Fennema, Note 6), however, have failed to replicate the earlier results. All these studies have used familial patterns or distributional analyses to test the X-borne recessive gene hypothesis. A study examining linkages with a marker trait, a more appropriate method of examining inheritance, also failed to find evidence of X-linkage with spatial ability though the results suggested possible X-linked inheritance of field dependence (Goodenough, Gandini, Olkin, Pizzamiglio, Thayer, & Witkin, 1977). As a consequence of these recent studies, the X-borne recessive gene hypothesis appears to be unlikely.

But even when it was viable, the genetic hypothesis did not account for all the evidence. Several genetic–hormonal anomalies exist showing a pattern of cognitive abilities different from that expected on the basis of a genetic explanation alone. Phenotypic females with Turner's syndrome (XO) are poor spatial visualizers (Alexander, Ehrhardt, & Money, 1966; Money & Alexander, 1966). Phenotypic females with the androgen insensitivity syndrome (XY) also show the usual female pattern of verbal superiority over spatial skill (Masica, Money, Ehrhardt, & Lewis, 1969). Genetic males feminized by a kwashiorkor-induced syndrome also show a female pattern of cognitive functioning (Dawson, 1967, 1972). What these three examples have in common is an endocrine abnormality, the first two existing prenatally and the third developing in early childhood. Perhaps the sex hormones, which produce somatic differences between the sexes, also influence cognitive functioning by affecting the brain. Hormones could influence the brain during the critical period of development that occurs prenatally in humans, or they could influence functioning with their increasing levels at puberty.

To study this endocrine hypothesis for cognitive functioning, Petersen (1976) correlated cognitive scores with ratings of somatic characteristics reflecting hormone influences. Actual hormone measures were unavailable, but the current state of endocrine methodology is such that somatic indices are a reasonable alternative measure. (See Petersen, in press-a, for a discussion of endocrine methodology). Petersen (1976) found that spatial ability was highest in both males and females who are more androgynous in physical characteristics, relative to those more sex stereotypic in body shape. In males, the relationship exists with a contrast between spatial ability and fluent production (the rapid and accurate production of symbolic codes or names). Androgynous males were better at spatial ability than fluent production while more physically masculine males were better at fluent production than spatial ability. Similarly, somatic masculinity was negatively related to spatial ability and positively related to fluent production. This result with males replicated the findings of Broverman and colleagues (Broverman, Broverman, Vogel, & Palmer 1964; Broverman & Klaiber, 1969; Klaiber, Broverman, & Kobayashi, 1968; Vogel, Broverman, & Klaiber, 1968). Note that for females, only spatial ability and not fluent production was related to the somatic characteristics. Petersen did not, however, find any relation between cognitive pattern and the timing of maturity in either sex. This differs from the Broverman results.

Another potential source of biological evidence for the verbal–spatial sex difference is the currently popular area of research on brain organization. Briefly, it is hypothesized that the left side of the brain is the primary focus (in right-handed individuals) for verbal skills. Similarly, it is thought that spatial skills are generally controlled by the right hemisphere.

Most recent evidence (e.g., McGlone & Davidson, 1973; Bryden, Note 7) suggests that the brains of males are more lateralized (e.g., left hemisphere dominant) while females' brains tend to be more equally lateralized (bilateralized).[1] Various hypotheses have emerged linking this sex difference in lateralization to the sex difference in spatial skill. For example, Levy (1972) argued that the bilateralization in females creates competition between the hemispheres and serves to reduce spatial ability in females. But the empirical support for both the hypothesized sex difference in lateralization and the relationship of lateralization to spatial and verbal skill is equivocal at present.

The sex difference in brain lateralization, if it exists, may be caused by another important biological sex difference: different rates of maturation (Waber, 1979). While male sexual differentiation is completed 4 weeks earlier than that of females (16 and 20 weeks from conception, respectively) (Hutt, 1972), the developmental retardation in males begins as soon as they have completed sexual differentiation (Hunt, 1966) and leaves them 4–6 weeks behind females at birth (Hutt, 1972).

The female human brain at age 4 shows greater left hemisphere myelination while with males the right is more advanced (Conel cited in Landsdell, 1964). Buffery and Gray (1972) argued that this left-hemisphere advancement and dominance in females, also documented by their data from ages 5 to 8, is maintained. The Buffery and Gray data, however, may simply represent a maturational advantage in lateralization for girls that, like height, declines and reverses with puberty. The hypothetical figure of Harshman and Remington (Note 8) for the development of lateralization by sex is strikingly similar to growth curves for height. Bock and others (Bock, Wainer, Petersen, Thissen,

---

[1] Buffery and Gray (1972) argued for the reverse sex pattern but their results remain unreplicated.

Murray, & Roche, 1973), in searching for a mathematical representation for growth in height, concluded that the adult sex difference in height is caused by the prepubertal component; girls are shorter because puberty, which both accelerates and ultimately curtails growth, begins earlier for them.

Similarly, perhaps boys are more lateralized because their maturation is later. There is not currently, however, sufficient data on the development of brain lateralization. Indeed some evidence suggests that lateralization, at least to some extent, is established early in development (e.g., Kinsbourne, 1975; Krashen, 1973).

With regard to the hypothesized relationship between lateralization and spatial or verbal skills, few studies in this area have measured verbal and spatial skills as they are generally operationalized in the individual differences paradigm typical of most sex-difference research. Rather the methods include dichotic listening tasks (in which sounds are presented in both ears and it is assumed that the sound reported first is the one processed in the dominant hemisphere) and tachistoscope tasks (images presented to both eyes). Verbal ability is inferred when the task involves words and spatial ability is inferred when visual images are used. Bryden (in press) has noted that strategy effects in performing the tasks (e.g., differential attention) may be operating along with or instead of underlying lateralization differences. In addition, Butler (Note 9) commented that we have not examined differential competence of perception in right-versus-left ears or eyes. Bryden (in press), in reviewing this literature, concludes that the evidence is less firm than the popular literature would have us believe. This is particularly true of the developmental aspects of brain lateralization.

How do sociocultural factors fit in here? There is some evidence that spatial skills are enhanced with practice (Goldstein & Chance, 1965; Kato, 1965), that girls are socialized to avoid courses or occupations requiring mathematics and spatial skills (Fennema & Sherman, 1977; Fox, 1976; in press), and that the nature of math and spatial tests themselves are frequently sex typed (Dwyer, 1979).

It is difficult, however, to explain the reverse hormonal-cognitive pattern found with boys by using any socialization argument. With mathematics and verbal skills, and with spatial ability for girls, we might argue that socialization and biology act synergistically, reinforcing each other. But the hormonal evidence related to spatial ability for boys is contrary to socializing influences. Boys who are good spatial visualizers seem to become so despite a less masculine appearance. Similarly, boys who are more masculine in physical attributes do not necessarily show good spatial skills. This argument assumes, however, that masculine bodies elicit masculine socialization. It is possible that the reverse actually occurs: less masculine males may receive more socialization pressure to perform like males. If this is the case, we must then explain why girls are not similarly socialized to compensate for sexually deviant appearance with sex-appropriate performance. But it may be that differential status operates here. Masculine performance is valued and rewarded in either sex. In addition, boys, especially less masculine boys, probably undergo rigorous socialization pressures toward maculinity and away from femininity. Society in general has more fears of the possible consequences of femininity in males than of masculinity in females.

What then can we conclude about the development of sex-related differences in cognitive abilities? Though there no longer is a viable genetic hypothesis that explains the cognitive sex-related differences, evidence exists that these traits are highly heritable (e.g., J. B. Block, 1968; Bock & Vandenberg, 1968; Bramble, Bock, & Vandenberg, 1969; Kolakowski, Bock, & Vandenberg, Note 10). The manifestion of genetic potentials may also require certain moderate levels of androgen influence (or perhaps the appropriate ratio of androgen to estrogen or some other endocrine mechanism). These sexually-differential levels may be important at the so-called critical period of development (prenatal in humans) to function in brain organization, hemi-spheric lateralization, and perhaps prefrontal development (Goldman & Mac-Brown, 1975; Gray & Buffery, 1975; Waber, Note 11). Brain organization may in turn serve to extend cognitive differences to verbal-versus-spatial skills with the spatial differences then also influencing some math skills. Socialization may serve to make it more likely that boys become good at math and spatial skills (and less likely for girls) while reinforcing verbal and fluency skills in girls. The appearance at adolescence of sex differences in these skills may be caused by increased sexually differential socialization at this time and/or by the activational influences of hormones at puberty, perhaps on the termination of brain lateralization.

Personality Differences

This paper has focused primarily on cognitive sex-related differences. I shall now attempt to review and organize the personality literature. There is little evidence of genetic influence on noncognitive personality traits, especial-ly any that would explain sex differences. Buss and Plomin (1975), in their study of four temperamental traits (emotionality, activity, sociability, and impulsivity), concluded that the first three show evidence of significant heritability. They also concluded that activity and sociability show sex-related differences, at least at some ages. At the same time they argued that the sex differences could not be explained by genetics. A genetic explanation would require evidence of sex linkage (i.e., that the trait is borne on the X chromosome); there is no such evidence for these traits. Furthermore, the developmental pattern of activity and sociability showing divergence between the sexes beginning at adolescence suggests socialization as the likely cause of sex-related differences, although they note that a hormonal hypothesis cannot be excluded by the data. Others (e.g., Eysenck, 1967; Klein & Cattell, Note 12) have found evidence for genetic components of personality traits, but none of these traits show sex-related differences. Hence there is little evidence of a genetic basis for sex-related differences in personality traits.

Similarly, there is little systematic evidence of brain organizational influences on sex differences in personality or social behavior. It should be noted, however, that these conclusions are not based on negative evidence but rather on meager evidence. In contrast to cognitive sex differences, there has been little systematic investigation of biological influences on sex differences in personality.

The primary exception to this is the work relating aggression to androgen influence. This research is new (of necessity since endocrine methodology was inadequate for these purposes until the last decade), and the preliminary results are not clear. In the first study, Persky, Smith, and Basu (1971) found that aggression was related to androgen, at least in younger men. Subsequent studies have produced contradictory results (e.g., Ehrenkranz, Bliss, & Sheard, 1974; Kreuz & Rose, 1972; Monti, Brown, & Corriveau, 1977; Persky, O'Brien, Fine, Howard, Kahn, & Beck, 1977). Thus the relationship between androgens and aggression is unclear at present.

Studies relating an extra Y chromosome to aggression are also relevant to this issue. While the current consensus suggests that XYY individuals are found in institutions (prisons and mental hospitals) more than expected (Gardner & Nieu, 1972; Jarvik, Klodin, & Matsuyama, 1973), recent evidence suggests that this may be because of lower intelligence rather than higher aggression (Witkin, Mednick, Schulsinger, Bakkestrom, Christiansen, Goodenough, Hirschorn, Lundsteen, Owen, Philip, Rubin, & Stocking, 1976).

Extending the concept of aggression to a wider range of social behaviors, Goldberg (1974) has suggested that dominance and compliance and perhaps other assertive–competitive differences are also related to androgen levels. In his volume titled *The Inevitability of Patriarchy,* Goldberg argued that hormonally induced male aggression leads to patriarchy, male dominance, and male attainment of high-status, nonmaternal roles. Although his historical analysis of male dominance and patriarchy is basically accurate (see also Rosaldo & Lamphere, 1974), his conclusion that male dominance is inevitable because of its biological origins is questionable.

It is tempting to argue that observed sex-related differences must be biologically determined if they have persisted over a long time. This is a common argument and the type made by Goldberg (1974). Since hormones differentiate the sexes, the appeal is generally to this factor as the determinative one, though sex chromosomes sometimes are also addressed. In the case of hormones determining the historical dominance relations between the sexes, we must raise serious questions. Hormones may play some role, but the current evidence is ambiguous. Furthermore, hormones may by influenced by social situations. Of particular importance here are the studies that show the influence of social factors on androgen level. High-androgen, aggressive monkeys show drastic decreases in androgen level when placed in a situation in which they are not dominant (Rose, Gordon, & Bernstein, 1972). Similarly, other forms of stress will cause androgen levels to decrease in humans (Kreuz, Rose, & Jennings, 1972) and in mice (Macrides, Bartke, & Dalterio, 1975). We see here an excellent example of the interaction of hormonal and psychological factors. We cannot say which is causal unless we know more about the specific circumstances and situation. In addition, while the sex differences in hormone levels are probably necessary to maintain reproductive capacity, why are hormones linked to a trait such as aggression? If this is not necessary for the survival of the species, and we cannot see an adaptive significance for dominance in these times, then such a linkage may disappear with time. But even more importantly there is little evidence to support the claim that androgens influence dominance, much less the whole array of characteristics included in the description of the aggressive person (Goldberg, 1974).

An alternative explanation for the sex differences in power and status is also based on biology: the reproductive role of women has traditionally kept them involved with childbearing and childrearing throughout much of the life cycle. This fact together with the greater strength of males could well have served to keep women from competing for positions of power.

But if it is true that sexually differential socialization is more extreme than sexually differential biological capacities, then an equally important question emerges. Why have societies evolved this system of socialization? Goldberg (1974) explained this by paternalism: males have protected females from highly probable failure. Such a benevolent hypothesis strikes us as unlikely. It seems more likely that throughout history some effort has been expended toward keeping women in their place. Goldberg himself provided an important rationale here, though he failed to recognize its significance.

> Nature has bestowed on women the biological abilities and bio-psychological propensities that enable the species to sustain itself. Men must forever stand at the periphery, questing after the surrogate powers, creativity, and meaning that nature has not seen fit to make innate functions of *their* biology. Each man knows that he can never again be the most important person in another's life for long and all know that they must reassert superiority in enough areas often enough to justify nature's allowing them to stay. (p. 227)

It is possible then that men strive for dominance because of their inadequacies. While sperm is necessary to produce a child, once inseminated a woman may depart with the product of her nurturance unless forced to remain by a stronger male. Hence male power becomes necessary for men to play some role in the reproductive process.

The preceding discussion portrays male–female relations in a very negative light. While it is more extreme than commonly experienced, we believe that the forces that influence strong sex-role differences also serve to make negative male–female relationships more likely. Both childrearing and suprafamilial responsibilities can be rewarding experiences. Being relegated solely to either seems unfair and unnecessary. While some may choose to focus only on childrearing or suprafamilial roles, others may desire alternative roles.

There are clear trends in the direction of more androgynous life styles and personalities. There is no evidence that maternal behavior and feelings are biologically linked to women, and some men are beginning to enjoy the maternal role. Similarly, we are seeing more and more women enjoying suprafamilial roles in our society. Those who are attempting such dual functions as parents and professionals are likely to conclude that this life style is easier when shared with another adult. Giving up a single, traditional sex role is difficult, especially for males given the higher status ascribed to the male roles in societies. But the rewards of both roles are great.

If the current minitrend toward androgynous role responsibilities continues, what will become of patriarchy, male dominance, and male status? I suspect that our societies will continue to thrive without such institutions. While the status quo may have a biological origin, it is not inevitable and there are some indications of changes. If changes occur, they will occur slowly. Sex-role stereotyping is far too prevalent in our society to disappear overnight or even in our generation. If the trends continue in the same direction, it will probably take several generations. Recent advances in birth control have hastened and to some extent enabled the recent rapid change in one generation toward changing views of sex roles, but it will take much longer for the larger society, especially the male portion who benefit least, to see the advantages of the change.

Another source for hormonal influences on personality, though now we are speaking of transient states rather than stable traits, is the menstrual cycle literature. There is some evidence that some women are more anxious and hostile premenstrually (Altmann, Knowles, & Bull, 1971; Benedek, 1959; Ivery & Bardwick, 1968; McCance, Luff, & Widdowson, 1937; Moos, Kopell, Melges, Yalom, Lunde, Clayton, & Hamburg, 1969; Paige, 1971), though other studies have not found this relationship, and Dan (1976) found that the cycle does not add variability in females. None of these studies have measured hormone levels, so it is unclear whether the results are from the change in hormone levels in general, from some particular hormonal level, or from expectations related to the cycle that are sociocultural in origin (e.g., see chapter 11). In any case, there is no evidence that these relationships with anxiety and hostility are related to androgen influences, since androgens also decrease premenstrually (Kim, Dupon, & Hosseinian, 1974). Finally, recall that there was not conclusive evidence for a sex difference in anxiety (Maccoby & Jacklin, 1974) and that men are more aggressive (hostile?) than women so that the menstrual cycle could not account for this sex difference.

Finally, in reviewing the literature, one is struck by the studies that describe the greater susceptibility to disease shown by males (e.g., Taylor & Ounsted, 1972). How did less healthy males attain positions of power over females? The conclusion proposed by Hoffman (1977) and Rosenblatt and Cunningham (1976) is that women have been physically vulnerable relative to stronger males and have been limited by their role as childbearers. The influence of physical health and strength on sex-role differentiation poses an interesting and open question that has received little theoretical or empirical analysis.

WHERE ARE WE NOW AND WHAT NEXT?

As occasionally noted in the preceding sections, there are gaps in our current knowledge of how sex differences develop. We know little about the specific influences of socialization on the cognitive abilities showing differences especially for various groupings such as high spatial ability boys and girls versus those with lower skills. How does socialization interact with brain organization in development? It may very well be that socialization, through differential practice, influences the developmental changes that we see in lateralization of boys versus girls. Cross-cultural differences in ways of thinking suggest that perhaps sociocultural values influence which side of the brain becomes the dominant one. For example, differential experience with verbal-versus-spatial tasks may enhance the development of one side of the brain or the other.

With personality differences, the research gaps are mainly in the biological area. Do brain organization or genes have anything to do with the sex differences in aggression and other traits?

More importantly, we need longitudinal research to determine when linkages between the biological or sociocultural influences and the traits showing sex differences begin to occur. Are hormones important from birth or only from puberty? Are hormone levels related to brain lateralization? And is brain lateralization development sexually differential? Does the development of lateralization correspond to the development of the cognitive abilities showing sex differences? How are the sexually differential cognitive and personality traits related? A broader but related question here is the relationship of socialization and sex typing to the various biological influences on the cognitive outcomes. It is time to begin examining the interactions of biological and sociocultural influences.

We are just beginning to learn what is happening in this field, and we need a great deal more systematic research that considers influences from all existing sources. Furthermore, we need theoretical models that consider biopsychosocial development. Using such a model we have noted where our past biases have been and where further research is needed. Why has most of the research with cognitive sex differences focused on biological influences? Similarly, why have we assumed that any personality differences between the sexes are mainly influenced by socialization? We are not questioning any results that have been obtained. Rather we suggest that the questions asked influence in a determinative way the results that have been obtained. We must not be misled by any initial biases in assumptions and hence research questions, but we must be aware of the larger universe of questions that could have been asked and which of these the particular piece of research supports or refutes.

REFERENCE NOTES

1. McDaniel, E. D., & Guay, R. B. *Spatial ability, mathematics achievement, and the sexes.* Paper presented at the annual meeting of the American Educational Research Association, San Francisco, April 1976.
2. Tiefer, L. *Some comments on hormone determinants of sex differences.* Paper presented at the National Institute of Mental Health Conference on Research Issues in the Biological and Cultural Bases of Sex Roles, 1972.
3. Aiken, L. E., Jr. *Affective variables and sex differences in mathematical abilities.* Paper presented at the annual meeting of the American Educational Research Association, Chicago, 1974.
4. Fennema, E. *Mathematics, spatial ability, and the sexes.* Paper presented at the annual meeting of the American Educational Research Association, Chicago, 1974.
5. Bouchard, T. *Sex differences in human spatial ability: Not an X-linked recessive gene effect.* Manuscript submitted for publication, 1976.
6. Sherman, J. A., & Fennema, E. *Distribution of spatial visualization and mathematical problem solving scores: A test of the sex-linked hypothesis.* Manuscript submitted for publication, 1977.
7. Bryden, P. *Sex differences in cerebral organization.* Paper presented to the International Neuropsychology Society, Toronto, 1976.
8. Harshman, R. A., & Remington, R. *Sex, language, and the brain, Part I: A review of the literature on adult sex differences in lateralization.* (Working Papers in Phonetics, No. 31) Unpublished manuscript, UCLA, 1975.
9. Butler, R. Personal communication, Chicago, August 1977.
10. Kolakowski, D., Bock, R. D., & Vandenberg, S. G. *Components of heritable variation in the Wechsler Adult Intelligence Scale.* Research Report No. 28, Louisville Twin Study, University of Louisville School of Medicine, 1967.
11. Waber, D. P. *Neuropsychological analysis of spatial ability in Turner's syndrome: Genetic implications.* Paper presented at the annual meeting of the American Psychological Association, Washington, D.C., September 1976.
12. Klein, T. W., & Cattell, R. B. *A preliminary analysis of the inheritance personality traits in male sibs.* Paper presented at the annual meeting of the Behavior Genetic Association, Chapel Hill, N.C., 1973.

REFERENCES

Abramovich, R. D. Human sexual differentiation—in utero influences. *Journal of Obstetrics and Gynecology,* 1974, *81,* 448–453.

Alexander, D. E., Ehrhardt, A. A., & Money, J. Defective figure drawing, geometric and human, in Turner's syndrome. *Journal of Nervous and Mental Disease,* 1966, *142,* 161–167.

Altmann, M., Knowles, E., & Bull, H. D. A psychosomatic study of the sex cycle in women. *Psychosomatic Medicine,* 1971, *3,* 199–225.

Archer, J. & Lloyd, B. Sex roles: Biological and social interactions. *New Scientist,* November 21, 1974, pp. 582–584.

Bem, S. L. The measurement of psychological androgyny. *Journal of Consulting and Clinical Psychology,* 1974, *42,* 155–162.

Benedek, T. F. Sexual functions in women and their disturbance. In S. Arieti (Ed.), *American handbook of psychiatry*. New York: Basic Books, 1959.

Block, J. B. Hereditary components in the performance of twins on the WAIS. In S. G. Vandenberg (Ed.), *Progress in human behavior genetics*. Baltimore: Johns Hopkins Press, 1968, 221–226.

Block, J. H. Debatable conclusions about sex differences. *Contemporary Psychology*, 1976, *21*, 517–522. (a)

Block, J. H. Issues, problems, and pitfalls in assessing sex differences. *Merrill-Palmer Quarterly*, 1976, *22* 283–308. (b)

Bock, R. D., & Kolakowski, D. F. Further evidence of sex-linked major gene influence on human spatial visualizing ability. *American Journal of Human Genetics*, 1973, *25*, 1–14.

Bock, R. D. & Vandenberg, S. G. Components of heritable variation in mental test scores. In S. G. Vandenberg (Ed.), *Progress in human behavior genetics*. Baltimore: Johns Hopkins Press, 1968, 233–260.

Bock, R. D., Wainer, H., Petersen, A. C., Thissen, D., Murray, J., & Roche, A. A parameterization for human growth curves. *Human Biology*, 1973, *45*, 63–80.

Bramble, W. J., Bock, R. D., & Vandenberg, S. G. *Components of heritable variation in the Primary Mental Abilities test*. Research Report, Institute for Behavioral Genetics, University of Colorado, 1969.

Broverman, D. M., Broverman, I. K., Vogel, W., & Palmer, R. D. The automatization cognitive style and physical development. *Child Development*, 1964, *35*, 1343–1359.

Broverman, D. M., & Klaiber, E. L. Negative relationships between abilities. *Psychometrika*, 1969, *34*, 5–20.

Bryden, P. Evidence for sex differences in cerebral organization. In M. A. Wittig & A. C. Petersen (Eds.), *Sex-related differences in cognitive functioning: Developmental issues*. New York: Academic Press, in press.

Buffery, A. W. H., & Gray, J. A. Sex differences in the development of spatial and linguistic skills. In C. Ounsted & D. C. Taylor (Eds.), *Gender differences: Their ontogeny and significance*. London: Churchill, 1972, 123–158.

Buss, A. H., & Plomin, R. *A temperament theory of personality development*. New York: Wiley, 1975.

Coltheart, M., Hull, E., & Slater, D. Sex differences in imagery and reading. *Nature*, 1975, *253*, 438–440.

Dan, A. *Patterns of behavioral and mood variation in men and women: Variability and the menstrual cycle*. Unpublished doctoral dissertation, University of Chicago, 1976.

Davis, J. *Stipends and spouses*. Chicago: University of Chicago Press, 1962.

Dawson, J. L. M. Cultural and physiological influences upon spatial perceptual processes in West Africa. *International Journal of Psychology*, 1967, *2*, 171–185.

Dawson, J. L. M. Effects of sex hormones on cognitive style in rats and men. *Behavior Genetics*, 1972, *2*, 21–42.

DeFries, J. C., Ashton, G. C., Johnson, R. C., Kuse, A. R., McClearn, G. E., Mi, M. P., Rashad, M. N., Vandenberg, S. G., & Wilson, J. R. Parent–offspring resemblance for specific cognitive abilities in two ethnic groups. *Nature*, 1976, *261*, 131–133.

Dwyer, C. A. Book review of *Psychology of sex differences*. *American Educational Research Journal*, 1975, *12*, 513–516.

Dwyer, C. A. The role of test bias in producing apparent sex-related differences. In M. A. Wittig & A. C. Petersen (Eds.), *Sex-related differences in cognitive functioning: Developmental issues*. New York: Academic Press, 1979.

Ehrenkranz, J., Bliss, E., & Sheard, M. H. Plasma testosterone: Correlation with aggressive behavior and social dominance in man. *Psychosomatic Medicine*, 1974, *36*, 469–475.

Emmerich, W. The complexities of human development. *Science*, 1975, *190*, 140–141.

Eysenck H. *The biological basis of personality*. Springfield, Ill.: Charles C Thomas, 1967.

Fennema, E. Mathematics learning and the sexes. A review. *Journal for Research in Mathematics Education,* 1974, *5,* 126–139.

Fennema, E. Influences of selected cognitive, affective, and educational variables on sex-related differences in mathematics learning and studying. In L. H. Fox, E. Fennema, & J. Sherman (Eds.), *Women and mathematics: Research perspectives for change* NIE Papers in Education and Work No. 8). Washington, DC: National Institute of Education, 1977.

Fennema, E., & Sherman, J. Sex-related differences in mathematics achievement, spatial visualization, and related factors. *American Educational Research Journal,* 1977, *4,* 51–71.

Fox, C. H. Women and the career relevance of mathematics and science. *School Science and Mathematics,* 1976, *26,* 347–353.

Fox, C. H. Sex differences: Implications for program planning for the academically gifted. In J. C. Stanley (Ed.), *The gifted and the creative: Fifty year perspective.* Baltimore: Johns Hopkins University Press, in press.

Frodi, A., Macaulay, J., & Thome, P. R. Are women always less aggressive than men? A review of the experimental literature. *Psychological Bulletin,* 1977, *84,* 634–660.

Gardner, L. I., & Nieu, R. L. Evidence linking an extra Y chromosome to sociopathic behavior. *Archives of General Psychiatry,* 1972, *26,* 220–222.

Goldberg, S. *The inevitability of patriarchy.* New York: Morrow, 1974.

Goldberg, J., & Meredith, W. A longitudinal study of spatial ability. *Behavior Genetics,* 1975, *5,* 127–135.

Goldman, P. S., & Mac Brown, R. The influence of neonatal androgen on the development of cortical function in the rhesus monkey. *Neuroscience Abstracts,* 5th Annual Meeting of the Society for Neuroscience, New York, 1975.

Goldstein, A. G., & Chance, J. E. Effects of practice on sex-related differences in performance on Embedded Figures. *Psychonomic Science,* 1965, *3,* 361–362.

Goodenough, D. R., Gandini, E., Olkin, I., Pizzamiglio, L., Thayer, D., & Witkin, H. A. A study of X-chromosome linkage with field dependence and spatial visualization. *Behavior Genetics,* 1977, *7,* 373–387.

Gove, W. R. & Herb, T. R. Stress and mental illness among the young: A comparison of the sexes. *Social Forces,* 1974, *53,* 256–265.

Gove, W. R., & Tudor, J. Adult sex roles and mental illness. *American Journal of Sociology,* 1973, *78,* 812–835.

Grave, G. D. Introduction. In M. M. Grumback, G. D. Grave, & F. E. Mayer (Eds.), *Control of the onset of puberty.* New York: Wiley, 1974.

Gray, J. A., & Buffery, A. W. H. Sex differences in emotional and cognitive behavior in mammals including man. *Acta Psychologica,* 1975, *35,* 89–111.

Gurin, G., Veroff, J., & Feld, S. *Americans view their mental health.* New York: Basic Books, 1960.

Guttman, D. Parenthood: A key to the comparative study of the life cycle. In N. Datan & L. H. Ginsburg (Eds.), *Life-span/developmental psychology: Normative life crises.* New York: Academic Press, 1975, 167–184.

Harris, G. W. Sex hormones, brain development and brain function. *Endocrinology,* 1964, *75,* 627–647.

Hoffman, L. W. Changes in family roles, socialization, and sex differences. *American Psychologist,* 1977, *32,* 644–657.

Hoffman, M. L. Sex differences in empathy and related behaviors. *Psychological Bulletin,* 1977, *84,* 712–722.

Horner, M. Toward an understanding of achievement related conflicts in women. *Journal of Social Issues,* 1972, *28,* 157–175.

Hunt, E. E. The developmental genetics of man. In F. Falkner (Ed.), *Human development.* Philadelphia: Saunders, 1966.

Hutt, C. Neuroendocrinological, behavioral and intellectual aspects of sexual differentiation in human development. In C. Ounsted & D. C. Taylor (Eds.), *Gender differences: Their ontogeny and significance.* London: Churchill, 1972, 73–121.

Hyde, J. S., Geiringer, E. R., & Yen, W. M. On the empirical relation between spatial ability and sex differences in other aspects of cognitive performance. *Multivariate Behavioral Research,* 1975, *10,* 289–309.

Ivey, M. E., & Bardwick, J. M. Patterns of affective fluctuation in the menstrual cycle. *Psychosomatic Medicine,* 1968, *30,* 336–345.

Jarvik, L. F., Klodin, V., & Matsuyama, S. S. Human aggression and the extra Y chromosome. *American Psychologist,* 1973, *28,* 674–682.

Kato, N. A fundamental study of rod-frame test. *Japanese Psychological Research,* 1965, *7,* 61–68.

Kim, M. H., Dupon, C., & Hosseinian, A. H. Plasma levels of estrogens, androgens and progesterone during normal and dexamethasone-treated cycles. *Journal of Clinical Endocrinology and Metabolism,* 1974, *39,* 706–712.

Kinsbourne, M. The ontogeny of cerebral dominance. *Annals of the New York Academy of Sciences,* 1975, *263,* 244–250.

Klaiber, E. L., Broverman, D. M., & Kobayashi, Y. The automatization cognitive style, androgens, and monoamine oxidase. *Psychopharmacologia,* 1968, *11,* 320–336.

Koeske, R. K. Theoretical perspectives on menstrual cycle research: The relevance of attributional approaches for the perception and explanation of premenstrual emotionality. In A. J. Dan, E. Graham, & C. Beecher (Eds.), *The menstrual cycle: Synthesis of interdisciplinary research.* New York: Springer, in press.

Kohlberg, L. A cognitive-developmental analysis of children's sex-role concepts and attitudes. In E. E. Maccoby (Ed.), *The development of sex differences.* Stanford: Stanford University Press, 1966, 82–172.

Krashen, S. D. Lateralization, language learning, and the critical period: Some new evidence. *Language Learning,* 1973, *23,* 63–74.

Kreuz, L. E., & Rose, R. M. Assessment of aggressive behavior and plasma testosterone in a young criminal population. *Psychosomatic Medicine,* 1972, *34,* 321–332.

Kreuz, L. E., Rose, R. M., & Jennings, J. R. Suppression of plasma testosterone levels and psychological stress. *Archives of General Psychiatry,* 1972, *26,* 479–482.

Landsdell, H. Sex differences in hemispheric asymmetries of the human brain. *Nature,* 1964, *203,* 550.

Lenney, E. Women's self-confidence in achievement settings. *Psychological Bulletin,* 1977, *84,* 1–13.

Levy, J. Lateral specialization of the human brain: Behavioral manifestations and possible evolutionary basis. In J. A. Kiger (Ed.), *The biology of behavior.* Corvallis, Oregon: University of Oregon Press, 1972.

McCance, R. A., Luff, M. C., & Widdowson, E. E. Physical and emotional periodicity in women. *Journal of Hygiene,* 1937, *37,* 571–611.

Maccoby, E. E., & Jacklin, C. N. *The psychology of sex differences.* Stanford: Stanford University Press, 1974.

McGlone, J., & Davidson, W. The relationship between cerebral speech laterality and spatial ability with special reference to sex and hand preference. *Neuropsychologia,* 1973, *11,* 105–113.

Macrides, F., Bartke, A., & Dalterio, S. Strange females increase plasma testosterone levels in male mice. *Science,* 1975, *189,* 1104–1105.

Marcus, R., & Korenman, S. G. Estrogens and the human male. *Annual Review of Medicine,* 1976, *27,* 357–370.

Masica, D. N., Money, J., Ehrhardt, A., & Lewis, V. G. IQ, fetal sex hormones and cognitive patterns: Studies in the testicular feminizing syndrome of androgen insensitivity. *The Johns Hopkins Medical Journal,* 1969, *124,* 34–43.

Mitchelmore, M. C. *The perceptual development of Jamaican students, with special reference to visualization and drawing of three-dimensional geometrical figures and the effects of spatial training.* Unpublished doctoral dissertation, Ohio State University, 1974.

Money, J., & Alexander, D. Turner's syndrome: Further demonstration of the presence of specific cognitional deficiencies. *Journal of Medical Genetics,* 1966, *3,* 42-48.

Money, J., & Ehrhardt, A. *Man and woman, boy and girl.* Baltimore: Johns Hopkins University Press, 1972.

Monti, P. M., Brown, W. A., & Corriveau, D. P. Testosterone and components of aggressive and sexual behavior in man. *American Journal of Psychiatry,* 1977, *134,* 692-694.

Moos, R. H., Kopell, B. S., Melges, F. T., Yalom, I. D., Lunde, D. T., Clayton, R. B., & Hamberg, D. A. Fluctuation in symptoms and moods during the menstrual cycle. *Journal of Psychosomatic Research,* 1969, *13,* 37-44.

Nash, S. Sex role as a mediator of intellectual functioning. In M. A. Wittig & A. C. Petersen (Eds.), *Sex-related differences in cognitive functioning: Developmental issues.* New York: Academic Press, 1979.

Offer, D., Ostrov, E., & Howard, K. I. The self-image of adolescents: A study of four cultures. *Journal of Youth and Adolescence,* 1977, *6,* 265-280.

Paige, K. E. Effects of oral contraceptives on affective fluctuations associated with the menstrual cycle. *Psychosomatic Medicine,* 1971, *33,* 515-537.

Parsons, J. E., Ruble, D. N., Hodges, K. L., & Small, A. W. Cognitive-developmental factors in emerging sex differences in achievement-related expectancies. *The Journal of Social Issues,* 1976, *32,* 47-62.

Persky, H., O'Brien, C. P., Fine, E., Howard, W. J., Kahn, M. A., & Beck, R. W. The effect of alcohol and smoking on testosterone function and aggression in chronic alcoholics. *American Journal of Psychiatry,* 1977, *134,* 621-625.

Persky, H., Smith, K. D., & Basu, G. K. Relation of psychologic measures of aggression and hostility to testosterone production in man. *Psychosomatic Medicine,* 1971, *33,* 265-277.

Petersen, A. C. Physical androgyny and cognitive functioning in adolescents. *Developmental Psychology,* 1976, *12,* 524-533.

Petersen, A. C. Puberty in adolescent girls and its psychosocial correlates. In M. Sugar (Ed.), *Female adolescent development.* New York: Brunner/Mazel, in press. (a)

Petersen, A. C. Puberty in girls: Its psychosocial significance. In A. J. Dan, E. Graham, & C. Beecher (Eds.), *The menstrual cycle: Synthesis of interdisciplinary research.* New York: Springer, in press. (b)

Petersen, A. C. Biological development in adolescence. In J. Adelson (Ed.), *Handbook of adolescent development.* New York: Wiley, in press. (c)

Petersen, A. C., & Kellam, S. G. The measurement of psychological well-being of adolescents: The psychometric properties and assessment procedures of the How I Feel. *Journal of Youth and Adolescence,* 1977, *6,* 229-248.

Reinisch, J. M. Effects of prenatal hormone exposure on physical and psychological development in humans and animals. In E. J. Sachar (Ed.), *Hormones, behavior, and psychopathology.* New York: Raven Press, 1976.

Reyes, F. I., Boroditsky, R. S., Winter, J. S. S., & Faiman, C. Studies on human sexual development. II. Fetal and maternal serum gonadotropin and sex steroid concentrations. *Journal of Clinical Endocrinology and Metabolism,* 1974, *38,* 612-617.

Riegel, K. F. The dialectics of human development. *American Psychologist,* 1976, *31,* 689-700.

Rosaldo, M. Z., & Lamphere, L. (Eds.), *Woman, culture, and society.* Stanford: Stanford University Press, 1974.

Rose, R. M., Gordon, T. P., & Bernstein, I. S. Plasma testosterone levels in the male rhesus: Influences of sexual and social stimuli. *Science,* 1972, *178,* 643-645.

Rosenberg, M., & Simmons, R. *Black and white self-esteem.* The Rose Monograph Series. Washington, D.C.: American Sociological Association, 1972.

Rosenblatt, P. C., & Cunningham, M. R. Sex differences in cross-cultural perspective. In B. Lloyd & J. Archer (Eds.), *Sex differences: An interactionist approach.* New York: Academic Press, 1976.

Rosenkrantz, P., Vogel, S., Bee, H., Broverman, I., & Broverman, D. Sex-role stereotypes and self-conceptions in college students. *Journal of Consulting Psychology,* 1968, *32,* 287–295.

Sameroff, A. J. Early influences on development: Fact or fancy. In S. Chess & A. Thomas (Eds.), *Annual progress in child psychiatry and child development.* New York: Brunner/Mazel, 1977, 3–33.

Scarr-Salapatek, S. Genetics and the development of intelligence. *Review of Child Development Research,* 1975, *4,* 1–57.

Sherman, J. A. Problem of sex differences in space perception and aspects of intellectual functioning. *Psychological Review,* 1967, *74,* 290–299.

Sherman, J. A. Field articulation, sex, spatial visualization, dependency, practice, laterality of the brain and birth order. *Perceptual and Motor Skills,* 1974, *38,* 1223–1235.

Sherman, J. A. The psychology of sex differences. (Book review) *Sex Roles,* 1975, *1,* 297–301.

Simmons, R., & Rosenberg, F. Sex, sex roles, and self-image. *Journal of Youth and Adolescence,* 1975, *4,* 229–258.

Taylor, D. C., & Ounsted, C. The nature of gender differences explored through ontogenetic analyses of sex ratios in disease. In C. Ounsted & D. C. Taylor, *Gender differences: Their ontogeny and significance.* London: Churchill, 1972, 215–240.

Tresemer, D. The cumulative record of research on "fear of success." *Sex Roles,* 1976, *2,* 217–236.

Ullian, D. Z. The development of conceptions of masculinity and feminity. In B. Lloyd & J. Archer (Eds.), *Exploring sex differences.* New York: Academic Press, 1976, 25–48.

Vogel, W., Broverman, D. M., & Klaiber, E. L. EEG, physique, and androgens. *Perceptual and Motor Skills,* 1968, *26,* 419–429.

Waber, D. P. Sex differences in cognition: A function of maturation rate? *Science,* 1976, *192,* 572–574.

Waber, D. P. The ontogeny of higher cortical functions: Implications for sex differences in cognition. In M. A. Wittig & A. C. Petersen (Eds.), *Sex-related differences in cognitive functioning: Developmental issues.* New York: Academic Press, 1979.

Witkin, H. A., Mednick, S. A., Schulsinger, F., Bakkestrom, E., Christiansen, K. O., Goodenough, D. R., Hirschorn, K., Lundsteen, C., Owen, D. R., Philip, J., Rubin, D. B., & Stocking, M. Criminality in XYY and XXY men. *Science,* 1976, *193,* 547–555.

Yen, W. M. Sex-linked major-gene influences on selected types of spatial performance. *Behavior Genetics,* 1975, *5,* 281–298.

Yen, S. S. C., Rebar, R. W., & Quesenberry, W. Pituitary function in pseudocyesis. *Journal of Clinical Endocrinology and Metabolism,* 1976, *43,* 132–136.

Young, W. C., Goy, R. W., & Phoenix, C. H. Hormones and sexual behavior. *Science,* 1964, *143,* 212–218.

3

Gonadal Hormones and Cognitive Functioning

Donald M. Broverman, Edward L. Klaiber,
and William Vogel
*Worcester State Hospital and The Worcester
Foundation for Experimental Biology*

We have been studying the relationship of gonadal hormones to mental processes in humans since 1963. At that time the hypothesis that the gonadal hormones might significantly influence human mentation was held in a high state of negative esteem. Our first paper in this area (Broverman, Broverman, Palmer, Vogel, & Klaiber, 1964), reporting correlations of secondary sex characteristics and abilities in young adult males, was rejected with the comment, "I'd sooner throw myself across the presses than permit this paper to be printed." Our first grant proposal in this area was rejected with the statement that "androgens and behavior have been intensively studied (in rats) for over 20 years and the feeling of the committee was that there was nothing more to be learned in this area." Physiologically oriented critics pointed out that the gonadal hormones could not possibly affect brain functions since they did not cross the "blood brain barrier," a belief now known to be in error (Pfaff, 1968).

With that early perspective in mind, it is most satisfying to see the interest and work now being devoted to gonadal hormones and mental functioning in humans, as demonstrated by the conference that resulted in this volume. Debate and criticism are no less abundant, but the issues now concern the details of the phenomena rather than whether the phenomena exist.

The following pages will attempt to trace the historic sequence of studies investigating gonadal steroid hormones and behavior that lead to our present investigations of gonadal hormone dynamics in depressed women and men.

INITIAL STUDIES INVOLVING THE AUTOMATIZATION COGNITIVE STYLE

The various studies to be described below derive from observations made in connection with the *automatization cognitive style*. Automatized behaviors are behaviors that have been so well practiced and overlearned that a minimum of conscious effort is required for their successful, efficient execution (Ach, 1905/1951). Such behaviors include the bulk of everyday activities, for example, maintaining one's balance, walking, writing, reading, talking, maintaining perceptual constancies, and so forth.

Bryan and Harter's (1899) "hierarchy of habits" theory argued that the ability to automatize a given task is a prerequisite to the acquisition of new higher level habits in which the lower level automatized habits are subunits (e.g., the ability to automatically recognize letters may be necessary before effective reading becomes possible). Similarly, Humphrey (1951) suggested that the automatic recognition of phonemes, the basic sounds of speech, may be necessary before facility with speech itself can develop. The ability to automatize successively over more complex levels of behavior can result, according to Bryan and Harter (1899), in an escalation of the general level of intellectual functioning. So enamored were these investigators with the potentiating effects of automatization on the psychic economy that they asserted, "automatism is not genius, but it is the hands and feet of genius" (p. 375).

Automatization Cognitive Style

The cognitive style approach to automatization assesses the strength of automatized responses relative to the individual's general level of mental ability rather than against performances of other individuals (Broverman, 1960a). Thus the automatization cognitive style is defined as greater ability (strong automatization) or lesser ability (weak automatization) to perform simple, highly practiced repetitive tasks (e.g., speed of naming repeated common objects or color hues) than expected from the individual's general level of ability (Broverman, 1964).

Indices of the automatization cognitive style computed in this ipsative manner have been experimentally validated; that is, such indices were significantly associated with the ability to achieve skill with extended practice on a novel, but intrinsically simple, repetitive coding task (Broverman, Broverman, & Klaiber, 1966).

Factor analyses of ipsative performance scores (deviations of specific task performances from the individual's general level of ability) have regularly produced bipolar factors that contrast performances of automatized tasks with perceptual restructuring tasks (Broverman, 1964). Perceptual restructuring tasks require individuals to inhibit, or set aside, initial automatized responses to obvious stimulus attributes in order that responses may be made to less obvious stimulus attributes. Examples of perceptual restructuring tasks are the Embedded Figures Task (Witkin, 1950) and the Block Designs and Object Assembly subtests of the Wechsler Adult Intelligence Scale (Wechsler, 1955).

Bipolarity, in this context, indicates that the greater the magnitude of the ipsative deviations, in one direction, of automatization task performances from the individual's mean level of cognitive performance, the greater are the deviations in the opposite direction of the individual's performances of perceptual restructuring tasks from his or her mean level of performance. Thus strong automatizers perform simple repetitive tasks better than their own level of general intellectual performance, and they perform perceptual restructuring tasks worse than their own level of general intellectual performance. Weak automatizers have the reverse pattern of abilities on these tasks.

Factor analyses of normative (nonipsatized) performance scores of cognitive tasks typically report separate factors of automatization and perceptual restructuring tasks (e.g., Podell & Phillips, 1959), suggesting that these two types of task performances are independent of each other. However, such analyses achieve statistical independence between factors by assigning portions of the first "general" (g) factor variance to each of the residual bipolar "special" factors via rotation of axes. The g factor variance is the same between-individual variance that is removed by ipsatization of data (Broverman, 1963; MacAndrew & Forgy, 1963). Thus the factorial independence achieved by rotation is normative, that is, it refers to relationships across individuals. In contrast, the bipolar ipsative factors are based on within-individual portions of variance remaining after extraction of the g, between-individual, variance. Ipsative factors, therefore, refer to intraindividual relationships (Broverman, 1961, 1962).

It has been suggested that the factorial bipolarity of automatization and perceptual restructuring tasks represents an artifact rising out of the ipsative procedure (MacAndrew & Forgy, 1963) rather than reflecting a true inverse functional relationship that occurs within individuals. This problem may be addressed on several levels.

Statistically the factorial bipolarity connotes, at a minimum, that maximum dissimilarity exists between automatization and perceptual restructuring task performances. Theoretically it can be argued that the stronger the initial automatized perceptual response to the obvious features of a perceptual restructuring task, the greater the difficulty there may be in setting that initial, erroneous response aside, and therefore the poorer the restructuring. Empirically, several types of studies indicate that negative relationships between these tasks do exist independent of the ipsative technique:

1. Significant negative correlations have been obtained from the raw scores of automatization and perceptual restructuring tasks when subjects were selected to represent extremes of a parameter known to be associated with the automatization cognitive style (Broverman & Klaiber, 1969).
2. Performances of automatization and perceptual restructuring tasks vary diurnally in opposite ways; that is, individuals perform automatization tasks better in the morning than in the afternoon, but these same individuals perform perceptual restructuring tasks better in the afternoon

than they do in the morning (Mackenberg, Broverman, Vogel, & Klaiber, 1974).

3. Performances of the two categories of tasks respond in opposite ways to adrenergic stimulants and to adrenergic depressants. For example, the adrenergic stimulant amphetamine facilitates performance of such automatized tasks as speed of naming color hues (Callaway & Stone, 1960) and reading speed (Florey & Gilbert, 1943) but impairs space perception in airplane pilots (Davis, 1947). On the other hand, the adrenergic depressant chlorpromazine impairs performance of automatized tasks such as tapping speed (Lehmann & Csank, 1957) and letter discrimination (Primac, Mirsky, & Rosvold, 1957) but facilitates the speed of counting backward, a task that requires suppression of the stronger habit of counting forward (Shatin, Rockmore, & Funk, 1956). A fuller review of relevant psychopharmacological studies involving these categories of tasks and drugs was presented in Broverman, Klaiber, Kobayashi, and Vogel (1968).

These specific drug-by-category-of-task interactions also give insight into the neural substrates that may underlie performances of automatization and perceptual restructuring tasks (Broverman et al., 1968).

The above findings suggest that the two categories of tasks are negatively related intrapsychically and that ipsative perceptual restructuring task performance scores negatively define the automatization cognitive style.

It is also of interest to note that the two categories of tasks have opposite patterns of sex differences: females perform automatized tasks better than males (Gainer, 1962; Norman, 1953; Staples, 1932; Stroop, 1935) while males perform perceptual restructuring tasks better than females (Bennett, 1956; Bieri, Bradburn, & Galinsky, 1958; MacMeeken, 1939; Witkin, Dyk, Faterson, Goodenough, & Karp, 1962).

The automatization cognitive style, positively defined by ipsative automatization task performance scores and negatively defined by ipsative perceptual restructuring task performance scores, has been found to be positively associated with occupational and social effectiveness in 50-year-old males: strong automatizers had higher level occupations and greater social status that weak automatizers matched for age, educational level, and general level of intelligence (Broverman, 1964). The strong automatizers were also more upwardly mobile socially than the weak automatizers (Broverman, 1964). Young adult male strong automatizers had greater resistance to distraction (Broverman, 1960b), while preadolescent male strong automatizers had more aggressive game playing (Sutton-Smith, Roberts, Kozelka, Crandall, Broverman, Blum, & Klaiber, 1967) and greater oral reading ability (Drake & Schnall, 1966; Eakin & Douglas, 1971) than like-aged groups of weak automatizers.

An interesting problem in values occurs at this point. The above arguments and empirical findings strongly favor the adaptive value of the strong automatization over the weak automatization cognitive style. On the other hand, developmental theorists and researchers have long espoused the developmental superiority inherent in good perceptual restructuring task performances (Werner, 1948; Witkin, Lewis, Hertzman, Machover, Meissner, & Wapner, 1954; Witkin et al., 1962). The basis of this developmental argument is twofold: (1) Werner's (1948) postulate that development entails an increasing ability to subordinate responses to immediate, concrete aspects of a stimulus situation in favor of responses to other, less perceptually salient stimuli, and (2) the fact that performance of perceptual restructuring tasks improves from childhood to adulthood. Performances of perceptual restructuring tasks, then, have been used as developmental indices, and numerous studies have reported adaptive superiority of individuals who perform perceptual restructuring tasks well compared to those who perform such tasks poorly (Witkin et al., 1962). However, these studies have been criticized (Zigler, 1963) for not having separated general level of intellectual ability from specific perceptual restructuring task performances (i.e., the developmentalists have not employed ipsative techniques). Their suggestion that good perceptual restructuring task performances are associated with greater adaptive value, therefore, could be in part, because of the association of such nonipsatized task performances with general intellectual ability.

At any rate a conflict exists in the value orientations of the automatization and developmental theories, and we have accepted as valid criticism that we have overenthusiastically focused on the advantages of strong automatization without equal attention to the positive features that may accompany a weak automatization (good perceptual restructuring) cognitive style. It is ironic therefore that in the first paper in which we attempted to restrain our own value prejudices in favor of strong automatization (Broverman et al., 1968) by omitting value considerations and restricting ourselves to descriptions of the task attributes, our work was interpreted within the wider cultural value system, which favors complexity over simplicity (Parlee, 1972). Consequently, when we argued that females were superior on simple repetitive automatization tasks and males superior on more complex perceptual restructuring tasks, we were perceived as being prejudiced against women. Our mistake was in failing to anticipate that the culturally determined value preference for complexity over simplicity would prevail over our own bias in favor of automatization ability.

Maturational and Anthropometric Correlates of the Automatization Cognitive Style

The conclusions reached from this initial set of studies is that gonadal hormones (estrogens in females, testosterone in males) tend to induce a strong automatization cognitive style, that is, better performances of automatized tasks than of perceptual restructuring tasks.

Our initial ventures into physiology were not prompted by theory but rather by our impressions that the strong and weak automatizing male undergraduate subjects in our various behavioral studies seemed to look different physically. The first study (Broverman et al., 1964) was undertaken then without a priori hypotheses, and the physiological measurements consisted simply of photographs of 50 male undergraduates stripped to the waist, plus a number of physical measurements. The photographs, which permitted crude assessments of body hair, strongly suggested that male strong automatizers had more body hair than male weak automatizers. Further, the strong automatizers appeared to be physically more muscular than were the weak automatizers. A second, younger, high school sample was immediately obtained with attention paid to frequency of shaving. The second sample confirmed the findings of the first and also indicated that strong automatizers tend to shave more often than weak automatizers (Broverman et al., 1964).

At this time Dr. Klaiber, an endocrinologist, joined the study. With his help the various findings were interpreted to indicate that the strong automatizing males tended to mature earlier than weak automatizing males. This conclusion has now been confirmed in an independent study by Waber (1976), who also extended her conclusions to females (i.e., early maturing persons of both sexes tend to be strong automatizers; late maturing individuals of both sexes tend to be weak automatizers). Petersen (1976) did not find this phenomenon in her data. However, Waber's subjects were selected extremes of early and late maturation, which may have facilitated the observation.

Rate of maturation at time of adolescence, of course, is essentially a reflection of the vigor of gonadal function. Hence these studies support the notion that strong automatizers within each sex have greater homotypical gonadal hormone stimulation than do weak automatizers of that sex.

Our second study (Klaiber, Broverman, & Kobayashi, 1967) was intended to provide somewhat more sophisticated clinical evidence of androgen (male hormone) differences in strong and weak automatizing males. In addition to physical measurements, assessments were made of pubic hair development from nude photographs after the manner described by Tanner (1962). Pubic hair development is considered the most sensitive anthropometric index of testosterone stimulation in both sexes. Urinary levels of 17-ketosteroids (testosterone metabolites) were also obtained. This study confirmed the expectations derived from our initial study: strong automatizing males had greater physical evidence of testosterone stimulation than did male weak automatizers, a finding that has since been confirmed by Petersen (1976). Petersen also extended her observations to female adolescents and found that physical evidence of testosterone stimulation in females was significantly associated with the weak automatization cognitive pattern. Thus testosterone in females is associated with cognitive functioning in a manner opposite to the way it is associated in males. At first this may seem odd. However, it should be kept in mind that testosterone is a potent antiestrogen (Price & Williams-

Ashman, 1961). Hence elevated testosterone activity in females would tend to oppose estrogen functions in females. It is possible then that the strong automatizing females in Petersen's study, who tended to have few signs of testosterone stimulation, had more estrogen stimulation than did the weak automatizing females in that sample.

An interesting aspect of the Klaiber et al. (1967) study is that the secondary sex characteristics (chest and biceps circumferences, pubic hair development) are all positively related to raw scores of the automatization tasks and negatively related to the raw scores of the perceptual restructuring tasks, in most cases, with statistical significance. This pattern of relationships again illustrates the intrinsic bipolarity of automatization and perceptual restructuring tasks; that is, the two types of tasks tend to reflect negatively related phenomena.

Blood Hormone Studies

Our third study was an attempt to more directly assess testosterone levels in male strong and weak automatizers by assaying blood concentrations of the hormone. Although the then recently developed assay (Riondal, Tait, Gut, Tait, Joachim, & Little, 1963) was extremely costly and time consuming, we did manage to assay, eventually, bloods from 60 male undergraduates. To our dismay we found virtually identical mean levels of testosterone in the bloods of strong and weak automatizing subjects (Klaiber & Broverman, Note 1). This setback forced consideration of other possibilities. Several were available. The concentration of testosterone circulating in the blood does not necessarily reflect the degree of testosterone utilization by the body. For instance, in order to be used the hormones must impinge upon an appropriate tissue receptor site. Utilization could be impaired by a lack of such tissue receptor sites. Still another possibility stemmed from the fact that testosterone, like most other hormones, circulates in the blood in two states: a bound state wherein the hormone molecule is attached to a specific protein molecule produced by the liver and a free state wherein the hormone molecule is unattached to any other molecule. Only the free hormone is physiologically active. Our assay measured total testosterone level, that is, bound and free combined. Methods for assaying the free testosterone level had not then been developed. However, the Worcester Foundation researchers had by then developed a radioactive infusion procedure for determining the dynamics of blood testosterone (i.e., the rate at which testosterone is metabolically cleared from the blood and the rate at which the body secretes testosterone into the blood) (Tait & Burstein, 1964). These dynamic aspects of testosterone are, presumably, closely related to the physiological activity of the hormone.

Testosterone metabolic clearance and production rates therefore were determined in a new sample of young adult males. This study (Klaiber,

Broverman, Vogel, & Mackenberg, 1974) revealed that the strong automatizers were producing and metabolically clearing over 50% more testosterone per time unit than were the weak automatizers. Again the mean blood concentrations of testosterone in the two groups did not differ. It should be emphasized that all the subjects were normal, healthy, well-functioning undergraduates of a prestigious northeastern college. Yet major differences in testosterone dynamics, associated with cognitive functioning, occurred in this sample. Clearly the category of "normal" covers as wide a range of individual difference in physiology as it does in personality and behavior.

Hormone Manipulations

Despite the impressive difference in testosterone dynamics found in male strong and weak automatizers the finding was still correlative, and correlations do not imply causation. In order to determine if testosterone were causatively influencing cognitive performances, manipulations of testosterone would have to be shown to induce changes in cognitive performance. This goal was pursued in our next study (Klaiber, Broverman, Vogel, Abraham, & Cone, 1971) wherein male undergraduates, matched for performance on a serial subtraction task, were infused either with saline or a saline-testosterone mixture. Strong and weak automatizers had been previously found to differ significantly in performance of this task (Vogel, Broverman, & Klaiber, 1968). All subjects thought they had volunteered for a 6-hour infusion of testosterone. Actually, all subjects were infused for the first 3 hours with saline. The serial subtractions test and an EEG examination were then administered. Half the subjects were then switched to the saline-testosterone mixture for the next 3 hours; the other half continued on saline. The testosterone dosage was high but within normal physiological limits. After the second 3 hours of infusion all subjects were again administered the serial subtractions task and EEG examination. Both groups of subjects performed the serial subtractions task more poorly on the second occasion than on the first. This fact may have been caused by the prolonged stress of the study (indwelling catheters were placed in both arms; the infusion pump connected to one arm, periodic blood samples being taken from the other). However, the deterioration in the saline group was approximately twice that of the testosterone-infused group ($F = 4.24$; $p < .05$). We had for the first time ever, then, evidence that the administration of testosterone acutely affected cognitive functioning in humans. Significant shifts in EEG alpha waves during task performances in a direction previously found associated with strong automatizers (Vogel et al., 1968) were also noted in the testosterone-infused group (Vogel, Broverman, Klaiber, Abraham, & Cone, 1971).

The magnitude and level of significance of the above main effects, however, were not very impressive. Therefore closer attention was given to the attributes of those subjects whose mental performance improved versus those whose mental performance did not improve in response to the administered testosterone. All the experimental subjects had received the same dosage of testosterone. Their postinfusion blood levels of testosterone, however, showed marked differences. The postinfusion testosterone concentrations in some subjects were elevated to levels not observable in normal individuals, whereas the postinfusion blood testosterone concentrations of other individuals had remained normal. The elevated postinfusion blood concentrations imply that these subjects were not clearing or using the administered hormone. Rather the administered hormones appeared to have been trapped in the circulating system, possibly because of a heightened degree of binding by specific binding proteins in the blood. At any rate, the deterioration in serial subtraction performance of the subjects with elevated post-infusion testosterone concentrations was comparable to that of the saline-infused subjects (i.e., the administered testosterone had no apparent effect upon these subjects).

On the other hand, those subjects infused with testosterone who maintained normal postinfusion blood concentrations of testosterone, implying that they cleared the administered hormone as rapidly as they received it, actually showed a slight improvement in their postinfusion cognitive performances. The difference in changes in performance of the high and low postinfusion blood testosterone groups was highly statistically significant: $F(1, 25) = 10.06$; $p < .002$.

The implication of the above finding is that major individual differences exist in response to administered gonadal hormones. The responses depend in part on the physiology of the person.

In an attempt to determine other attributes of the good and poor responders to testosterone, we noted that the poor responders with high postinfusion testosterone concentrations tended to have less pubic hair development than did the better responders with normal postinfusion testosterone concentrations. This finding suggests the possibility that the relatively low level of chronic testosterone stimulation evidenced by the scant pubic hair development of the poor responders may result from a chronic inability to utilize their own endogenous testosterone.

PROPOSED MECHANISMS OF ACTION OF THE GONADAL HORMONES ON THE CENTRAL NERVOUS SYSTEM

We hypothesize that the gonadal hormones, estrogen and testosterone, achieve their effects on the central nervous system (CNS) via their regulatory influence on the activity of the enzyme monoamine oxidase (MAO). MAO is found predominantly within the adrenergic neurons of the body where it metabolizes various monoamines thought to be the neurotransmitters for adrenergic nerves.

The adrenergic (sympathetic) or *ergotropic* portion of the central autonomic nervous system is believed to regulate behavioral activity, alertness, sensory reactivity, and so forth, while the cholinergic (parasympathetic) or *trophotropic* part of the central autonomic nervous system is thought to control appetite, relaxation, sleep, inhibition of ergotropic activity, and the like (Hess, 1954). The two systems are frequently in competition and the final effect depends on the relationship of the momentary activities of the two systems (Hess, 1954).

The monoamine norepinephrine is believed to be a primary neural transmitter of the central adrenergic nervous system. Neuronal norepinephrine is synthesized within adrenergic neurons. Levels of norepinephrine are controlled in part by the intraneural metabolic activity of the enzyme MAO. Elevated MAO activity may act to diminish neural stores of norepinephrine with a subsequent impairment of neural adrenergic activity (Kopin, 1964). Chronic suppression of MAO activity, however, also impairs adrenergic functioning by allowing the neural accumulation of "false neurotransmitter" monoamines that displace norepinephrine and then act as inefficient neurotransmitters (Kopin, 1968). Adequate central adrenergic functioning, then, requires that MAO activity stay at intermediate levels.

The hypothesis that the gonadal hormones achieve their effects on the CNS via their influence on MAO originated from an unplanned observation that our male strong automatizers had significantly lower plasma MAO activity than did the weak automatizers (Klaiber et al., 1967). This observation occurred when one of our colleagues at the Worcester Foundation for Experimental Biology, Dr. Yutaka Kobayashi, asked us for human blood samples to test a new assay he had developed for MAO activity. Blood samples from our subjects sharply differentiated the strong and weak automatizers. The possible implications quickly became evident. A review of the literature revealed two prior MAO, gonadal hormone reports. Wurtman and Axelrod (1963) had found that female rats had lower MAO activity in various tissues than did male rats and that estrogens administered to male rats lowered their MAO activity to the female range. Testosterone administered to female rats, on the other hand, raised the MAO activity into the male range. These findings suggest that each steroid hormone tends to bring MAO activity into a range associated with that hormone. Hence the hormones act as MAO regulators.

Kobayashi, Kobayashi, Kato, and Minaguchi (1966) had reported that ovariectomized rats had higher hypothalamic MAO activity than normal female rats. The administration of estrogens to ovariectomized rats resulted in hypothalamic MAO activity not significantly different than normal female rats.

The behavioral implications of these gonadal hormone manipulations of MAO activity may be gleaned from various studies of wheel-running in rats. Wheel running in the rat appears to be an adrenergic dependent behavior. For instance, adrenergic stimulants such as amphetamine (Tainter, 1943; Zieve,

1937) and caffeine (Tainter, 1943) increase wheel running; while adrenergic depressants such as chlorpromazine reduce wheel running (Mirsky, White, & O'Dell, 1959).

The gonadal hormones act like adrenergic stimulants on wheel running, possibly through their effects on MAO activity. Thus female rats, which are reported to have lower MAO activity than male rats (Wurtman & Axelrod, 1963), run more than male rats (Hitchcock, 1925). Administration of large amounts of estrogens to castrated male rats induced female levels of wheel-running activity (Hoskins & Bevin, 1941; Wang, Richter, & Guttmacher, 1925). Removal of the ovaries from female rats causes a reduction in wheel-running activity (Richter, 1927; Wang, 1923); the administration of estrogens to ovariectomized female rats restores their wheel-running activity (Young & Fish, 1945). Similarly, castration sharply reduces the wheel running of adult male rats (Hoskins, 1925; Richter, 1933), and the administration of testosterone to castrated male rats restores their activity level to normal (Jackubezak, 1965).

The above animal studies seem to make a good case for the gonadal hormones acting as stimulants on the central adrenergic nervous system via their influence on MAO activity. No comparable MAO work had been done on humans at this time (circa 1966) because of the absence of a convenient blood assay for MAO activity. Kobayashi's plasma MAO assay (Otsuka & Kobayashi, 1964) filled this void and enabled us to undertake such studies.

Our first planned MAO study consisted of daily blood samples from 19 ovulating student nurses across one complete menstrual cycle (Klaiber, Kobayashi, Broverman, & Hall, 1971). Daily basal body temperatures were recorded to assure that ovulation had occurred. For comparison purposes the six bloods preceding and including the basal body temperature nadir (time of ovulation) were selected as a period when blood estradiol levels are known to be peaking; and the six blood samples immediately preceding the first day of flow were selected as a period when both blood estradiol and blood progesterone levels are known to be elevated. Progesterone, in many respects, is an antiestrogen.

The mean plasma MAO activity of the premenstrual phase of the menstrual cycle, characterized by high estrogen opposed by high progesterone levels, was approximately double that of the preovulatory phase when estrogen levels are high and progesterone levels are low ($t = 4.02; p < .001$). If plasma MAO activity is reflective of brain MAO activity, this result would imply that the premenstrual phase of the cycle is characterized by reduced central adrenergic functioning compared to the preovulatory phase. We noted with interest that the various symptoms reported for the "premenstrual tension" syndrome (i.e., headaches, fatigue, appetite surges, etc.) were largely consistent with what would be predicted from decreased central adrenergic functioning as implied by heightened MAO activity.

Wineman (1971) has reached an opposite conclusion about the pattern of adrenergic function over the menstrual cycle. She reports that sympathetic (adrenergic) autonomic indices of arousal are maximal during the postovulatory (premenstrual) phase of the cycle. However, Wineman's (1971) conclusions are based on peripheral indices that are responsive to adrenal medullary secretions of catecholamines, whereas we are concerned with CNS adrenergic processes that depend upon catecholamines synthesized within the brain. We have hypothesized (Broverman, Klaiber, Vogel, & Kobayashi, 1974) that prolonged adrenergic impairment in the brain may act as a stressor that stimulates the partially compensatory release of peripheral adrenal catecholamines. Thus depressed patients, who are believed to be suffering from a central catecholamine deficiency (Schildkraut, 1965), are reported to have elevated levels of circulating catecholamines (Wyatt, Portnoy, Kupfer, Snyder, & Engelman, 1971). The administration of an MAO inhibitor, an adrenergic stimulant, to these patients resulted in reduced levels of circulating catecholamines. This study illustrates the long-term inverse relationship that may exist between central and peripheral adrenergic functioning. This formulation makes Wineman's conclusions and ours compatible. If the premenstrual elevation of plasma MAO activity represents central adrenergic impairment, that impairment could act as a stressor, inducing the release of adrenal catecholamines with subsequent arousal of peripheral autonomic indices.

The above-described menstrual cycle–plasma MAO activity relationships are correlative in nature. In order to determine if the hormonal changes associated with the menstrual cycle were actually causing the changes in plasma MAO activity, manipulations of the hormones were required. Therefore two groups of patients known to be estrogen deficient, young amenorrheic women and older menopausal women, were studied (Klaiber, Kobayashi, Broverman, & Hall, 1971).

Each group of patients had pretreatment means of plasma MAO activity that were grossly and significantly elevated over the values observed in regularly menstruating women. Treatment consisted of 21 days of oral conjugated estrogen, 5 mg/day, with a progestin added for the last 5 days. In each group the estrogen treatment produced a major decrease in the plasma MAO activity, while the estrogen–progestin combination resulted in significantly higher levels of MAO activity than estrogen alone but not as high as the pretreatment values (Klaiber et al., 1971). These results indicate that the gonadal hormones significantly affect plasma MAO activity.

Plasma MAO Activity as an Index of Central Adrenergic Functioning

A critical issue is whether the MAO activity in plasma tends to reflect brain MAO activity. Our approach to this issue has rested largely on the EEG "driving" response to photic stimulation. When a bright flashing light is placed before the closed eyes of a subject, the EEG rhythms often synchronize with the flashing light. This is called an EEG driving response to photic stimulation.

The phenomenon appears to be adrenergic dependent; that is, adrenergic stimulants such as amphetamine (Shetty, 1971) or infused norepinephrine (Floru, Costin, Nestianu, & Sterescu-Volanschi, 1962) tend to prevent the response from occurring, while adrenergic depressants such as chlorpromazine increase the frequency of the response (Killam, Killam, & Naquet, 1967).

We have found that EEG driving responses occur significantly more often in weak automatizing than strong automatizing males (Vogel, Broverman, Klaiber, & Kun, 1969) and more often in the premenstrual phase of the cycle than in the preovulatory phase (Vogel, Broverman, & Klaiber, 1971). More important, the frequency of EEG driving responses were significantly correlated with plasma MAO activity in young adult males (Vogel, Broverman, Klaiber, & Kobayashi, 1974) and in depressed women (Klaiber, Broverman, Vogel, Kobayashi, & Moriarty, 1972). Also, the administration of an MAO inhibitor drug (Marplan) significantly depressed both plasma MAO activity and frequency of EEG driving responses in young adult males (Vogel et al., 1974).

Similar results have been obtained with gonadal steroid hormones; that is, estrogens administered to amenorrheic (Vogel et al., 1969) and depressed women (Klaiber et al., 1972) significantly decreased EEG driving rates, as did testosterone administered to hypogonadal males (Stenn, Klaiber, Vogel, & Broverman, 1972). Hence plasma MAO activity does appear to reflect the state of adrenergic processes in the brain.

Criticisms of the Plasma MAO Assay

Several criticisms have been made of the Otsuka and Kobayashi (1964) plasma MAO assay. The first was by Robinson, Lovenberg, Keiser, and Sjoerdsma, (1968), who reported that standard MAO inhibitor drugs did not inhibit plasma MAO activity. However, although Robinson et al. stated that they used the Otsuka and Kobayashi plasma method, the method actually described was that of McEwen (1965). Our method includes the addition of aminoguanidine to inhibit the activities of three other enzymes (spermine oxidase, diamine oxidase, and benzylamine oxidase) that are present in human plasma. All three enzymes, if not inhibited, could oxidize the radioactive substrate used by Robinson et al. (1968) and would yield evidence of oxidative activity in the presence of an MAO inhibitor drug. McEwen's assay does not call for the addition of aminoguanidine. Hence the results obtained from the procedure do not uniquely reflect MAO activity. The Otsuka and Kobayashi method has repeatedly indicated that MAO inhibitors do inhibit plasma MAO activity (Vogel et al., 1974; Kobayashi, 1966).

Another criticism of plasma MAO activity is that since the MAO enzyme is a discrete, insoluble particle, it is not likely to be present in clear plasma from which discrete particles have been supposedly removed. For many years we could not answer this criticism. Recently we have found that the standard clinical centrifugal preparation of plasma does not completely remove all the blood platelets from the plasma. A small but significant number of platelets remain that can only be removed by ultracentrifugation or microfiltration. When these procedures are employed the plasma is devoid of MAO activity. In short, the plasma MAO assay has actually been measuring the MAO activity of residual platelets in the plasma. Much of the variability that we have encountered in the plasma MAO activity values appears to have resulted from variations in the number of residual platelets. We are now counting the number of residual platelets per cc plasma by a rapid method utilizing a Coulter Counter and expressing the activity per 100,000 platelets (Klaiber, Broverman, & Vogel, Note 2). This procedure should improve the reliability of the MAO data. Meanwhile, our modified plasma method continues to be a quick, economical method of measuring MAO activity.

Finally, suggestions have been made that monoamine oxidase consists of several isoenzymes, and that the isoenzyme found in the blood is not the same as that found in brain tissue (Gomes, Igaue, Kloepfer, & Yasunobu, 1969). More recently, however, the appearance of various isoenzymes have been reported to be caused by differential tissue affinities for various monoamine substrates and that in fact no true isoenzymes exist (Tipton, Houslay, & Garrett, 1973). These various criticisms therefore do not seem substantial enough to warrant turning away from the useful empirical results being obtained from plasma MAO measures.

APPLICATION OF THE RESEARCH: HORMONAL THERAPY OF DEPRESSION

At this stage of our research it became evident that the theoretical formulation we had developed to explain the relationship of the gonadal hormones to cognitive processes also had implications for the affective disturbance of mental depression. Unfortunately, the ensuing series of studies exploring these implications in samples of depressed patients did not produce meaningful data relevant to our earlier concern with cognitive processes, primarily because the relatively small numbers of patients studied varied widely in age and level of education.

MAO has been of interest to psychiatrists since the late 1950s when drugs that inhibit the activity of this enzyme were found to alleviate the symptoms of depression (Kline, 1959). MAO inhibitors were the first effective anti-depressant drugs. Because a convenient blood assay of MAO activity was not available for many years, no evidence had been obtained that depressed individuals had abnormally elevated MAO activity that required inhibition. With the advent of the Otsuka and Kobayashi (1964) plasma MAO assay, we were able to investigate this possibility. Our original sample consisted of 17 moderately depressed, regularly menstruating outpatient women. Blood samples from these women revealed the highest plasma MAO activity that we had thus far encountered: the mean level of MAO activity of our depressed patients in the preovulatory phase of the menstrual cycle was 700% greater than that of nondepressed regularly menstruating women and 200% greater than that found in amenorrheic women (Klaiber et al., 1972). Nies et al. (1971) simultaneously reported elevated platelet MAO activity in depressed women and men.

Since our depressed women had abnormally elevated plasma MAO activity, it seemed reasonable to attempt to inhibit the enzyme's activity with estrogens as we had done with amenorrheic and menopausal women. The same treatment procedure, 5 mg/day oral conjugated estrogen, again significantly lowered their elevated plasma MAO activity (Klaiber et al., 1972). At the same time, the patients reported to their psychiatrists that they felt better. However, that study was not done in double-blind fashion; the patient's reports could have resulted from suggestion. We therefore undertook a double-blind study of estrogens as a treatment for depression. At the suggestion of our funding agency, the study was performed with inpatients in order to better control their diet, accessibility to other drugs, and other factors. Depression, however, is now for the most part an outpatient illness. Only the most severe, therapy-resistant depressives now require prolonged hospitalization. Furthermore, for ethical reasons we limited ourselves only to those patients who had failed to respond to conventional antidepressant therapies (i.e., chemotherapy, psychotherapy, electric shock therapy). Such patients are extremely rare and only approximately 8 patients volunteered and completed the studies per year. After 5 years, we now have $n = 40$ completed patients, 23 who received estrogen, 17 who received placebos. The study period lasted 4 months. During the first month all patients received placebos and the data obtained in this period served as baseline measures. Patients then received either estrogen or placebos for the next 3 months. Approximately two-thirds of the patients were premenopausal; one-third postmenopausual. All had histories of at least 2 years of chronic depression; most for much longer periods.

Pilot study work indicated that much higher dose levels of estrogen would be required to inhibit plasma MAO activity in these very severely depressed patients. Hence our treatment doses ranged from 5–25 mg/day of oral conjugated estrogen. Twenty-five milligrams of conjugated estrogen is approximately 20–40 times the dose levels conventionally prescribed for menopausal symptoms. Pap smears and endometrial biopsies were performed before and after treatment.

Our results indicate that 65% of the patients treated with estrogen showed significant improvement; a few to a very marked extent (repeated measures t test $= 5.17$; $p < .001$). The placebo treated patients, on the other hand, were slightly worse after 3 months of treatment (Klaiber, Broverman, Vogel, & Kobayashi, 1976). Plasma MAO activity in the two groups followed the same pattern: grossly elevated in both groups prior to treatment; significantly reduced after 3 months in the estrogen-treated group; and slightly higher after placebos in the placebo group.

Side Effects of Estrogen Therapy

The possible side effects of large doses of estrogen are a major concern. In fact, few side effects were observed. Breast tenderness has been minimal and tended to disappear completely after a month of therapy. No thrombotic or embolic episodes have been observed. There has never been a documented report of thrombosis or embolism attributable to conjugated estrogen in the more than 20 years that this medication has been widely used in women (Boston University Drug Surveillance Program, 1974).

Several studies have reported increased risks of endometrial cancer in postmenopausal women on estrogen therapy because of menopausal symptoms (Mack, Pike, Henderson, Pfeffer, Gerkins, & Arthur, 1976; Smith, Prentice, Thompson, & Herrmann, 1975; Weiss, Szekely, & Austin, 1976; Ziel & Finkle, 1975). However, none of these studies included groups of women in which the estrogens were administered cyclically and in conjunction with progesterone at the end of each cycle, as was done with our patients.

The concern about estrogen in relation to endometrial carcinoma has historically centered around endometrial hyperplasia, which can be caused by sustained estrogen stimulation (Lipsett, 1974). Endometrial hyperplasia precedes adenomatous hyperplasia, which has been shown to be a precursor to endometrial carcinoma in some cases (Gusberg, 1974).

Endometrial hyperplasia can be avoided if periodic shedding of the endometrial lining is induced by administering estrogen in a cyclic manner with progestin added near the end of each cycle (Kistner, 1971). All our patients were treated in this manner; none had excessive uterine bleeding, and endometrial biopsies, which were performed after 3 months of estrogen therapy and periodically during aftercare, have revealed endometrial hyperplasias in only two of our patients. In each case the hyperplasia was corrected by increasing the dose of progesterone to provide a more adequate shedding of the uterine lining.

Other studies indicate that approximately 994 women out of every 1000 receiving estrogen therapy do not develop endometrial cancer in a given year (Weiss, 1975); that the overall incidence of cancers of all varieties in women on long-term estrogen therapy is decreased by over 50% (Burch, Byrd, & Vaughn, 1974). However, these studies involved much lower doses of estrogen than used in the present study.

Several factors must be considered in the risk–benefit ratio of estrogen therapy with these patients. Of the 40 patients, 25 (62.5%) had made serious suicide attempts prior to inclusion in the program. All our patients admitted to suicidal thoughts ranging from mild to severe during the time of the study, and a number of suicide attempts occurred during the study period. In addition to the suicide risk, these women faced an extremely high risk of lifelong debilitation from a severe chronic depressive state. In comparison, the risks of endometrial carcinoma or thromboembolic disease seem considerably less. Thus we feel that the risk–benefit ratio, which must be considered in the use of all drugs, is well met by this estrogen therapy. The risk of endometrial carcinoma seems a relatively remote threat to these patients compared with the almost certain risk of lifelong debilitation by their depressive illness.

Obviously, the estrogen doses employed in our study are markedly higher than the doses of estrogen usually employed. The number of patients in our study is still relatively small, and the patients have been followed over a relatively short time. Thus any statements about the long-term effects of large doses of estrogen administered cyclically with respect to such problems as thromboembolic disease or cancer are impossible at this time.

Testosterone Therapy of Depression in Males

We have also successfully treated in an initial open study therapy-resistant male depressives with very large doses of a testosterone analogue (Vogel, Klaiber, & Broverman, Note 3).

Gonadal Hormone Therapy and MAO Inhibition

If the gonadal steroids are achieving their effects via regulation of MAO activity, it is reasonable to ask why these patients did not respond positively to MAO inhibition therapy. The reason may be the same reason that MAO inhibitors are no longer widely used in the treatment of depression.

A characteristic of the MAO inhibitors is that their alleviation of depressive symptoms tends to be temporary. After a period of time the effectiveness of the drugs diminished. Without a convenient method of assessing the patient's MAO activity, psychiatrists faced with this problem typically increased the dosage but to no avail. At the same time various other physiological indices indicated that the drugs were having paradoxical effects (i.e., patients would develop hypotension instead of hypertension). After the plasma MAO assay was developed, the effects of various MAO inhibitors on plasma MAO activity were examined (Kobayashi, 1966). The drugs were found to be extremely potent inhibitors; for example, a single clinical dose of a commonly used antidepressant (Parnate) completely inhibited all plasma MAO in a normal individual for 14 days. It seems likely therefore that depressed patients tended to be overdosed with MAO inhibitors. Kopin (1968) has pointed out that chronic excessive MAO inhibition results in the accumulation of slowly synthesized other monoamines that infiltrate adrenergic neurons, displace norepinephrine, and act as false neurotransmitters. The false neurotransmitters are not able to achieve adequate synaptic action. Hence adrenergic functions become impaired when the MAO enzyme is maintained at too low a level of activity for an extended period of time. The steroid hormones may be more effective because they seem to move the MAO activity into a biologically appropriate range of activity.

Hormonal Functioning of Depressed Patients

The need for massive doses of hormones to alleviate depressive symptoms is most puzzling. We are therefore studying the characteristics of hormonal functions in depressed women and men. Our results are beginning to clarify this unusual situation. Our first observation was that before treatment depressed women had abnormally elevated levels of circulating estrogens (estrone and estradiol) (Klaiber, Broverman, & Vogel, Note 4). Yet, paradoxically, the estrogens did not seem to be working adequately. One immediately thinks of our male subjects who retained but did not respond to their infused testosterone. Possibly the depressed women were doing the same to their own estrogens. Studies of the metabolic clearance rates of these patients further support this possibility. Metabolic clearance refers to the rate at which a hormone leaves the bloodstream and is available for tissue utilization or metabolism and excretion. Depressed women had significantly lower clearance rates of estradiol than did nondepressed women (Klaiber et al., Note 2).

Still another abnormal hormonal aspect of the depressed women was a grossly elevated (approximately 500%) production of testosterone compared to nondepressed women (Klaiber et al., Note 2). Testosterone is a potent antiestrogen. Much of the failure of estrogen to function normally in these women therefore could be caused by interference from testosterone.

Depressed men were also found to be hormonally aberrant although in a manner not quite parallel to depressed women. Like the women the men produce too much of the wrong hormone, estradiol in this case. However, unlike the women the depressed men have significantly lower levels of circulating testosterone and significantly elevated metabolic clearance rates of testosterone. This last aspect is most puzzling since an elevated metabolic clearance rate is normally thought to reflect usage. However, it is also possible that increased metabolic clearance rates reflect a heightened level of metabolism and excretion. The depressed men do respond well to large doses of administered testosterone (Vogel et al., Note 3).

Our work in this area is continuing and obviously much more work is needed. However, in both sexes the excess production of heterologous hormones (testosterone in women and estradiol in men) make more understandable the need for large doses of the appropriate gonadal hormone to restore the proper hormonal balance.

CONCLUSIONS

1. The gonadal hormones are psychoactive. Both estrogens and testosterone appear to exert similar effects upon the central nervous system; that is, both appear to act as central adrenergic stimulants possibly through their regulatory effects upon the enzyme MAO. Adrenergic stimulants appear to facilitate performances of automatized tasks and impair performances of

perceptual restructuring tasks. Within each sex, individuals with greater amounts of anthropometric or developmental evidence of sex-appropriate gonadal hormone stimulation tend to be strong automatizers (they perform automatized tasks better than perceptual restructuring tasks), while individuals within each sex with lesser amounts of anthropometric or developmental evidence of sex-appropriate gonadal hormone stimulation tend to be weak automatizers with the reverse pattern of cognitive abilities.

Two sex differences in cognition that have been reported—feminine superiorities in performance of automatization tasks and masculine superiorities in performance of perceptual restructuring tasks—may be the result of the greater potency of estrogens as adrenergic stimulants compared to testosterone.

2. Blood levels of the gonadal hormones are poor indicators of degree of hormonal stimulation; metabolic clearance and production rates of the gonadal hormones seem to be more closely related to anthropometric indices of gonadal hormone stimulation and to cognitive and affective functioning.

3. Major individual differences exist within normals in response to administered gonadal hormones; that is, some individuals do not respond well to administered hormones. This resistance to exogenously administered hormones appears to an even greater extent in the disturbed affective state of depression.

4. High doses of sex-appropriate gonadal hormones appear to alleviate depressive symptoms. The requirement of high doses may be because of abnormally high production rates of sex-inappropriate gonadal hormones in depressed patients of each sex (elevated production rates of testosterone in depressed women; elevated production rates of estradiol in depressed men).

REFERENCE NOTES

1. Klaiber, E. L., & Broverman, D. M. *Physiological and psychological development.* Progress Report, USPHS Grant HD–02557-01, 1967.
2. Klaiber, E. L., Broverman, D. M., & Vogel, W. *Relationship of steroids to brain, plasma monoamine oxidase activity and behavior.* Progress Report, USPHS Grant MH-26424-02, 1977.
3. Vogel, W., Klaiber, E. L., & Broverman, D. M. *Treatment of depressed males with a synthetic androgen (Mesterolone).* Proceedings of the VI World Congress of Psychiatry, Honolulu, Hawaii, August 28–September 3, 1977.
4. Klaiber, E. L., Broverman, D. M., & Vogel, W. *Relationships of steroids to brain, plasma monoamine oxidase activity and behavior.* Progress Report, USPHS Grant MH-26424-01, 1976.

REFERENCES

Ach, N. Ueber die Willenstaetigkeit un das Kenen. Trans. in D. Rapaport (Ed.), *Organization and pathology of thought.* New York: Columbia University Press, 1951. (Originally published, 1905.)

Bennett, D. H. Perception of the upright in relation to body image. *Journal of Mental Science*, 1956, *102*, 487–506.

Bieri, J., Bradburn, W. M., & Galinsky, M. D. Sex differences in perceptual behavior. *Journal of Personality*, 1958, *26*, 1–12.

Boston University Drug Surveillance Program. Surgically confirmed gall bladder disease, venous thrombo-embolism and breast tumor in relation to postmenopausal estrogen therapy. *New England Journal of Medicine*, 1974, *290*, 15–19.

Broverman, D. M. Cognitive style and intra-individual variation in abilities. *Journal of Personality*, 1960, *28*, 240–256. (a)

Broverman, D. M. Dimensions of cognitive style. *Journal of Personality*, 1960, *28*, 167–185. (b)

Broverman, D. M. Effects of score transformation in Q and R factor analysis techniques. *Psychological Review*, 1961, *68*, 68–80.

Broverman, D. M. Normative and ipsative measurement in psychology. *Psychological Review*, 1962, *69*, 295–305.

Broverman, D. M. Comments on the note by MacAndrew and Forgy. *Psychological Review*, 1963, *70*, 119–120.

Broverman, D. M. Generality and behavioral correlates of cognitive styles. *Journal of Consulting Psychology*, 1964, *28*, 487–500.

Broverman, D. M., Broverman, I. K., & Klaiber, E. L. Ability to automatize and automatization cognitive style: A validation study. *Perceptual and Motor Skills*, 1966, *23*, 419–437.

Broverman, D. M., Broverman, I. K., Palmer, R. D., Vogel, W., & Klaiber, E. L. The automatization cognitive style and physical development. *Child Development*, 1964, *35*, 1343–1359.

Broverman, D. M., & Klaiber, E. L. Negative relationships between abilities. *Psychometrika*, 1969, *34*, 5–20.

Broverman, D. M., Klaiber, E. L., & Vogel, W. Short- vs. long-term effects of adrenal hormones upon behaviors. *Psychological Bulletin*, 1974, *81*, 672–694.

Broverman, D. M., Klaiber, E. L., Vogel, W., & Kobayashi, Y. Roles of activation and inhibition in sex differences in cognitive abilities. *Psychological Review*, 1968, *75*, 23–50.

Bryan, W. L., & Harter, N. Studies on the telegraphic language: The acquisition of a hierarchy of habits. *Psychological Review*, 1899, *4*, 345–375.

Burch, J. C., Byrd, B. F., Jr., & Vaughn, W. K. The effects of long-term estrogen on hysterectomized women. *American Journal of Obstetrics and Gynecology*, 1974, *118*, 778–782.

Callaway, E., III, & Stone, G. Reevaluating focus of attention. In L. Uhr & J. G. Miller (Eds.), *Drugs and behavior*. New York: Wiley, 1960, pp. 393–398.

Davis, D. R. Psychomotor effects of analeptics and their relation to fatigue phenomena in air crew. *British Medical Bulletin*, 1947, *5*, 43–45.

Drake, C., & Schnall, M. Decoding problems in reading. *Pathways in Child Guidance*, 1966, *3*, 1–12.

Eakin, S., & Douglas, V. I. Automatization and oral reading problems in children. *Journal of Learning Disabilities*, 1971, *4*, 31–33.

Floru, R., Costin, A., Nestianu, V., & Sterescu-Volanschi, M. Researches concerning the effect of noradrenaline upon the electrical activity of the central nervous system and upon the evoked rhythm of intermittent photic stimulation in cats with chronic electrodes. *Electroencephalography and Clinical Neurophysiology*, 1962, *14*, 566.

Flory, C. D., & Gilbert, J. The effects of benzedrine sulphate and caffeine citrate on the efficiency of college students. *Journal of Applied Psychology*, 1943, *27*, 121–134.

Gainer, W. L. The ability of the WISC subtests to discriminate between boys and girls of average intelligence. *California Journal of Education Research*, 1962, *13*, 9–16.

Gomes, B., Igaue, I., Kloepfer, H. G., & Yasunobu, K. T. Amine oxidase XIV. Isolation and characterization of the multiple beef liver amine oxidase components. *Archives of Biochemistry and Biophysics*, 1969, *132*, 16.

Gusberg, S. B. Precursors of corpus carcinoma, estrogens, and adenomatous hyperplasia. *American Journal of Obstetrics and Gynecology*, 1947, *54*, 905.

Hess, W. R. *Diencephalon, autonomic and extrapyramidal function.* New York: Grune and Stratton, 1954.

Hitchcock, F. A. Studies in vigor. V. The comparative activity of male and female albino rats. *American Journal of Physiology*, 1925, *75*, 205–210.

Hoskins, R. G. Studies in Vigor. II. The effect of castration on voluntary activity. *American Journal of Physiology*, 1925, *72*, 324–330.

Hoskins, R. G., & Bevin, S. The effect of fractionated chorionic gonadotropic extract on spontaneous activity and weight of elderly male rats. *Endocrinology*, 1941, *27*, 929–931.

Humphrey, G. *Thinking.* New York: Wiley, 1951.

Jackubezak, L. Relative effects of testosterone and nortestosterone on the running activity of castrated male rats. *Animal Behavior*, 1965, *13*, 419–422.

Killam, K. F., Killam, E. K., & Naquet, R. An animal model of light-sensitive epilepsy. *Electroencephalography and Clinical Neurophysiology*, 1967, *22*, 497–513.

Kistner, R. W. *Gynecology principles and practice.* Chicago: Year Book Medical Publishers, 1971.

Klaiber, E. L., Broverman, D. M., & Kobayashi, Y. The automatization cognitive style, androgens and monoamine oxidase. *Psychopharmacologia* (Berl.), 1967, *11*, 320–336.

Klaiber, E. L., Broverman, D. M., Vogel, W., Abraham, G. E., & Cone, F. L. Effects of infused testosterone on mental performances and serum LH. *Journal of Clinical Endocrinology Metabolism*, 1971, *32*, 341–349.

Klaiber, E. L., Broverman, D. M., Vogel, W., & Kobayashi, Y. The use of steroid hormones in depression. In T. M. Itil, G. Laudahn, & W. M. Hermann (Eds.), *Psychotropic action of hormones.* Holliswood, NY: Halsted Press, 1976.

Klaiber, E. L., Broverman, D. M., Vogel, W., Kobayashi, Y., & Moriarty, D. Effects of estrogen therapy on plasma MAO activity and EEG driving responses of depressed women. *American Journal of Psychiatry*, 1972, *128*, 1492–1498.

Klaiber, E. L., Broverman, D. M., Vogel, W., & Mackenberg, E. J. Rhythms in cognitive functioning and EEG indices in males. In M. Ferin, F. Halberg, R. M. Richart, & R. L. Vande Wiele (Eds.), *Biorhythms and human reproduction.* New York: Wiley, 1974.

Klaiber, E. L., Kobayashi, Y., Broverman, D. M., & Hall, F. Plasma monoamine oxidase activity in regularly menstruating women and in amenorrheic women receiving cyclic treatment with estrogens and a progestin. *Journal of Clinical Endocrinology Metabolism*, 1971, *33*, 630–638.

Kline, N. S. Use of reserpine, the newer phenothiazines and iproniazid. *Research Publication Assn. Nervous Mental Disease*, 1959, *37*, 218–244.

Kobayashi, Y. The effect of three monoamine oxidase inhibitors on human plasma monoamine oxidase activity. *Biochemical Pharmacology*, 1966, *15*, 1287–1294.

Kobayashi, T., Kobayashi, T., Kato, J., & Minaguchi, H. Cholinergic and adrenergic mechanisms in the female rat hypothalamus with special reference to feedback of ovarian steroid hormones. In G. Pincus, T. Nakao, & J. Tait, (Eds.), *Steroid dynamics.* New York: Academic Press, 1966, pp. 305–307.

Kopin, I. J. Storage and metabolism of catecholamines: The role of monoamine oxidase. *Pharmacological Reviews*, 1964, *16*, 179–191.

Kopin, I. J. False adrenergic neurotransmitters. *Annual Review of Pharmacology*, 1968, *8*, 377–394.

Lehmann, H. E., & Csank, J. Differential screening of phrenotropic agents in man: Psychophysiologic test data. *Journal of Clinical and Experimental Psychopathology*, 1957, *18*, 222–235.

Lipsett, M. B. Endocrine responsive cancers of man. In R. H. Williams (Ed.), *Textbook of endocrinology* (5th ed.) Philadelphia: Saunders, 1974.

MacAndrew, W., & Forgy, E. A note on the effects of score transformations in Q and R factor analysis technique. *Psychological Review*, 1963, *70*, 116–118.

McEwen, C. M. Human plasma monoamine oxidase. I. Purification and identification. *Journal of Biological Chemistry*, 1965, *240*, 2003–2010.

Mack, T. M., Pike, M. C., Henderson, B. E., Pfeffer, R. I., Gerkins, V. R., & Arthur, M. Estrogens and endometrial cancer in a retirement community. *New England Journal of Medicine*, 1976, *294*, 1262–1267.

Mackenberg, E. J., Broverman, D. M., Vogel, W., & Klaiber, E. L. Morning-to-afternoon changes in cognitive performances and in the electroencephalogram. *Journal of Educational Psychology*, 1974, *66*, 238–246.

MacMeeken, A. M. *The intelligence of a representative group of Scottish children.* London: University of London Press, 1939.

Mirsky, J. H., White, H. D., & O'Dell, T. B. Central nervous system depressant effects of some indolylethylpyridines. *Journal of Pharmacology and Experimental Therapy*, 1959, *125*, 122–127.

Nies, A., Robinson, A. S., Ravaris, C. L., & Davis, J. M. Amines and monoamine oxidase in relation to aging and depression in man. *Psychosomatic Medicine*, 1971, *33*, 470.

Norman, R. D. Sex differences and other aspects of young superior adult performance on the Wechsler Bellevue. *Journal of Consulting Psychology*, 1953, *17*, 411–418.

Otsuka, S., & Kobayashi, Y. A radioisotopic assay for monoamine oxidase determinations in human plasma. *Biochemical Pharmacology*, 1964, *13*, 995–1006.

Parlee, M. B. Comments on "Roles of activation and inhibition in sex differences in cognitive abilities." *Psychological Review*, 1972, *79*, 180–184.

Petersen, A. C. Physical androgyny and cognitive functioning in adolescence. *Journal of Developmental Psychology*, 1976, *12*, 524–533.

Pfaff, D. W. Autoradiographic localization of radioactivity in rat brain after injection of tritiated sex hormones. *Science*, 1968, *161*, 1355–1356.

Podell, J. E., & Phillips, L. A developmental analysis of cognition as observed in dimensions of Rorschach and objective test performance. *Journal of Personality*, 1959, *27*, 439–463.

Price, D., & Williams-Ashman, H. G. The accessory reproductive glands of mammals. In W. C. Young (Ed.), *Sex and internal secretions* (Vol. I). Baltimore: Williams & Wilkins, 1961.

Primac, D. W., Mirsky, A. F., & Rosvold, H. E. Effects of centrally acting drugs on two tests of brain damage. *Archives of Neurology and Psychiatry*, 1957, *77*, 328–332.

Richter, C. P. Animal behavior and internal drives. *Quarterly Review of Biology*, 1927, *2*, 307–343.

Richter, C. P. The effect of early gonadectomy on the gross body activity of rats. *Endocrinology*, 1933, *17*, 445–450.

Riondel, A., Tait, J. F., Gut, M., Tait, S. A. S., Joachim, E., & Little, B. Estimation of testosterone in human peripheral blood using S^{35}-thiosemicarbazide. *Journal of Clinical Endocrinology and Metabolism*, 1963, *23*, 620.

Robinson, D. S., Lovenberg, W., Keiser, H., & Sjoerdsma, A. Effects of drugs on human blood platelet and plasma amine oxidase activity *in vitro* and *in vivo*. *Biochemical Pharmacology*, 1968, *17*, 109–119.

Schildkraut, J. J. The catecholamine hypothesis of affective disorders: A review of supporting evidence. *American Journal of Psychiatry*, 1965, *122*, 509–522.

Shatin, L., Rockmore, L., & Funk, I. C. Response of psychiatric patients to massive doses of thorazine. II. Psychological test performance and comparative drug evaluation. *Psychiatric Quarterly*, 1956, *30*, 402–416.

Shetty, T. Photic responses in hyperkinesis of childhood. *Science*, 1971, *174*, 1356-1357.

Smith, D. C., Prentice, R., Thompson, D. J., & Herrmann, W. L. Association of exogenous estrogen and endometrial carcinoma. *New England Journal of Medicine*, 1975, *293*, 1164-1167.

Staples, R. The responses of infants to color. *Journal of Experimental Psychology*, 1932, *15*, 119-141.

Stenn, P. G., Klaiber, E. L., Vogel, W., & Broverman, D. M. Testosterone effects on photic stimulation of the EEG and mental performances of humans. *Perceptual Motor Skills*, 1972, *34*, 371-378.

Stroop, J. R. Studies of interference in serial verbal reactions. *Journal of Experimental Psychology*, 1935, *18*, 643-672.

Sutton-Smith, B., Roberts, J. M., Kozelka, R. M., Crandall, V. J., Broverman, D. M., Blum, A., & Klaiber, E. L. Studies of an elementary game of strategy. *Genetic Psychology Monographs*, 1967, *75*, 31.

Tainter, M. L. Effects of certain analeptic drugs on spontaneous running activity of the white rat. *Journal of Comparative Psychology*, 1943, *36*, 143-155.

Tait, J. F., & Burstein, S. *In vivo* studies of steroid dynamics. In G. Pincus, K. V. Thimann, & E. B. Astwood (Eds.), *The hormones* (Vol. V). New York: Academic Press, 1964.

Tanner, J. M. *Growth at adolescence*. Oxford, England: Blackwell Scientific Publications, 1962.

Tipton, K. F., Houslay, M. D., & Garrett, N. J. Allotropic properties of human brain monoamine oxidase. *Nature*, 1973, *246*, 213.

Vogel, W., Broverman, D. M., & Klaiber, E. L. EEG and mental abilities. *Electroencephalography and Clinical Neurophysiology*, 1968, *24*, 166-175.

Vogel, W., Broverman, D. M., & Klaiber, E. L. EEG responses in regularly menstruating women and in amenorrheic women treated with ovarian hormones. *Science*, 1971, *172*, 388-391.

Vogel, W., Broverman, D. M., Klaiber, E. L., Abraham, G., & Cone, F. L. Effects of testosterone infusions upon EEGs of normal male adults. *Electroencephalography and Clinical Neurophysiology*, 1971, *31*, 400-403.

Vogel, W., Broverman, D. M., Klaiber, E. L., & Kobayashi, Y. EEG driving responses as a function of monoamine oxidase. *Electroencephalography and Clinical Neurophysiology*, 1974, *36*, 205-207.

Vogel, W., Broverman, D. M., Klaiber, E. L., & Kun, K. J. EEG response to photic stimulation as a function of cognitive style. *Electroencephalography and Clinical Neurophysiology*, 1969, *27*, 186-190.

Waber, D. P. Sex differences in cognition: A function of maturation rate? *Science*, 1976, *192*, 572-574.

Wang, G. Relation between "spontaneous" activity and estrous cycle in the white rat. *Comparative Psychology Monographs*, 1923, *2*, 1-27.

Wang, G. H., Richter, C. P., & Guttmacher, A. F. Activity studies of male castrated rats with ovarian transplants, and correlation of the activity with the histology of the grafts. *American Journal of Physiology*, 1925, *73*, 581-598.

Wechsler, D. *Wechsler Adult Intelligence Scale*. New York: Psychological Corporation, 1955.

Weiss, N. S. Risks and benefits of estrogen use. *New England Journal of Medicine*, 1975, *293*, 1200-1202.

Weiss, N. S., Szekely, D. R., & Austin, D. F. Increasing incidence of endometrial cancer in the United States. *New England Journal of Medicine*, 1976, *294*, 1259-1262.

Werner, H. *Comparative psychology of mental development*. New York: International Universities Press, 1957.

Wineman, E. W. Autonomic balance changes during the human menstrual cycle. *Psychophysiology*, 1971, *8*, 1-6.

Witkin, H. A. Individual differences in ease of perception of embedded figures. *Journal of Personality*, 1950, *19*, 1-15.

Witkin, H. A., Dyk, R. B., Faterson, H. F., Goodenough, D. R., & Karp. S. A. *Psychological differentiation,* New York: Wiley, 1962.

Witkin, H. A., Lewis, H. B., Hertzman, M., Machover, K., Miessner, P. B., & Wapner, S. *Personality through perception.* New York: Harper & Row, 1954.

Wurtman, R. J., & Axelrod, J. Sex steroids, cardiac ³H-norepinephrine, and tissue monoamine oxidase levels in the rat. *Biochemical Pharmacology,* 1963, *12,* 1417–1419.

Wyatt, R. J., Portnoy, B., Kupfer, D. J., Snyder, F., & Engelman, K. Resting plasma catecholamine concentrations in patients with depression and anxiety. *Archives of General Psychiatry,* 1971, *24,* 65–70.

Young, W. C., & Fish, W. R. The ovarian hormones and spontaneous running activity in the female rat. *Endocrinology,* 1945, *36,* 181–189.

Ziel, H. K., & Finkle, W. D. Increased risk of endometrial carcinoma among users of conjugated estrogens. *New England Journal of Medicine,* 1975, *293,* 1167–1170.

Zieve, L. Effect of benzedrine on activity. *Psychological Record,* 1973, *1,* 393.

Zigler, E. Review of *Psychological differentiation: Studies of development* by Witkin, H. A., Dyk, R. B., Faterson, H. F., Goodenough, D. R., & Karp, S. A. *Contemporary Psychology,* 1963, *8,* 133–135.

4

Human Sex-Hormone Abnormalities Viewed from an Androgynous Perspective: A Reconsideration of the Work of John Money

Alexandra G. Kaplan
University of Massachusetts/Amherst

Biological and psychological researchers have for a long time assumed that it was both professionally profitable and ethically justifiable to look primarily at the biological underpinnings and behavioral manifestations of human sex differences. Now, however, we are not quite so sure of this. Those who are concerned with the interrelationship between societal values and scientific research (e.g., Bernard, 1976) have stressed that research on sex differences can serve to support and promote the discriminatory treatment of women and the inflexibility of sex-role options. In addition, careful examinations of the literature on sex differences are finding, first, that the accumulated results do not point to nearly the extent of sex differences that are commonly assumed to exist (Maccoby & Jacklin, 1974) and, second, that by focusing on sex differences many aspects of behavior that reflect not differences but similarities between the sexes tend to be ignored (Bem, Note 1).

One of the effects of this emphasis on sex differences is the tendency to attempt to classify the specific parameters of whatever one is studying under the rubrics of feminine or masculine according to a priori notions of what is appropriate for each sex or to seek out or emphasize those findings that most clearly discriminate between females and males. But it does not suffice merely to decry the potentially oppressive uses to which such emphasis can be put, not to bemoan the loss of that data that could not be incorporated into a sex-difference perspective. Far more productive at this point are approaches that seek to learn more about previously unexplored areas of behavior or that attempt to reanalyze old findings from a perspective that is more sensitive to the subtle aspects of behavioral descriptors than is a sex-difference, feminine *or* masculine, approach. This chapter represents one step in line with the latter approach. Its purpose is a preliminary reexamination of John Money's findings on the behavioral correlates of human sex-hormone abnormalities from the perspective of androgyny. This analysis requires, however, that we first identify more specifically some of the ways that scientific research has been limited by a sex-difference perspective and, second, that we define and illustrate the concept of androgyny.

LIMITATIONS OF A SEX-DIFFERENCE PERSPECTIVE

Limitations in research design that frequently appear within a sex-difference framework can be categorized into three basic problem areas:

1. When only one sex is being studied, there is a tendency to investigate only the hormonal correlates of behavior that are stereotypically expected of that sex. For example, far more research has been done on the hormonal correlates of sexual assertiveness in male rats than female rats, probably because the very existence of sexual assertiveness in females tends to go unrecognized (Doty, 1974). Similarly, there is a large body of data on the emotional and behavioral correlates of hormone cyclicity in the female but virtually none on the same phenomenon in males despite some evidence that similar relationships may well exist in men (Ramey, 1972). In other words, researchers' choices of traits to be investigated tend to be determined by preconceived and culturally supported notions of what behaviors one might expect to be exhibited by each sex. For the most part the hormonal underpinnings of nonspecific behaviors such as competence tend not to be investigated.

2. When only one sex is being studied, findings that pertain to that sex are assumed to reflect sex differences without any attempt to empirically verify this assumption. The most classic example of this concerns findings on women's emotional instability and physical symptomatology associated with menstrual cyclicity. There is widespread acceptance of the notion that such findings reflect greater instability and symptomatology in women than in men, despite the fact that women's reaction patterns are seldom if ever compared to those of their male peers (Parlee, 1973). This sort of reasoning by negation (if one sex has it then the other sex must not) serves to bias interpretations of large bodies of data.

3. When both sexes are being studied, the specific traits under investigation tend to be defined and operationalized according to the ways that they are expressed by the sex with which they are stereotypically linked. Thus aggression tends to be defined according to the male pattern of expression, while parenting behavior is defined based on the female pattern. This, of course, greatly increases the likelihood that males but not females will be found to be aggressive and that females more than males will evidence

parenting behaviors. Female patterns of aggression that are unlike those of their male peers and male parenting behaviors that are of a fashion other than those used by their female peers tend either to be ignored or called by another name.

These three pitfalls in research design exist in part because investigators conceptualize sex-role behaviors in terms of a bipolar model (Constantinople, 1973). This model assumes that masculine and feminine characteristics are polar ends of a single continuum, such that the presence of a given trait as characteristic of one sex implies that the opposite trait must be characteristic of the other sex. If men are active then women are passive; if women are emotional then men are rational. Such a line of reasoning has been strongly criticized by Constantinople (1973), Bem (1974), and others who argue that masculinity and femininity are better conceptualized as independent, orthogonal constructs. Within this model, femininity and masculinity would vary independently, such that the presence or absence of traits associated with either one of these would have no predictive value for the presence or absence of traits associated with the other of these. A person then could be both active and passive, rational and emotional, depending on his or her mood and the nature of the situation.

ANDROGYNY

Bem (1974) first suggested the use of the term *psychological androgyny* to signify a sex-role orientation in which positively valued aspects of both feminine and masculine characteristics are incorporated. Androgyny in its simplest form signifies an equal balance between masculine and feminine characteristics. In further elaborations of this construct Spence, Helmreich, and Stapp (1975) have stressed that the androgynous individual is one who not only has an equal balance of masculinity and femininity but also is above the median on both these characteristics. A person with equally present but minimal representations of masculine and feminine characteristics would be considered not androgynous but indeterminate. Kaplan (Note 2) has further suggested that masculine and feminine characteristics can be combined, at any point in time, into hybrid characteristics that represent a blending of the original sex-linked behavioral roots. Thus, for example, an individual could exhibit what one might call assertive-dependency, recognizing and accepting one's legitimate dependency needs and seeking ways in which these might realistically be met.

Androgyny is proposed not just as an alternative to femininity and masculinity but as an option that is more adaptive than the other two. Androgynous individuals can respond to a situation on the basis of what is appropriate for that situation rather than on the basis of what is expected for someone of their sex. They are freer to express their own personality styles without the constraints of arbitrarily imposed sex-role expectations. It is also assumed that such individuals will not manifest extremes of either sex-role stereotype, being able to avoid the traps of either the macho male or the helpless female that result from an undue emphasis on the value of sex-appropriate behavior. Androgynous individuals, for the purpose of this chapter, would include those who show evidence of a balance of positively valued masculine and feminine characteristics and for whom this distribution of traits results in adaptive functioning. Evidence that the appellation of androgynous better fits some of Money's subjects than either masculine or feminine could lend construct validity to the concept of androgyny. Further, this third option for the classification of sex-role behaviors in his subjects might provide new insights into the behavioral correlates of human sex-hormone abnormalities.

HUMAN SEX–HORMONE ABNORMALITIES

The term *human sex-hormone abnormalities* is a basic name for a broad spectrum of conditions varying widely as to causality, symptomatology, and amenability to alterations. These conditions are reflected in developmental abnormalities during one or several of the five stages of prenatal sexual dimorphism (genetic, gonadal, hormonal, internal genitalia, external genitalia) and also have impact on the two postnatal stages (sex of assignment and rearing and sex-role identity). The shared element across the several syndromes is an upset in the balance of sex hormones caused usually by an excess of androgens (the adrenogenital syndrome in genetic males and females and progestin-induced excess androgens in genetic females) or by deficiencies in amounts of or reactions to sex-appropriate hormones (Turner's syndrome individuals and the androgen insensitivity syndrome in genetic males).

These abnormalities have both behavioral and anatomical effects, and the anatomical effects produce an additional problem: identification of the child's true sex. Individuals with Turner's syndrome and genetic males with the adrenogenital syndrome have no discrepancy between their chromosomal sex and external genitalia, so that their sex of assignment does not pose any difficulties. Genetic females with adrenogenital syndrome, however, are born with partial-to-pronounced masculinization of the external genitalia, making possible a male or female sex of assignment. Genetic males with androgen insensitivity syndrome are born with intact female external genitalia but also with testes, which may or may not be discovered. If they are there is some chance that the individual would be assigned and reared as male. If they are not the individual would in all likelihood be assigned and reared as female. The various combinations of hormonal abnormalities and sex of rearing yield the following clinical groupings: individuals with Turner's syndrome reared as females, genetic males with androgen insensitivity syndrome reared as males or as females, genetic females with adrenogenital syndrome reared as males or females, and genetic males with adrenogenital syndrome.

For each of these groupings we will examine those behavioral descriptions that are available in the literature by Money and his colleagues and explore whether the behavioral labels applied to the various conditions fit the specific descriptions offered. Additionally, we will attempt to determine whether the concept of androgyny serves as a better descriptor of certain behavioral conditions, allows for a better differentiation between the behavioral correlates of the various conditions, and alters in any way estimates of the adjustment levels associated with the syndromes under consideration.

Turner's Syndrome

Individuals born with Turner's syndrome were portrayed by Money (1970) as follows: "[These] girls not only conform to the style of femininity idealized in our cultural definitions of femininity, but they are also (long before they know the prognosis of their condition) maternal in their childhood play and adult aspirations" (p. 258).

Elsewhere, Money and Ehrhardt (1972) reported that:

Despite the handicap of their stature and infertility which all the older Turner's girls know about, all but one explicitly hoped to get married one day. They all reported daydreams and fantasies of being pregnant and wanting to have a baby to care for one day. All but one had played with dolls exclusively, and the one preferred dolls even though she played with boy's toys occasionally. Twelve of them had a strong interest in taking care of babies, tending to their younger siblings, or babysitting for other parents; two had a moderate interest in such maternalistic activities; for the one remaining girl, information was missing. (p. 107)

Money (1973) additionally pointed out that there was a "complete lack of tomboyish traits" in these girls and that they outdid their controls "in conformity to the traditions of femininity." He thereby concluded that these girls "develop a postnatal feminine gender identity with spontaneous ease" and "tend to be free of personality pathology."

Our conclusions about these behavioral characteristics, from an androgynous perspective, would have a somewhat different emphasis. In the absence of sex-appropriate hormones, paradoxical as it may seem, these females evidence an overextension, an exaggeration of culturally valued feminine traits. They seem locked into developing the nurturant side of themselves at the expense of their more assertive, self-oriented, independence-striving potential. If androgyny is posited as a model of mental health, then these females cannot be seen as free of personality pathology. Rather than appropriately feminine we would call them insufficiently androgynous in that they seem characterologically to lack the potential for pursuing a variety of life-styles. Their insufficiency is not that they are following a traditionally feminine pattern, but that, at least in the examples offered by Money, there is no indication of styles that vary from that pattern.

Androgen Insensitivity Syndrome

The closest parallel in genetic males to the females with Turner's syndrome are the males with androgen insensitivity. These individuals born with testes that produce androgen but that their bodies cannot absorb are occasionally assigned and reared as males. Money reported the behavioral correlates of this condition with somewhat less clarity, perhaps because the numbers are so small. He stated (1973) that "their masculine gender identity is characterized by a quality that has no name of its own and is the opposite of tomboyism, while not being sissyness." In the absence of greater specificity we can only assume that the characteristics to which Money was referring are more consistent with a feminine than a masculine gender identity. In the same article Money stated that these men may be "adequately masculine even to the point of overcompensation, to the extent that their physique permits, in the tradition of the most rugged masculine stereotype" (p. 261). One gets the picture from these descriptions of individuals who vary between extremes of stereotypically feminine and stereotypically masculine behavior. It is no doubt the latter that led Money to label these individuals adequately masculine, but it is unclear how the former characteristics fit this appellation. From our perspective, although these individuals contain aspects of masculinity and femininity, we would hesitate to call them adequately androgynous. Their sex-typed traits, somewhat like the individuals with Turner's syndrome, seem to involve extremes of behavior rather than falling within the broader and more varied range that could produce the effective, flexible characteristics of androgynous individuals. Money's own position is consistent with our conclusion that these individuals are not well adjusted; he concludes that although these are genetic males "they should have been assigned and reared as girls" (1973; p. 260).

Genetic males with androgen insensitivity assigned and reared as females seem, according to Money's (1973) description, to be surprisingly similar in personality to the females with Turner's syndrome. He described the typical woman with this condition as one who "gives priority to marriage over a nondomestic career, who likes domestic activities . . . who anticipated the mother role in her childhood play and was definitely not a tomboy. She is content in her role as a female and prefers and follows the feminine fashion in clothing styles and cosmetics." Elsewhere, Masica, Money and Ehrhardt (1971) described these women as conforming "closely to the conventional feminine stereotype: regarding explicit satisfaction with female sex role and with cosmetic and clothing interests, the androgen-insensitive group was characteristically feminine" (p. 131). These individuals, like those we have just discussed, seem also to lack the behavioral flexibility and diversity that would render them in keeping with a model of androgyny.

In all the above examples then the absence of sufficient or normally produced sex hormones appropriate for one's genetic sex seems to be associated with evidence of extremes of sex-role related behaviors. It should be noted that this is the case regardless of the sex of rearing (in the case of androgen insensitivity syndrome) and regardless of which hormone is lacking. For those reared as female, regardless of their genetic makeup, these extremes are in a feminine direction. For those reared as male these extremes extend in both masculine and feminine directions.

Adrenogenital Syndrome

Let us now turn for comparison to genetic males and females with excess androgens. This grouping includes those with the adrenogenital syndrome as well as a group of women born in the 1950s who were partially masculinized *in utero* from artificial progestins given their mothers to avoid miscarriage. These artificial progestins had the effect of partially masculinizing the girls external genitalia, but their influence did not continue after birth. In the majority of cases the partial masculinization of the external genitalia was surgically corrected soon after birth. This group is of special interest, partly because of the depth to which they have been studied and the clarity with which their personalities have been described and partly because of the ways in which their characteristics can be understood within an androgynous framework. Reports of girls with this syndrome range from Ehrhardt and Money's (1967) initial study to Ehrhardt and Baker's (1974) elaboration of associated familial factors. The composite picture that emerges is of individuals who considered themselves to be tomboys but were not dissatisfied to be girls. They were active and energetic but no more aggressive or dominance seeking than matched controls. They preferred utilitarian, simple clothing but were not loath to dress up when necessary. They showed no predisposition for primping, although they valued cleanliness. Along with their distaste for female games they showed less interest as youngsters in doll play and other rehearsals of adult maternal roles. They anticipated marriage and a family, but this tended to be subordinated to planning for a career. They were further reported to reveal "independence and self-reliance, to have minimal personality disturbances, to be good students, socially mature, easy to get along with, flexible and reasonable in response to reasonable demands" (Ehrhardt & Money, 1967). Money labeled these girls as masculinized, but from our perspective they seem to offer a remarkably consistent and accurate portrait of one style of an androgynous personality. The term masculinized seems to do an injustice to the subtle distinctions between Ehrhardt and Money's data and the stereotypical masculine paradigm. These girls were active but did not demonstrate the associated aggressiveness and dominance-seeking behaviors often found in boys (Bardwick, 1971). Although utilitarian in their clothing, they seemed more concerned with appearance than one would typically expect in boys. They did not reveal the academic or emotional problems that are up to four times as common in boys as in girls (Oakley, 1972). They were more rather than less socially mature, as one would expect in boys. In sum these girls were neither simply masculinized nor simply feminized. Rather, their absence of extreme sex-typed reactions, their high level of emotional adjustment, their ability to combine planning for a family and a career in thinking about the future, all speak to a healthy integration of masculine and feminine attributes in a manner befitting our concept of androgyny.

Similar though less detailed descriptions can be found for genetic males with excess androgens (adrenogenital syndrome). For these individuals the influence of the excess adrenal androgens continues postnatally, until the condition is discovered and corrected. Money (1973) reported that these individuals, although pubertally precocious, were "shy and reticent in sexual partnerships, and . . . are not sexually aggressive and do not impose themselves on unwilling partners. They are not prone to be fighters or otherwise aggressive. Rather they tend to be gentle, as though protecting their smaller age mates against the power of their own precocious physique . . . and they tend to show the same tendency to high IQ as do their genetic female counterparts" (p. 257). Money used the label boyism to characterize these individuals, but this term in the absence of further justification seems to be a disservice to the descriptors provided. There is not the clear evidence here of optimal functioning nor of a healthy integration of masculine and feminine characteristics that would permit us to label these boys androgynous with the same ease that we could apply the term to the progestin-exposed girls. Yet they seem free from the sex-typed extremes of passivity and aggressiveness and without some of the limited flexibility found in the conditions associated with insufficient sex hormones. We therefore feel justified in calling these boys potentially androgynous to emphasize the qualitative difference between their behavioral traits and those of the males with the androgen insensitivity syndrome. Money's labels of boyism for males with adrenogenital syndrome and adequately masculine for males with the androgen insensitivity syndrome do not, in our opinion, make this distinction sufficiently clear.

Prenatal Exposure to Artificial Estrogens

Thus in contrast to the sex-role rigidity concurrent with insufficient amounts of normally produced sex-appropriate sex hormones, there seems to be evidence, especially with girls, that slight to moderate amounts of excess androgens are associated with sex-role flexibility and increased behavioral options consistent with the concept of androgyny. One might question, however, whether this is caused by excess androgens per se, or whether excesses of estrogens or progesterones would be associated with similar effects. While Money's work does not provide us with material with which to address this question, some very tentative speculations can be made from findings of

Yalom, Green, and Fisk (1973) in their data on characteristics, in male children, associated with prenatal exposure to artificial estrogens given to their diabetic mothers to prevent miscarriage. These boys were studied at ages 6 and 16 as to their relative degrees of masculinity and femininity on several measures, compared to controls who were sons of diabetic mothers not treated with artificial estrogens. The findings indicated, in general, that the 6-year-old boys differed from the controls only in being less assertive and less athletically able, while the 16-year-olds were significantly less masculine in terms of interest areas, assertiveness, and performance on a variety of personality tests.

If these boys, especially the 16-year-olds, were less masculine in the eyes of the researchers, might they be more androgynous from our perspective? This question is not addressed in the study, so it is possible that some data pertinent to our inquiry are not available. However, the evidence that is presented suggests patterns that seem more typical of sex-role extremes than of androgyny. For example, on two personality tests the boys scored at extremes of masculinity and femininity. Similar patterns were also reported based on interview material. The authors concluded that these boys were "psychologically conflicted," which further speaks against their evidencing androgynous personality styles.

One can raise serious questions, however, as to whether the psychological conflict associated with increased estrogen in these boys is a function of hormonal influence or cultural attitudes toward sex-appropriate behavior in males and females. There is increasing evidence that, especially for males, positive self-concepts and high adjustment levels are associated more with masculine than androgynous sex-typing (Jones, Chernovitz, & Hanson, 1978). This seems to reflect the fact that in our culture masculine traits in general are valued more than feminine traits. Thus it is possible that these boys evidenced an initial potential for androgyny that was gradually thwarted as society failed to reinforce those traits not consistent with a masculine stereotype. However, much more detailed observations of behavior, including those looking specifically for androgynous components, would be required before these thoughts could be developed beyond mere speculations.

CONCLUSION

This chapter has offered a preliminary reconceptualization of Money's behavioral descriptions associated with several syndromes caused by sex-hormone abnormalities. We have attempted to demonstrate that the addition of the concept of androgyny permits us to categorize behavior in ways that (1) more accurately reflect the descriptors provided, (2) more clearly differentiate between one syndrome and another, and (3) provide a more appropriate assessment of the behavioral states associated with each syndrome. In some ways the additional utility provided by the concept of androgyny should not come as a surprise. By broadening the possible categories from two (masculine and feminine) to three (masculine, feminine, or androgynous) one is by definition increasing the subtlety of one's descriptive ability. The ultimate utility of this perspective, however, awaits researchers' attempts to collect and analyze data within a perspective that includes androgyny. This might mean that certain behavioral traits that were not sought out under the old framework would be under the new. It could also mean that some of the inventories now being developed to identify psychological androgyny could be used with these subjects (Bem, 1974; Spence, Helmreich, & Stapp, 1975; Berzins & Welling, Note 3). In these ways, questions about the validity of this approach could be assessed.

The work of Money and his colleagues (Money & Ehrhardt, 1972) has demonstrated the enormous complexities in prenatal sexual dimorphism. One's biological sex, we now know, is determined not by a one-stage, genetic differentiation but rather by a seven-stage process including five levels of prenatal development and two additional postnatal events of sex of assignment and sex of rearing. It is certainly consistent to propose that one's psychological sex is similarly more complicated than the traditional divisions of femininity and masculinity. Perhaps all that this chapter is suggesting is that we begin to bring our understanding of psychological sex somewhat closer to the sophistication to which Money has led us in understanding the complexities of determining biological sex.

REFERENCE NOTES

1. Bem, S. L. *Psychology looks at sex roles: Where have all the androgynous people gone?* Paper presented at UCLA Symposium on Women, 1972.
2. Kaplan, A. G. *Clarifying the concept of androgyny: Implications for treatment.* Paper presented at the annual meeting of the American Psychological Association, Washington, D.C. 1976.
3. Berzins, J. I., & Welling, M. A. *The PRF ANDRO scale: A measure of psychological androgyny derived from the Personality Research Form.* Unpublished manuscript, University of Kentucky, 1974.

REFERENCES

Bardwick, J. M. *Psychology of women: A study of bio-cultural conflicts.* New York: Harper & Row, 1971.
Bem, S. L. The measurement of psychological androgyny. *Journal of Consulting and Clinical Psychology,* 1974, *42,* 155–162.
Bernard, J. Where are we now? Some thought on the current scene. *Psychology of Women Quarterly,* 1976, *1,* 21–37.
Constantinople, A. Masculinity–femininity: An exception to a famous dictum. *Psychological Bulletin,* 1973, *80,* 389–407.
Doty, R. A cry for the liberation of the female rodent: Courtship and copulation in rodentia. *Psychological Bulletin,* 1974, *81,* 159–172.
Ehrhardt, A. A., & Baker, S. Fetal androgens, human CNS differentiation, and behavioral

sex differences. In Friedman (Ed.), *Sex differences in behavior.* New York: Wiley, 1974.

Ehrhardt, A. A., & Money, J. Progestin-induced hermaphroditism: IQ and sexual identity in a study of 10 girls. *Journal of Sex Research,* 1967, *3,* 83–100.

Jones, W. H., Chernovetz, M. E. O'C., & Hanson, R. O. The enigma of androgyny: Differential implications for males and females. *Journal of Consulting and Clinical Psychology,* 1978.

Maccoby, E., & Jacklin, C. *The psychology of sex differences.* Stanford: Stanford University Press, 1974.

Masica, D. N., Money, J., & Ehrhardt, A. Fetal feminization and gender identity in the testicular feminizing syndrome of androgen insensitivity. *Archives of Sexual Behavior,* 1971, *1,* 131–141.

Money, J. Sexual dimorphism and homosexual gender identity. *Psychological Bulletin,* 1970, *74,* 425–440.

Money, J. Effects of pre-natal androgens and de-androgenization on behavior in human beings. In W. Ganong & M. Luciano (Eds.), *Frontiers in neuroendocrinology.* New York: Oxford University Press, 1973.

Money, J., & Ehrhardt, A. A. *Man and woman, boy and girl.* Baltimore: Johns Hopkins University Press, 1972.

Oakley, A. *Sex, gender, and society.* New York: Harper & Row, 1972.

Parlee, M. B. The premenstrual syndrome. *Psychological Bulletin,* 1973, *80,* 454–465.

Ramey, E. Men's cycles (they have them too, you know). *Ms Magazine,* Spring 1972.

Spence, J. T., Helmreich, R., & Stapp, J. Ratings of self and peers on sex-role attributes and their relation to self-esteem and concepts of masculinity and femininity. *Journal of Personality and Social Psychology,* 1975, *32,* 29–39.

Yalom, I. D., Green, R., & Fisk, N. Prenatal exposure to female hormones. *Archives of General Psychiatry,* 1973, *28,* 554–561.

II

SEXUALITY

5

Biochemical and Neurophysiological Influences on Human Sexual Behavior

Florence Ledwitz-Rigby
Northern Illinois University

The literature concerning the biological influences on sexual behavior is filled with speculation, controversy, and relatively little solid data. Much of the problem with research in this area is that many basic biochemical and neurophysiological questions must first be answered before we can even know what questions are meaningful to ask about the biology of human sexuality. As will be explained in this chapter, there are many instances where we do not know precisely which hormones are responsible for causing specific biological actions, which specific nerves in the brain are involved in certain functions, how these nerves are organized into pathways, or how hormones influence the portions of the nervous system controlling sexual behavior. Rather than presenting an exhaustive review of the current literature, I have chosen to cite only examples of the attempts to determine the biological contributions to sexual potency, libido, and sexual orientation and to emphasize where the gaps in our knowledge of basic physiology prevent resolution of these controversial topics. I should point out that my perspective is that of a cellular reproductive endocrinologist and not that of a researcher in the field of human sexuality.

BIOCHEMICAL INFLUENCES

Potency

The influence of biological factors on sexual potency is perhaps the best understood of the three areas to be considered. Estrogenic hormones (primar-

The assistance of Dr. Brian Rigby, Department of Biological Sciences, Northern Illinois University, in editing this chapter is gratefully acknowledged.

ily 17β-estradiol) are essential for the maturation and maintenance of function of the female reproductive tract, including the size of the vagina and maintenance of the structure and lubrication of the vaginal lining (Labhart, 1976). In the male, androgenic hormones (primarily testosterone) are required for fetal development, adult maturation, and maintenance of size and function of the male reproductive tract. Drastic reductions in these hormones can interfere with the ability to function sexually (Labhart, 1976). However, it is often difficult to demonstrate a direct correlation between the level of estrogen or androgen circulating in an individual's blood and level of potency.

To understand why hormone levels and behavior do not always correlate it is necessary to understand how hormones act. Before either an estrogenic or androgenic hormone can stimulate changes in a target cell such as growth or secretion, it must bind to a specific cytoplasmic receptor protein. The binding of a hormone to its specific receptor alters the receptor protein so that it can interact with other molecules within the cell's nucleus and initiate changes in cell activities (O'Malley & Means, 1974). Individuals vary in their sensitivities to hormones just as they do in size, shape, or ability to tolerate alcohol. Hormone sensitivity can be influenced by the amount of a specific receptor protein present in cells, by the binding affinity of the receptor for the hormone, and in the case of testosterone by the ability of the target cell to convert testosterone or other androgens to dihydrotestosterone (DHT), which is the only androgen that can activate most androgen receptors found outside the central nervous system (CNS) (Wilson & Gloyna, 1969). Similarly, estrogens (except for the synthetic compound diethyl stilbesterol) must be converted to 17β-estradiol before they can alter cell function. Alteration in any of these factors can result in an individual who has normal sex hormone levels but decreased responsiveness or an individual who is functionally normal with either excessive or diminished levels of sex hormones in the blood.

In addition to variation in sensitivity to specific hormones among individuals, there are variations in sensitivity to hormones among the various cell types found in one individual. Androgens, for example, can stimulate beard growth and the development of baldness in either males or females whose hair follicle cells are genetically predisposed to respond to androgens. North American Indians lack the genes for beard growth and remain beardless in spite of normal plasma androgen levels and normal masculinization of genital organs and other secondary sex characteristics (Labhart, 1976). Other tissues, including nervous tissue, that normally respond to the sex hormones might also show genetic variability in response. This could produce individuals whose hormone levels are sufficient to make them appear sexually normal but whose sexual behavior is in some way deviant from normal.

17β-estradiol and testosterone are known to antagonize each other's actions, although the mechanism for this remains to be determined (Marcus & Korenman, 1976). As a result the absolute level of each hormone is less important than the ratio of estrogen–androgen. Androgens and estrogens have opposite actions on many tissues and essentially compete with each other. For example, estrogens stimulate the growth of breast tissue and androgens inhibit it. Women develop breasts because they have a low androgen–estrogen ratio in their blood. Men have enough estrogen in their blood to stimulate breast development but do not do so because of their high androgen–estrogen ratio. If a man is injected with estrogen, as is done to treat some prostate cancers, his androgen–estrogen ratio is lowered and some femalelike breast development will occur. Similarly breast development will occur in a male if the amount of estrogen is kept constant but the androgen activity is effectively lowered. This occurs in a syndrome referred to as *androgen insensitivity* or *testicular feminization*. The person with this syndrome is genetically XY and has plasma androgen and estrogen levels close to that of a normal male. However, the cells of this individual are unable to respond to androgens. In effect it is as if the individual has no androgens at all (Bullock & Bardin, 1972). Normal male levels of estrogen in the absence of competing androgens completely feminize the individual's external appearance. The individual with the testicular feminization syndrome is also an extreme example of variability in sensitivity to hormones.

Many studies of the importance of androgens and estrogens in human sexual behavior fail to take the concepts of hormone sensitivity and hormone ratios into consideration. The most common type of study is to measure androgen levels in men with normal potency versus impotent men. Although most aging males experience a decline in testosterone levels and a rise in estrogen levels (Marcus & Korenman, 1976) only about 25% of impotency from physiological causes is associated with a deficiency of androgens and responds to androgen treatment. Most cases of male impotency are thought to be due to psychological and social factors (Labhart, 1976). Even castration, which removes the major source of testosterone, does not always result in impotency (Ellis & Grayhack, 1963). The adrenal gland secretes androgens, and in men who are sufficiently androgen sensitive and have positive psychological attitudes this androgen may be sufficient to maintain functioning. The testis is also the major source of estrogen in men (Marcus & Korenman, 1976), and castration may thus reduce estrogen levels, allowing the adrenal androgen to maintain an androgen–estrogen ratio that supports normal potency.

Women who lose the function of their ovaries, whether through surgery or menopause, experience a decline in plasma estrogens. Not all such women experience a change in the structure or function of their genital organs. In some women the adrenal secretes sufficient estrogen to maintain the genital organs (Filler & Drezner, 1944).

Libido

Androgens are considered the prime hormones responsible for libido in both male and female humans. If a male is castrated before puberty, libido fails to develop (Labhart, 1976). After puberty castration may not be followed by loss of libido if the adrenal secretes sufficient androgens. Administration of androgen to men with declining libido caused by declining androgens can stimulate libido (Masters & Johnson, 1966). Women do not experience a loss of libido with loss of their ovaries, as their adrenals have always been their major source of androgens (Filler & Drezner, 1944). Women who lose their adrenals do experience a reduction of libido, which is restored by the administration of androgens (Foss, 1951). Although estrogens have been demonstrated to be essential for sexual receptivity in rats, monkeys, and other lower animals (Goy & Resko, 1971), the need for estrogens for human female libido is not clearly established.

As in the discussion of potency the individual's sensitivity to androgens and estrogens and the ratio of these two hormones are more important to libido than the absolute levels of hormones in the body. The observation that the administration of identical quantities of synthetic estrogens (as oral contraceptives) to millions of women enhanced libido in some, reduced it in others, and produced no change in others may be because of these differences in sensitivity (Goldzieher, Moses, Averkin, Scheel, & Taber, 1971). While a change in libido may also be explained by the woman's psychological reaction to being protected from conception, many women who experienced a change in libido on one dose of synthetic steroids have experienced a restoration to prepill libido when switched to an equally effective birth control pill containing a different dose of steroids.

One curious anomaly is that individuals with testicular feminization have been reported to exhibit normal female libido (Labhart, 1976; Money & Tucker, 1975). However, these reports do not explain the criteria for measuring female libido. Possibly, libido in these individuals has been estimated on the basis that they marry and are sexually receptive rather than on a measurement of desire for sexual activity. An alternative possibility is that the sexual centers in the brains of these individuals are responsive to androgens (or to whichever metabolites of androgens these cells respond to) even though their nonnervous cells are not responsive to androgens. Most studies of androgen insensitivity have been performed on cells obtained from outside the CNS (Strickland, 1969). Recent reports have suggested that although tissues such as the prostate respond only to DHT, neurons within the hypothalamus respond to other androgens (Kao & Weisz, Note 1). In some physiological responses androgens must first be converted to estrogens by the target cells before the hormones can influence brain function (Naftolin, Ryan, & Petro, 1972). In other cases the identity of the hormone that is finally responsible for influencing brain function has yet to be determined (Gay, Note 2). In looking for endocrine differences between individuals who exhibit different sexual behaviors, we therefore may not know which hormones to measure, whether to measure their absolute concentrations or ratios, and whether we should be determining these values in the general circulatory system, in the cerebrospinal fluid, or in specific target tissues.

Sex Choice

The literature on the role of biological factors influencing sex choice is the most contradictory. Studies in which female homosexuals have been compared with female heterosexuals have resulted in the following conclusions: (1) female homosexuals have greater stature, shoulder width, and look older than their age but have no detectable hormonal differences (Griffiths, Merry, Browning, Eisinger, Huntsman, Lords, Polani, Tanner, & Whitehouse, 1974); (2) female homosexuals have higher levels of luteinizing hormone (LH) (Loraine, Adamopoulos, Kirkham, Ismail, & Dove, 1971); and (3) female homosexuals have higher urinary levels of testosterone (Loraine, Ismail, & Adamopoulos, 1970). Studies comparing male homosexuals with male heterosexuals have reported (1) male homosexuals had lower plasma testosterone (Kolodny, Masters, Hendryx, & Toro, 1971); (2) lower urinary androgens (Loraine et al., 1970); (3) a different ratio of urinary androgens (androsterone-etiocholanolone) (Evans, 1972; Margolese & Janiger, 1973); (4) smaller stature and bone development and less muscle mass (Evans, 1972); and (5) lower LH levels (Loraine et al., 1971). Many studies have found no differences at all between homosexual and heterosexuals (Barlow, Abel, Blanchard, & Mavissakalian, 1974; Birk, Williams, Chasin, & Rose, 1973; Brodie, Gartrell, Doering, & Fhue, 1974; Tourney, Petrilli, & Hatfield, 1975).

All the problems previously mentioned under potency and libido may apply to the studies on homosexuals. In addition it is quite possible that there are many different reasons for homosexuality. These could include a number of different biological syndromes as well as psychological and social influences. The conflicting studies on homosexuals have often been performed on distinct social groups. The study on homosexual women with no hormonal differences but differences in body size was done on women who belonged to one social club (Griffiths et al., 1974). It is quite possible that the women preselected themselves and represented a particular subset of homosexual. Male homosexuals who sought out psychotherapy for their homosexuality had normal plasma testosterone levels (Birk et al., 1973) while male homosexual college students who were psychologically well adjusted had subnormal testosterone levels (Kolodny et al., 1971). These observations probably tell more about the influence of testosterone on one's acceptance of one's homosexuality than whether testosterone levels are the cause of homosexuality.

Treatment of male homosexuals with androgens does not alter sexual orientation but in some cases can increase libido (Williams, 1974). Antiandrogens have been used to treat sex offenders, including homo- and heterosexual pedophiles, exhibitionists, fetishists, and individuals who have committed indecent assault, sex murders, incest, and sodomy (Laschet, 1973). Such treatment reduces the incidence of the above behaviors but does not alter the direction of the sex deviation. The antiandrogens most probably work by reducing libido and potency.

For every endocrine difference mentioned above, there are cases of male and female heterosexuals who exhibit the same endocrine deviations without any sexual deviation (Labhart, 1976). Thus even if an endocrine abnormality may predispose an individual to homosexuality, the endocrine difference cannot explain the development of homsexuality by itself. Studies on twins have yielded the same conclusions concerning the contribution of genetics. Some identical twins are concordant for sex choice (Kallman, 1952) while others are discordant (Klintworth, 1962). Both authors reported on case histories without providing statistical analyses of their data. Thus it is not possible to determine if more twins were concordant for sex choice than would be expected by chance.

NEUROPHYSIOLOGICAL INFLUENCES ON HUMAN SEXUALITY

The literature on neurophysiological influences on human sexuality has at least as many problems as the endocrine literature.

The genitals will function well with only input from the lower portion of the spinal cord. Erection, orgasm, and ejaculation are controlled by spinal reflexes involving the autonomic nervous system. Individuals who are paralyzed from the waist down because of severed spinal cords can still experience these sexual events if properly stimulated (Williams, 1965). The brain, however, certainly has a major role in modifying the input to the autonomic nerves. Potency, libido, and sex choice appear to be modified by events in specific regions of the brain.

Research in this area has centered on attempts to locate the anatomical regions of the brain that are involved in sexual behavior and to find correlations between levels of specific neurotransmitters in the brain and aspects of sexual behavior. Most of our understanding of these topics comes from studies on animals other than humans. Often there are marked differences between results obtained with rats, mice, dogs, or cats. Deciding which of these species are closest to human beings in terms of sexual behavior is a highly controversial topic. Studies done directly on humans are often very imprecise and the data that result are often uninterpretable. Attempts to correlate human brain dysfunction with sexual dysfunction yield a small number of individuals in whom abnormal function (such as convulsions) in a specific region of the brain is correlated with a specific type of sexual abnormality (such as fetishes) (Epstein, 1973). However, large numbers of individuals have been found with similar neurological disorders and no sexual abnormality (Klintworth, 1962).

The studies on neurotransmitters have suggested that the two chemicals most likely to alter sexual behavior are dopamine and serotonin. Serotonin is thought to suppress sexual behavior while dopamine stimulates it (Gessa & Tagliamorite, 1974; Zitrin, Dement, & Barchas, 1973). Much of the data supporting the hypothesis that serotonin inhibits sexuality has been obtained from studies in which parachlorophenylalanine (PCPA) has been administered to animals. In some species PCPA is thought to specifically inhibit serotonin synthesis (Gessa & Tagliamorite, 1974). PCPA has been reported to increase sexual behavior of male rats and cats who had previously exhibited low libido but to have no influence on previously normal rats and cats (Gessa & Tagliamorite, 1974). When administered to human males (either normal volunteers or patients with serotonin-producing tumors), profound effects were observed in terms of depression, anxiety, gastrointestinal ailments, and so forth, but sex drive was not stimulated (Zitrin et al., 1973).

The initial report that PCPA inhibits serotonin synthesis was made in rats (Gessa & Tagliamorite, 1974). This does not appear to be the case in mice (Gessa & Tagliamorite, 1974). Some authors suggest that PCPA may cause general autonomic stimulation by itself, leading to heightened arousal to all stimuli. An increase in sexual behavior would be just one of its effects.

Serotonin has been demonstrated to be important in many different types of behavioral activities, including decreasing sensitivity to pain, decreasing general arousal, inducing sleep and increasing the contractility of the digestive system (Gessa & Tagliamorite, 1974). In animal experiments in which serotonin or PCPA has been injected directly into or measured in small specific regions of the brain, some understanding of serotonin's roles in specific functions have been obtained. However, in the studies done with humans drugs are injected intravenously and influence many systems at once. A human male who is experiencing fatigue, nausea, constipation, headache, and depression in response to PCPA should not be expected to exhibit increased sexuality even if the depression of serotonin levels in the brain center controlling sex drive could have such an effect.

Studies of dopamine have similar problems. Administration of monoamine oxidase (MAO) inhibitors decreases the rate of destruction of dopamine in the brain and thus increases the effectiveness of dopamine synthesized and released in the brain. Such drugs can influence many behaviors besides sexuality, including stimulating aggressive behavior, general alertness, and altering motor control. The increase in sexual behavior may be a result of the alterations in these other functions rather than a direct influence of dopamine on "sex centers." Many studies done with a variety of tranquilizers such as reserpine and tetrabenazine, which suppress the secretion of dopamine and other adrenergic transmitters, have reported the suppression of sexual activity to the point of impotency (Gessa & Tagliamorite, 1974). These drugs have so many depressing effects on many regions of the brain that the studies often make me think of a similar one that could be done with a sledge hammer, that is, if you knock someone unconscious and then measure sexual behavior, you are likely to observe a decrease.

Attempts to identify specific regions of the brain associated with sexual behavior have suggested that there is a sex center located in the anterior hypothalamus (Patton, Sundsten, Crill, & Swanson, 1976). Lesions induced in this portion of the brain can completely eliminate mating behavior in animals. The hypothalamus receives input from many other regions of the nervous system, all of which can modify its activity. The limbic system and the amygdaloid nucleus are both major sources of input, and occasionally lesions in these regions are found in individuals who exhibit abnormal sexual behavior. For example, Epstein (1973) has reported on individuals with fetishes and on exhibitionists with convulsive type EEGs in the limbic region. Treatment with anticonvulsive drugs decreased exhibitionist behavior in one such individual. Epstein also found a pedophilic homosexual who had lesions in the ventromedial nucleus of the hypothalamus, as well as individuals with deep anterior lobe tumors who exhibited excessive sex drive. The limbic region is, however, a rather large area of the brain, which influences almost the entire spectrum of human behavior and control of the vegetative functions. The control of specific functions does not appear to be well localized within the limbic system and many individuals with convulsive activity in the limbic region (as observed in a study of 40,000 epileptics) do not exhibit any sexually abnormal behavior (Klintworth, 1962).

CONCLUSION

Much basic physiological research needs to be done before we can legitimately approach the questions of what biological factors contribute to human sexual behavior. There are undoubtedly many biological factors such as hormones, neurotransmitters, and the organization of specific neuronal pathways within specific regions of the brain that can modify human sexual behavior. However, as external stimuli such as sociological factors work directly to alter nervous activity, which in turn can influence hormone levels, it is impossible to completely separate biological factors from social and psychological influences.

For each human sexual behavior there are likely to be many different biological factors that could predispose an individual to act in a specific way. While the biological factors may predispose toward certain behavior or cause an increased sensitivity to certain stimuli, the social or psychological stimuli may be essential to actually provide an alteration in behavior.

REFERENCE NOTES

1. Kao, L. W. L., & J. Weisz. *5α reduction and testosterone feedback regulation of luteinizing hormone secretion.* Paper presented at the 9th annual meeting of the Society for the Study of Reproduction, Philadelphia, 1976. (Abstract #142.)

2. Gay, V. L. *Species variation in the metabolism of dihydrotestosterone: Correlation with reported variations in behavioral responses.* Paper presented at the 9th annual meeting of the Society for the Study of Reproduction, Philadelphia, 1976. (Abstract #23.)

REFERENCES

Barlow, D. H., Abel, G. G., Blanchard, E. B., & Mavissakalian, M. Plasma testosterone levels and male homosexuality: A failure to replicate. *Archives of Sexual Behavior,* 1974, *3,* 571–575.

Birk, L., Williams, G. H., Chasin, M., & Rose, L. I. Serum testosterone levels in homosexual men. *New England Journal of Medicine,* 1973, *289,* 1236–1238.

Brodie, H. K. H., Gartrell, N., Doering, C., & Fhue, T. Plasma testosterone levels in heterosexual and homosexual men. *American Journal of Psychiatry,* 1974, *131,* 1.

Bullock, L. P., & Bardin, C. W. Androgen receptors in testicular feminization. *Journal of Clinical Endocrinology,* 1972, *35,* 935–937.

Ellis, W. J., & Grayhack, J. T. Sexual function in aging males after orchiectomy and estrogen therapy. *Journal of Urology,* 1963, *89,* 895–899.

Epstein, A. W. The relationship of altered brain states of sexual psychopathology. In J. Zubin & J. Money (Eds.), *Contemporary sexual behavior.* Baltimore: Johns Hopkins University Press, 1973, pp. 297–310.

Evans, R. B. Physical and biochemical characteristics of homosexual men. *Journal of Consulting and Clinical Psychology,* 1972, *39,* 140–147.

Filler, W., & Drezner, N. The results of surgical castration in women under forty. *American Journal of Obstetrical Gynecology,* 1944, *47,* 122–124.

Foss, G. L. The influence of androgens on sexuality in women. *Lancet,* 1951, *1,* 667–669.

Gessa, G. L., & Tagliamorite, A. Role of brain monoamines in male sexual behavior. *Life Sciences,* 1974, *14,* 425–436.

Goldzieher, J. W., Moses, L. E., Averkin, E., Scheel, C., & Taber, B. Z. A placebo controlled double blind crossover investigation of the side effects attributed to oral contraceptives. *Fertility and Sterility,* 1971, *22*(9), 609–623.

Goy, R. W., & Resko, J. A. Gonadal hormones and behavior of normal and pseudo-hermaphroditic nonhuman female primates. *Recent Progress in Hormone Research,* 1971, *28,* 707–734.

Griffiths, P. D., Merry, J., Browning, M. C. K., Eisinger, A. J., Huntsman, R. G., Lords, E. J. A., Polani, P. E., Tanner, J. M., & Whitehouse, R. H. Homosexual women: An endocrine and psychological study. *Journal of Endocrinology,* 1974, *63,* 549–556.

Kallman, F. J. Comparative twin study on the genetic aspects of male homosexuality. *Journal of Nervous and Mental Diseases,* 1952, *115,* 283.

Klintworth, G. K. A pair of male monozygotic twins discordant for homosexuality. *Journal of Nervous and Mental Diseases,* 1962, *135,* 113–125.

Kolodny, R. C., Masters, W. H., Hendryx, J., & Toro, G. Plasma testosterone and semen analysis in male homosexuals. *New England Journal of Medicine,* 1971, *285,* 1170–1173.

Labhart, A. *Clinical endocrinology theory and practice.* New York: Springer-Verlag, 1976.

Laschet, U. Antiandrogen in the treatment of sex offenders. In J. Zubin & J. Money (Eds.), *Contemporary sexual behavior.* Baltimore: Johns Hopkins University Press, 1973, pp. 311–319.

Loraine, J. A., Adamopoulos, D. A., Kirkham, K. E., Ismail, A. A. A., & Dove, G. A. Patterns of hormone excretion in male and female homosexuals. *Nature* (London), 1971, *234,* 552–554.

Loraine, J. A., Ismail, A. A. A., & Adamopoulos, D. A. Endocrine function in male and female homosexuals. *British Medical Journal,* 1970, *4,* 406-408.

Marcus, R., & Korenman, S. G. Estrogens and the human male. *Annual Review of Medicine,* 1976, *27,* 357-370.

Margolese, S. M., & Janiger, O. Androsterone:etiocholanolone ratios in male homosexuals. *British Medical Journal,* 1973, *3,* 207-210.

Masters, W. H., & Johnson, V. E. *Human sexual response.* Boston: Little, Brown, 1966.

Money, J., & Tucker, P. *Sexual signatures: On being a man or a woman.* Boston: Little, Brown, 1975.

Naftolin, F., Ryan, K. J., & Petro, F. Aromatization of androstenedione by the anterior hypothalamus of adult male and female rats. *Endocrinology,* 1972, *90,* 295-298.

O'Malley, B. W., & Means, A. R. Female steroid hormones and target cell nuclei. *Science,* 1974, *183,* 610-620.

Patton, H. D., Sundsten, J. W., Crill, W. E., & Swanson, P. D. *Introduction to basic neurology.* Philadelphia: Saunders, 1976.

Strickland, A. L., & French, F. S. Absence of response to dihydrotestosterone in the syndrome of testicular feminization. *Journal of Clinical Endocrinology,* 1969, *29,* 1284-1286.

Tourney, G., Petrilli, A., & Hatfield, L. M. Hormonal relationships in homosexual men. *American Journal of Psychiatry,* 1975, *132,* 288-292.

Williams, J. G. Sex and the paralyzed. *Sexology,* 1965, *31,* 453-456.

Williams, R. H. *Textbook of endocrinology.* Philadelphia: Saunders, 1974.

Wilson, J. D., & Gloyna, R. E. The intranuclear metabolism of testosterone in the accessory of organs of reproduction. *Recent Progress in Hormone Research,* 1969, *26,* 309-329.

Zitrin, A., Dement, W. C., & Barchas, J. D. Brain serotonin and male sexual behavior. In J. Zubin & J. Money (Eds.), *Contemporary sexual behavior.* Baltimore: Johns Hopkins University Press, 1973, pp. 321-338.

6

Homosexual Orientation in Women and Men: A Hormonal Basis?

Heino F. L. Meyer-Bahlburg

State University of New York at Buffalo

INTRODUCTION

In the context of the biopsychology of sex-role related behaviors one of the most persistent goals of sex research has been the explanation of homosexuality. There have been marked ups and downs in the predominance of biological or social-psychoanalytic etiologies, with theories and clinical actions often going far beyond the given empirical basis. With radical, biologically based therapies in the offing again the purpose of this paper is to review our current state of knowledge of the psychoneuroendocrinology of sexual orientation. This is the area in which most of the current biologically oriented research on homosexuality is being done, whereas relatively little recent work has been done on the genetics of sexual orientation.

Terms

Since there is no generally accepted standard nomenclature in this area of behavioral research, I need to clarify several terms used in this review. *Sex-dimorphic behavior* refers to all overt and covert behaviors in which males and females differ in a given society. Some of its major subcategories are: *gender identity,* the basic identification of oneself as being male or female; *sexual orientation,* the degree of erotic responsiveness toward the same or other sex (homo- or heterosexual); and *gender-role behavior,* all remaining sex-dimorphic behaviors, for example, aggression and parenting. This terminology implies that sexual orientation is a phenomenon of male–female differentiation (i.e., it develops under the influence of the same factors that govern the differentiation of sex-dimorphic behavior in general), and this is in fact

Ms. Virginia A. Huson and Ms. Joanne M. Pagan provided secretarial assistance.

the working hypothesis of all biological theories of homosexuality and the approach examined in this review. The use of homosexuality as a subcategory of sex-dimorphic behavior does not necessarily imply an etiology based on biological sex differentiation; the polarization of sexual orientation and related behaviors in a masculine-feminine dimension could as well be the result of social influences, with society just superimposing its sex-role concepts and sex-typing pressures from early childhood on and the individual responding by conforming to such role prescriptions. Sexual orientation can also be conceptualized in ways not primarily linked to sex-dimorphic behavior, for instance, in terms of the development of sex-object preferences, along with the various paraphilias. Here the preference for certain sex objects is the result of conditioning in situations of high sexual arousal, and the initial selection of sex objects may be caused by a variety of circumstantial factors (cf. the "social episode model of human sexual behavior" by Meyer & Freeman, 1976-1977).

Homosexual orientation needs to be distinguished from *homosexual behavior.* The latter refers to any sexual acts between members of the same sex. In contrast, *homosexual orientation* refers to a sexual responsiveness to and preference for the same sex expressed in sexual fantasies, attractions, and (not necessarily) actual sexual experiences. Following Kinsey, Pomeroy, and Martin (1948), sexual orientation is operationalized as a rating scale continuum ranging from 0, exclusive heterosexuality, to 6, exclusive homosexuality. This operational definition provides a simple descriptive measure for the assessment of sexual orientation without negating the possibility that there may be various etiological types of homosexuality (as well as of heterosexuality) as implied, for instance, in the psychoanalytic distinction between true and pseudohomosexuality (Ovesey, 1969). The question of how to assess sexual orientation with or without implying certain personality and etiological types is somewhat comparable to the measurement of weight in various forms of obesity: although many physiological and psychological factors contribute to body weight and its variations, the weight measure is a very useful assessment tool to start with.

Sex Hormones and Sexual Orientation

Most hormonal research on sexual orientation has focused on indicators of a decrease of male sex hormones and less frequently of an increase of female sex hormones in male homosexuals and of the reverse situation in female homosexuals. Again the underlying assumption is that homosexuality is an intersexual phenomenon based upon sex hormone patterns that deviate from the gender-typical ones. Massive differences exist between the sexes in hormone levels and production patterns after puberty, and recent research has established similarly strong differences in pre- and perinatal life, whereas early and middle childhood are characterized by only small differences of questionable significance. (Details on sex-dimorphic endocrinology are given in Chapter 5 of this volume.)

It is important to perceive the complexity of the endocrine system. In the search for a hormonal basis for homosexuality, investigations may be directed at many different aspects. Hormone production, including biochemical synthesis and release, may be influenced by a multitude of factors. Hormone levels in blood are affected by the rate of metabolic clearance of hormones from blood. Most of the measurable hormone in blood is bound to specific proteins, whereas only the small and variable fraction of free (unbound) hormone is believed to be biologically active. The utilization of hormones by body tissues including the nervous system involves several steps, each of which may be disturbed: for instance, the conversion of the hormone into the effective metabolite, binding to an intracellular receptor, or transport into the cell nucleus where the hormone will stimulate the formation of new genetic material. There are a great many sex hormones, and only some of their interactions are known so far. Hormone levels fluctuate tremendously, because of biological factors such as episodic secretion, circadian rhythms, and the menstrual cycle, and biological stresses such as traumas and diseases. In addition the endocrine system responds to psychological stimuli such as sexually arousing material (Pirke, Kockott, & Dittmar, 1974) or psychological–emotional stress (Kreuz, Rose, & Jennings, 1972; Rose, Bourne, Poe, Mougey, Collins, & Mason, 1969). All these factors have to be considered for the pre- and perinatal condition as well as for the pubertal and postpubertal situation. Thus negative findings with regard to a particular endocrine aspect do not automatically rule out the involvement of other endocrine factors. On the other hand, positive findings do not necessarily indicate that a given hormone abnormality is causally linked to a homosexual orientation. It is also possible that homosexuality itself as a psychological status influences hormone levels; consider, for instance, the stressful psychosocial repercussions in our society.

In searching for a biological basis of sexual orientation we consider man the most recent product of a long evolution of mammalian brain and behavior. Therefore I will first describe animal models of homosexuality before discussing the human research.

ANIMAL MODELS OF HOMOSEXUALITY

Homosexual behavior, especially in the form of mounting, has been observed in many mammalian species. In contrast, a sexual preference for partners of the same sex has been observed in only a few cases of (captive) animals (Erwin & Maple, 1976; Ford & Beach, 1951, pp. 141–146). Consequently, nobody has compared sex hormone levels of "homosexual animals" with those of "heterosexual animals," which would be the paradigm of the typical human study.

The absence of such a spontaneous animal model of homosexuality is not necessarily an argument against the assumption of a biological basis for human homosexuality. It is plausible that the selection pressures in wild as well as in domesticated animals are strongly against preferential homosexuality, whereas the selection pressures have considerably eased in human evolution. Moreover, animal sex-dimorphic behavior in general and sex-dimorphic mating behavior in particular can be drastically influenced by hormonal manipulations, especially in the early stages of development; the neuroendocrine systems involved in these modifications appear to exist in the human brain as well.

The "Homosexual" Rat

In the male rat, typical mating behavior involves mounting, intromission, and ejaculation. Typical female mating behavior involves lordosis, that is, a downward arching of the back in response to the male's mounting. To some degree these behaviors can be modulated by hormone manipulations in adulthood, but it is usually not possible to achieve a sex-role inversion in this way. However, sex-role inversions can be brought about by prenatal or perinatal hormone manipulation. For instance, one can produce lordotic behavior in male rats by experimentally inducing a deficiency of androgens, via surgical or hormonal (by antiandrogens) castration curing a critical phase in perinatal development, followed by administration of sex hormones in adulthood. Analogously genetic female rats can become malelike in their behavior by perinatal administration of androgens; that is, under appropriate sex-hormone replacement in adulthood they will show less lordotic and more mounting and intromission behavior than the unmanipulated female rat. Perinatal manipulation of androgens has decisive effects not only on later mating behavior but also on other sex-dimorphic behaviors, such as aggression or maternal behavior, and on cyclic-female versus tonic-male patterns of gonadotropin release (Montagna & Sadler, 1974).

Studies with similar results have been performed by many researchers on a variety of subprimate mammals. Naturally it is tempting to extrapolate from the sex-role inversion of lower mammals to human homosexuality. The major proponent of such an extrapolation is Dörner (1972, 1976) in East Berlin who has applied the term homosexuality to rat behavior (Dörner, 1968; Dörner & Hinz, 1968). He equates homosexuality of the male rat with an increased readiness to display lordosis and/or a decreased readiness to show mounting and intromission behavior; homosexuality of the female rat is denoted by the reverse changes. Since these mating behaviors are strongly dependent on the early androgen situation, Dörner concludes that in humans also the early androgen production predisposes for a certain sexual orientation.

The Pseudohermaphroditic Rhesus Monkey

The effects of hormonal manipulation during early development on sex-dimorphic behavior is not restricted to subprimate mammals but also has been found in primates, as demonstrated in intensive investigations by Goy and his co-workers (Goy & Resko, 1972). Prenatal androgenization of female rhesus monkeys has marked effects on their later behavior, placing them between normal females and normal males: there is an increase of sham threat behavior, rough-and-tumble play, chasing play, mounting behavior, and play initiation. After prenatal treatment with high doses of androgens administration of testosterone in adulthood led to further changes in behavior, and one out of three monkeys studied developed a complete pattern of male copulatory behavior. Normal adult females treated with testosterone in adulthood also showed some changes, although different ones. There was no significant increase in mounting behavior. One female developed clitoral hypertrophy with self-induced stimulation on a female partner's back in a nonmale position. One has to take into consideration, however, that the prenatally androgenized females were pseudohermaphroditic; that is, they had phalluses from birth on, a fact that may have behavioral consequences of its own. Also, the number of animals observed in the various treatment groups was very small. Nevertheless, the overall similarity of these findings to those in lower mammals permits the conclusion that prenatal androgen treatment of female rhesus monkeys has long-lasting masculinizing effects on various sex-dimorphic behaviors, including aspects of mating behavior, thereby again suggesting a similar etiology for human sexual orientation.

Extrapolation to Humans

Prenatal Prophylaxis

If indeed the homosexual rat is a valid model for human homosexuality, then human homosexuality should be the result of prenatal hormone abnormalities. Consequently Dörner (1976) suggests that "in genetic males, androgen deficiency during the hypothalamic differentiation phase results in a more or less female differentiation of the brain; i.e., a neuroendocrine predisposition for male hypo-, bi- or even homosexuality; . . . in genetic females, on the other hand, overdoses of androgen . . . during the hypothalamic differentiation phase lead to more or less male differentiation of the brain, i.e., . . . a neuroendocrine predisposition for female hypo-, bi- or homosexuality" (p. 194). Many mechanisms could theoretically account for such assumed hormonal abnormalities *in utero:* genetic abnormalities of hormone production or timing, various drugs, and stress. With regard to stress factors, for example, Ward (1972, 1977) has demonstrated that the male offspring of pregnant rats

undergoing severe gestational stress tend in fact to exhibit decreased masculine
and increased feminine (lordotic) behavior.

Dörner's theory implies that homosexuality cannot be treated by endocrine manipulations in adulthood since the decisive changes have taken place
during a critical hypothalamic organization phase *in utero*. It follows that
primary prevention of homosexuality would require treatment during prenatal
life. In pursuit of this goal Dörner has successfully developed procedures to
assess both sex chromosomes and androgen levels *in utero* by amniocentesis.
He is currently advocating prenatal androgen treatment for male fetuses who
were found to have low androgen exposure *in utero*. Whether the psycho-
endocrine data on human homosexuality provide a sufficient empirical basis
for Dörner's clinical proposal will be discussed in later sections of this chapter.

Hypothalamic Surgery as Cure

The concept of the homosexual rat has supported still another approach
to the treatment of homosexuality. Male rats that have been castrated at birth
and then show increased lordotic (homosexual) behavior in adulthood can be
treated with electrolytic lesions of the ventromedial nucleus of the hypothalamus, a nucleus close to the stalk of the pituitary gland and also in close
proximity to those centers that regulate gonadotropin secretion and, thereby,
sex hormone production. After such hypothalamic lesions, male mating
behavior prevails (Dörner, 1976, pp. 139-140). On the basis of several
pertinent experiments Dörner (1976) considers the ventromedial nucleus to be
the female mating center. A similar effect had been demonstrated by
Schreiner and Kling (Note 1) in cats: these authors produced hypersexuality
by lesions in the amygdala and the pyriform cortex, and the deviant behavior
could be abolished after destruction of the hypothalamic ventromedial nuclei,
although this was accompanied by the appearance of aggressiveness. The
results by Schreiner and Kling and by Dörner provided the experimental base
for a group of neurosurgeons in West Germany (Roeder, Orthner, & Müller,
1972) to try a stereotaxic treatment of homosexuality by destruction of the
ventromedial nucleus (mostly unilaterally, on the nondominant side). They
used a side electrode for the electrocoagulation of 50–70 mm^3 of brain tissue,
which is about three-fourths of the nucleus. The first operation was done in
1962 on a 60-year-old man who was socially isolated and had sexual contacts
with 12-14-year-old boys involving mutual masturbation. He was psychiatric-
ally classified as an "inhibition" homosexual and confined to a psychiatric
hospital according to the penal code. He was unresponsive to psychotherapy
and had been sentenced to imprisonment repeatedly. Follow-up for $9\frac{1}{2}$ years
after surgery showed that his sexual interest in young adolescent boys had
vanished altogether; potency was weakened but preserved. Occasionally the
man had normal relationships with women. There was a steady professional
rehabilitation. The authors considered this a "complete cure!" (Roeder et al.,
1972, p. 93).

The next cases were operated on in 1968, and by 1973 a total of 23 cases had had hypothalamus operations for various diagnoses, not all involving sexual disorders (Müller, Orthner, Roeder, König, & Bosse, 1974). All patients were male; many had a history of brain trauma. Of the 23 patients 15 were pedophilic or ephebophilic (13 homosexual, 2 heterosexual); 1 was hyper-heterosexual; 4 were exhibitionists (3 heterosexual, 1 homosexual-pedo-philic—he was operated on bilaterally); 1 had a contact neurosis misdiagnosed as latent homosexuality; 2 were alcohol and drug addicts. The latter were also lesioned in the posterior lateral hypothalamus in order to prevent an increase of the eating drive. The patients with heterosexual behavior disturbances had additional lesions in the mediobasal section of the preoptic area, the latter being the male mating center in Dörner's dual mating center theory.

The general results in terms of recidivism are claimed to have been favorable. The patients generally experienced a decrease of the compulsiveness of their sex drive, often a loss of their deviant sexual interests. Some of them returned to heterosexuality without loss of potency, although sometimes with delayed ejaculations. There was no major endocrine deficiency following the surgery and no other major side effects, except for one patient who died from a virus pneumonia 6 days after hypothalamotomy. Unfortunately pretreatment and posttreatment comparisons, both with regard to psychology and endo-crinology, employed relatively poor methods so that we are not really certain of the side effects on patients. The whole issue is currently a matter of heated controversy in West Germany (Schorsch, Sigusch, Schmidt, & Meyer, Note 2), which has led to a temporary moratorium on this psychosurgical approach.

For our discussion this approach is noteworthy in two respects. One is theoretical: the ventromedial nucleus of the hypothalamus has been shown to take up sex steroids in both lower mammals and subhuman primates (McEwen, 1976), and there is no doubt that it participates in the regulation of sexual behavior in lower mammals. It is extremely likely that comparable uptake studies in humans would also show a specific steroid sensitivity in this area. The success of psychosurgery in reducing the recidivism rate of various sexual problems demonstrates that the hypothalamic nuclei are involved in human sexual behavior also. This result may result from a general reduction in sexual motivation; the available clinical data are not sufficient to permit any conclusions as to a specific neurophysiological basis of homosexuality.

The other point is an ethical one in the area of comparative research: When do animal studies give us enough evidence for drawing conclusions on human behavior and its neurophysiological basis and for taking clinical action? As Aronson and Cooper (Note 3) have demonstrated, cats with lesions in the amygdala or related areas do not show hypersexuality in a clinical sense but rather indiscriminate object selection, which may include animals of other species as well as inanimate objects; they are certainly not homosexual in any sense of the word. As to Dörner's theory the homology of rat homosexuality and human homosexuality has also not been established (Meyer-Bahlburg,

1977). Consequently the psychosurgical approach appears premature. However, one has to acknowledge that it was at least partially successful in terms of reducing recidivism, although the costs in terms of side effects have not been documented satisfactorily. The issue is not an easy one to decide because withholding of medical interventions tends to result in long-term or repeated imprisonment with serious psychosocial consequences for many of the males engaging in pedophilic and other tabooed sexual behaviors.

SEXUAL ORIENTATION IN HUMANS: PSYCHONEUROENDOCRINOLOGY

Hormone Manipulation of Adult Homosexuals

When the sex hormones were identified and synthesized and their functions became more and more known, many clinicians believed that they were the key to the etiology of homosexuality and tried treating homosexual males by the administration of male sex hormones (Glass & Johnson, 1944; Heller & Maddock, 1947, pp. 419–422). However, this treatment approach had little success and was subsequently given up. Male homosexuality did not seem to be caused by sex hormone deficiency in adulthood. Quite the contrary, the sexual activity, potency, and libido of male homosexuals, as well as heterosexuals, can be decreased through reduction of androgen levels by surgical castration (e.g., Bremer, 1958; Cornu, 1973) without a change in sexual orientation. The same results can be achieved by (reversible) "hormonal castration," that is, the use of synthetic hormones to suppress the production of testosterone or to block its effectiveness (Bancroft, Tennent, Loucas, & Cass, 1974; Money, 1970; Murray, Bancroft, Anderson, Tennent, & Carr, 1975; Raspé & Bernhard, 1972). In a few cases castration was even followed by a change in sexual activity from homosexual or homosexual–pedophilic to heterosexual (e.g., Bremer, 1958, pp. 100, 106). It is doubtful, however, that the latter changes indicated genuine alterations of sexual orientation rather than just self-limitation of sexual behavior to the societal norm, made possible by the reduction of sexual libido.

From the results of both androgen treatments and deandrogenization of intact adult men, we have to conclude that the manipulation of male sex hormone levels in adulthood has little effect on sexual orientation. There are no data on the effects of castration on sexual orientation in women.

Hypogonadism

If homosexuality were caused by gross deficiencies in the gender-appropriate sex hormones, the various syndromes of male and female hypogonadism should show increased frequencies of homosexuality, but this is not the case. A recent review (Meyer-Bahlburg, 1977) of detailed studies of 49 male patients with a variety of hypogonadal syndromes (Bobrow, Money, & Lewis, 1971; Clopper, Adelson, & Money, 1976; Johnson, Myhre, Ruvalcaba, Thuline, & Kelley, 1970; Money & Alexander, 1967; Money & Clopper, 1975; Meyer-Bahlburg & Aceto, Note 4) showed a predominantly homosexual or bisexual orientation in only 10%, that is, no increase above expectations for the general population. Likewise, an increased frequency of homosexual orientation in hypogonadal females, as in Turner's syndrome, has not been reported and is not clinically apparent (Ehrhardt, Note 5). Hypogonadism in both males and females is correlated with hyposexuality in general, which may even persist after hormone replacement, especially if the latter is not started before late adolescence or young adulthood.

Homosexuality and Body Build

Males and females differ in various aspects of body build, some of which are already becoming apparent in fetal development. The endocrine changes of puberty have a marked influence on somatic development and accentuate the sexual dimorphism of body build (Tanner, 1975). It has therefore been of interest to study whether homosexual orientation is correlated with an intersexual body build. In fact several studies suggest such a correlation, although the differences found are rather subtle.

Males

In Germany, Schlegel (1962) has made comprehensive studies of the pelvis in male homosexuals as compared with unselected males and females. From the 4th month of fetal life (Goss, 1973, p. 237), there is a very clear-cut sex difference in the transverse diameter of the pelvic outlet, with males having the smaller diameter (adult male range 6.5–11.5 cm, mode 8.5 cm; female range 9.5–14.5 cm, mode 12 cm; Schlegel, 1962). A group of 150 homosexual men showed a statistically significant shift of the diameter measure toward the gynecomorphic side (mode 9.5 cm). Unfortunately Schlegel did not discuss whether and to what degree physical activity level or aging correlate with the pelvic diameter, factors that were apparently not controlled.

In a recent study in this country (Evans, 1972) involving detailed anthropological measurements in 44 homosexual and 111 heterosexual men aged 22–47 years, the homosexual men showed a significantly (although only slightly) lower shoulder–pelvis ratio (in terms of Tanner's [1951] discriminant androgyny score), a more linear or ectomorphic body build, less muscularity, and less muscular strength than the heterosexuals. The pelvic diameter was not measured in this study. Evans's results in part replicate a study by Coppen (1959), who found that 31 homosexual patients had significantly lower shoulder–pelvis ratios than 53 normal controls; however, they did not differ from a group of 22 neurotic patients. Coppen's homosexuals had attended the

Maudsley Hospital in London primarily for homosexuality; the majority had been referred from the courts after they had been convicted of homosexual offenses. By contrast Evans's subjects were members of a homosexual organization, and the selection criteria included being healthy, employed, Caucasian, aged 21–47, with at least a high school education, no history of mental disorder, and no perceived need for psychotherapy. Thus the difference in the androgyny scores between homo- and heterosexuals cannot be explained by the relationship between neuroticism and androgyny scores as suggested by Coppen.

It is unknown if these differences in body build are caused by sex hormones or by the many other factors that influence growth and body build. For instance, the body build differences may be due (at least in part) to the timing of puberty rather than the rate of hormone production itself. As we know from the California Growth Study, late-maturing males have a less masculine (less mesomorph) body build in adolescence than early or average-maturing males. The delayed adolescents catch up in their body build development later, and the two groups are almost indistinguishable in body build at age 33 (Jones, 1957). Unfortunately, the available reports on body build differences between homo- and heterosexuals do not allow for such a timing-oriented analysis.

Even if such body build differences are replicable, they do not necessarily imply a neuroendocrine basis for homosexuality. Clinical experience suggests that a nonmasculine body build itself (possibly compounded by delayed puberty) may bring about self-image problems for a male, which may then increase the risk for (a nonassertive, submissive, passive form of) homosexual behavior.

Females

For female homosexuality the data are even more scant. Using self-reported (by questionnaires) body measures, Kenyon (1968a) compared 123 lesbians contacted through an organization devoted to the interests of lesbians and a similar number of normal heterosexual women contacted through an organization of married women. The lesbians were heavier with bigger busts and waists. Exclusively homosexual women did not differ significantly from the predominantly homosexual groups (Kenyon, 1968b).

The only study involving careful multiple anthropometric measurements in a nonpatient sample is by Griffiths et al. on 42 members of a lesbian organization who were compared to a control group of like-aged mothers of a sample of normal children (Griffiths, Merry, Browning, Eisinger, Huntsman, Lord, Polani, Tanner, & Whitehouse, 1974). They found that the lesbians were significantly greater in stature; statistically significant but small differences in shoulder width and the Tanner androgyny score (the lesbians being greater in masculinity) disappeared when body height was controlled for. The authors also found that the somatotypes of the lesbians covered a wide range, and they concluded that "there is no such thing as a lesbian physique." They considered their "only striking finding" the visual impression that the lesbian subjects mostly looked older than their ages and sometimes strikingly so.

In summary we can conclude that there may be slight group differences in body build (with extensive overlap) between heterosexuals and homosexuals (although replicability has not been established yet) but that such differences seem to be very small in comparison to the considerable differences in sexual orientation. Thus body build is not a likely determinant of sexual orientation, although it may be a contributing factor in at least a subgroup of homosexuals.

Hormone Measurements

Males

With the improvement in hormone-assay methodology in the 1960s endocrine studies on homosexuals have proliferated. The recent upswing of such research started with Loraine and co-workers who studied 3 homosexual men and 4 lesbian women (Loraine, Adamopoulos, Kirkham, Ismail, & Dove, 1971; Loraine, Ismail, Adamopoulos, & Dove, 1970). Two of the three men, both practicing exclusive homosexuality during the time of the study, showed significantly lowered excretion of testosterone and epitestosterone with normal excretion of luteinizing hormone (LH) in repeated urine collections, whereas the third man, a bisexual, was only slightly but not significantly lower in his testosterone excretions than the controls who were mainly staff members. The findings were corroborated in the studies on 30 male homosexual students by Kolodny and colleagues (Kolodny, Jacobs, Masters, Toro, & Daughaday, 1972; Kolodny, Masters, Hendryx, & Toro, 1971). Compared to a student control group subjects with exclusive or almost exclusive homosexuality (Kinsey score 6 or 5) showed significantly decreased plasma testosterone levels with decreased sperm count and increased plasma gonadotropins [LH and follicle-stimulating hormone (FSH)]. Subsequent endocrine research, however, was contradictory. The available studies on males, most of which have been described elsewhere in detail (Meyer-Bahlburg, 1977), will be summarized briefly.

On testosterone in male homosexuality 14 more studies (including one report on transsexuals) have been reported. Excluding data on identifiable subjects with agonadism, castration, or current estrogen treatment, all data available so far permit the conclusions that follow.

1. Most male homosexuals investigated had testosterone levels within the normal range of male samples unselected for sexual orientation. Gross deficiencies of testosterone levels are conspicuously rare, even in those few studies that report statistically lower values for homosexuals compared to heterosexuals.

2. There is no uniform trend in the results. Four studies found significantly lower testosterone means for homosexual than for heterosexual subjects (Kolodny et al., 1971; Loraine et al., 1970; Pillard, Rose, & Sherwood, 1974; Starká, Šipová, & Hynie, 1975). Three of these lack adequate control groups, and the result of the fourth study (Kolodny et al., 1971) seems to be confounded by the fact that the homosexual group had a high number of drug abusers; many psychotropic drugs have been found to depress testosterone levels. By contrast, eight studies show no systematic difference between homosexuals and controls or between homosexuals with different Kinsey ratings (Barlow, Abel, Blanchard, & Mavissakalian, 1974; Birk, Williams, Chasin, & Rose, 1973; Doerr, Kockott, Vogt, Pirke, & Dittmar, 1973; Dörner, Rohde, Stahl, Krell, & Masius, 1975; Friedman, Dyrenfurth, Linkie, Tendler, & Fleiss, 1977; Parks, Korth-Schütz, Penny, Hilding, Dumars, Frasier, & New, 1974; Stahl, Dörner, Ahrens, & Graudenz, 1976; and Migeon, Rivarola, & Forest, 1968, on transsexuals). An additional particularly interesting report has been published by Friedman, Wollesen, and Tendler (1976). They described a pair of monozygotic twins discordant for sexual orientation who had equivalent (normal) blood levels of testosterone. Two studies showed elevated levels of testosterone in homosexuals (Brodie, Gartrell, Doering, & Rhue, 1974; Tourney & Hatfield, 1973, republished in Tourney, Petrilli, & Hatfield, 1975). The almost linear negative correlation between Kinsey score and testosterone levels found by Kolodny has not been demonstrated again. Decreased testosterone levels have not been found in those studies that are methodologically the soundest, that is, employing careful patient selection procedures and multiple blood sampling (Brodie et al., 1974; Parks et al., 1974).

A particularly important aspect is the blood production rate of testosterone because it takes into account the metabolic clearance rate. The only investigation concerned with this (Migeon et al., 1968) did not find a deviation from normal in untreated male transsexuals. Two studies have been published on unbound testosterone (i.e., the biologically active fraction in plasma): one finds an elevation in homosexuals (Doerr, Pirke, Kockott, & Dittmar, 1976), the other a decrease in comparison to controls (Stahl et al., 1976). No correlations could be found between testosterone and the preferred role (active, passive, alternately active and passive) in sexual activities (Doerr et al., 1973), nor between testosterone and degree of effeminacy in general gender-role behavior (Pillard et al., 1974).

Data on gonadotropin levels in male homosexuals are similarly variable. Two studies found elevations (Doerr et al., 1976, in a group of subjects ranging from Kinsey score 3 to 6; Kolodny et al., 1972, in Kinsey score 5 and 6 subjects), whereas seven studies did not find a systematic difference (Brown, Zajac, & Steiner, 1971; Dörner, Rohde, Seidel, Haas, & Schott, 1976; Dörner, Rohde, Stahl, Krell, & Masius, 1975; Friedman et al., 1977; Loraine et al., 1970, 1971; Parks et al., 1974; Tourney et al., 1975). The design of many of these studies leaves much to be desired, especially in terms of control group selection and sampling, but the conclusion is certainly justified that male homosexuals as a group do not show gross central under- or overstimulation of gonadotropin production or release or deficient negative-feedback sensitivity in the hypothalamic–pituitary–gonadal axis.

A few investigators were concerned with other hormones that are of interest in the area of sexual differentiation. For instance, Kolodny et al. (1972) found an elevation of plasma prolactin levels in Kinsey score 6 subjects, but this finding was not confirmed in a new study by Friedman and Frantz (1977). Doerr et al. (1973, 1976) reported elevated plasma estrogens in homosexuals, whereas Friedman et al. (1977) found no difference in plasma estradiol and plasma estrone levels between 20 homosexuals and 18 heterosexual men, confirming their earlier report of comparable plasma estradiol levels in their homosexual and heterosexual twin brothers (Friedman et al., 1976).

Of particular interest is the finding by Friedman et al. (1976) that the blood levels of androstenedione, a weak androgen usually of adrenal origin, were significantly elevated in the homosexual twin. Similarly Friedman et al. (1977) described a significant elevation of androstenedione along with cortisol in their group of 20 homosexual men. The authors offer as the most likely explanation for the apparent alteration of adrenal functioning the fact that the group differs from heterosexuals with regard to emotional stress, since the homosexuals belong to a repressed minority group in a homophobic culture. Equally likely seems the hypothesis that they showed a stronger transient emotional response to the one-time venipuncture. The replicability of the data by Friedman et al. is in doubt since Tourney and Hatfield (1973) did not find significant differences in plasma androstenedione between 13 homosexuals and 11 control males.

The only hormonal difference between homosexual and heterosexual males that has been reported relatively consistently concerns the ratio between two androgen metabolites, androsterone and etiocholanolone. After puberty there is a clear-cut sex difference in the androsterone–etiocholanolone ratio, with women being lower than men (Zumoff, Bradlow, Finkelstein, Boyar, & Hellman, 1976). Three available studies (Evans, 1972; Margolese, 1970; Margolese & Janiger, 1973) showed a significant decrease in homosexuals as compared to heterosexuals, particularly in Kinsey score 5 and 6 individuals, and the fourth report (Tourney & Hatfield, 1973) showed a negligible difference in the same direction. However, the patterns of the levels of androsterone and of etiocholanolone across the Kinsey scale categories vary between the four studies, and the androsterone–etiocholanolone ratios are very sensitive to various influences, especially diseases. Also, the biological function of these metabolites as well as their indicator function for metabolic deviations are quite unknown.

The heterogeneity of the findings of different endocrine studies is surprising. This must result from problems with sample selection, especially of control subjects, and also from problems with the endocrine methodology. At any rate the data available make it seem highly unlikely that deviations in peripheral hormone levels and production in adulthood can be held responsible for the development of male homosexuality in general. This conclusion does not exclude the possibility that such endocrine irregularities may be a contributing factor in some homosexual individuals.

Females

Studies involving hormone measures on female homosexuals and transsexuals are exceedingly rare. Loraine et al. (1970, 1971) described four lesbian women who showed elevated testosterone excretion and decreased estrone excretion. Three of these subjects had a history of irregular menstrual cycles. Apart from Loraine's reports there are only three other studies; two are concerned with transsexuals. Fulmer (1973) determined plasma testosterone in nine female transsexuals (aged 18-50 years), none of whom was known to have received prior androgen therapy. Four of these patients had levels above the normal range for women, and two had levels in the very high female range. Unfortunately the report lacks data on the subjects on which the normative values are based; also, single blood samples were drawn without regard to time of day or stage of the menstrual cycle. Jones and Samimy (1973) studied three female transsexuals (age not given) whose previous testosterone medication (duration of 1-3 years) had been discontinued 8 weeks prior to testing. Two had plasma testosterone concentrations typical of normal control subjects (22 student nurses with regular menstrual patterns and without endocrine abnormality), that is, 0.02 μg/100 ml; and the third female transsexual had a testosterone concentration of 0.06 μg/100 ml comparable to those reported on hirsute, anovulatory patients with the polycystic ovary syndrome. Adrenal and ovarian suppression and stimulation studies on the latter patient indicated an ovarian source of the elevated testosterone, as expected.

Griffiths et al. (1974) studied 42 volunteering members of a lesbian organization in regard to urinary hormone excretion (in 24-hour urine samples); 36 of the group (aged 22-55 years) provided urine specimens. Of these subjects 10 had elevated testosterone levels, 2 of them also had high epitestosterone levels. In 2 subjects no testosterone or epitestosterone could be detected in urine, probably because of their use of oral contraceptives; the other subjects were within the normal female range. All results on estrogens fell within normal limits for females when allowance was made for the stage in the menstrual cycle, menopause, and those subjects taking oral contraceptives.

Only the study by Loraine et al. included gonadotropins: FSH was within normal range in three subjects and abnormally low in the fourth subject. Mean LH excretion was within normal range in one subject but significantly raised in the remaining three. These findings await replication.

We can conclude that the majority of female homosexuals appear to have testosterone and estrogen levels within normal range, whereas there may be a subgroup with an elevation of male sex hormone levels. Much caution, however, is required in the interpretation of these results before they have been replicated on a larger scale and with a higher degree of methodological sophistication.

Neuroendocrine Studies

An important potential indicator of prenatal sex hormone effects is the positive estrogen feedback effect on LH. Adult female rats respond to increasing levels of estrogen with an LH surge. This response to estrogen cannot be elicited in neonatally androgenized female rats or in males castrated in adulthood (Neill, 1972), although some recent results (Dörner, Götz, & Rohde, 1975) suggest that the difference is more quantitative than absolute. Such a positive feedback effect is well known in human females. Recent studies in human males demonstrate a positive estrogen feedback in some (but not all) subjects studied (Kulin & Reiter, 1976), especially after castration and estrogen priming (Dörner, Rohde, & Schnorr, 1975). However, the response is clearly much smaller and less consistent in males than in females. If, as Dörner suggested, homosexuality is caused by an irregularity of prenatal androgen effects on the brain and if this is accompanied by changes of the positive feedback mechanism, then homosexuals (and transsexuals) should show deviations in the positive feedback phenomenon.

Males

For male homosexuals this has been demonstrated by Dörner's group in three investigations (Dörner, Rohde, & Krell, 1972; Dörner, Rohde, Seidel, Haas, & Schott, 1976; Dörner, Rohde, Stahl, Krell, & Masius, 1975 [incorporating the earlier data]). As a group these intact homosexual men showed a positive feedback effect of estrogen priming on LH, whereas intact heterosexual men did not. In the homosexuals the response was weaker and delayed for 24 hours when compared to the response in women. However, the response pattern was far from uniform in the homosexual men and was not shown by all of them, and a positive response occurred in some heterosexual men as well, although in a smaller proportion of the sample. Dörner et al. (1976) studied several transsexual men; two transsexual men with homosexual behavior and intact testicular function showed a similar delayed positive estrogen feedback action on LH. In contrast the positive feedback effect was not found in four transsexual men with hypo- or asexuality. One of these men had Klinefelter's syndrome, a second one agonadism from autocastration, and the other two were suspected of having possible atrophy of hypothalamic regions.

Females

In the same paper Dörner et al. (1976) reported on four transsexual women (aged 24-25 years). Three had homosexual behavior and oligo- and/or hypomenorrhea and only a weak or at best moderate positive estrogen feedback action on LH release was evocable in them, similar to the findings in castrated and estrogen-primed heterosexual men. However, in one transsexual woman with bisexual behavior and eumenorrhea a normal female positive estrogen feedback action on LH secretion could be evoked. Analogous data have been reported by Seyler et al. (1978), who studied nine transsexual women with a somewhat different method. He investigated the effects of luteinizing hormone-releasing hormone (LHRH) administration on the LH response over 7 days of daily administration of estrogens (2 mg/day of diethylstilbestrol). Heterosexual women typically show an increase of the LH response over the week (a positive feedback effect); heterosexual men respond with a diminished LH response (negative feedback effect); the nine transsexual women (aged 20-40 years) as a group did not show the strongly increased responsiveness typical for normal women but remained unchanged, although the individual effects varied between moderate increase and decline. It is not quite clear how Seyler's method compares to Dörner's. Two male transsexuals and four male homosexuals studied by Seyler did not differ significantly from normal males in their LH response to LHRH after treatment with diethylstilbestrol.

Comments

The new data on irregularities of the positive estrogen feedback effect in homosexuals and transsexuals are in striking contrast to the lack of correlation of the sexual conditions with other endocrine or somatic abnormalities. Potentially these findings are of great theoretical interest. However, a word of caution is in order: the available reports are sorely lacking in details on sample characteristics, and most of the samples are rather small. Thus very careful replications are needed. In addition one needs to analyze baseline differences in LH and in steroid hormones that may influence the hypothalamic–pituitary sensitivity to estrogens. Explanations of the phenomenon, if replicable, could involve temporary deficiencies in prenatal hormone production as well as changes in central target organ sensitivities to normal levels of circulating androgens. The latter theory would not be in conflict with the well-documented lack of abnormalities in primary and secondary sex characteristics in the majority of homosexuals, since the utilization of androgens in the periphery may be dependent on biochemical mechanisms different from those in central utilization. Hypothetical temporary irregularities (deficiencies in males, excesses in females) in androgenization must occur so late in prenatal development as not to interfere with normal peripheral differentiation since homosexuals are not characterized by genital intersexuality; the irregularities must be reversible because the postnatal gonadal hormone production of most homosexuals appears to be normal. In the male these conditions are most easily met by a hypothetical premature decline of the peak testosterone production by the fetal testes, which ordinarily occurs toward the end of the 4th month of pregnancy, or by a delayed onset of hypothalamic differentiation, which, according to Dörner (1976), takes place during the second trimester of pregnancy. In the case of females one has to speculate about potential sources of unusual androgen levels, for instance, from the adrenal, or unusual tissue sensitivities to androgens (or estrogens) during pregnancy. In both sexes many other factors including hypothalamic lesions and prenatal drugs that influence prenatal differentiation could be involved as well.

Endocrine Syndromes with Prenatal Hormone Abnormalities

Investigating the positive estrogen feedback effect is an indirect method of tracing prenatal hormone abnormalities in humans. A more direct approach is the study of human subjects with known endocrine syndromes involving prenatal sex hormone abnormalities.

Males

If in human males the effective presence of androgens in prenatal life is predisposing for masculine development including a heterosexual orientation, then prenatal androgen deficiency should lead to homosexuality and androgen excess to heterosexuality. This hypothesis can be examined in several endocrine syndromes.

In the syndrome of complete androgen insensitivity or testicular feminization sex hormone production is largely normal, but the target organs are insensitive to androgen. At birth these patients show female external genitalia in spite of their male 46,XY genotype, and they are reared female. Money and co-workers (Masica, Money, & Ehrhardt, 1971; Money, Ehrhardt, & Masica, 1968) studied 10 such patients (aged 16-33 years) in detail and found that they were sexually attracted to males, as are genetically normal XX heterosexual women. All 8 patients with sexual partner experiences had exclusively heterosexual relations and no homosexual erotic dreams and fantasies. Of the 2 remaining patients 1 had exclusively heterosexual dreams and fantasies and the other did not report any erotic imagery. All 10 patients had repeated dreams and fantasies about raising a family.

A recent preliminary report (Lewis, Note 6) describes an intense study of nine androgen-insensitive women (aged 17-38 years) all reared and identified as female. One of them, however, had developed self-doubts about her gender identity after she had secretly discovered her medical diagnosis. (Lewis, Note 7, reinvestigated six patients from the earlier reports by Money's group and studied 3 additional ones.) Seven of the nine women were exclusively heterosexual with no homosexual imagery. The other two were primarily heterosexual but reported a trivial history of homosexual relations. Obviously sex chromosomes do not have an overriding effect on sexual orientation. However, the effects of the sex hormones and of the sex of rearing cannot be distinguished because these patients are sensitive only to the female portion of their sex hormones and are reared female.

Patients with partial androgen insensitivity are typically born with inter-sex external genitalia and may be reared in either sex. A study by Money and Ogunro (1974) of 10 such patients showed that their sexual orientation seemed to follow their sex of rearing. That is, the patients usually had a heterosexual orientation relative to their sex of rearing: one patient who was gender-ambivalent, in correspondence with a history of ambiguous rearing, was bisexual. Money has published a number of case reports on other intersexes with similar results (Money & Ehrhardt, 1972). A study of my own on 10 patients with bilateral cryptorchidism, in which some late prenatal hormone (gonadotropin) deficiency may be suspected, showed heterosexuality in all patients (Meyer-Bahlburg, McCauley, Schenck, Aceto, & Pinch, 1974). Finally, a study by Money and Alexander (1969) on 14 males with prenatal hyperandrogenization (i.e., congenital adrenal hyperplasia) showed hetero-sexuality as expected.

Females

The major paradigm for prenatal androgen influences on human females is the syndrome of congenital adrenal hyperplasia (CAH) (Ehrhardt, 1975), in which an enzyme defect within the adrenal shifts the bulk of steroid hormone production from cortisol to androgens (Lee, Plotnick, Kowarski, & Migeon, 1977). Typically, genetic females affected with CAH are born with various degrees of intersexed genitalia, and some of them can appear totally male so that they will be reared in the male gender. If the diagnosis is made in time, the genitalia will be surgically feminized in infancy and permanent cortisone administration will allow the girl to develop normally. There are reports on three studies with information on sexual orientation in such women. Ehrhardt, Evers, and Money (1968) interviewed 23 CAH women (aged 19–55 years) whose cortisone treatment had started relatively late; thus they had many years of severe somatic virilization in addition to the prenatal effects. It is remarkable that by experience the majority of these patients were heterosexual, some were bisexual, none was exclusively homosexual; considering dreams, half of them were heterosexual, the other half bisexual, and none exclusively homosexual. One more recent study (Money and Schwartz, 1977) on 17 young women (aged 16–25 years) with early onset of cortisone treatment (15 in infancy, 2 at age 2 years), who did not have a prolonged history of virilization, showed that heterosex-uality dominated in these groups also. Of the 8 patients with sexual partner experi-ence, 5 had exclusively heterosexual experience, 2 bisexual experience, and 1 infre-quent exclusive homosexual experience. Eleven patients reported erotic dreams and/or fantasies that were exclusively heterosexual in 6, bisexual in 4 (and assumed to be bisexual in a 12th patient), and exclusively homosexual in 1. Unfortunately there were no matched control groups, so it is impossible to estimate if the observed incidence of women with bisexuality or homosexuality in the CAH groups was above normal expectations. It is remarkable, however, that in both studies on patients with congenital adrenal hyperplasia there were more patients with bisexual or homosexual experience and/or fantasies than in the previously mentioned group of genetically male females with complete androgen insensitivity.

Money and Daléry (1976) described three genetic females with congenital adrenal hyperplasia (aged 18-26 years) who had been reared male. By the time of the investigation they had been ovarectomized and hysterectomized and received continuous testosterone therapy to maintain pubertal virilization. All three showed exclusive heterosexuality relative to their sex of rearing (or exclusive homosexuality relative to their genetic and original gonadal sex).

Comments

In spite of the small samples published, several conclusions seem warranted.

1. Prenatal androgenization certainly does not determine homosexuality in genetic females, and it has not even been established yet that prenatal androgenization "predisposes" them at all in a neuroendocrine sense to a homosexual development.

2. Conversely partial deandrogenization of males *in utero* does not determine their development as homosexuals. Whether complete androgen insensitivity per se determines the sexual orientation of genetic males toward the male sex is an open question because the available data do not permit an ascertainment of the hormonal effects independently of the sex of rearing.

3. The available data on intersex patients make the sex of rearing appear to be the decisive variable not only for gender identity formation but also for the establishment of sexual orientation in these patients. Does this conclusion apply to normal males and females? One can argue with Zuger (1970) that intersex patients are exposed to intermediate levels of prenatal androgens and therefore are more malleable postnatally than normal males and females. Yet this argument apparently does not hold true for extreme degrees of prenatal masculinization in females with congenital adrenal hyperplasia, some of whom have been diagnosed in newborn age or infancy and assigned to and reared in the female sex, while others were reared male; their sexual orientation agreed with the sex of rearing in either case. Clearly, many more such cases have to be described in detail as to physical status and development as well as to the development of sex-dimorphic behavior and sexual orientation before a more definite judgment can be rendered on this issue.

Human studies on gender-role behaviors such as physical activity expenditure, maternal behavior, and, to a lesser degree, aggression have delineated a significant contributing (but not determining) role for prenatal sex hormones in their development (Ehrhardt, 1975; Money & Ehrhardt, 1972). In this context the frequent occurrence of cross-gender role behaviors in homosexuals, especially the varying degrees of effeminacy in the majority of male homosexuals (Freund, 1974), also raises the question of contributing endocrine factors. Currently, however, we have more data linking effeminacy to childhood rearing (e.g., Green, 1974) than to prenatal hormone conditions; also, the effects of rearing on sex-dimorphic behavior in general are relatively well documented (Feshbach, 1970; Maccoby & Jacklin, 1974; Mischel, 1970).

CONCLUSIONS

1. Neither manipulation of sex hormone levels nor endogenous deficiencies of gonadal steroids in adulthood are typically associated with homosexuality. The majority of male and female homosexuals have normal sex hormone levels after puberty; there are no differences (that have been established with satisfactory replicability) between homo- and heterosexual subjects in any hormone or metabolite studied. This means that on the basis of our current knowledge homosexuality in general cannot be explained by endocrine abnormalities in adulthood.

2. The absence of endocrine abnormalities also indicates that the majority of homosexual individuals studied do not show signs of chronic stress in the endocrine systems tested.

3. Several recent reports present evidence for differences in gonadotropin regulation in homosexuals and transsexuals as compared to heterosexuals. Animal research suggests that such differences may be related to prenatal hormone effects. The findings are not uniform, however, and their replicability and interpretation are still open. In the majority of intersex patients with known prenatal hormone abnormalities the sexual orientation follows the sex of rearing. Consequently one has to assume that prenatal hormone conditions do not determine sexual orientation. It seems possible that prenatal hormone abnormalities contribute to the development of sexual orientation, at least in a minority of homosexual subjects, but this has not been sufficiently documented.

4. The endocrine data available at present are still compatible with the theory that sexual orientation is acquired primarily by social learning, with hormones possibly playing an indirectly facilitating role via their effects on body build or gender-role behavior. Such a concept would allow for the development of a uniform theory of the development of sex-object preference covering sexual orientation as well as the paraphilias (Meyer-Bahlburg, 1977).

5. The empirical evidence available so far does not provide a basis sufficient for justifying the biological treatment approaches outlined earlier.

6. Most endocrine studies of homosexuality seem to imply a uniform syndrome (or trait) of homosexuality varying along an intensity scale. In such a working model the degree of homosexuality depends on the extent of the

past or present hormonal influences or is determined by a random combination of all somatic and environmental factors contributing to the development of sexual orientation. In an alternate working model homosexuality would encompass a group of etiologically heterogeneous syndromes, one or more of which may involve hormonal factors in their development.

The situation may be similar to that of obesity. The latter may be conceptualized as a psycho-somatic phenomenon involving metabolic processes as well as hypothalamic CNS systems that regulate behavior. The degree of overweight is uniformly expressed in weight standards. The term *obesity,* however, applies to various syndromes with different etiologies, some of them involving gross endocrine abnormalities (e.g., Cushing's syndrome or hypothyroidism), others developing on the basis of early childhood feeding patterns or behavior–hormone interactions in adulthood (e.g., middle-age obesity). Moreover, body weight regulation is influenced by cultural standards, and in some cultures obesity is deliberately induced in selected individuals. Only in the rare cases of gross endocrine abnormalities are hormones the primary cause of obesity. By contrast obesity itself is often associated with secondary endocrine changes. With respect to homosexuality only a detailed and comprehensive case-by-case analysis can bring about the delineation of distinct etiological entities, if indeed they really exist.

Note added in proof. For a detailed review of the psychoendocrinology of female homosexuality see: Meyer-Bahlburg, H. F. L.: Sex hormones and female homosexuality: A Critical examination. *Archives of Sexual Behavior,* 1979, *8,* 101–119.

REFERENCE NOTES

1. Schreiner, L., & Kling, A. *Behavioural changes following paleocortical injury in rodents, carnivores, and primates.* Film presented at the First International Congress of Neurological Science, Brussels, July 21–28, 1957. (Quoted by Roeder, Orthner, & Müller, 1972.)
2. Schorsch, E., Sigusch, V., Schmidt, G., & Meyer, A.-E. *Stellungnahme zu stereotaktischen Hirnoperationen bei Menschen mit abweichendem Sexualverhalten.* Unpublished manuscript, Deutsche Gesellschaft für Sexualforschung, Hamburg, Frankfurt, 1976.
3. Aronson, L. R., & Cooper, M. L. *A new look at hypersexuality following basolateral amygdala and periamygdala cortical lesions in male cats.* Paper presented at the 8th Annual Meeting of the Eastern Conference on Reproductive Behavior, Saratoga Springs, New York, June 13–16, 1976.
4. Meyer-Bahlburg, H. F. L., & Aceto, T., Jr. *Psychosexual status of adolescents and adults with idiopathic hypopituitarism.* Paper presented at the 33rd Annual Meeting of the American Psychosomatic Society, Pittsburgh, Pa., March 26–28, 1976.
5. Ehrhardt, A. A. Personal communication, June 1977.
6. Lewis, V. G. *Androgen insensitivity syndrome: Erotic component of gender identity in nine women.* Paper presented at the Second International Congress of Sexology, Montreal, Quebec, October 28–31, 1976.
7. Lewis, V. G. Personal communication, July 1977.

REFERENCES

Bancroft, J., Tennent, G., Loucas, K., & Cass, J. The control of deviant sexual behavior by drugs. 1. Behavioural changes following oestrogens and anti-androgens. *British Journal of Psychiatry*, 1974, *125*, 310-315.

Barlow, D. H., Abel, G. G., Blanchard, E. B., & Mavissakalian, M. Plasma testosterone levels and male homosexuality: A failure to replicate. *Archives of Sexual Behavior*, 1974, *3*, 571-575.

Birk, L., Williams, G. H., Chasin, M., & Rose, L. I. Serum testosterone levels in homosexual men. *New England Journal of Medicine*, 1973, *289*, 1236-1238.

Bobrow, N. A., Money, J., & Lewis, V. G. Delayed puberty, eroticism, and sense of smell: A psychological study of hypogonadotropinism, osmatic and anosmatic (Kallmann's syndrome). *Archives of Sexual Behavior*, 1971, *1*, 329-344.

Bremer, J. *Asexualization: A follow-up study of 244 cases.* Oslo: Oslo University Press, 1958.

Brodie, H. K. H., Gartrell, N., Doering, C., & Rhue, T. Plasma testosterone levels in heterosexual and homosexual men. *American Journal of Psychiatry*, 1974, *131*, 82-83.

Brown, G. M., Zajac, A. S., & Steiner, B. W. Solid phase human luteinizing hormone (HLH) radioimmunoassay (RIA): Findings in intact and castrated transsexuals. *Clinical Research*, 1971, *19*, 770.

Clopper, R. R., Jr., Adelson, J. M., & Money, J. Postpubertal psychosexual function in male hypopituitarism without hypogonadotropinism after growth hormone therapy. *Journal of Sex Research*, 1976, *12*, 14-32.

Coppen, A. J. Body-build of male homosexuals. *British Medical Journal II*, 1959, *5164*, 1443-1445.

Cornu, F. *Katamnesen bei Kastrierten Sittlichkeitsdelinquenten aus Forensisch-Psychiatrischer Sicht.* Basel: Karger, 1973.

Doerr, P., Kockott, G., Vogt, H. J., Pirke, K. M., & Dittmar, F. Plasma testosterone, estradiol, and semen analysis in male homosexuals. *Archives of General Psychiatry*, 1973, *29*, 829-833.

Doerr, P., Pirke, K. M., Kockott, G., & Dittmar, F. Further studies on sex hormones in male homosexuals. *Archives of General Psychiatry*, 1976, *33*, 611-614.

Dörner, G. Hormonal induction and prevention of female homosexuality. *Journal of Endocrinology,* 1968, *42*, 163-164.

Dörner, G. *Sexualhormonabhängige Gehirndifferenzierung und Sexualität.* Wien: Springer, 1972.

Dörner, G. *Hormones and brain differentiation.* Amsterdam: Elsevier, 1976.

Dörner, G., Götz, F., & Rohde, W. On the evocability of a positive oestrogen feedback action on LH secretion in female and male rats. *Endokrinologie*, 1975, *66*, 369-372.

Dörner, G., & Hinz, G. Induction and prevention of male homosexuality by androgen. *Journal of Endocrinology*, 1968, *40*, 387-388.

Dörner, G., Rohde, W., & Krell, L. Auslösung eines positiven Östrogen-feedback-Effekt bei homosexuellen Männern. *Endokrinologie*, 1972, *60*, 297-301.

Dörner, G., Rohde, W., & Schnorr, D. Evocability of a slight positive oestrogen feedback action on LH secretion in castrated and oestrogen-primed men. *Endokrinologie*, 1975, *66*, 373-376.

Dörner, G., Rohde, W., Seidel, K., Haas, W., & Schott, G. On the evocability of a positive estrogen feedback action on LH-secretion in transsexual men and women. *Endocrinology*, 1976, *67*(1), 20-25.

Dörner, G., Rohde, W., Stahl, F., Krell, L., & Masius, W.-G. A neuroendocrine predisposition for homosexuality in men. *Archives of Sexual Behavior*, 1975, *4*, 1-8.

Ehrhardt, A. A. Prenatal hormonal exposure and psychosexual differentiation. In E. J. Sachar (Ed.), *Topics in psychoendocrinology.* New York: Grune & Stratton, 1975, pp. 67-82.

Ehrhardt, A. A., Evers, K., & Money, J. Influence of androgen and some aspects of sexually dimorphic behavior in women with the late-treated adrenogenital syndrome. *Johns Hopkins Medical Journal,* 1968, *123,* 115-122.

Erwin, J., & Maple, T. Ambisexual behavior with male-male anal penetration in male rhesus monkeys. *Archives of Sexual Behavior,* 1976, *5,* 9-14.

Evans, R. B. Physical and biochemical characteristics of homosexual men. *Journal of Consulting and Clinical Psychology,* 1972, *39,* 140-147.

Feshbach, S. Aggression. In P. H. Mussen (Ed.), *Carmichael's manual of child psychology* (3rd ed.), (Vol. II). New York: Wiley, 1970, pp. 159-259.

Ford, C. S., & Beach, F. A. *Patterns of sexual behavior.* New York: Harper & Row, 1951.

Freund, K. W. Male homosexuality: An analysis of the pattern. In J. A. Loraine (Ed.), *Understanding homosexuality: Its biological and psychological bases.* New York: American Elsevier, 1974, pp. 25-81.

Friedman, R. C., Dyrenfurth, I., Linkie, D., Tendler, R., & Fleiss, J. L. Hormones and sexual orientation in men. *American Journal of Psychiatry,* 1977, *134,* 571-572.

Friedman, R. C., & Frantz, A. G. Plasma prolactin levels in male homosexuals. *Hormones and Behavior,* 1977, *9,* 19-22.

Friedman, R. C., Wollesen, F., & Tendler, R. Psychological development and blood levels of sex steroids in male identical twins of divergent sexual orientation. *Journal of Nervous and Mental Diseases,* 1976, *163,* 282-288.

Fulmer, G. P. Testosterone levels and female-to-male transsexualism. *Archives of Sexual Behavior,* 1973, *2,* 399-400.

Glass, S. J., & Johnson, R. W. Limitations and complications of organotherapy in male homosexuality. *Journal of Clinical Endocrinology,* 1944, *4,* 540-544.

Goss, C. M. (Ed.) *Anatomy of the human body, by Henry Gray* (29th American ed.). Philadelphia: Lea & Febiger, 1973.

Goy, R. W., & Resko, J. A. Gonadal hormones and behavior of normal and pseudo-hermaphroditic nonhuman female primates. *Recent Progress in Hormone Research,* 1972, *28,* 707-734.

Green, R. *Sexual identity conflict in children and adults.* New York: Basic Books, 1974.

Griffiths, P. D., Merry, J., Browning, M. C. K., Eisinger, A. J., Huntsman, R. G., Lord, E. J. A., Polani, P. E., Tanner, J. M., & Whitehouse, R. H. Homosexual women: An endocrine and psychological study. *Journal of Endocrinology,* 1974, *63,* 549-556.

Heller, C. G., & Maddock, W. O. The clinical uses of testosterone in the male. *Vitamins and Hormones,* 1947, *5,* 393-432.

Johnson, H. R., Myhre, S. A., Ruvalcaba, R. H. A., Thuline, H. C., & Kelley, V. C. Effects of testosterone on body image and behavior in Klinefelter's syndrome: A pilot study. *Developmental Medicine and Child Neurology,* 1970, *12,* 454-460.

Jones, J. R., & Samimy, J. Plasma testosterone levels and female transsexualism. *Archives of Sexual Behavior,* 1973, *2,* 251-256.

Jones, M. C. The later careers of boys who were early- or late-maturing. *Child Development,* 1957, *28,* 113-128.

Kenyon, F. E. Physique and physical health of female homosexuals. *Journal of Neurological and Neurosurgical Psychiatry,* 1968, *31,* 487-489. (a)

Kenyon, F. E. Studies in female homosexuality, VI. The exclusively homosexual group. *Acta Psychiatrica Scandinavica,* 1968, *44,* 224-237. (b)

Kinsey, A. C., Pomeroy, W. B., & Martin, C. E. *Sexual behavior in the human male.* Philadelphia: Saunders, 1948.

Kolodny, R. C., Jacobs, L. S., Masters, W. H., Toro, G., & Daughaday, W. H. Plasma gonadotrophins and prolactin in male homosexuals. *Lancet*, 1972, *II*(7766), 18–20.

Kolodny, R. C., Masters, W. H., Hendryx, J., & Toro, G. Plasma testosterone and semen analysis in male homosexuals. *New England Journal of Medicine*, 1971, *285*, 1170–1174.

Kreuz, L. E., Rose, R. M., & Jennings, J. R. Suppression of plasma testosterone levels and psychological stress. *Archives of General Psychiatry*, 1972, *26*, 479–482.

Kulin, H. E., & Reiter, E. O. Gonadotropin and testosterone measurements after estrogen administration to adult men, prepubertal and pubertal boys, and men with hypogonadotropism: Evidence for maturation of positive feedback in the male. *Pediatric Research*, 1976, *10*, 46–51.

Lee, P. A., Plotnick, L. P., Kowarski, A. A., & Migeon, C. J. (Eds.) *Congenital adrenal hyperplasia*. Baltimore: University Park Press, 1977.

Loraine, J. A., Adamopoulos, D. A., Kirkham, K. E., Ismail, A. A. A., & Dove, G. A. Patterns of hormone excretion in male and female homosexuals. *Nature*, 1971, *234*, 552–555.

Loraine, J. A., Ismail, A. A. A., Adamopoulos, D. A., & Dove, G. A. Endocrine function in male and female homosexuals. *British Medical Journal*, 1970, *4*, 406–408.

Maccoby, E. E., & Jacklin, C. N. *The psychology of sex differences*. Stanford: Stanford University Press, 1974.

McEwen, B. Interactions between hormones and nerve tissue. *Scientific American*, 1976, *235*, 48–58.

Margolese, M. S. Homosexuality: A new endocrine correlate. *Hormones and Behavior*, 1970, *1*, 151–155.

Margolese, M. S., & Janiger, O. Androsterone/etiocholanolone ratios in male homosexuals. *British Medical Journal*, 1973, *3*, 207–210.

Masica, D. N., Money, J., & Ehrhardt, A. A. Fetal feminization and female gender identity in the testicular feminizing syndrome of androgen insensitivity. *Archives of Sexual Behavior*, 1971, *1*, 131–142.

Meyer, R. G., & Freeman, W. A social episode model of human sexual behavior. *Journal of Homosexuality*, 1976–1977, *2*, 123–131.

Meyer-Bahlburg, H. F. L. Sex hormones and male homosexuality in comparative perspective. *Archives of Sexual Behavior*, 1977, *6*, 297–325.

Meyer-Bahlburg, H. F. L., McCauley, E., Schenck, C., Aceto, T., Jr., & Pinch, L. Cryptorchidism, development of gender identity and sex behavior. In R. C. Friedman, R. M. Richart, & R. L. Vande Wiele (Eds.), *Sex differences in behavior*. New York: Wiley, 1974, pp. 281–299.

Migeon, C. J., Rivarola, M. A., & Forest, M. G. Studies of androgens in transsexual subjects: Effects of estrogen therapy. *Johns Hopkins Medical Journal*, 1968, *123*, 128–133.

Mischel, W. Sex-typing and socialization. In P. H. Mussen (Ed.), *Carmichael's manual of child psychology* (3rd ed.), (Vol. II). New York: Wiley, 1970, pp. 3–72.

Money, J. Use of an androgen-depleting hormone in the treatment of male sex offenders. *Journal of Sex Research*, 1970, *6*, 165–172.

Money, J., & Alexander, D. Eroticism and sexual function in developmental anorchia and hyporchia with pubertal failure. *Journal of Sex Research*, 1967, *3*, 31–47.

Money, J., & Alexander, D. Psychosexual development and absence of homosexuality in males with precocious puberty: Review of 18 cases. *Journal of Nervous and Mental Diseases*, 1969, *148*, 111–123.

Money, J., & Clopper, R., Jr. Postpubertal psychosexual function in post-surgical male hypopituitarism. *Journal of Sex Research*, 1975, *2*, 25–38.

Money, J., & Daléry, J. Iatrogenic homosexuality: Gender identity in seven 46,XX chromosomal females with hyperadrenocortical hermaphroditism born with a penis, three reared as boys, four reared as girls. *Journal of Homosexuality*, 1976, *1*, 357-371.

Money, J., & Ehrhardt, A. A. *Man and woman, boy and girl.* Baltimore: Johns Hopkins University Press, 1972.

Money, J., Ehrhardt, A. A., & Masica, D. N. Fetal feminization induced by androgen insensitivity in the testicular feminizing syndrome: Effect on marriage and maternalism. *Johns Hopkins Medical Journal*, 1968, *123*, 105-114.

Money, J., & Ogunro, C. Behavioral sexology: Ten cases of genetic male intersexuality with impaired prenatal and pubertal androgenization. *Archives of Sexual Behavior*, 1974, *3*, 181-205.

Money, J., & Schwartz, M. Dating, romantic and nonromantic friendships, and sexuality in 17 early-treated adrenogenital females, aged 16-25. In P. A. Lee, L. P. Plotnick, A. A. Kowarski, & C. J. Migeon (Eds.), *Congenital adrenal hyperplasia.* Baltimore: University Park Press, 1977, pp. 419-431.

Montagna, W., & Sadler, W. A. (Eds.). *Reproductive behavior.* New York: Plenum Press, 1974.

Müller, D., Orthner, H., Roeder, F., König, A., & Bosse, K. Einfluss von Hypothalamus-läsionen auf Sexualverhalten und gonadotrope Funktion beim Menschen. Bericht über 23 Fälle. (English summary). In G. Dörner (Ed.), *Endocrinology of sex.* Leipzig: Barth, 1974, pp. 80-105.

Murray, M. A. F., Bancroft, J. H. J., Anderson, D. C., Tennent, T. G., & Carr, P. J. Endocrine changes in male sexual deviants after treatment with anti-androgens, oestrogens, or tranquilizers. *Journal of Endocrinology*, 1975, *67*, 179-188.

Neill, J. D. Sexual differences in the hypothalamic regulation of prolactin secretion. *Endocrinology*, 1972, *90*, 1154-1159.

Ovesey, L. *Homosexuality and pseudohomosexuality.* New York: Science House, 1969.

Parks, G. A., Korth-Schütz, S., Penny, R., Hilding, R. F., Dumars, K. W., Frasier, S. D., & New, M. I. Variation in pituitary-gonadal function in adolescent male homosexuals and heterosexuals. *Journal of Clinical Endocrinology and Metabolism*, 1974, *39*, 796-801.

Pillard, R. C., Rose, R. M., & Sherwood, M. Plasma testosterone levels in homosexual men. *Archives of Sexual Behavior*, 1974, *3*, 453-458.

Pirke, K. M., Kockott, G., & Dittmar, F. Psychosexual stimulation and plasma testosterone in man. *Archives of Sexual Behavior*, 1974, *3*, 577-584.

Raspé, G., & Bernhard, S. (Eds.) Schering Symposium über Sexualdeviationen und Ihre Medikamentöse Behandlung. Berlin, 17. und 18. Mai 1971. *Life Sciences Monographs* 2. Oxford: Pergamon Press, 1972.

Roeder, F., Orthner, H., & Müller, D. The stereotaxic treatment of pedophilic homosexuality and other sexual deviations. In E. Hitchcock, L. Laitinen, & K. Vaernet (Eds.), *Psychosurgery.* Springfield, Ill.: Charles C Thomas, 1972, pp. 87-111.

Rose, R. M., Bourne, P. G., Poe, R. O., Mougey, E. H., Collins, D. R., & Mason, J. W. Androgen responses to stress. II. Excretion of testosterone, epitestosterone, androsterone, and etiocholanolone during basic combat training and under threat of attack. *Psychosomatic Medicine*, 1969, *31*, 418-436.

Schlegel, W. S. Die konstitutionsbiologischen Grundlagen der Homosexualität. *Zeitschrift für menschliche Vererbungs- und Konstitutionslehre*, 1962, *36*, 341-364.

Seyler, L. E., Jr., Canalis, E., Spare, S., & Reichlin, S. Abnormal gonadotropin secretory responses to LRH in transsexual women after diethylstilbestrol priming. *Journal of Clinical Endocrinology and Metabolism*, 1978, *47*, 176-183.

Stahl, F., Dörner, G., Ahrens, L., & Graudenz, W. Significantly decreased apparently free testosterone levels in plasma of male homosexuals. *Endokrinologie*, 1976, *68*, 115-117.

Starká, L., Šipová, I., & Hynie, J. Plasma testosterone in male transsexuals and homosexuals. *Journal of Sex Research,* 1975, *11,* 134–138.

Tanner, J. M. Current advances in the study of physique. *Lancet,* 1951, *1,* 574–579.

Tanner, J. M. Growth and endocrinology of the adolescent. In L. I. Gardner (Ed.), *Endocrine and genetic diseases of childhood and adolescence* (2nd ed.). Philadelphia: Saunders, 1975, pp. 14–63.

Tourney, G., & Hatfield, L. M. Androgen metabolism in schizophrenics, homosexuals, and normal controls. *Biological Psychiatry,* 1973, *6,* 23–36.

Tourney, G., Petrilli, A. J., & Hatfield, L. M. Hormonal relationships in homosexual men. *American Journal of Psychiatry,* 1975, *132,* 288–290.

Ward, I. L. Prenatal stress feminizes and demasculinizes the behavior of males. *Science,* 1972, *175*(4017), 82–84.

Ward, I. L. Exogenous androgen activates female behavior in noncopulating, prenatally stressed male rats. *Journal of Comparative and Physiological Psychology,* 1977, *91,* 465–471.

Zuger, B. Gender role determination: A critical review of the evidence from hermaphroditism. *Psychosomatic Medicine,* 1970, *32,* 449–467.

Zumoff, B., Bradlow, H. L., Finkelstein, J., Boyar, R. M., & Hellman, L. The influence of age and sex on the metabolism of testosterone. *Journal of Clinical Endocrinology and Metabolism,* 1976, *42,* 703–706.

7

A Social Psychological Model of Human Sexuality

Toni Falbo
University of Texas at Austin

In Chapters 5 and 6 Ledwitz-Rigby and Meyer-Bahlburg address the topic of the biological foundations of human sexual function and dysfunction. As a social psychologist I am impressed that both writers repeatedly speculate about the possible psychological factors intervening in and even directing the biological processes. I would like to follow up on these speculations by proposing a social psychological model of human sexuality. Essentially the model combines cognitive, social learning, and social psychological theories to describe the cognitive structures underlying one's understanding and organization of human sexual behavior. The model is primarily social psychological because the processes by which the contents of the cognitive structures are acquired, maintained, and changed are brought about by interpersonal interactions.

The specific contents of the cognitive structures that trigger human sexual behavior are determined by the individual's experiences within a culture. Thus language, cultural values, and each individual's unique experiences within a culture provide most of the contents of these triggering mechanisms. Because I am writing for a U.S. audience and because I am more familiar with U.S. culture than any other, the issues I address and the examples I give are all drawn from the U.S. experience. However, I believe that the model can be applied to human sexual behavior in other cultures.

It is essential to begin the presentation of the model by integrating it into a biological context because most scientific explanations for human sexuality have taken a biological perspective. This is not surprising because sexuality is a critical element in reproduction, and the perpetuation of the species has been an important topic for biologists. Furthermore the taking of a biological perspective has been fostered by the tendency in U.S. culture to regard sexual dysfunction as a medical problem. In contrast my position is that most everyday sexuality is determined primarily by social and psychological factors not biological processes. To support this point I will present the results of biologically oriented research that refute a popular assumption about the supremacy of biological over psychological factors in human sexuality.

This assumption is that sex chromosomes (XX or XY) determine the process whereby boys become boys and girls become girls. That is, it has been thought that genes determine gender identity or the persistent belief of an individual that he is a male or she is a female. The work reported by Money and Ehrhardt (1972) clearly demonstrates that this is not true. They reported considerable success at reassigning children to a sex inconsistent with the child's genetic endowment. This has been done for basically two reasons: (1) male babies who suffer severe injury to their penises are reassigned to the female sex and (2) hermaphrodites who have the genitalia of both sexes are mistakenly assigned to the sex inconsistent with their chromosomal sex. According to Money and Ehrhardt (1972), the success of both types of reassignment is contingent on surgery and hormone therapy so that the child looks like the sex of assignment. However, they have also written, "It is absolutely prerequisite that the parents have no doubt or ambiguity as to whether they are raising a son or daughter" (p. 152). This certainty is apparently essential because then and only then can parents and others behave toward the child in ways that are specifically sex typed. Money and Ehrhardt also report that sex reassignment has a greater likelihood of success if it occurs early in life, before 2 years of age. After this age children are more likely to experience ambivalence about their gender identity. Although much more could be said about this topic, I will leave it by pointing out that one of the criteria of success concerns sexual behavior. Sex reassignment is considered successful if the reassigned child expresses heterosexual interests. That is, successfully reassigned patients select as targets of sexual expression members of the sex opposite to their sex of assignment and identical to their chromosomal sex. Money and Ehrhardt report that even in cases in which the reassigned sex is in conflict with chromosomal sex, successful patients adopt a heterosexual orientation.

Thus it would appear that an essential element in the acquisition of a gender identity is the presence of a sex label (e.g., he is a boy; she is a girl) that is applied with certainty by others to the child during the first years of life.

THE MODEL

The model portrays the cognitive structures underlying human sexuality as self-schemata regarding sex and sexuality. According to Markus (1977), self-schemata "are cognitive generalizations about the self, derived from past experience, that organize and guide the processing of self-related information contained in the individual's social experiences" (p. 64). As used here, self-schemata are described as consisting of labels and significances. Labels are the nouns, pronouns, or adjectives that we apply to ourselves regarding our sex (e.g., I am a woman) and sexuality (i.e., I am a heterosexual). We acquire these labels in several ways: sometimes we adopt the labels that others apply to us; sometimes we label ourselves on the basis of our own assessment of our behavior; sometimes we label ourselves as a result of social comparison; and so on. Some labels we comfortably express publicly (e.g., I am married), and some we hide from others, generally because we feel that these labels will elicit social disapproval (e.g., I am homosexual).

Labels possess an extensive array of significances. As used here, significances are cognitive representations that direct behavior and feelings associated with the label. For example, women (a label) have babies (a behavioral significance), or being impotent (a label) arouses shame and embarrassment (a feeling significance). Significances are thematically organized so that the contents are compatible. This content consistency aids in the retrieval of behavioral and affective units. The sum of all significances associated with the basic sex label represents the contents of the individual's understanding of his or her sex role.

DEVELOPMENT

Chronologically the first sex-related label acquired by an individual is the basic sex label. Secondary sex labels include sex-typed names and characteristics that bolster the basic sex label. The major significance of the baby's sex label for others is that they then know how to think of and behave toward the child. Thus the child not only encounters repetitions of the label but also is treated in ways dependent upon the label. Evidence currently exists to demonstrate that parents behave differently toward boys and girls from birth (Moss, 1967; Thoman, Leiderman, & Olson, 1972), expect them to have sex-stereotyped characteristics (Rubin, Provenzano, & Luria, 1974), and even interpret their behavior differently depending on the sex label (Condry & Condry, 1977). Thus the sex of the child determines both the child's physical (toys, clothing) and social environments, which in turn limit and control the types of experiences the child has. It is through these experiences that children learn to assign the label boy or girl to themselves.

Several lines of evidence suggest that this self-labeling about sex occurs at a critical time in the child's development—at the period when children begin speaking (around 18 months). This behavioral event is generally considered to herald the onset of the symbolic abilities within the child and the emergence of the self-concept (Amsterdam, 1972; Gallup, 1977). The self-concept represents the integrated combination of all the labels we assign to ourselves. Evidence indicates that one of the earliest labels attached to the self is that of sex. Gesell and colleagues found that the majority of 3 year olds could correctly identify their own sex (Gesell, Halverson, Thompson, Ilg, Castner, Ames, & Amatrudo, 1940). A similar result was reported by Thompson (1975), who also found that the majority of 3 year olds could correctly identify the sex of others and many sex-role expectations. Furthermore Thompson found that the 3-year-old children consistently used same-sex labels to guide their selection of behavior. Thus not only is the label appropriately self-assigned by 3 years for most children, but also the knowledge of one's sex is already directing behavior. There is also evidence that the sex label is directing feelings by this age. Kohlberg (1966) reports that around the age of 3 years children demonstrate a chauvinism regarding their own sex. That is, at this age children value anything like themselves as being better than things not like themselves, and sex is a distinguishing characteristic. Boys learn to feel that boylike behavior and traits are better than girllike behavior and traits and girls learn the reverse. Later, around 5 to 6 years, children learn that society as a whole values male-typed behaviors and traits more than female-typed behaviors and traits, which probably confirms the belief most males already have while leaving females more ambivalent about their own sex.

This research evidence suggesting that the adoption of sex labels and the behavioral and affective significance of sex occurs between the age of 2 and 3 years explains why the success of sex reassignments is dependent on two factors: (1) early occurrence and (2) parental confidence about the sex label. The process of adopting sex labeling and its significance probably begins at birth and crystallizes around the period of the emergence of the self-concept. If children encounter ambiguous messages regarding what sex they are, they will fail to adopt a firm understanding of their sex.

This last statement should not be regarded to mean that all we ever know about our sex is learned around age 3 or that people who try to raise their children in a nonsexist fashion are going to end up with children confused about their sex. At age 3 most children have learned that they are girls or boys and that these labels are important in determining appropriate behavior and feelings regarding behavior. The sex label and the centrality of the sex label in determining behavior and feelings are indeed fixed by the age of 3 for most people. However, 3 year olds possess fewer and different significances of the sex label than adults because of their relative cognitive immaturity and lack of experience. As used here, cognitive immaturity represents children's general intellectual inability to process and retain information in ways similar to adults. While cognitive immaturity accounts for some of the discrepancies in content and quality of the sex-related significances, the major determinant of this difference between children and adults concerns experience. Children generally are not exposed to all the information necessary for the acquisition of adultlike significances of the sex label. A more adultlike accumulation of sex-related significances usually does not occur until puberty or thereafter.

Nonsexist child raising is generally aimed at altering the significance of the sex label not the sex label itself. Ideally this alteration is away from a traditional separation of appropriate behavior for girls and boys. Also, nonsexist childrearing would involve the acquisition of nonsexist feelings associated with the sex label. For example, in nonsexist training girls are not taught to feel generally inferior to boys and boys are not taught to feel generally superior to girls. It is quite possible for a child to learn that men have penises and women have ovaries without attaching the additional significance that only men can play baseball, only women can cry, and so forth. Unfortunately parents who try to raise their children in nonsexist fashion frequently complain that children acquire sexist significances despite their efforts. Of course they do. A child, like any other naive observer of U.S. culture, will see that men are more likely to be the breadwinners while women are more likely to be the caretakers. They will no doubt observe that all the players in the World Series are men, all U.S. presidents are men, most physicians, and so on. All these observations are potential input for the development of more traditional significances.

Label changes are infrequent, but when they occur they bring about major changes in the significances. Examples of common label changes are from virgin to nonvirgin, heterosexual to homosexual (or the reverse), single to married (or the reverse). Obviously the most drastic change occurs when the basic sex label is changed.

Significances can lead to the acquisition of new labels. For example, a person who labels himself as a boy learns that one of the significances of being a boy is that he is supposed to be attracted to girls. As he grows older he dates, develops a special attachment to a particular girl, and marries her. Thus he adds to his secondary sex labels the label married and then adopts the significances associated with this label. In this fashion adults are continuously accumulating new sex-related significances and, at a slower rate, sex-related labels.

In addition to changes that occur as a result of the accumulation of new experience, sex-related significances can change when new significances replace old ones. Thus a 12-year-old girl learns that it is no longer acceptable for her to go swimming bare chested. According to the model the processes whereby old significances are replaced or superseded by new ones are generally social psychological in nature. Processes such as described by the theories of social comparison (Festinger, 1954), social learning (Bandura, 1971), cognitive dissonance (Festinger, 1957), and self-perception (Bem, 1967) operate to bring about changes in the significances associated with the basic sex label as well as changes in secondary sex labels. For example, a girl who was brought up to believe that she should preserve her virginity until marriage would probably experience some discomfort and eventual change in this significance if she were to discover that she was the only virgin in her college dormitory.

However, the changes that can occur to the secondary sex labels and their significances are limited by the fact that the links between labels and significances are self-reinforcing. That is, by virtue of our observing our performance of sex-related behavior we confirm the sex label. Furthermore these observations of our own behavior and the positive reactions of others to it arouse positive feelings that reinforce the sex label. This is one of the reasons why labels that are adopted early in life, such as the basic sex label, are fairly resistant to change.

The social psychological model of human sexuality is presented in Figure 1. The processes of change as well as the processes of perpetuation are represented in the feedback loops (portrayed here as dotted lines). Feelings and behaviors are portrayed as feeding back to the labels.

The figure also portrays a feedback loop interconnecting behavior and feelings. These affect each other in that behavior can elicit feelings and feelings can elicit behavior. The feedback loop between the two also indicates the process whereby the significances that directed them is perpetuated or changed. That is, the association of positive feelings with a behavior reinforces the behavior and increases the likelihood of it happening again. The association of bad feelings with a behavior leads to an inhibition of the behavior, which decreases the likelihood that the behavior will occur again.

This model contains elements in common with Kohlberg's (1966) cognitive developmental model of sex-role identification and Mischel's (1966) social learning theory. The proposed social psychological model differs from Kohlberg's model in that the proposed model reduces the importance of anatomical differences in the development of a child's knowledge of his or her own sex. The proposed model presents the basic sex label as acquired as a consequence of the repetition of sex-typed labels and significances. Although anatomical sex differences are probably observed early in life and attached to sex labels (e.g., I am a girl; I will have breasts), it is possible with the social psychological model for the 3 year old to correctly label his or her sex without associating anatomical sex differences with it.

The proposed model incorporates social learning (Bandura, 1971) as a major process whereby significances and to a lesser degree labels are acquired and perpetuated. The social psychological model is more comprehensive in that it adds the cognitive structures of labels and significances to the observational learning process. Furthermore the proposed model includes social psychological processes, such as social comparison, to account for changes that occur in significances and labels.

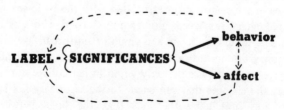

FIGURE 1   Representation of the social psychological model of human sexuality.

HUMAN SEXUALITY

Up to this point the model is a general one that could be applied to any sex-related behavior or feeling. I will now narrow the scope of the model to focus it onto the topic of human sexuality. To demonstrate the usefulness of the social psychological model I will apply it to the most common sexuality label, heterosexual.

Probably soon after the basic label of sex is adopted, children acquire the significance that sexuality is supposed to be expressed toward members of the opposite sex. Information relevant to drawing this conclusion is easily obtained by most children. The appropriateness of the heterosexual choice of a sex partner is demonstrated by most children's observation that men marry women and that one of their parents is male and the other female. Furthermore they notice that other parents also come in a mixed sex pair. This simple observation leads most children to conclude that opposite sex pairs are a basic component of social organization.

The behavioral content of sexuality is probably fairly vague during the early years but gradually is acquired through experience. Children observe their parents expressing affection toward each other, they listen to older sisters gossiping about boyfriends, and they watch love stories on television. Later in life they study sex manuals. Despite the large amount of observational learning that goes on, it seems likely that most knowledge of sexual behavior is acquired by experience with a sexual partner.

Feelings of sexual arousal are associated early in life with cues related to characteristics of the opposite sex. The association process can occur in a variety of ways. One phenomenon in American culture that facilitates the pairing of sexual arousal with opposite sex cues is the existence of a special relationship between mothers and sons, fathers and daughters. Evidence for this special relationship can be found in the research literature. Rubin et al. (1974) found that among parents of newborns, mothers rated sons as more cuddly than did fathers, and fathers rated daughters more cuddly than did mothers. Similarly Rothbart and Maccoby (1966) found that mothers were more indulgent of boys' requests and fathers were more indulgent of girls' requests.

In addition to learning arousal cues children acquire feelings regarding the social acceptability of sexual arousal. Children who come from families that regard sexuality as disgusting or sinful will probably learn to associate sexuality with shame. Children from such backgrounds may marry but practice sex rarely, or they may remain unmarried and be relatively asexual. Impotence, frigidity, and the general avoidance of sex are more common among such people (Coleman, 1964). Children who come from families that regard sexuality as acceptable will be more likely to acquire positive feelings about sexuality. This allows them to exhibit normal levels of libido and potency. Feelings about the appropriateness of sexuality are communicated to children even in the absence of parental communications regarding sexuality. Other cultural agents (such as peers, teachers, and priests) can inform the child about the appropriate feelings they should have about sexuality.

People who label themselves heterosexual actually represent a wide variety of sexual behaviors and feelings. Within a group of self-designated heterosexuals we can find spouses who have not engaged in sexual intercourse for the last 10 years, people who have sex with opposite sex partners everyday, and so on. There will also be people who try to pass as heterosexual but who are predominantly asexual, unisexual (via masturbation), or covertly homosexual.

DEVIANCE

There is a wide range of possible significances and labels a person can acquire about sexuality. The only limits to this range are imposed by the limits of an individual's experience. Nonetheless within a given culture certain trends emerge that represent the most common labels and significances. Behavior that approximates the normal trends are regarded as normal, while behavior that deviates significantly from the norm is regarded as deviant. The U.S. culture recognizes two important trends regarding sex and sexuality, which when violated lead the violators to be regarded as deviant. The first is that the sex label is continuous within an individual. Transsexuals deviate from this trend. The second popular trend is that sexuality is expressed between members of the opposite sex. Obviously homosexuals deviate from this trend. Because of the idiosyncratic nature of each person's experience, people become transsexuals or homosexuals for a variety of reasons. I will apply the social psychological model of human sexuality to explain one possible route to becoming transsexual or homosexual.

Transsexuals are people who publicly take on the appearance of the opposite sex but only after submitting to extensive medical procedures that make them look like the opposite sex. Retrospective self-reports of transsexuals indicate that from their earliest memories they think of themselves as members of the opposite sex (Money & Ehrhardt, 1972). To avoid social disapproval they go along with the socially applied sex label, some of them getting married to members of the sex opposite to their socially labeled sex. Some even have children before deciding to undergo the medical procedures necessary to become the sex that they always thought they were.

Transsexuality may be caused by the interaction of two factors. First, people who become transsexuals were exposed to insufficient quantities of social labeling regarding their sex. Thus they were confused or vague regarding their sex label. Second, these children were exposed to an imbalance of information about men and women that make the sex opposite to their socially labeled sex seem more desirable. Perhaps these children observe that opposite sex persons seem to get more rewards (e.g., mothers prefer boys) or are allowed to do more desirable activities (e.g., girls can cry). Being the opposite sex may seem so desirable that these children privately relabel themselves to be the sex with the more desirable significances.

This explanation is consistent with the clinical observation that more men than women undergo sex change procedures (Money & Ehrhardt, 1972). While this sex difference may be partially a result of the fact that it is surgically more feasible to create females than males, it probably also reflects the fact that more men want to become women than women want to become men. This preference is puzzling in view of the well-documented finding that the male role is more socially desirable than the female role (Broverman, Vogel, Broverman, Clarkson, & Rosenkrantz, 1972). I would like to argue that from a baby's perspective girls may seem to have an easier and more pleasant life than boys. Furthermore the fact that most caretakers are women means that the major experience of boys with adults consists of an experience with an opposite sex person carrying out the opposite sex role. Because the mother is often the most powerful person in the child's experience, the child could conclude that the female sex label and sex role are more desirable than the male counterpart. It seems likely then that from a child's perspective the desirability of being a female may seem greater than the desirability of being a male.

Transsexuals appear willing to live with the discrepancies that inevitably result from the pursuit of one sex role followed by the pursuit of the other. An example is provided by Morris (1974) who fathered four children, worked as a war correspondent, and climbed part way up Mt. Everest before becoming a woman. She writes of her experience,

> The more I was treated as a woman, the more woman I became. I adapted willy-nilly. If I was assumed to be incompetent at reversing cars, or opening bottles, oddly incompetent I found myself becoming. . . . It amuses me to consider, for instance, when I am taken out to lunch by one of my more urbane men friends, that not so many years ago that fulsome waiter would have treated *me* as he is now treating *him*. (p. 149)

Because of the strong motivation or tendency to maintain consistency between sex labeling and sex significances, transsexuals shift their sex targets when they shift their sex (Money & Ehrhardt, 1972). They engage in sexual relationships with members of the sex opposite to their newly acquired sex. This somewhat anomalous situation demonstrates that people who engage in sexual behavior with members of the same chromosomal sex are not necessarily homosexual. Furthermore there are people engaging in sexual behaviors with members of the socially labeled same sex who also do not consider themselves homosexual. Besides the obvious case of those who deny the label because it is socially disapproved, many male prostitutes ("Chickenhawks," 1973) and prisoners (Moore, 1976) apparently do not think of themselves as homosexuals, although they openly declare that they engage in sexual behaviors with members of the same sex. The social psychological model would explain this phenomenon in terms of inadequate justification (Aronson, 1976). That is, male prostitutes can interpret their homosexuality and prostitution as a consequence of their inability to earn enough money otherwise. Similarly because prisons contain only members of the same sex, if sexual behavior other than masturbation is desired, homosexual partners are the only possibility. Thus male prostitutes and prisoners who engage in homosexual behavior do not need to alter their self-label regarding sexual orientation because they can easily explain their behavior as caused by situational factors outside their control. Only homosexual behavior that is perceived as freely chosen would lead an individual to change the label that he or she has assigned to the self.

This leaves us with what I would call genuine homosexuals, people who label themselves (covertly or overtly) as homosexual. Like heterosexuals, homosexuals acquire early the basic sex label that others apply to them. What differs homosexuals from heterosexuals is that the former learn to associate sexual arousal with same sex cues, while the latter associate sexual arousal with opposite sex cues. The association of sexual arousal with same or opposite sex cues probably occurs haphazardly and without awareness or remembrance of parents or children. In principle sexual cues can as readily be associated with same sex cues as with opposite sex cues. In practice, however, sexual arousal is more likely to be associated with heterosexual cues because of the greater frequency of heterosexual cues in our culture. Possible sources of homosexual cues include the reversal of the opposite sex parent–child preferences described earlier or the presence of same sex siblings or homosexual parents. Although the latter may seem farfetched, children occasionally have the opportunity to observe homosexual behavior. The following example comes from a portrayal of the difficulties gay parents have in raising children: "Nan's year-and-a-half-old son spent the summer with her on a lesbian farm. He seldom saw men. One day he saw two men swimming nude, and he immediately took off his clothes and started playing with his penis" (Boston Women's Health Book Collective, 1976, p. 95).

Because homosexual or heterosexual arousal cues become part of the basic self-concept near the time of its initial organization, these cues cannot be changed by simple conditioning or other simple therapies. Nothing short of a total reorganization of the basic self-concept could alter the homosexual or heterosexual orientation.

Several lines of evidence suggest that there are more male homosexuals than female homosexuals (Money & Ehrhardt, 1972). If this is the case, one reason may be the greater likelihood of males acquiring same sex cues for sexuality than females. I propose that this greater likelihood of homosexual cues among males may be a consequence of the combination of two factors. First, penile erections are more readily observable than vaginal lubrication. Second, penises are a distinguishing characteristic of males. If the boy associates his erections with the distinguishing characteristic of maleness, this pairing is enough to bring about the connection of sexuality with the same sex cues.

As in the case of heterosexuals, feelings about the appropriateness of the label *homosexual* lead to several variations in homosexual behavior and self-labeling. In the most positive case an overt homosexual living within a context of social acceptance can feel at least mildly positive about the homosexual label. In fact, to the extent that homosexuals see themselves as superior to nonhomosexuals, the label can serve as a source of pride. However, since homosexuality is generally viewed negatively by society, the self-application of the label frequently brings about negative feelings about the self and the desire to hide the label. This leads some homosexuals to seek therapy, to practice homosexuality covertly, to marry and practice bisexuality, and so forth.

In conclusion the proposed model helps to explain possible routes to heterosexuality, transsexuality, and homosexuality in terms of interpersonal events. Clearly more could and should be stated about this social psychological model of human sexuality. This brief presentation, however, is designed to indicate the approach that one social psychologist takes. Further elaboration will be left for future papers.

REFERENCES

Amsterdam, B. Mirror self-image reactions before age two. *Developmental Psychobiology,* 1972, *5,* 297–305.

Aronson, E. *The social animal* (2nd ed.), San Francisco: Freeman, 1976.

Bandura, A. *Social learning theory.* Morristown, NJ: General Learning Press, 1971.

Bem, D. J. Self-perception: An alternative interpretation of cognitive dissonance phenomena. *Psychological Review,* 1967, *74,* 183–200.

The Boston Women's Health Book Collective, *Our bodies, ourselves.* New York: Simon & Schuster, 1976.

Broverman, I. K., Vogel, S. R., Broverman, D. M., Clarkson, F. E., & Rosenkrantz, P. S. Sex-role stereotypes: A current appraisal. *Journal of Social Issues,* 1972, *28*(2), 59–78.

Chickenhawks: Young male hookers hunting homosexuals. *Newsweek,* 1973, *81,* 42.

Coleman, J. C. *Abnormal psychology and modern life.* Glenview, Ill.: Scott, Foresman, 1964.

Condry, J., & Condry, S. Sex differences: A study of the eyes of the beholder. *Child Development,* 1977, *47*(3), 812–820.

Festinger, L. A theory of social comparison processes. *Human Relations,* 1954, *7,* 117–140.

Festinger, L. *A theory of cognitive dissonance.* Stanford: Stanford University Press, 1957.

Gallup, G. G. Self-recognition in primates: A comparative approach to the bidirectional properties of consciousness. *American Psychologist,* 1977, *32*(5), 329–338.

Gesell, A. A., Halverson, H. M., Thompson, H., Ilg, F. L., Castner, B. M., Ames, L. B., & Amatrudo, C. S. *The first five years: A guide.* New York: Harper & Row, 1940.

Kohlberg, L. A cognitive-developmental analysis of children's sex-role concepts and attitudes. In E. E. Maccoby, *The development of sex differences.* Stanford: Stanford University Press, 1966.

Markus, H. Self-schemata and processing information about the self. *Journal of Personality and Social Psychology,* 1977, *35*(12), 63–78.

Mischel, W. A social-learning view of sex differences in behavior. In E. E. Maccoby, *The development of sex differences.* Stanford: Stanford University Press, 1966.

Money, J., & Ehrhardt, A. A. *Man and woman: Boy and girl.* Baltimore: The Johns Hopkins University Press, 1972.

Moore, W. E. How to end sex problems in our prisons. *Ebony,* 1976, *32,* 83.

Morris, J. *Conundrum.* New York: Harcourt Brace Jovanovich, 1974.

Moss, H. A. Sex, age, and state as determinants of mother-infant interaction. *Merrill-Palmer Quarterly,* 1967, *13*(1), 19–36.

Rothbart, M. K., & Maccoby, E. E. Parents' differential reactions to sons and daughters. *Journal of Personality and Social Psychology,* 1966, *4*(3), 337–343.

Rubin, J. Z., Provenzano, F. J., and Luria, Z. The eye of the beholder: Parents' view on sex of new-borns. *American Journal of Orthopsychiatry,* 1974, *44,* 512–519.

Thoman, E. B., Leiderman, P. H., & Olson, J. P. Neonate-mother interaction during breast feeding. *Developmental Psychology,* 1972, *6,* 110–118.

Thompson, S. K. Gender labels and early sex role development. *Child Development,* 1975, *46,* 339–347.

III

WOMEN'S REPRODUCTIVE SYSTEM AND LIFE CYCLES

8

American Birth Practices: A Critical Review

Susan Reed Hahn
University of California, Berkeley

Karen Ericksen Paige
University of California, Davis

The social and technical practices associated with childbirth in our society have become the focus of increasing public debate and controversy in recent years. The medical benefits of many standard obstetrical procedures and scientific validity of medical advice about sexual and social conduct during pregnancy and postpartum are beginning to be questioned. Increasing numbers of women have resorted to "natural" childbirth accompanied by their husbands or others, and there is even some advocation of a return to home deliveries and midwifery.

Public debate and individual attempts to challenge standard medical birth practices have only recently begun to stimulate empirical research and critical evaluation of present-day American birth practices (Haire, 1973; Mead & Newton, 1967; Newton, 1963, 1967, 1975; Rich, 1975; Rossi, 1977; Wertz & Wertz, 1977). Within social science the theoretical significance of childbirth practices in this society has been virtually ignored, despite a long tradition of research on the human life cycle, fertility and reproduction, and the evolution and structure of social beliefs and institutions. One of the objectives of this review is to stimulate interest in developing a broad empirically based comparative framework within which contemporary birth practices can be more fully understood. This chapter will begin by describing preindustrial patterns of childbirth practices followed by a critical overview of standard obstetrical procedures and the natural childbirth methods in our own society. The extent to which the major features of natural childbirth represent a radical departure from standard obstetrical practices is also evaluated.

PREINDUSTRIAL WORLD PATTERNS

A number of cross-cultural surveys of ethnographic materials have described the beliefs, rituals, and taboos associated with childbearing; the social expectations about how individuals should behave during the birth process; and the technical procedures associated with labor and delivery in world societies (see especially Ayres, 1954, 1967; Ford, 1964; Naroll, Naroll, & Howard, 1961; Paige & Paige, 1973; Saucier, 1972; Whiting, 1964). There is, for example, a widespread belief that the behavior and thoughts of pregnant women have a significant influence on the birth process. In nearly all societies women engage in numerous ritual observances during pregnancy, such as avoiding certain thoughts, objects, and individuals or wearing special clothing and charms, in order to influence the health and character of the fetus and determine success of delivery. Nutritional taboos are also observed throughout the birth process in a majority of societies, although there is enormous cross-cultural variation in the particular foods considered beneficial or harmful to mother and fetus. In a survey conducted by Paige and Paige[1] at least one food was avoided by mothers in 83% of the sample societies. In addition sexual relations are usually strictly avoided during the last trimester of pregnancy and not resumed for months or even years postpartum.[2] It is generally believed that sexual activity will not only be harmful to the mother and offspring but will also be dangerous to the woman's husband. Women are often regarded as dangerous to all men throughout the birth process, and restrictions on their social contacts can be extreme. One-fourth of the societies in the Paige and Paige sample even resorted to physical segregation of pregnant women during the last few months before delivery, restricting them to their own households, removing them to specially built dwellings, or sending them to their own natal communities.

Although detailed descriptions of preindustrial delivery procedures are rare, broad cross-cultural patterns regarding the location of delivery, social characteristics of the assistants, and some features of the technical procedures involved can be outlined (see especially Ford, 1964, pp. 55–69; Naroll et al., 1961). With few exceptions the delivery process is a strictly feminine event. Women usually go through labor in the presence of female relatives, and only in cases of serious difficulty is a male allowed to participate. Final preparations for delivery begin once the pregnant woman begins experiencing uterine contractions. If she is not already secluded at the place of delivery, at the onset of labor she is removed to the appropriate location, and only those female relatives who will assist the delivery are allowed entry. An analysis of unpublished data collected on 105 societies of the Paige and Paige (1973) sample showed that childbirth most often takes place in the woman's own dwelling (40% of the cases), in a special house built for the occasion (27%), or less frequently in the home of her own parents (16%). Only rarely does birth

---

[1] See Paige and Paige (1973, Table 3) for proportional distribution of maternal and husband practices cross-culturally.

[2] Estimates are derived from analysis of incidence of postpartum abstinence in world societies as coded by Barry and Paxson (1971) and from Whiting (1964).

take place in the bush, and even when it does a special well-protected place is prepared some distance from the community in the presence of another female assistant. In no society examined was a woman expected to give birth casually and without assistance. Such a stereotypic "primitive" delivery procedure is always the exception in a preindustrial society.

Delivery is usually supervised by an experienced older woman, most often a relative of the expectant woman or of her husband. In a few cases a professional midwife in the community supervises. In 78% of the cases in the Paige and Paige sample at least one or more additional women assisted in the delivery. Among 40% of these societies representatives of both the woman's and her husband's relatives are present, although in an additional 33% only the woman's own kinswomen attend. (In 5% of the cases kin relations between witnesses and mother could not be ascertained). If the husband's relatives are not allowed within the place of delivery, they and other members of the local community commonly may wait nearby until the outcome is announced. Rarely are those relatives who are permitted to witness delivery mere observers; all assist the process in some way such as soothing the mother during the hours of labor and supporting her body when the fetus and placenta are finally expelled. When husbands are allowed to observe (15% of the societies mentioned instances), their role in the birth is an active one.

Once the expulsion of the fetus is imminent, the delivering mother assumes one of three positions: Assisted by one or two attendants she almost always assumes an upright position, held in back by one woman, with an additional woman sitting in front watching for the fetus to appear. She may also kneel or squat, although these positions are less common cross-culturally than the sitting position (Ford, 1964; Naroll et al., 1961). If necessary, her assistants support her arms and ankles, with the woman behind her frequently squeezing her abdomen to assist the passage of the fetus. If the delivery is successful, the fetus drops onto a soft pad or into the hands of a female attendant. After the expulsion of the afterbirth the umbilical cord is cut and mother and newborn are washed. The washing procedure may continue for days or even weeks, and the cutting and disposal of the cord may be the focus of elaborate ceremony.

The remarkable characteristic of deliveries described in the ethnographic literature is the virtual absence of direct physical intervention in the labor process. There were no instances in the Paige and Paige or Ford samples of attendants routinely attempting to physically assist the fetus or afterbirth through the birth canal. Only if the life of either mother or fetus was in serious danger would mechanical intervention be used. In cases of such difficulties the mother and often the husband and members of the community may be held responsible, accused of ignoring birth taboos, entertaining evil thoughts, committing adultery, or other malfeasance (Paige & Paige, in press).

Subsequent to a successful delivery the mother and infant typically remain secluded in the place of delivery. Strict seclusion commonly lasts from

2 to 7 days, although a semiseclusion may be observed for an additional month or two. Throughout the postpartum period sexual relations are almost always prohibited, with the husband usually sleeping separately from the mother and nursing infant (Barry & Paxson, 1971; Whiting, 1964). According to recent data a postpartum sex taboo is observed in 93% of world societies (with 53% abstaining for up to 6 months), and in 79% of world societies the father sleeps apart from the mother and infant during the nursing period, which averages 2.5 years.[3]

The historical analysis of childbirth in preindustrial America by Wertz and Wertz (1977, pp. 7-39) documents similar patterns, such as the location of birth at home or a nearby "borning room," the assistance by female relatives and friends, minimal intervention by a local midwife, and delivery in upright position, often with the aid of a "birth stool" to support the mother's back. As in other preindustrial societies the husband was rarely present during the delivery but remained nearby with other relatives awaiting word of the outcome.

Although they are not allowed to observe delivery in preindustrial societies, it is not uncommon for husbands to observe food taboos and perform a variety of special rituals throughout a wife's pregnancy, delivery, and postpartum period. The most extreme form of paternal ritual involvement in the birth process is the so-called couvade, which refers to the observance of a period of postpartum seclusion by a husband (Paige & Paige, 1973, Table 2). Despite the cross-cultural infrequency of couvade seclusion, the ritual has been the focus of much speculation and research. Much more common is the paternal observance of food and work taboos. In the Paige and Paige sample the classic couvade seclusion ritual was observed in only 16.2% of the societies compared to 29.7% observing work taboos and 44.1% observing food taboos, with these and less elaborate paternal birth practices ordered into a Guttman-type scale.

CONTEMPORARY BIRTH IN THE UNITED STATES

A number of studies have documented similarities in pregnancy and postpartum behavior and beliefs between U.S. and preindustrial societies, such as the adherence to social, nutritional, and sexual restrictions. The social avoidance of pregnant women, for example, has been observed empirically (Taylor & Langer, 1977), and institutional prohibitions against pregnant women working (e.g., school teachers) partly reflect enduring cultural prohibitions against pregnant women appearing in public. An immense variety of pregnancy food and personal taboos have also been documented, many of

---

[3] Barry and Paxson's (1971) codes pertain to a sample of 186 societies selected to best represent all world societies and minimize the effects of cultural diffusion. The sample was developed by Murdock and White (1969).

which are based on the belief that a woman's behavior and eating habits will influence the success of delivery and even determine the physique and behavior of the newborn (Ferreira, 1969; Newman, 1969). Pregnancy and postpartum sexual taboos are also commonly observed, despite abundant evidence demonstrating that sexual relations during these periods cannot be hazardous (Boston Children's Medical Center, 1972; Brecher & Brecher, 1966; Clark & Hale, 1974; Falicov, 1971; Paige, 1977; "Sex Soon After," 1976; SEICUS, 1970, pp. 50-51; Solberg et al., 1973).

Despite these similarities in beliefs and taboos between preindustrial societies and the United States, the social context and technology of delivery are dramatically different. Those features that best characterize standard delivery procedures in most U.S. hospitals today and that are currently subject to controversy will be reviewed below. We will present the medical rationale for such procedures as well as empirical evidence suggesting that many of these practices have little or no medical value and may even be hazardous to both mother and infant. We will begin by evaluating the medical necessity for performing deliveries in hospitals, then discuss practices associated with each of the three phases of labor.

Standard Obstetrical Practices

Location and Attendants

With few exceptions childbirth today takes place in hospitals. This trend began after the turn of the century and was completed by the mid-1950s. In 1900, for example, only 5% of women delivered in hospitals, but by World War II at least half of deliveries occurred in hospitals, and by 1955 all but a small minority of women gave birth in the hospital (Hellman & Eastman, 1966; Wertz & Wertz, 1977, p. 144). The transition from home to hospital deliveries reflects a number of social changes occurring in this century coinciding with the rural–urban transition, such as the reduction in the size and structure of family dwelling units and changes in the organization of medical practice. Relevant examples of the latter include the professionalization of obstetrics, the decline of family doctors, and the increasing number of local community hospitals.

The transition to hospital deliveries has often been considered a major advance in obstetrical care and is frequently cited by the medical profession as a primary cause of the reduction in infant and maternal mortality. On the contrary there is evidence that until recent decades the relocation of deliveries from homes to hospitals actually increased the dangers of childbirth by increasing the chances of infection by puerperal fever (Wertz & Wertz, 1977, pp. 131-139, 245-246), and the rapid decline in maternal mortality prior to World War II actually preceded the introduction of those drugs and hospital procedures that do reduce the dangers of birth. The substantial decrease in maternal mortality rate in Philadelphia from 68 to 23 per 10,000 live births between 1931 and 1940, for example, antedated the widespread use of sulfa drugs, antibiotics, and blood banks in local hospitals and the improved quality of obstetric training in medical schools.[4] Similarly, low infant mortality rates are not causally associated with hospital births. One of the lowest infant mortality rates in the world (11.1 per 1000 births) is reported for the Netherlands, where a substantial proportion of births takes place in the home (53% in 1971 and 40% in 1973). A recent evaluation of the relative health and safety of home and hospital deliveries among 2000 "low-risk" women in the U.S. indicated that home births may in fact offer some health benefits that hospital deliveries do not. (See Haire, 1973, and Chase, 1972, for discussions of the reliability of statistics on infant mortality. See also Arms, 1975, pp. 255–291, for a description of obstetrical services and midwifery in England, Denmark, and Holland; and MacFarlane, 1977, p. 29, for a description of the Dutch birth process.)

One of the major consequences of hospital births has been the transfer of social and legal control of childbirth from families and folk practitioners to the established medical profession in the U.S. Childbirth has become a pathological and medical event rather than a natural and social event, and each delivery is treated as if it were a medical emergency requiring the supervision of numerous highly trained specialists. These specialists include an obstetrician, an anesthesiologist, and specially trained nurses and other hospital personnel; in addition, gynecologists, pediatricians, and other medical specialists are involved throughout pregnancy and the postpartum period and in cases of complicated deliveries. Unlike preindustrial societies family and friends in the U.S. are rarely allowed to participate in the birth process and are strictly excluded from the delivery procedure in many hospitals. Only recently have some hospitals and obstetricians consented to permit the husband to stay with his wife during labor in the hospital, although the American College of Obstetricians and Gynecologists warns that a husband may remain with his wife only "if physical facilities and hospital policy permit, and if the patient, her husband, and the obstetrician agree that it is desirable," and emphasizes that allowing a husband even minimal participation in a hospital delivery is a "privilege to be granted, not a right to be demanded" (American College, 1969, p. 32; Goetsch, 1966, p. 104). One of the rationales for prohibiting family participation is obstetricians' anxiety

---

[4] P. F. Williams, quoted in Marmol, Scriggins, and Vollman (1969). The authors of this article imply that the decline in maternal mortality might be attributed to the effects of the introduction of routine investigation of all maternal deaths. However, this decline might also be associated with improving economic conditions. In the 15th edition of *Williams Obstetrics* (Pritchard & MacDonald, 1976, p. 4), the decline in maternal mortality rates is attributed to a large extent to the introduction of blood banks, antibiotics, and techniques for the maintenance of fluid, electrolyte, and acid-base balance, and to improved quality of obstetric training.

about having people "looking over their shoulder" or "hanging around and listening in" (Sehgal, 1974; Shu, 1973).

Within the hospital setting the social and technical practices associated with each of the three stages of labor are substantially different from those observed in preindustrial societies. A medically supervised labor may be considerably less time consuming and more convenient for the attendants, but the psychological and medical benefits of many of the hospital practices for the mother and fetus can be seriously questioned.

First Stage of Labor

There are four practices associated with the first stage of labor whose medical value is not easy to justify empirically: shaving the genital hair, giving enemas, nutritional prohibitions, and manipulating the timing of delivery. The practices of perineal shaving and inserting an enema are both purported to decrease the chances of bacterial infection; the enema is also advocated as a mechanism for speeding labor (Davis & Rubin, 1966, pp. 279-280; Ingalls, 1967, pp. 136-138; Pritchard & MacDonald, 1976, pp. 325-326). One study found that 54% of obstetricians routinely ordered enemas given to women in labor, and 60% advocated routine perineal shaving, despite the fact that neither practice is based on scientific evidence of efficacy in reducing the chances of infection (Lake, 1976).[5] In fact our comprehensive search of the medical literature compiled in *Index Medicus* revealed that no study had been conducted during the last 10 years to evaluate the necessity of administering enemas. One study of 7600 women did evaluate the effects of perineal shaving on reducing infection and found no significant difference between shaved and unshaved women in bacterial growth (Burchell, 1964; Kantor, Rember, Tabio, & Buchanon, 1965). A study demonstrating the same negative results was reported in 1922 by the author of one of the most influential obstetrical texts at the time. Despite the finding that perineal shaving did not affect infection rates, J. W. Williams, the author of the authoritative *Williams Obstetrics,* wrote, "I am not yet prepared to advocate abandoning the time-honored method of preparing the genitalia, even though I am skeptical concerning its value" (quoted in Burchell, 1964, p. 272). However, as one recent critic has written, "Isn't it time we dispense with these rituals of such questionable value, both of which contribute so much discomfort?" (Miller, 1966, p. 106).

A third questionable practice associated with the first stage of labor is the prohibition of food and drink. While a woman in labor may be allowed to suck on a damp washcloth and occasionally be given ice chips, according to standard medical procedure the stomach must be empty to proceed with delivery. The rationale underlying this nutritional taboo is the possible need for general anesthesia during the fetal delivery which could induce vomiting

---

[5] Pritchard and MacDonald (1976) have also added that "the infamous '3H' enema (high, hot, and a hell of a lot) has no place in modern obstetrics" (p. 326).

and aspiration of gastric contents (Newton, 1975, pp. 38-39). It should be pointed out, however, that the prohibition of food and nourishment during labor does not guarantee that the stomach will be empty; when either labor or fasting is prolonged, gastric juices collect in the stomach regardless of the time since the last meal (Phillips, 1974, p. 173). Moreover, women giving birth for the first time average about 14 hours of labor, and for subsequent births average 9 hours (Pritchard & MacDonald, 1976, p. 328), so that enforced nutritional prohibitions for such a lengthy period not only are unsuccessful in emptying the stomach by the time delivery takes place, but also almost certainly cause considerable physical discomfort and may exacerbate fatigue and dehydration (Newton, 1975). As will become clear, one delivery practice is often used to counteract the effects of other practices. Nutritional prohibition during the long hours of labor are instituted to counteract the risks associated with the use of general anesthesia. General anesthesia is not only rarely necessary but also potentially hazardous, with between 3% and 16% of maternal deaths attributable to complications associated with anesthesia (Phillips & Hulka, 1965; Pritchard & MacDonald, 1976, p. 351). It is possible to perform almost every major obstetrical procedure, including Caesarian section, under regional anesthesia (such as spinal or epidural anesthesia), which should eliminate the need for stringent nutritional prohibitions throughout labor.

While enemas, genital shaving, and nutritional restrictions cause unnecessary psychological and physical discomfort, a fourth practice, the direct manipulation of the length of labor, carries serious medical risks. Drugs and even mechanical methods are commonly used to prolong, speed, or even initiate the natural course of labor. The prolongation of labor through mechanical procedures in order to fit the timing of delivery into a doctor's schedule has always been a standard joke among nursing staffs, who might attempt to prevent fetal expulsion by crossing a woman's legs until the obstetrician was available. However, labor can be more reliably prolonged by the use of analgesics. Administered early in the first stage of labor, these pain medications will make uterine contractions less forceful and alter the rhythm of the contractions (Flowers, 1967, p. 68). (See also Davenport-Slack, 1975, p. 272, for a list of studies that have correlated medication use with increased labor length.)

Far more common than prolonging labor is the practice of initiating (inducing) and speeding (enhancing) labor. Labor can be initiated or speeded through the administration of artificial hormones, such as oxytocin. The hormones stimulate uterine contractions in conjunction with amniotomy, which involves rupturing the amniotic sac surrounding the fetus (Cibils, 1972; Fields, 1968; "A Time," 1974[6]). In a study of 55,000 deliveries in 15

---

[6] This editorial, which appeared in a prestigious English medical journal, provides a strongly worded criticism of the practice of inducing labor for social and medical convenience.

university hospitals from 1959 to 1965 it was found that such methods were used to initiate labor in 10% of white women and 5% of black women and to speed labor in an additional 36% of white and 34% of black women (The Collaborative Study, 1972; Rindfuss, Ladinsky, Coppock, & Marshall, Note 1). While there is good empirical evidence that induction or enhancement of labor can be medically beneficial under special circumstances, a leading authority estimates that the practice of inducing labor through oxytocin injections is unnecessary in as many as 90% of all cases (Caldeyro-Barcia quoted in Arms, 1975, p. 56).[7] Scientific and clinical data indicate the considerable risks associated with speeding or initiating labor through oxytocin. Two infrequent but serious dangers associated with the hormone are intrauterine fetal asphyxia due to prolonged hypercontractility and the rupture of the uterus due to overstimulation. In addition, induced labor may cause premature delivery, as indicated by one study of 1200 births in which prematurity resulting from induced labor occurred in 3.3% of the births (Fields, 1968). Despite warnings of the questionable medical necessity of manipulating the course of labor for the large majority of women and the risks of physically harming both mother and fetus, the percentage of "induced labor for daylight deliveries" is actually increasing each year (Dillon & Friedman, 1971).[8] Rindfuss et al. (Note 1) have analyzed national data in both Canada and the U.S. that provide provocative indirect evidence of an increasing trend toward elective (i.e., not medically indicated) induction of labor. By inspecting birth registration data they could compute the average deviation from the number of expected births to occur on any given day of the week. They found that in 1971 there were substantially fewer births on weekends than would be expected by chance, and that this trend has increased dramatically since the early 1950s when oxytocin was made available to induce labor. These researchers point out that the increasing trend toward the induction of labor for the sake of convenience rather than medical necessity entails medical risks not only to those being induced but to all other women giving birth as well. If the trend toward reducing weekend deliveries continues at the same rate observed since 1951, hospitals may begin reducing the number of hospital personnel available on weekends so that any complications arising among nonscheduled weekend births may have to be handled by fewer and probably less qualified personnel.

The practices of speeding and prolonging labor by the use of drugs are

[7] The classic indication for the induction of labor is the case in which continuation of pregnancy would provide a clear-cut threat to the life or well-being of the woman or her child. Examples of this include severe preeclampsia, diabetes, Rhesus isoimmunization (Rh incompatibility), antepartum hemorrhage, and prolonged pregnancy (Cibils, 1972; "A Time," 1974).

[8] A particularly substantial increase is reported by Rana, Lewis, and Crook (1975), who state that the induction rate in the English hospital in which they practice increased from less than 20% in 1971 to over 60% in 1974.

even known to be used sequentially on a single mother in labor. If analgesics are administered early in labor, either to prolong labor or inhibit pain, the effects of this medication on diminishing uterine contractions may then require the use of oxytocin to speed the contractions. But since oxytocin stimulation may increase the pain of labor, pain-deadening analgesics may have to be administered once again.

The practice of inducing amnesia, or "twilight sleep," through the drug scopolamine is now largely abandoned but does further illustrate the health hazards associated with standard obstetrical practices during the first stage of labor. As a mechanism to control the pain of labor through amnesia, scopolamine was favored by numerous middle-class women during the 1930s as well as by obstetricians. In 1941 Eastman wrote that "doctors who specialize in maternity work pride themselves on the large proportion of mothers who retain little or no memory of their labor" (p. 134). Scopolamine is a belladonna derivative with hallucinogenic properties. Although it does induce memory loss of the pain of labor, it also slows the labor process, induces infant depression, and requires constant supervision of the mother (Hellman & Eastman, 1966, p. 460). The stereotype of maternity wards comprising a bunch of "moaning, screaming women . . . behaving in a generally regressed and helpless way" (Lomas, 1966, p. 207) was probably based on the behavioral effects of scopolamine, which causes restlessness and agitation.

Throughout the first stage of labor a woman is also subjected to periodic cervical examinations in order to gauge the extent of cervical dilation. These examinations, which can be very painful, are used not only to check on the physical condition of the mother and fetus but also to determine the time at which the mother must be transferred into the delivery room. As Rothman (Note 2) points out, unlike hospitals in most other countries in U.S. hospitals women experience a first and second stage of labor in separate rooms frequently attended by entirely different personnel. Presumably to decrease the time a woman must spend in the delivery room requiring the attention of the most specialized and costly personnel, it is critical that some physical indicator be used to determine the time at which it becomes absolutely necessary for a woman to make use of the delivery room and its personnel. The extent of cervical dilation is by no means a foolproof indicator of the timing of fetal expulsion. Women may deliver earlier than expected, in the hallways between the labor room and delivery room (called a precipped delivery), or much later than expected, spending an hour in the delivery room before fetal expulsion begins (Rothman, Note 2).

Second Stage of Labor: Fetal Delivery

A number of standard delivery room procedures are of questionable benefit to mother and fetus and are the subject of current debate—specifically, delivery in the lithotomy position, episiotomy, and the use of anesthesia. Once in the delivery room the woman is strapped to a table with her legs wide apart, high in the air, and held in place by stirrups. Despite both public and medical criticism of delivery in the lithotomy (or supine) position, there has been little attempt until recently to abandon this practice. Articles questioning its use date back to the 1930s, and even *Williams Obstetrics* (Pritchard & MacDonald, 1976, pp. 187–188) makes clear the variety of complications that delivery in the lithotomy position can produce. One problem is maintenance of normal blood pressure. In the lithotomy position the large uterus compresses the venous system returning blood from the lower half of the body, leading to difficulties in filling the heart and thus reducing the output of blood from the heart. Although blood pressure could be maintained by encouraging peripheral movement in the delivering mother, such a procedure is not possible with an anesthetized patient. Delivering in the lithotomy position may even slow labor and interfere with the regularity of uterine contractions, and this in turn may increase the likelihood that artificial hormones will be used to stimulate labor. The lithotomy position also puts additional strain on the muscles surrounding the perineum, thus justifying the practice of episiotomy (Blankfield, 1965; Hellman & Eastman, 1966, pp. 259, 429; Mitre, 1974; Yuen Chou Liu, 1974). Despite the seemingly widespread agreement of the potential harm of the lithotomy position, *Williams Obstetrics* contains no references suggesting alternative positions such as the upright position common in most world societies. The only argument presented in support of the lithotomy position is that it enables the obstetrician to see better.

While there is some chance that the lithotomy position may be abandoned in the future as more women urge their obstetricians to allow them an upright delivery position, the practice of performing episiotomies shows no sign of declining popularity. Episiotomy refers to the surgical practice of making a deep cut several inches in length through the skin and muscles of the perineum, the region between the vagina and the anus. Begun in the 1930s, this surgical technique has now become routine in U.S. obstetrics but is far less widespread in other industrialized countries. In the United States episiotomies are now performed in as many as 75–90% of deliveries in some hospitals, and as many as half of all obstetricians report in surveys that they always perform episiotomies in delivery. According to hospital reports, the rate is less than 10% in the Netherlands, 30% in Australia, and between 12 and 26% in Britain (Arms, 1975; Beischer, 1967; "Episiotomy," 1968; Lake, 1976). In preindustrial societies such an incision is truly exceptional. One rationale for this practice is that it facilitates the use of forceps to ease the head through the vaginal opening (called low forceps delivery). In fact it has been remarked that "the combination of (low) forceps deliveries and early episiotomies has been the hallmark of modern obstetrics for the past three decades" (McCall, 1975, p. 129).

Even when forceps are not used, it is thought that episiotomies must still be performed to prevent jagged tearing of the perineum during fetal expulsion

(Bekhit, 1976; McCall, 1975; Pritchard & MacDonald, 1976, pp. 346-349). It is highly unlikely, however, that prior to the widespread use of episiotomies in the U.S. women necessarily delivered "by stretch or by tear" (McCall, 1975). As Arms (1975, p. 81) points out, if the woman is able to restrain the urge to bear down as the fetal head is crowning (i.e., appears at the vaginal opening) and if the strength of uterine contractions is not unduly augmented by the use of oxytocin, the vaginal tissue will stretch naturally to accommodate adequately the fetal head. The use of episiotomy is still advocated, however, to prevent irreparable stretching and a sagging perineum, said to result from the natural expansion of the vaginal opening (McCall, 1975). (See also DeLee, 1920-1921, who states that with episiotomies "virginal conditions are often restored.") Whatever stretching does occur can be remedied by pelvic-tightening exercises and general good health habits, making cutting through pelvic musculature and nerves quite unnecessary (Haire, 1973). The popular euphemism for episiotomy, husband's stitches, points to an additional medical rationale for its use (Lake, 1966). An enlarged vaginal opening is thought to be repugnant to a woman's sexual partner, and episiotomy is thought to restore a new mother's sexual apparatus to its prior nonmaternal state. (The effects of the size of the vaginal opening on sexual satisfaction have not to our knowledge been documented in the empirical literature.)

Finally, routine episiotomies have been advocated as early as 1920 as a means of preventing perineal battering, a term used to describe the variety of possible damages that may result from the fetus pushing its head against the perineum during expulsion (DeLee, 1920-1921). Three-fourths of obstetricians in one survey indicated that prevention of such potential injuries was the major reason for performing episiotomies (Lake, 1976). A particularly vivid statement by Le Boyer describes the widespread fear of fetal injury during expulsion:

> It is she who is the enemy. She who stands between the child and life . . . The monster drives the baby lower still. And not satisfied with crushing, it twists it in a refinement of cruelty. And the infant's head—bearing the brunt of the struggle . . . why doesn't the head give way. The monster bears down one more time. (quoted in Rich, 1975)

Despite such fears, there is enough evidence to indicate no increased incidence of neurological deficits in newborns specifically associated with the normal time necessary to pass out of the vaginal opening without perineal surgery (Niswander & Gordon, 1973).[9]

The use of drugs in labor is the third standard practice that requires careful empirical scrutiny. It has been pointed out that obstetric analgesics

---

[9] Although this article attempts to evaluate the "protecive" function of low forceps, the data demonstrate that increased length of the second stage of labor was not associated with a greater risk of abnormality during infancy or early childhood.

and anesthetics are among the most powerful agents known to prevent pain and that labor is indeed a painful event (Moore, 1964, p. 14). A study of Swedish primiparas found that 35% reported intolerable pain and 37% reported severe pain during childbirth, and in a study of U.S. women 97% reported that birth was the most painful experience they had ever had (Davenport & Boylan, 1974; Nettelbladt, Fugerstrom, & Uddenberg, 1976). Drugs used throughout the labor process fall into two broad classes: analgesics (which dull the perception of pain) and anesthetics (which eliminate sensation or feeling). Included in the first group are narcotics and sedatives, which are administered during the first as well as second stage of labor. The second group can be subdivided into general and local anesthetics, most likely administered only during the second stage. General anesthetics relieve pain through depression of the nervous system and are administered either intravenously or by inhalation (Flowers, 1967, p. 38). Local anesthesia, or conduction blocks, are effected by the injection of an anesthetic into nerves, thus blocking the transmission of impulses to or from the central nervous system. Included in this group are the pudendal and paracervical blocks, and spinal, caudal, and lumbar epidural blocks.

Both the general anesthetics and analgesics are systemic drugs; that is, they are carried in the bloodstream, traverse the placenta, and exert a significant effect on the fetus. *Williams Obstetrics* notes that the respiratory center of the infant is highly vulnerable to sedative and anesthetic drugs, and the use of systemic medications may jeopardize respiration after birth (Pritchard & MacDonald, 1976, p. 351). Flowers (1967, p. 74) cites five studies in which it was found that infants of women who had received meperidine (i.e., Demerol, the most widely used analgesic) showed decreased oxygen concentration in their blood and decreased APGAR scores. In addition it has been reported that meperidine in combination with a narcotic antagonist can lead to poor feeding behavior for at least 10 days (Richards & Bernal cited in Brackbill, Kane, Manniello, & Abramson, 1974, p. 383).

Bowes (1970) reports that as recently as 1962 well-known authorities in analgesia concluded that no untoward drug effect on the fetus resulted from the use of local anesthetics, although he summarizes the results of five studies demonstrating that drugs used to produce local anesthesia do traverse the placenta, producing such effects as slowing of the fetal heart and fetal depression. It has also been reported that infants delivered of women who received local–regional anesthesia were more irritable and motorically less mature at 3 days after birth than infants whose mothers were not medicated (Standley, Soule, Copans, & Duchowny, 1974).

These drugs carry risks for the mother as well. The use of general anesthesia presents a significant risk to any patient. Shock following spinal anesthesia has been the second most common cause of those maternal deaths attributable to anesthesia. Eliminating the use of the lithotomy position might reduce this risk (Davis & Rubin, 1966, p. 298; Pritchard & Macdonald, 1976,

p. 364). If spinal or epidural anesthesia are administered too early in labor, labor can be slowed or stopped (Pritchard & MacDonald, 1976). Additionally the introduction of local anesthetics into the spinal fluid has been associated with spinal headaches and bladder dysfunction after delivery. The use of anesthesia can inhibit the mother from expelling the fetus through a series of spontaneous uterine contractions throughout labor. Depending on the type of anesthesia used, it can prevent the natural expulsion of the fetus through the cervix, vaginal canal, and vaginal opening, thereby making direct physical intervention in the delivery process a necessity. The use of anesthesia, then, provides an important rationale for the lithotomy position and episiotomy as well as the use of forceps. Even with the decline in the use of general anesthesia, low forceps are still used in conjunction with local anesthesia as the fetus is crowning. According to the cliché heard in maternity wards, "If the woman can't push, the doctor will pull," that is, use forceps.

The selection of anesthetic or analgesic methods depends on the preference of the physician who uses them, so that methods vary from hospital to hospital. However, current data indicate that most women receive pain-relieving drugs during labor. In the study cited earlier of 55,000 women (The Collaborative Study, 1972, p. 388) some form of anesthesia was used for 73.7-92.1% of deliveries, with rates varying by class and race. In another study of 80,000 births that occurred at the Boston Hospital for Women between 1960 and 1971 more than 94% of all women received anesthetics. During this period the use of inhalation anesthesia declined from 30 to 4%, spinal anesthesia declined from 63 to 47%, and epidural anesthesia increased from 2 to 47% (Weiss, 1974). Comparable rates of analgesic (narcotic or sedative) use could not be ascertained.

The potential hazards associated with the lithotomy position, episiotomy, and use of drugs refer, of course, to vaginal deliveries. Although fetal delivery in hospitals currently still makes use of the process of labor contractions (however modified by medicinal and mechanical intervention) to expel the fetus through the vaginal canal, the practice of nonvaginal, or Caesarian, deliveries is increasing in popularity. According to a recent survey, 11% of U.S. births nationwide are now delivered by Caesarian section, ranging up to 24% in some hospitals (Hibbard, 1976; Wedemeyer, 1977). Caesarian section, of course, is major surgery and therefore involves a considerable health risk. Since nonvaginal deliveries are not yet a standard medical birth practice, the literature on this practice will not be evaluated here, although the rationale for the procedure and the causes of its increasing popularity should be carefully examined in future research.

Third Stage of Labor and Postdelivery Procedures

Once the fetus has been expelled, with or without medical intervention, three essential steps remain before delivery is complete: clamping and severing of the umbilical cord, the expulsion of the placenta, and suturing of the episiotomy wound.

The time at which the cord is severed is currently the subject of some debate. If it is clamped and severed too quickly, the newborn can suffer a loss of hemoglobin, which may lead to respiratory distress, because at birth as much as 25% of the newborn's blood can be in placental circulation (Pritchard & MacDonald, 1976, pp. 339-340). However, delayed clamping and severing may augment the red blood cell volume by 50%, a development that can lead to hyperbilirubinemia (i.e., increased bilirubin in the blood) (Saigal, O'Neill, Yeldandi, LeBeng, & Usher, 1972). The scant research on the effects of cord-clamping procedures on the mother has concentrated primarily on the advantages and disadvantages of double clamping, that is, the practice of clamping the cord in two places and severing the cord between the clamps. The alternative is to use a single clamp and sever the cord on the placental side of the clamp. After a review of the literature on clamping procedures and their effects, Botha (1968) found that the two major reasons offered in favor of double clamping were the prevention of stains on bed linens and that it provided a method to evaluate the progress of placental separation. Single clamping, on the other hand, was found to significantly decrease maternal blood loss (Botha, 1968). In the one study (Walsh, 1968) on the effects on 120 mothers of the timing of cord clamping it was found that early clamping increased the chances of placental fragments being retained in the birth canal, since the residual blood remaining in the placenta interfered with successful placental separation. The removal of all placental fragments as well as immediate repair of any internal tears resulting from labor is critical in preventing damage to a mother's health, in particular puerperal (or childbed) fever, a consequence of bacterial infection of the site of placental attachment or wounds of the cervix, vagina, or external genitalia. Only completely antiseptic conditions can prevent this deadly infection, although antibiotic therapy can usually cure the fever of those infected.[10]

The possible risks to both mother and infant of early clamping and severing of the umbilical cord may be considered necessary in order to control other potential hazards produced by medical procedures used during the first and second stages of delivery. The deep cut produced by an episiotomy, for example, requires immediate suturing to prevent both bacterial infection and blood loss. Moreover, the physical status of the birth canal must be immediately evaluated because of the possibility of internal hemorrhaging, tears, and lacerations.

Neither suturing nor thorough inspection of the status of the reproductive apparatus can begin until the placenta is expelled. The gradual expulsion of the placenta through the natural series of uterine contractions may either be

[10]Wertz and Wertz (1977) describe the history of the eventual control of puerperal fever, which was responsible for a significant proportion of maternal deaths until the 1930s. As they make clear, this deadly disease was a consequence of the medical control of births since it was caused by inadequate antiseptic procedures when practitioners began directly intervening in the delivery. The bacteria causing the infection was most often carried on the doctor's hands and instruments inserted into the birth canal.

considered too time consuming or in fact be difficult or even impossible if the mother has received anesthesia during fetal delivery. Therefore in addition to early clamping of the umbilical cord the third stage of labor may also be medically manipulated through the administration of yet another drug, ergonovine, to hasten placental expulsion by artificially stimulating uterine contractions.

Early clamping of the umbilical cord may also be necessary to separate the newborn from its mother so that the potentially dangerous effects of delivery techniques can be evaluated. Particularly serious are the risks to infants associated with hormones, analgesics, and anesthetics administered to the mother as discussed above. The APGAR scale, a standard method of assessing the health status of infants after delivery, is based on evaluation of heart rate, respiratory effort, muscle tone, reflex response, and color. Since studies using this scale have shown that the depressive effects of drugs on infants seem to disappear over time (Windle, 1969), some researchers have suggested that the effects of medication on infants are not particularly hazardous. However, the APGAR scale itself has been criticized as too gross a measure to detect either the short- or the long-term effects of anesthesia or narcotics on infants. A recent editorial in the prestigious *New England Journal of Medicine* noted that the APGAR scale did not reveal the effects of drug administration on infants that other measures detected as late as the third day after delivery ("Psychoprophylaxis in Labor," 1976). A study by Brackbill et al. (1974) illustrates this problem in its evaluation of the effects of the analgesic Demerol on a mother's infant. This evaluation of 25 infants, 13 of whose mothers had received the drug, indicated that although the drugged and nondrugged infants did not produce significantly different APGAR scores, other measures did reveal differences between the two groups, with the size of the effects depending on the time at which the medication was administered, the dosage, and whether the medication was used in combination with other pharmacologic agents. The recently renewed interest in maternal attachment (discussed in Chapter 9 of this volume) may direct further attention to the measures used in obstetrics to evaluate the health effects of delivery procedures, especially the effects of drugs, on both infant and mother.

Comments

The evidence presented here does make clear the substantial differences between contemporary birth practices in the U.S. and those observed among preindustrial societies. Since there is little if any systematic accounting of the extent to which preindustrial delivery practices contribute to the higher maternal and infant mortality and morbidity rates in those societies, it is difficult to estimate the extent to which the technological interventions into the birth process are responsible for delivery-related morbidity and mortality rates in U.S. society. As Wertz and Wertz (1977) make clear, however, maternal and infant mortality and morbidity in the United States are more closely linked to the quality of pre- and postnatal care than to delivery procedures. It is plausible, then, that the high mortality and morbidity rates associated with childbearing reported for many preindustrial societies (Nag, 1968) also largely result from less adequate pre- and postnatal care (and inadequate health care generally) rather than the absence of technical advances of modern obstetrics. In fact the delivery procedures described in cross-cultural surveys appear in many important respects significantly less hazardous than those used in most hospitals in the United States, particularly the absence of direct medicinal or mechanical intervention in the natural course of labor (although the effects of herbal remedies often given mothers are unknown), the positioning of the mother for fetal and placental expulsion in an upright rather than lithotomy position, and the absence of episiotomy. The apparent greater safety of standard delivery procedures in preindustrial societies is probably not a consequence of greater wisdom among individuals in these societies, but, as Paige and Paige (1973) have argued, rather a serendipitous consequence of sociopolitical considerations inhibiting individuals from interfering in the natural process of birth and therefore being held responsible for abnormalities or deaths.

Certainly the technological and social procedures of contemporary obstetrics have reduced the risks associated with abnormal births. However, the common practice of treating every delivery in U.S. hospitals as if it were a pathology seems, in our view, to be motivated at least in part by hospital's and practitioners' desire to reduce the time required for delivery. When medical assistance in birth is based on fee-for-service, technical and medicinal intervention in the birth process not only speeds delivery and thus maximizes organizational efficiency but also increases the financial costs of birth through the use of expensive equipment and highly trained personnel.

Natural Childbirth

The most significant change in the experience of childbirth during the past two decades has been the inclusion of so-called natural birth procedures in some hospital deliveries. Since the 1960s, increasing numbers of pregnant women, often accompanied by their husbands, have participated in private or hospital-supervised classes that offer training in special physical and psychological methods to control pain in order to enhance the emotional experience of birth. One recent study estimates that between one-third and one-half of the pregnant women in the U.S. today now receive special training in preparation for natural birth, most of whom seem to be middle-class (see especially Davis & Marrone, 1962; MacFarlane, 1977; Werts, Gardener, Mitchell, Thompson, & Oliver, 1975).

It is difficult to estimate precisely the size of this natural childbirth movement in the U.S., since it includes a wide variety of pregnancy and delivery practices. It is not unified under a single nationwide organization;

antenatal education classes can be organized by any group or individual who chooses to do so, and private obstetricians even hire their own instructors to supervise classes. Moreover, whether a woman has experienced a natural birth depends a great deal on individual interpretation, although the term *natural childbirth* was actually first introduced in the 1930s in reference to a specific birth procedure (Dick-Read, 1933). For some a birth may not be considered natural if medication was used during labor even if the woman attended natural childbirth classes during pregnancy. For others a natural birth could refer to a delivery not preceded by special training but in which the expectant mother was assisted by her husband, controlled labor and pain through breathing, and refused medication. Even the mere presence of the father in the delivery room can be termed a natural birth. The medical profession in fact has resisted the use of natural in reference to these modifications and prefers the less evaluative term *prepared* childbirth. The term natural, it is said, "implies that delivery performed in any other manner is wrong or unnatural" (Blankfield, 1968, p. 24).

Whatever the appropriate definition of a natural childbirth and the actual number of participants, the currently intense feeling about the procedure is indicated by the importance many women attach to successfully meeting the ambiguous criteria of natural birth practices. An organization has even been formed to "combat the guilt of Caesarian section" (Wedemeyer, 1977). This organization, called C/SEC (Caesarian/Support, Education, Concern), was founded in 1972 by a woman who had attended natural childbirth classes and then experienced guilt and disappointment when she failed to deliver vaginally. In 1977 C/SEC had 3000 members and had helped found 80 other similar organizations. Although much of the natural childbirth literature cautions women about being harsh on themselves if their delivery process does not meet ideal standards, many women do become extremely disappointed if the delivery does not proceed according to expectations. An obstetrician on the board of C/SEC commented, "It's frightening what they [the members of C/SEC] think. They hated their doctors and a lot of them hated themselves because they had failed" (Wedemeyer, 1977).

The theoretical foundations of the current U.S. natural childbirth movement derive largely from two European obstetricians, Dick-Read and Lamaze. Dick-Read's *Childbirth Without Fear*, published in 1933, outlines a theory about how the pain of birth can be controlled through psychological training (Buxton, 1962, p. 39; see also Heardman, 1959). He believed that it was modern women's fear of childbirth itself that produced physical pain and that women could have painless childbirth if they were taught how to relax and to value the sanctity of motherhood. The major feature of the method is its emphasis on passive relaxation.

The Lamaze method, which originated in the Soviet Union, superceded the Dick-Read approach and is more popular in the U.S. today. This method is based on the conditioning principles of Pavlovian psychology: its goal is to reduce pain through reinforcement techniques rather than through reduction of fear. It is thought that women will perceive no pain in birth if the brain can be conditioned not to interpret signals it receives as pain. Toward this end the woman is trained to concentrate on special breathing techniques. Indeed, the hallmark of the Lamaze method has become the particular pattern of breathing and panting to aid the course of labor. (See Lamaze, 1970, for a full description of the Pavlovian base of the psychoprophylactic method.) Despite its Soviet origins and popularity among politically leftist Europeans, the idea received support from Pope Pius XII (Chertok, 1967). The Roman Catholic Church believes that the Lamaze method humanizes natural functions, emphasizing motherhood and the female nature, the dignity of effort, and the value of self-mastery (Chertok, 1967).

The theoretical distinctions often made between the passive Dick-Read and active Lamaze methods obscure their basic similarities. Both methods emphasize the role of fear in the etiology of childbirth pain, the emotional significance of birth to women, avoidance of unnecessary pain medication, and the need for "verbal asepsis" (e.g., a uterine contraction should never be called labor pain) (Buxton, 1962, p. 29). These and other methods offer childbirth education classes in which instructors provide basic information about the physiology of childbirth, teach pain control, encourage full participation in labor through physical exercises and breathing techniques, and stress the importance of support during labor. In fact the role of helpers in these psychophysical methods has now become their outstanding feature. Originally expectant mothers were to be aided throughout the labor process by women trained in the technique. A shortage of teachers and a refusal of hospitals and obstetricians to permit childbirth instructors into the delivery room, however, made it necessary to formulate a new approach. Instructors would train the husband so that he could supervise his wife's training and assist her during labor (Bing, 1972, pp. 71-73).[11]

The research within the medical profession attempting to evaluate the effects of natural childbirth on the course of women's labor has yet to produce convincing empirical evidence of either the benefits or potential difficulties that various procedural modifications produce. Many studies are flawed by inadequate measures and research design, and some are clearly biased for or against the natural childbirth techniques under investigation. Our review of the medical literature revealed a tendency to present data demonstrating the benefits of natural (or prepared) methods during the 1950s and data suggesting absence of effects or empirically ambiguous effects in the 1960s. (Polemical essays and advice manuals throughout these two decades do

---

[11] Other material advocating natural childbirth in both the U.S. and Europe includes Anderson, 1976; Arms, 1975, for a number of vivid descriptions of home births; Bean, 1972; Bradley, 1965; Buxton, 1965; Frey, 1972; Lamaze, 1970; Vellay, 1972; Velvovski, 1972.

not reveal this trend.) An early advocate of the European theories of natural childbirth, Thoms (1954) reported in 1951 and 1954 that such methods shortened labor, minimized the need for anesthesia, and possibly reduced risks to the fetus. However, in the absence of control groups systematic comparisons of these health benefits could not be causally linked to the method. Similarly another study (St. van Eps, 1955) reported that preparation of women prior to delivery increased the proportion of satisfactory results for 60–80%, although the criteria used to determine satisfactory results, the procedures used in preparing women, and how these procedures differed from standard ones are not described.

The emerging negative medical response to natural birth methods in the 1950s is illustrated by one evaluation (Mandy, Mandy, Farkas, & Sher, 1952) in which the researchers begin by stating that natural childbirth threatens to undermine the progress made by modern obstetrics, then proceed to describe how such methods lengthened rather than shortened the first and second stages of labor in a study of 628 women. One of the best of the 1960s studies is that of Davis and Marrone (1962), whose comparison of 463 "prepared" women with 108 "unprepared" women produced no group differences in either the length of labor or amounts of medication administered. In a follow-up study Davis and Curi (1968) suggest that the failure to find significant group differences could have been affected by the standard obstetrical procedures used in the community in which the study took place. That is, many of the physicians in the community had directly or indirectly been influenced by the natural birth advocate, Thoms, and were therefore likely to have used less analgesia and anesthesia regardless of whether women were prepared for delivery. Other evaluations of the effects of natural methods on the course of labor have been flawed by failure to take into consideration such factors as maternal age, use of oxytocin, induction and stimulation of labor, positions of presentation, and birth weights of infants—each of which is known to significantly affect the course of labor. One recent study (Scott & Rose, 1976) found that women who had participated in a Lamaze training program were given fewer narcotics, received less conduction anesthesia, and had a higher number of spontaneous vaginal deliveries than women who had not been Lamaze trained. However, these group differences in medication use and type of delivery did not in turn affect length of labor, number and type of maternal complications, and infant well being as measured by the APGAR scale. An editorial ("Psychoprophylaxis in Labor," 1976) in the journal issue in which the study was reported argued that results were difficult to interpret given the inadequacy of the APGAR scale and small sample size. Clearly a systematic evaluation of the effects of natural childbirth practices on the biological course of labor, obstetrical procedures, and the physical health of mother and infant has yet to be presented.

Even the effects of natural childbirth-training techniques on women's emotional responses to labor and delivery and attitudes about the newborn remain unclear, despite the psychological focus of training procedures. The relationship between attendance in childbirth classes during pregnancy and such psychological factors as maternal anxiety, reaction to the newborn, and irritability and tension during labor has been reported (e.g., Doering & Entwisle, 1975; Klusman, 1975; Tanzer, 1973; Zax, Sameroff, & Farnum, 1975), although until recently studies have not controlled for self-selection bias of groups studied, specifically a greater likelihood for participants in training programs to be better educated, less anxious, and more positive in their attitudes toward motherhood than women who receive no special preparation. Therefore whatever emotional and attitudinal differences occur between trained and untrained women could be spurious. Since natural childbirth classes are usually of short duration, typically consisting of six 1-hour classes during the last trimester of pregnancy, Davis and Marrone's (1962) assertion that "the type of person who elects preparation is more important in determining its effects than the preparation itself" (p. 1200) clearly must be taken into account in evaluation research.

Studies (Norr, Block, Charles, Mayering, & Meyers, Note 3; Leonard, 1973) have indicated that better educated women not only tend to elect natural child-birth training during pregnancy but are also more likely to have planned and wanted the pregnancy, to elect breastfeeding, and to score healthier on indices of mental health, all factors that could contribute to a positive response to birth whatever the procedure. One study (Werts et al., 1975) has reported that indicators of women's emotional states in labor are causally associated with educational level; better educated women scored lower on measures of body tenseness, writhing, moaning, and complaining during labor. Even the effects of the husband's presence or absence on labor behavior were eliminated when women's educational level was taken into account.

Quite different results are reported by Norr et al. (Note 3), who examined the relative effects of background characteristics, pregnancy experiences, labor process, labor setting, and medication factors on two important psychological birth experiences, pain and enjoyment, among 249 patients in a large teaching hospital. Although their sample was quite skewed, with substantially more higher status participants than would appear in a representative sample (43% either held college degrees or were married to professional husbands), higher social status still predicted participation in Lamaze classes ($r = .40$), the likelihood of husband participation in the labor process ($r = .44$), and the use of pain control techniques during labor ($r = .27$). Higher status women also reported greater enjoyment during the labor process ($r = .28$). However, when the degree of enjoyment experienced during the birth process was regressed simultaneously on these and 17 additional variables the results showed, first, that the independent effects of social status on enjoyment were almost completely eliminated ($b = .08$) and, second, that the most powerful predictor of enjoyment was the intensity of pain experienced ($b = -.43$), with greater pain decreasing enjoyment. The only social psychological factors to exert

statistically significant independent effects on enjoyment were husband participation in labor ($b = .24$), marital closeness ($b = .13$), feeling poorly during
pregnancy ($b = -.21$), and experiencing a difficult delivery ($b = -.17$).
Participating in Lamaze classes and using pain control techniques showed no
significant independent effects on enjoyment, suggesting that their high
zero-order correlations with enjoyment (.46 and .40, respectively) could be
because of their associations with husband participation. Husband participation was correlated .67 with Lamaze preparation and .52 with the use of pain
control techniques. These data suggest that higher social status women enjoy
childbirth more than lower status women because of the greater likelihood of
having husbands participate in the labor process, feeling better during the
pregnancy, and perceiving greater marital closeness, although pain intensity is
still the best single predictor of enjoyment.

In their analysis of predictors of pain intensity experienced during birth
Norr et al. found that participation in Lamaze classes and the use of analgesics
were two of only three variables to exert statistically significant unique effects
on pain, with each about equally powerful in its predictive ability (i.e.,
$b = .27$ for analgesic use and $b = -.24$ for Lamaze preparation). Interestingly
a measure of self-concept also significantly affected pain perception independent of the other 20 variables in the regression equation ($b = -.20$), with a
more negative self-concept associated with greater pain. Unlike the results for
enjoyment the woman's social status had no zero-order effect on pain
intensity ($r = -.06$) or the use of analgesics during labor ($r = .04$). However, the data suggest that indeed Lamaze preparation is an alternative to
analgesics as source of pain control, and it is through greater participation in
Lamaze that high social status may lead to lower pain in birth. The
independent effect of self-concept on pain intensity is difficult to interpret,
not only is positive self-concept negatively associated with social status
($r = -.18$) but also with Lamaze preparation ($r = -.21$). It seems that
women with a positive self-concept experience less pain in birth regardless of
their social status, prior preparation, or analgesic use.

A study by Quinlan (Note 4) with a much smaller sample of patients
($n = 100$) produced similar trends, with husband participation having no effect
on pain intensity but a substantial effect on the wife's enjoyment. Quinlan has
constructed a path model in which extent of husband participation was the
single exogenous variable, whose influence on the wife's feelings during birth
(as measured by a 5-item scale on self-reported emotional and physical
well-being) is seen to be indirect through its effects on pain intensity and level
of consciousness (i.e., extent of medication, if any). The path coefficients in
his diagram indicate that in fact husband participation has a significant direct
effect on the wife's experience regardless of pain intensity and level of
consciousness each affect experience regardless of whether the husband participates. Nearly 53% of the variance in experience is explained by this three-step
model.

Both the Norr et al. and Quinlan studies present some of the most intriguing data currently in the natural childbirth literature and suggest leads regarding the role of social psychological factors in the birth experience that should be followed up on larger and more representative samples.

Whatever future research may reveal about the direct effects of natural childbirth techniques on the psychology and biology of birth, the immense interest in natural childbirth and increasing participation in training sessions reflect important changes in the social meaning of childbirth in recent years. The mixed response of medical practitioners could be partly based on fears that the movement will revolutionize standard obstetrical practice as some natural birth advocates suggest. There is also concern about an increase in malpractice suits now that a conscious patient and her helper may monitor the procedure; as one doctor laments, the presence of the "layman witness" in the delivery room could present serious problems for the defense in any malpractice suits (Morton, 1966). One study (Prill & Schneider, 1974) found that 20% of the husbands who elected to witness the delivery did so specifically because they "had no confidence in doctors and personnel" (p. 389), and one doctor has warned his fellow practitioners "not to panic in the presence of a mentally alert patient and the husband/father" (Shu, 1973, p. 94). There are even warnings that the special training techniques are actually dangerous. In an essay titled "The Lamaze Lament" one doctor argues that "there is more than casual observation to suggest that some natural childbirth babies are depressed when they arrive at the nursery" and that natural childbirth methods increase perineal battering, thereby producing a "shocky" newborn that requires resuscitation (McCall, 1975, p. 128). He also warns that natural childbirth will lead to pelvic floor relaxation in the mother, causing a "gaping, relaxed vaginal barrel" that is both unattractive and sexually dissatisfying.

The increased willingness of many hospitals and obstetricians to permit minor procedural modifications, reduce medication, and allow some participation by husbands or others could be partly based on increasing recognition that the movement actually upholds rather than challenges those aspects of contemporary U.S. medicine about which doctors are most sensitive. First, the complete authority of obstetrician and hospital staff over delivery has never been seriously questioned by natural childbirth advocates. The natural childbirth literature repeatedly warns women of the obstetrician's prerogatives and even attempts to appease medical skepticism by reassuring that the doctor is not only still in charge but is now given the additional benefit of a tractable patient. Thus the literature emphasizes that "the patient is carefully instructed that the obstetrician is in charge of her medical care" (Scott & Rose, 1976, p. 1205); "the mothers . . . are more fully cooperative in their medical management" (Davis & Curi, 1968, p. 120); "the doctor is never questioned about the conduct of labor" (Yahia & Ulin, 1965, p. 948); "sound psychophysical preparation for childbirth has its foundations in the patient's unswerving faith in the technical skills and judgments of her obstetrician" (Yahia & Ulin, 1965, p. 944); "trainees are told they must cooperate with their obstetricians as much as possible" (Zax et al., 1975, p. 190); and "the husband should not be permitted to walk around the delivery room to oversee the delivery of the immediate management of the infant" (Shu, 1973, p. 94). According to Zax et al. (1975) it is such recognition by natural childbirth proponents of traditional medical authority over the birth process that is responsible for the high rate of acceptance among obstetricians in one large city.

Second, natural childbirth proponents have not yet seriously challenged most of the technical procedures of delivery outlined earlier, with the important exception of modified drug use. Therefore the practices of nutritional taboos, enemas, and genital shaving during the first stage of labor are not questioned, nor are episiotomies, the timing of cord clamping, or the doctor's right to perform any procedure (such as Caesarian section, forceps, or anesthesia) that he or she deems necessary. Moreover the practice of lying in (keeping mother and newborn together for days after birth) is not a widespread hospital practice even among natural childbirth participants, although rooming in in some hospitals represents an important modification.

Finally the increased popularity of natural childbirth does not represent a serious challenge to the considerable financial costs that obstetrical supervision of birth represents. In 1974 it was estimated that the average cost of delivery and postnatal care across the nation was $1000, although it is well known that the cost can vary considerably from one hospital to another depending on hospital policies as well as the number of services, length of hospital stay, and special procedures involved in any one childbirth (Caspar Weinberger cited in Watson, 1975). For example, in 1974 the obstetrician's fees in New York City averaged $400 to $700 in addition to the average $1000 required for hospital services (Watson, 1975, p. 233). In San Francisco in 1976 these costs were even higher, with the cost of a standard delivery and 3-day hospital stay averaging $1200 in addition to an average $1000 obstetrician's fee (Anderson, 1976). These figures are really estimates of minimal expenses; Caesarian section, intensive care for the newborn, or any additional nonstandard services would add considerably to the costs. There is some anecdotal evidence that a delivery may cost as much as $4000 in San Francisco, with at least part of this figure including the cost of contraceptive sterilization that is increasingly becoming included in deliveries.

Health insurance coverage for maternity expenses has been notoriously inadequate. Coverage may specifically exclude hospitalization for prenatal complications and for the first 14 days postpartum when intensive care may be necessary. Many insurance companies also require a waiting period of up to 11 months before coverage for maternity care may begin, so that any care needed before that time must be financed entirely by family earnings. The reimbursement that insurance companies do offer may cover only from one-fourth to one-third of the total cost of childbirth, and many employers' group insurance plans may not even offer maternity benefits (Watson, 1975, p. 234). The financial costs of medical assistance in childbirth may be a major determinant of a woman's choice to consult a lay midwife in the community or general practitioner rather than a skilled obstetrician and an important reason why some women neglect prenatal and postnatal care. The substantial racial and social class differences in the prevalence of childbirth complications and maternal and infant mortality in the U.S. are to a large extent attributable to differences in the ability to finance a healthy birth (see Rindfuss et al., Note 1, footnote 17).

In many respects a natural birth remains a medical birth, located in a hospital under the direction of medical and hospital personnel who retain ultimate authority over the procedure and financial costs. Increased participation in natural birth, however, indicates one particularly significant change in contemporary birth practices. This movement recognizes the immense social and emotional significance of childbirth to both women and men. Natural childbirth in its present form could be interpreted as a temporary compromise between women's psychological needs and the requirements of hospitals and obstetricians, and natural births will continue to be tolerated in many U.S. hospitals as long as the procedures required to enhance women's experience of birth do not challenge the authority of medical practitioners, become too time consuming, upset hospital routine, or reduce the expense of delivery and maternal care. Today women and their husbands may participate more fully in delivery, but they cannot control it. In some states women are even required by law to deliver in hospitals under the supervision of a licensed physician (MacFarlane, 1977, p. 24). Not only does the medical profession have legal authority over childbirth, but its procedures are monitored only by the practitioners themselves, who may not always subject obstetrical practices to careful review. The natural childbirth movement could be called a protest movement but certainly not a revolution.

Other Directions

There is increasing recognition that the real challenge to the medical management of childbirth will originate elsewhere, perhaps as an outgrowth of the newly emerging interest in home birth in some communities, but most likely from social legislation shifting much of the responsibility of monitoring obstetrical practices from private medical professionals to the public.

The extent to which a return to home births offers a revolutionary alternative to standard medical birth practices must be considered first. Transferring the location of labor and delivery phases of childbearing back to homes, of course, represents a radical departure from post-World War II birth practices and reintroduces the ceremonial elements of childbirth characteristic of most preindustrial births. In home deliveries a woman can be assisted by friends and relatives, the delivery may be supervised by a midwife or sympathetic doctor with minimum technical or medicinal interference, and the infant remains close to the mother postpartum. We also discussed earlier that there is convincing evidence of the safety of current home births in the U.S. A recent study comparing 1000 home births and 1000 hospital births among women with similar social and reproductive characteristics found that delivering at home did not affect the health of mother or infant and in many important respects actually reduced the health hazard. Among the home birth group less anesthesia and labor-speeding drugs were used, there were fewer occasions in which forceps were used, and there was a much lower likelihood of episiotomy and use of the lithotomy position. Physical damage to the mother, such as perineal tears and wounds and postpartum hemorrhage, was also less frequent (Mehl et al., Note 5). The response of the established medical community to home births or even homelike births in institutional settings has been one of outrage, arguing that such radical departures from standard obstetrical practice are unsafe, despite evidence to the contrary (Wertz & Wertz, 1977, p. 244).

While the empirical evidence in both the U.S. and the Netherlands clearly suggests that safety need not be reduced if home births are adequately supervised, at least among low-risk women, the concern of the medical profession is certainly understandable. A return to home births on a massive scale would not only seriously jeopardize and even eliminate the authority of hospitals and obstetricians over childbirth and demonstrate that elaborate technology, heavy medication, and routine social procedures of hospitals are unnecessary for the vast majority of births but would also clearly reduce the financial cost of bearing children. The fee for a delivery and 48-hour stay in an alternative birth unit in San Francisco, for example, is only $350 (Anderson, 1976). Given the immense political power, organization, and legal status of U.S. medicine, a complete transition to home or homelike delivery is not likely in the near future. Moreover, giving birth at home may be undesirable, impossible, or hazardous for a substantial proportion of women. Not all expectant mothers have a home in which to deliver, nor do they all have husbands or families to assist them throughout labor. Many do not consider birth a joyous event, particularly those who are unmarried, did not want to become pregnant in the first place, or cannot afford to support a child once it is born. There are also women for whom childbearing involves medical risks and who will require the technical facilities of a well-equipped hospital and special training of skilled personnel.

It must also be recognized that childbirth involves more than labor and delivery and that a substantial proportion of the risks associated with childbearing can be reduced by providing high-quality, low-cost pre- and postnatal care and safe environmental conditions during pregnancy for all women regardless of race, socioeconomic status, delivery preferences, and emotional meaning of the birth event. It is widely recognized that the major hazards of childbearing have not been reduced by modern delivery technology and efficient hospital procedures and that class differences in the safety of childbearing persist. The poor and nonwhite mothers and infants are far more likely to die from lack of proper health and adquate prenatal and postnatal supervision than are the white middle class. As Wertz and Wertz (1977) state,

> It is a sad comment on our medical system that while increasing amounts of money are spent on research, experimentation, and sophisticated treatments for rare and unusual births, the most basic care and the simplest preventive measures are not reaching women of all classes. (p. 249)

We must agree with these authors, whose historical analysis of childbirth in the United States argues persuasively that the current interest and debate about U.S. birth practices should be directed at the major source of maternal and infant health difficulties—inadequate care during pregnancy and post-partum—as well as the health benefits of standard and natural delivery procedures. Equal access to adequate care throughout the birth process could not help but enhance the emotional experience of delivery that the primarily middle-class, natural childbirth participants now seem to enjoy.

REFERENCE NOTES

1. Rindfuss, R., Ladinsky, J., Coppock, E., & Marshall, V. *Convenience and the occurrence of births: Induction of labor in the U.S. and Canada.* Paper presented at the 72nd Annual Meeting of the American Sociological Association, Chicago, Sept. 5, 1977.
2. Rothman, B. K. *The social construction of birth: A symbolic interactionist analysis of in-hospital "prepared" childbirth.* Paper presented at the 72nd Annual Meeting of the American Sociological Association, Chicago, Sept. 5, 1977.
3. Norr, K. L., Block, C., Charles, A., Meyering, S., & Meyers, E. *Explaining pain and enjoyment in childbirth.* Paper presented at the 72nd Annual Meeting of the American Sociological Association, Chicago, Sept. 5, 1977.
4. Quinlan, D. C. *Husband participation in labor and delivery and the woman's birth experience: A multivariate analysis.* Paper presented at the 72nd Annual Meeting of the American Sociological Association, Chicago, Sept. 5, 1977.
5. Mehl, L. E., et al. *Home birth versus hospital birth: Comparisons of outcomes of matched populations.* Paper presented at 104th Annual Meeting of the American Public Health Association, Miami Beach, Oct. 20, 1976. (As summarized by Wertz & Wertz, 1977, pp. 239-240.)

REFERENCES

American College of Obstetricians and Gynecologists. *Standards for obstetric-gynecologic hospital services.* Chicago: American College of Obstetricians and Gynecologists, 1969.
Anderson, J. Home birth at the hospital. *San Francisco Chronicle,* June 8, 1976, p. 15.
Arms, S. *Immaculate deception.* Boston: Houghton Mifflin, 1975.

Ayres, B. *A cross-cultural study of factors relating to pregnancy taboos.* Unpublished doctoral dissertation, Harvard University, 1954.

Ayres, B. Pregnancy magic: A study of food taboos and sex avoidances. In C. Ford (Ed.), *Cross-cultural approaches: Readings in comparative research.* New Haven: HRAF Press, 1967.

Barry, H., & Paxson, L. M. Infancy and early childhood: Cross-cultural codes. *Ethnology,* 1971, *10,* 466–508.

Bean, C. *Methods of childbirth.* Garden City, N.Y.: Doubleday, 1972.

Beischer, N. A. The anatomical and functional results of mediolateral episiotomy. *Medical Journal of Australia,* 1967, *54,* 189–195.

Bekhit, S. M. The use of episiotomy. *Nursing Times,* August 1976, *72*(32), 1231–1233.

Bing, E. O. Psychoprophylaxis and family-centered maternity: A historical development in the U.S.A. In *Psychosomatic medicine in obstetrics and gynecology* (3rd International Congress, London, 1971). Basel: Karger, 1972.

Blankfield, A. The optimum position for childbirth. *Medical Journal of Australia,* 1965, *56*(2), 606–608.

Blankfield, A. Natural childbirth: Its origins, aims, and implications. *Medical Journal of Australia,* 1968, *1*(24), 1064–1067.

Boston Children's Medical Center. *Pregnancy, birth, and the newborn baby.* New York: Delacorte Press, 1972.

Botha, M. C. The management of the umbilical cord in labour. *South African Journal of Obstetrics and Gynecology,* 1968, *6*(2), 30–33.

Bowes, W. A. Obstetrical medication and infant outcome: A review of the literature. *Monographs of the Society for Research in Child Development,* 1970, *35*(4, Series 137).

Brackbill, Y., Kane, J., Manniello, R. L., & Abramson, D. Obstetric premedication and infant outcome. *American Journal of Obstetrics and Gynecology,* 1974, *118*(3), 377.

Bradley, R. A. *Husband-coached childbirth.* New York: Harper & Row, 1965.

Brecher, R., & Brecher, E. (Eds.). *An analysis of human sexual response.* New York: Signet-New American Library, 1966.

Burchell, R. C. Predelivery removal of pubic hair. *Obstetrics and Gynecology,* 1964, *24,* 272.

Buxton, C. L. *A study of psychophysical methods for relief of childbirth pain.* Philadelphia: Saunders, 1962.

Buxton, C. L. Differences in European and American attitudes toward psychosomatic childbirth preparation. In *Proceedings of the First International Congress of Psychosomatic Medicine and Childbirth* (Paris, July 1962). Paris: Gauthier-Villars, 1965, 125–128.

Chase, H. C. The position of the United States in international comparisons of health status. *American Journal of Public Health,* 1972, *62,* 581–589.

Chertok, L. Psychosomatic methods of preparation for childbirth. *American Journal of Obstetrics and Gynecology,* 1967, *98*(5), 698–707.

Cibils, L. Enhancement and induction of labor. In S. Aladjem (Ed.), *Risks in the practice of modern obstetrics.* St. Louis: Mosby, 1972.

Clark, A., & Hale, R. Sex during and after pregnancy. *American Journal of Nursing,* 1974, *74,* 1430–1431.

The collaborative perinatal study of the National Institute of Neurological Diseases and Stroke. *The women and their pregnancies.* Philadelphia: Saunders, 1972.

Davenport, B., & Boylan, C. B. Psychological correlates of childbirth pain. *Psychosomatic Medicine,* 1974, *36*(31), 215–223.

Davenport-Slack, B. A comparative evaluation of obstetrical hypnosis and antenatal childbirth training. *International Journal of Clinical and Experimental Hypnosis,* 1975, *23*(4).

Davis, C. D., & Curi, J. A comparative clinical study of a prepared childbirth program. *Connecticut Medicine*, 1968, *32*, 113-121.

Davis, C. D., & Marrone, F. A. An objective evaluation of a prepared childbirth program. *American Journal of Obstetrics and Gynecology*, Nov. 1, 1962, 1196-1201.

Davis, M. E., & Rubin, R. *DeLee's obstetrics for nurses* (18th ed.). Philadelphia: Saunders, 1966.

DeLee, J. B. The prophylactic forceps operation. *American Journal of Obstetrics and Gynecology*, 1920-1921, *1*, 34-44.

Dick-Read, G. *Natural childbirth*. London: Heinemann, 1933.

Dillon, T. F., & Friedman, R. K. Induction of labor: Symposium. *Journal of Reproductive Medicine*, 1971, *6*(1), 24.

Doering, S. G., & Entwisle, D. R. Preparation during pregnancy and ability to cope with labor and delivery. *American Journal of Orthopsychiatry*, 1975, *45*(5), 825-837.

Eastman, N. J. *Expectant motherhood*. Boston: Little, Brown, 1941.

Episiotomy. *The Lancet*, Jan. 13, 1968, p. 75.

Falicov, C. Sexual adjustment during first pregnancy and postpartum. *American Journal of Obstetrics and Gynecology*, 1971, *117*, 991-1000.

Ferreira, A. J. *Prenatal environment*. Springfield, IL: Thomas, 1969.

Fields, H. Induction of labor: Methods, hazards, complications, and contraindications. *Hospital Topics*, 1968, *46*(12), 63-66.

Flowers, C. E. *Obstetrical analgesia and anesthesia*. New York: Hoeber, 1967.

Ford, C. *A comparative study of human reproduction*. New Haven: HRAF Press, 1964.

Frey, K. S. Childbirth should involve the whole family. *Canadian Nurse*, August 1972, 19-20.

Goetsch, C. Fathers in the delivery room: Helpful and supportive. *Hospital Topics*, 1966, *44*, 104.

Haire, D. Cultural warping of childbirth. *Journal of Tropical Pediatrics and Environmental Child Health*, 1973, *19*(2), 172-191.

Heardman, H. *Physiotherapy in obstetrics and gynecology* (2nd ed.). London: Livingstone, 1959.

Hellman, L. M., & Eastman, N. J. *William's obstetrics* (13th ed.). New York: Appleton-Century-Crofts, 1966.

Hibbard, L. T. Changing trends in Caesarian section. *American Journal of Obstetrics and Gynecology*, 1976, *125*(6), 798.

Ingalls, A. J. *Maternal and child health nursing*. St. Louis: Mosby, 1967.

Kantor, H., Rember, R., Tabio, P., & Buchanon, R. Value of shaving the pudendal-perineal area in delivery preparation. *Obstetrics and Gynecology*, 1965, *25*(4), 509-512.

Klusman, L. E. Reduction of pain in childbirth by alleviation of anxiety during pregnancy. *Journal of Consulting and Clinical Psychology*, 1975, *43*(2), 162-165.

Lake, A. Childbirth in America. *McCall's*, Jan. 1976, p. 128.

Lamaze, F. *Painless childbirth*. Chicago: Regnery, 1970.

Leonard, R. Evaluation of selection tendencies of patients preferring prepared childbirth. *Obstetrics and Gynecology*, 1973, *42*, 371-377.

Lomas, P. Ritualistic elements in the management of childbirth. *British Journal of Medical Psychology*, 1966, *39*, 207.

McCall, J. O. The Lamaze lament. *Transactions of the Pacific Coast Obstetrical and Gynecological Society*, 1975, *42*.

MacFarlane, A. *The psychology of childbirth*. Cambridge, MA: Harvard University Press, 1977.

Mandy, A. J., Mandy, T. E., Farkas, R., & Sher, E. Is natural childbirth natural? *Psychosomatic Medicine*, 1952, *14*, 431-438.

Mead, M., & Newton, N. Cultural patterning in perinatal behavior. In S. A. Richardson &

A. F. Guttmacher (Eds.), *Childbearing: Its social and psychological aspects.* Baltimore: Williams & Wilkins, 1967.

Miller, J. Return the joy of home delivery. *Hospital Topics,* 1966, *44,* 106.

Mitre, I. N. The influence of the upright position on duration of the active phase of labor. *International Journal of Gynecology and Obstetrics,* 1974, *12*(5), 181–183.

Moore, D. C. *Anesthetic techniques for obstetrical anesthesia and analgesia.* Springfield, Ill.: Charles C Thomas, 1964.

Morton, J. H. Fathers in the delivery room: An opposition standpoint. *Hospital Topics,* 1966, *44,* 103.

Murdock, G., & White, D. R. Standard cross-cultural sample. *Ethnology,* 1969, *8,* 329–369.

Nag, M. *Factors affecting human fertility in nonindustrial societies: A cross-cultural study.* New Haven, CT: HRAF Press, 1968.

Naroll, F., Naroll, R., & Howard, F. The position of women in childbirth. *American Journal of Obstetrics and Gynecology,* 1961, *82,* 943.

Newman, L. Folklore of pregnancy: Wives' tales in Contra Costa County, California. *Western Folklore,* 1969, *27,* 112–135.

Nettelbladt, P., Fagerstrom, C. F., & Uddenberg, N. The significance of reported childbirth pain. *Journal of Psychosomatic Medicine,* 1976, *20*(3), 215–221.

Newton, N. Emotions of pregnancy. *Clinical Obstetrics and Gynecology,* 1963, *6*(3), 639–668.

Newton, N. Psychologic aspects of lactation. *New England Journal of Medicine,* 1967, *277,* 4–12.

Newton, N. Birth rituals in cross-cultural perspective: Some practical applications. In D. Raphael (Ed.), *Being female: Reproduction, power, and change.* The Hague: Mouton, 1975.

Niswander, K. R., & Gordon, M. Safety of the low forceps operation. *American Journal of Obstetrics and Gynecology,* 1973, *117*(5), 619.

Paige, K. E. Sexual pollution: Reproductive sex taboos in American society. *Journal of Social Issues,* 1977, *33,* 144–165.

Paige, K. E., & Paige, J. M. Politics of birth practices: A strategic analysis. *American Sociological Review,* 1973, *38,* 663–676.

Paige, K. E., & Paige, J. M. *Politics and reproductive rituals.* Berkeley: University of California Press, in press.

Phillips, O. C. Preferable methods of pain relief in labor, delivery and late pregnancy complications. In D. E. Reid & C. D. Christian (Eds.), *Controversy in obstetrics and gynecology, II.* Philadelphia: Saunders, 1974.

Phillips, O. C., & Hulka, J. F. Obstetric mortality. *Anesthesiology,* 1965, *26,* 433–446.

Prill, H. J., & Schneider, H. Sharing the birth experience. In H. Hirsch (Ed.), *The Family: Fourth International Congress of Psychosomatic Obstetrics and Gynecology.* Basel: Karger, 1975.

Pritchard, J. A., & MacDonald, P. C. *William's obstetrics* (15th ed.). New York: Appleton-Century-Crofts, 1976.

Psychoprophylaxis in labor and delivery. *New England Journal of Medicine,* 1976, *294*(22), 1235–1236.

Rana, S., Lewis, B. V., & Crook, E. Patient response to planned accelerated induction of labour. In H. Hirsch (Ed.), *The Family: Fourth International Congress of Psychosomatic Obstetrics and Gynecology.* Basel: Karger, 1975.

Rich, A. The theft of childbirth. *New York Review of Books,* Oct. 2, 1975, 25–30.

Rossi, A. A biosocial perspective on parenting. *Daedalus,* Spring 1977, *106*(2), 1–31.

Saigal, S., O'Neill, A., Yeldandi, S., LeBeng, C., & Usher, R. Placental transfusions and hyperbilirubinemia in the premature. *Pediatrics,* 1972, *49*(3), 406.

St. van Eps, L. W. Psychoprophylaxis in labour. *The Lancet,* July 16, 1955, 112–115.

Saucier, J. F. Correlates of the long postpartum sex taboo: A cross-cultural study. *Current Anthropology,* 1972, *13*(2), 238–249.

Scott, J. R., & Rose, N. B. Effect of psychoprophylaxis (Lamaze preparation) on labor and delivery in primiparas. *New England Journal of Medicine,* 1976, *294*(22), 1205–1207.

Sehgal, N. H. Husbands in the delivery room: Potential for problems. *Medical Times,* 1974, *102*(2), 50.

Sex soon after baby's born. *San Francisco Chronicle,* Nov. 14, 1976, p. 29.

Shu, C. Y. Husband–father in delivery room? *Hospitals J.A.H.A.,* 1973, *47,* 92.

SEICUS. *Sexuality and man.* New York: Scribner, 1970.

Solberg, D. Sexual behavior in pregnancy. *New England Journal of Medicine,* 1973, *288,* 1098–1103.

Standley, K., Soule, A. B., Copans, S., & Duchowny, M. F. Local–regional anesthesia during childbirth: Effect on newborn behaviors. *Science,* November 15, 1974, *186,* 634–635.

Sweeney, W. *Woman's doctor.* New York: Morrow, 1969.

Tanzer, D. Natural childbirth. In C. Tavris (Ed.), *The female experience: Psychology today.* Communications, 1973.

Taylor, S. E., & Langer, E. J. Pregnancy: A social stigma? *Sex Roles,* 1977, *3*(1), 22–35.

Thoms, H. Two thousand consecutive deliveries under a training for childbirth program. *American Journal of Obstetrics and Gynecology,* 1954, *18,* 279–284.

A time to be born. *The Lancet,* Nov. 1974, *2,* 1183–1184.

Vellay, P. Painless labour: A French method. In J. C. Howells (Ed.), *Modern perspectives in psycho-obstetrics.* Edinburgh: Oliver & Boyd, 1972.

Velvovski. Psychoprophylaxis in obstetrics: A Soviet method. In J. C. Howells (Ed.), *Modern perspectives in psycho-obstetrics.* Edinburgh: Oliver & Boyd, 1972.

Walsh, S. Z. Maternal effects of early and late clamping of the umbilical cord. *The Lancet,* May 11, 1968, *1,* 996–997.

Watson, R. L. The effect of cost on patterns of maternity care. *Nursing Clinics of North America,* 1975, *10*(2), 232.

Wedemeyer, D. Mothers organizing to combat the guilt of Caesarian birth. *New York Times,* March 28, 1977.

Weiss, J. B. Preferable methods of pain relief in labor, delivery, and late pregnancy complications. In D. E. Reid & C. D. Christian, *Controversy in obstetrics and gynecology, II.* Philadelphia: Saunders, 1974.

Werts, C. E., Gardener, S. H., Mitchell, K., Thompson, J., & Oliver, J. Factors related to behavior in labor. *Journal of Health and Human Behavior,* Winter 1975, *6,* 238–242.

Wertz, R. W., & Wertz D. C. *Lying-in: A history of childbirth in America.* New York: Free Press, 1977.

Whiting, J. W. M. Effects of climate on certain cultural practices. In W. H. Goodenough (Ed.), *Explorations in cultural anthropology.* New York: McGraw-Hill, 1964.

Windle, W. F. Brain damage by asphyxia at birth. *Scientific American,* Oct. 1969, p. 78.

Yahia, C., & Ulin, P. R. Preliminary experience with a psychophysical program of preparation for childbirth. *American Journal of Obstetrics and Gynecology,* 1965, *93,* 948.

Yuen Chou Liu. Effect of an upright position during labor. *American Journal of Nursing,* 1974, *74,* 2203.

Zax, M., Sameroff, A., & Farnum, J. Childbirth education, maternal attitudes, and delivery. *American Journal of Obstetrics and Gynecology,* 1975, *123*(2), 185–190.

9

Sources of Maternal Stress in the Postpartum Period: A Review of the Literature and an Alternative View

Elisabeth M. Magnus
Institute of Gerontology
University of Michigan

The purpose of this chapter is to critically examine the nature and origins of postpartum emotional disturbances. The postpartum period is variously defined as ranging from a few weeks to a few months after childbirth. Emotional disturbances usually have their onset in the first month postpartum and range in severity from mild and transient emotional upsets to long-lasting psychoses and depressive reactions. First, I will describe how an implicit or explicit "motherhood ideology" permeating much of the postpartum literature may have contributed to a delay in investigating several areas of research that I consider relevant to the study of postpartum disorders. I will then review the medical and psychological literature on these disorders. I will present an alternative approach, describing stresses of the postpartum period that are most frequently mentioned by mothers themselves in firsthand accounts and structured surveys and discussing possible sources of each stress. Finally I will present a hypothesis, based on this material, on the origins of postpartum emotionsl disturbances.

THE MOTHERHOOD IDEOLOGY

In our culture numerous popular beliefs describe how women should react to childbirth and assumption of the mothering role. Many of these beliefs are reflected in the medical and psychological literature on postpartum emotional disturbances. The most prevalent assumptions permeating both the theoretical and the empirical literature are: (1) the desire to have a child is every woman's instinctive wish; (2) having a child is the highest fulfillment for a woman and most deeply satisfies her creative potential; (3) the extent of a woman's desire and ability to bear and rear children is a gauge of her femininity and psychological health; (4) women possess instinctive capacities for sensitivity toward and caretaking of their infants that men do not possess; (5) women have a natural tendency to love their infants at birth, and this love generally outweighs the strains and frustrations of adjusting to the arrival of the infant; and (6) mothers have the obligation to be the prime caregivers for their children not only in infancy but throughout early childhood, and this care cannot be adequately provided to any great extent by others.

The acceptance of these beliefs as truths rather than cultural ideals may have contributed to the delay, until recently, in investigating several areas of research. For example, belief in women's instinctive wish to have a child may have contributed to a delay in researching social influences on the decision to have children. Belief in childbearing and rearing as the highest fulfillment for a woman may have contributed to neglect in researching the importance of other sources of fulfillment (such as work) in women's lives, how these sources of fulfillment are affected by the birth of a child, and how women's psychological health is affected by changes in these sources brought about by childbearing. Belief in a cultural ideal of femininity and its relation to motherhood may have led to a failure to examine conflicts inherent in the traditional female role itself, particularly the maternal role, in this society. Belief in maternal instinct may have contributed to a delay in exploring which aspects of early mother-infant interaction are innate and which are learned. Belief in mother love may have contributed to neglect in researching exactly how mothers become attached to their babies and what determines variations in attachment and also in researching the extent and causes of infanticide and child abuse. Finally belief in women's obligation to act as the prime caregiver may have led to neglect in researching the development of fathers' attachment to their infants, the ways in which and extent to which infants can become attached to fathers as well as mothers or to other figures besides the mother, the effects of multiple attachment on infant psychological health, and the age at which infants can first be separated from the mother for brief or longer periods without psychological damage. While many of these areas have become a focus of research during the last decade, few have been considered in relation to maternal stress in the postpartum period. The first part of this chapter will illustrate how research on postpartum disorders has been guided by a need to explain them without relinquishing the assumptions of the motherhood ideology. The second part, presenting an alternative approach, will examine some of the areas of research described above in an attempt to show their relevance to the etiology of postpartum disorders.

INCIDENCE OF POSTPARTUM DISTURBANCES

There is an enormous medical literature on emotional and psychiatric disturbances postpartum. Almost all of it is on the rarest and severest forms—psychiatric hospital admissions for severe depression and psychosis. Kaij and Nilsson's (1972) review of the literature summarizes current estimates as a figure of 1 to 2 cases of psychotic complications per 1000 deliveries. At the other extreme is the "baby blues," a transient syndrome of mood swings and crying episodes for 10 days or so postpartum, estimated by several studies to occur among a majority (50-80%) of parturient women (Davidson, 1972; Pitt, 1973; Robin, 1962; Yalom, Lunde, Moos, & Hamburg, 1968). Between these two extremes lies a broad range of reactions indicating varying degrees of emotional disturbance. As Pitt (1968) has pointed out, the frequent occurrence of symptoms of emotional disturbance less severe than psychoses and suicidal depression but far more persistent and disabling than the transient blues has received relatively little investigation.

Two Swedish studies have attempted to determine the occurrence and character of such symptoms. Nilsson and Almgren (1970) followed a representative sample of 152 women from late pregnancy through 6 months postpartum to measure such symptoms of emotional disturbance as insomnia, headaches, increased fatigue, loss of appetite, tension, mood swings, feelings of inferiority, anxiety, and depression. During the 6-month postpartum period approximately 19% of the women reported pronounced psychiatric symptoms (a large number of symptoms or symptoms of a serious nature such as depression and weariness with life). Another 26% reported moderate symptoms (a moderate number of symptoms clearly affecting well-being). Jacobson, Kaij, and Nilsson (1965) investigated the frequency of similar symptoms of emotional disturbance postpartum in an unselected sample of 404 women who had delivered 3, 6, 9, and 12 months before. The women answered a questionnaire comparing their physical and mental states for the 3 months before the investigation to those for the year before the pregnancy. Over one-fourth of the women reported a distinct increase in mental symptoms during the postpartum period. The commonest were fatigue, irritability, tension, and anxiety.

Meares, Grimwade, and Wood (1976) distinguish three kinds of emotional disturbance postpartum: (1) depressive disorder (not only severe mood change but also hopelessness, guilt, and self-depreciation) persisting for a month or more postpartum; (2) equally profound mood changes persisting for a month or more postpartum but not accompanied by the other symptoms of depressive illness; and (3) the transient postpartum blues. In his sample of 49 subjects Meares found an incidence of 19% for depressive disorder as judged by depression-rating scales. Adding cases of profound and persistent mood change without the other symptoms gave an incidence of 28%, and adding cases of brief episodes of mood change (the blues) gave an incidence of 70%.

Pitt's (1968) long-term study of 305 women from late pregnancy through 6-8 weeks postpartum revealed 10.8% of the subjects developing "atypical" depression (not suicidal, with the prominence of neurotic symptoms such as anxiety, irritability, and phobias overshadowing the depression) as judged by depression-rating scales at 6–8 weeks postpartum, and another 6.2% with new or exacerbated psychiatric symptoms, classified as doubtfully depressed. Pitt cites a questionnaire circulated by the Association for the Improvement of Maternity Services in 1965, which found 65% of mothers describing depression postpartum and in 25% of these symptoms that continued for longer than a few weeks.

TRADITIONAL APPROACHES TO POSTPARTUM DISTRESS

These studies describe a picture of new motherhood considerably at variance with the idealized picture. Researchers who wish to explain the phenomenon of emotional disturbance among a large group of mothers during the postpartum period without relinquishing the assumptions about motherhood described above have traditionally used one of two approaches: the biomedical approach, searching for physiological bases of postpartum emotional difficulties; or the psychoanalytic approach, concentrating on the most extreme cases (postpartum psychoses) and searching for "psychic insufficiencies" in the mother, attributing postpartum difficulties to deviance from the female psychological norm.

Biomedical Approach

The first researchers of postpartum psychiatric illness in the 1800s and early 1900s considered it a disease entity distinct from nonpostpartum psychiatric illness and in some way causally linked to the organic changes of childbearing (Jones, R., 1902; Marcé, 1858). This assumption was supported by the observation of a high incidence of delirious reactions involving clouding of consciousness, loss of orientation, hallucinations, and restlessness—an illness resembling the delirium of typhoid fever rather than nonpostpartum mania. As late as 1926 about one-third of postpartum psychosis cases were found to involve acute delirium (Kilpatrick & Tiebout, 32%; Strecker & Ebaugh, 34%). Recent researchers have tended to regard the frequent occurrence of delirious reactions in the past as a result of a higher incidence of infections acquired during confinement. By the 1950s the incidence of delirium in postpartum psychiatric cases had dropped to under 5% (Paffenbarger, 1961), and several studies had illustrated that postpartum psychiatric illness took on the forms of a variety of psychiatric disorders (Hemphill, 1952; Stevens, 1971; Vislie, 1956).

Nevertheless some contemporary researchers, notably Hamilton (1962), Karacan and Williams (1970), and Paffenbarger (1964), still assert that there is adequate evidence to suggest that postpartum psychiatric illness is a distinct pathological entity with an underlying organic, presumably endocrine, cause. During pregnancy, estrogen builds up continuously to about 10 times the normal level and after delivery drops rapidly so that it is no longer found in the blood after the third day. Progesterone increases during pregnancy till in the third trimester it reaches a concentration of 25 times the corpus luteum norm. After delivery it drops abruptly to a very low level. Both estrogen and progesterone remain at low levels until the menstrual cycle resumes. Hamburg, Moos, and Yalom (1968) have compared this hormonal decline to that of the premenstruum, which has also been considered a stressful period. While the decline in progesterone level a few days before menstruation involves fairly small amounts, the drop in progesterone level from the end of pregnancy to postpartum is much larger and more abrupt. Hamburg et al. have suggested that genetically determined abnormalities in progesterone metabolism may make certain women especially vulnerable to postpartum difficulties. Partial metabolic defects, which might be masked under ordinary circumstances, might become clinically significant under extreme conditions such as those occurring at the end of pregnancy.

Karacan and associates (Karacan, Heine, Agnew, Williams, Webb, & Ross, 1968; Karacan, Williams, Hursch, McCaulley, & Heine, 1969) have demonstrated that sleep patterns are disturbed postpartum, with marked deficiencies in REM and non-REM sleep, apparently caused by the large drop in progesterone level at delivery. Although these disturbances generally disappear within a few weeks following delivery, for some subjects the sleep stage fluctuations continue for several months. Since prolonged sleep and dream deprivation in normal subjects may result in psychoticlike symptoms, Karacan et al. have hypothesized that disturbed sleep patterns may be an etiological factor in postpartum psychosis. Their future research will compare sleep patterns of patients with postpartum psychiatric illness with those of normal mothers postpartum.

The thyroid and anterior pituitary also enlarge during pregnancy. It is thought that the enlarged pituitary produces an increased amount of several hormones, including thyrotropic hormone, and that this substance is primarily responsible for an enlargement of the thyroid gland and probably for an increase in its secretions. Some investigators have suggested that there is a long-lasting thyroid deficiency postpartum that might be especially pronounced in postpartum psychiatric cases. The evidence for this hormonal change is more disputed than that for estrogen and progesterone. Danowski and associates have published several studies (Danowski, Gow, Mateer, Everhart, Johnston, & Greenman, 1950; Danowski, Hedenburg, & Greenman, 1949; Danowski, Huff, Mrvos, Wirth, George, & Mateer, 1953) in which levels of protein-bound iodine (PBI) were examined in pregnant subjects. They report that on the average PBI levels during pregnancy are significantly higher than in the nonpregnant state, while PBI levels over the first 9 months postpartum are 40% lower than the last pregnancy determination. This change might be said to reflect a corresponding change in the level of the production of thyroxine. Melges (1968), however, reports that PBI levels of his sample of postpartum psychiatric patients are well within the normal range.

As yet there have been no studies comparing endocrine or other physiological changes in postpartum psychiatric patients with those of normal parturient women; thus much of the evidence for an organic basis of postpartum psychiatric illness is circumstantial. It has been based primarily on reports of the following characteristics: an element of confusion and delirium pervading all the psychiatric syndromes; a latent period, in which no psychiatric symptoms occur, for the first 2 days postpartum, median onset at 4 days postpartum, and onset within the first month postpartum for a large majority of cases; history of menstrual distress and periodic relapse during the premenstrual phase; successful treatment with progesterone; and successful treatment with thyroid derivatives and triiodothyronine. None of these characteristics make a clear case for the role of organic factors in postpartum psychiatric illness. Many are based only on clinical observation or studies without control groups, have been contradicted by other studies, or can be explained just as logically by social and psychological factors.

Hamilton (1962) has been the main contemporary proponent of the view that postpartum psychiatric illnesses are characterized by delirium. He claims the presence not only of clouding of consciousness and hallucinations but also of high pulse rate and fever. These assertions are not borne out by other studies. A study by Melges (1968) of 100 postpartum psychiatric patients and a control group of 50 general hospital psychiatric patients indicated no electroencephalographic or cognitive test evidence of delirium in the postpartum group despite the common occurrence of some confusion and disorientation. Melges cites a study by Carlson (1958) describing an acute nonorganic confusional state in relatively healthy college students, usually arising at the time of psychosocial shifts and new commitments, and suggests that confusion among postpartum psychiatric cases could have similar causes.

The existence of a latent period after delivery, in which no psychiatric symptoms occur, has also been disputed. Of Melges' 100 patients 16% had onset of symptoms within the first 24 hours. In his study the median onset of symptoms was 4 days postpartum; almost two-thirds of the sample experienced the onset within the first 10 postpartum days and 82% within the first month. However, the time of onset might just as easily be related to psychological factors. The fourth day postpartum coincides with the time that most women are discharged from the hospital to assume full responsibility for caretaking of the infant, and the first month postpartum coincides with the time of greatest difficulties in adapting to the arrival of the infant.

Melges notes that 51% of his sample of 100 postpartum psychiatric patients had a history of severe premenstrual tension (i.e., anxiety, irritability, and depression that disrupted their everyday activities) and 31% had moderate premenstrual tension. Other studies have also remarked on a high incidence of menstrual distress in postpartum psychiatric patients (Hamilton, 1962; Kline, 1955; Zilboorg, 1928b). There is much disagreement about the extent and severity of menstrual distress in the general population, but even assuming that Melges' figures are considerably higher than those for the general population, a history of menstrual distress among postpartum psychiatric patients does not necessarily indicate a hormonal etiology. Recent research by Paige (1971, 1973) has suggested that women's reports of their menstrual distress are strongly influenced by social and psychological factors. In a study of 352 unmarried university women Paige (1973) found the reporting of a high number of mood symptoms and physical changes on the Moos Menstrual Distress Questionnaire (MDQ) was related to psychological stress and illness behavior. Women who reported physical discomfort and psychological stress during menstruation tended to report such symptoms in other situations as well. Over the whole sample those who reported a high number of symptoms on the MDQ were significantly more likely to report high psychological stress, greater use of drugs, more aches and pains, and illnesses. Thus it may be that a history of menstrual distress among postpartum psychiatric patients merely indicates that these women are generally anxious and nervous, are under considerable psychological stress in their daily lives, and treat reproductive events in their lives as illnesses.

Reports of relapse or exacerbation of symptoms during the premenstrual phase are clinical observations of a few isolated cases. No study has been done to indicate that relapse occurs during the premenstrual phase for a majority of cases.

In general the prognosis for postpartum psychiatric illness is good compared to other psychiatric illness, and periods of care are on the whole short (Jansson, 1964; Wilson, Bargelow, & Shipman, 1972). Therefore any trials of drug therapy must take into account the possibility of spontaneous remission regardless of treatment and must include control groups given placebos. Few studies have even attempted to do so. Two frequently cited reports of progesterone treatment, Schmidt (1943) and Blumberg and Billig (1942), concern only one case. Billig and Bradley (1946) treated 12 cases, only 4 of which were postpartum cases. This study also illustrates a drawback common to several: the mixture of several kinds of therapies in addition to progesterone, making unique effects of progesterone impossible to detect. Patients were given combinations of electroshock, insulin, and progesterone therapy in varying numbers of courses. Similarly Bower and Altschule (1956), while using a larger sample of 39 postpartum psychiatric cases, used progesterone both alone and in combination with electroshock and insulin; the controls were a group of patients given differing kinds and amounts of electroshock, insulin, psychotherapy, and their combinations. Tucker (1962) tested progesterone on 44 patients with postpartum psychiatric reactions and 13 patients with nonpostpartum schizoaffective reactions as controls but treated patients in both groups not only with progesterone but also with electroshock, tranquilizers, and in some instances thorazine. Of the 13 controls 7 responded well to progesterone and 6 did not; of the 44 test patients the 25 depressives either recovered completely with the use of electroshock only or did not respond to progesterone, and the 19 schizoaffective patients recovered with the use of electroshock but relapsed unless progesterone was used to maintain recovery. As Tucker himself states, "the statistical results in this kind of study are difficult to evaluate," and "the results reported in this study are suggestive only and tests are inadequate" (pp. 152, 153). Hamilton (1962) treated 29 patients successfully with desiccated thyroid but without using a control group. Another study (Ballachey, Campbell, Claffey, Escamilla, Footer, Hamilton, Harter, Litteral, Lyons, Overstreet, Poliak, Schaupp, Smith, & Vooris, 1958) introduced the use of controls, but on a very limited sample: 12 patients were given triiodothyronine and 2 of these were given both triiodothyronine and a placebo in a double-blind cross-over technique. The authors achieved maintained remission for all patients, and the 2 patients in the control study showed exacerbation of symptoms upon substitution of placebos and remission upon reintroduction of triiodothyronine; these results are suggestive but far from conclusive. Hamilton suggests that patients whose symptoms begin after the 4th week postpartum are the best candidates for thyroid treatment, but as the large majority of postpartum psychiatric cases have their onset during the first month postpartum, the role of thyroid changes in postpartum psychiatric illness is unclear.

Psychological Approach

While rejecting the hypothesis of postpartum psychiatric illness as a disease entity, many researchers have accepted the importance of taking into account the physiological changes that occur in all women postpartum because of their possible role in contributing to a state of increased vulnerability and stress that for certain women may be sufficient to trigger psychosis and for others to produce the milder forms of disturbance found in this period. This model requires consideration of psychological factors in distinguishing which women react most severely to the physiological stresses. Still other researchers give psychological factors even greater importance, arguing that physiological changes are insignificant in comparison to the profound psychological changes that women experience in having a child.

Most of those holding a psychological perspective have based their work on psychoanalytic theories, particularly three assumptions: (1) that postpartum psychiatric illness is a manifestation of conflict over mothering; (2) that this conflict arises from rejection of or ambivalence toward one's femininity; and (3) that these attitudes are a sign of psychological malfunctioning from abnormal personality development.

Several investigators who emphasize the role of psychological factors in the causation of postpartum psychiatric illness have noted that their patients manifest difficulty in assuming a mothering role, guilt, fear and anxiety, and hostility toward baby and husband (Brew & Seidenberg, 1950; Deutsch, 1945; Hamilton, 1962; Heiman, 1965; Jones, E., 1950; Kline, 1955; Melges, 1968;

Ostwald & Regan, 1957; Robin, 1962; Smalldon, 1940; Zilboorg, 1928a, 1931, 1957). Fear and anxiety have also been noted among normal mothers during pregnancy and postpartum (Deutsch, 1945; Goodrich, 1961; Gruenberg, 1967; Hall & Mohr, 1933; Pleshette, Asch, & Chase, 1956). In general psychoanalytic theorists have contended that symptoms of psychiatric disturbance postpartum arise from a process of regression during pregnancy that reaches its farthest point at the moment of parturition. During regression, women relive conflicts and newly aroused unconscious ideas of early childhood, and at parturition their regression is heightened by their identification with their new child (Deutsch, 1945; Heiman, 1965; Jones, E., 1950; Zilboorg, 1928a, 1931). Thus after a woman has become pregnant her personality undergoes a psychological process that even in a very "normal" case is conflicted and dangerous. For mothers with incomplete resolution of psychosexual conflicts the risks are even greater; regression may become extreme and result in the emergence of psychosis. Zilboorg (1928a) suggests that postpartum psychiatric patients typically have failed to resolve the oedipal crisis and thus manifest either strong unresolved ties to their fathers or a father identification and rejection of the feminine role. He further claims that these women are unable to renounce their desire for a penis and replace it by the desire for a child; thus they manifest a castration complex of the revenge type, hating and envying masculine men. The baby is unconsciously equated with a penis; it therefore evokes "murderous hostility" sometimes disguised as excessive fears for the child's well-being (Zilboorg, 1931, p. 950). Schizophrenic reactions in particular are stated to be typified by complete masculine identification and rejection of the feminine role. The birth of a child as testimony to the anatomical femininity that these women wish to deny provokes a flight from reality. Depressive reactions are stated to be characterized by a lesser, though still present, masculine identification that conflicts with a partial acceptance of femininity; depressive patients manifest ambivalence toward marital partners, children, and themselves, and their hostility to their children provokes strong feelings of guilt. Other psychoanalytic writers have similarly suggested oedipal and castration complexes and rejection of femininity as central to postpartum psychiatric reactions (Heiman, 1965; Jones, E., 1950; Ostwald & Regan, 1957).

Difficulties in assuming the mothering role have been attributed not only to hostility caused by the castration complex but also to extreme dependency caused by insufficient mothering in early life or strong dependent ties to the father (Astrachan, 1965; Kline, 1955), to hatred and fear of the mother and thus unwillingness to compete with or replace her (Kline, 1955), or to domineering egocentrism caused by rejection of femininity, making mothers incapable of the "maximum masochistic reaction of giving" that parturition and caretaking of an infant require (Zilboorg, 1928a). Fears specifically have been related to the arousal of unconscious ideas and identification with the infant brought about by regression; these fears may be present among normal mothers also but become obsessional among psychiatric cases (Jones, E., 1950; Heiman, 1965). Heiman, for example, suggests that feelings of entrapment with resultant anxiety arise from identification with the infant and feelings of being enclosed.

To support these theories several psychoanalytic investigators have sought to link postpartum psychiatric illness with traits showing abnormal sexual tendencies, abnormal relations to parents, and rejection of femininity. Regarding abnormal sexual tendencies, they have reported a high incidence of frigidity, excessive eroticism, excessive masturbation, latent or open homosexuality, promiscuity, and aloofness or shyness in the presence of men (Brew & Seidenberg, 1950; Kline, 1955; Ostwald & Regan, 1957; Zilboorg, 1928a, 1928b, 1931). For abnormal relations to parents they have reported faulty mothering experience in childhood, mother as dominant parent, early death of a parent or parents, divorce during childhood, and father identification (Astrachan, 1965; Kline, 1955; Melges, 1968; Nilsson & Almgren, 1970; Zilboorg, 1928a). For rejection of femininity they have reported depreciatory attitudes toward feminine interests and activities; inability to do certain tasks usually thought of as feminine; avoidance of femininity in dress, make-up, hairstyle, and manner; extended tomboy phase; being one of the boys rather than socializing with women; lack of love for husband, lack of a passive-submissive attitude toward others; lack of interest in doll play in childhood; lack of interest in own or others' children; scoring high on the masculine end of masculinity-femininity scales; rating masculine traits on such scales as more desirable than feminine traits; having any of the sexual tendencies described above; being independent and self-supporting; having a career; being bored with housework and having a desire for more stimulating work; deferring marriage and childbirth as long as possible; and desiring equality with men (Kline, 1955; Melges, 1968; Ostwald & Regan, 1957; Zilboorg, 1928b). Menstrual disorders, explained from the biomedical perspective as a result of hormonal imbalances, are explained from the psychological perspective as a result of rejection of femininity (Kline, 1955; Zilboorg, 1928a).

From the above description postpartum psychiatric patients are obviously a contradictory lot, being both independent and dependent, shy and aloof with men and preferring to socialize with men, highly erotic and also frigid. While some researchers have reported late marriage and prolonged courtship (Zilboorg, 1928b), others do not find this trend (Paffenbarger, 1961), and while some report mother as dominant parent (Ostwald & Regan, 1957), others report father as dominant parent (Zilboorg, 1931). Further most of these reports lack reliability because they are based on clinical observations and case histories of a few patients rather than formal studies (Astrachan, 1965; Heiman, 1965; Jones, E., 1950; Zilboorg, 1928a, 1928b, 1931, 1957). Still others have examined larger samples with some attempt at defining their measures and have indicated statistically the incidence of each trait in their samples, but control groups of nonpostpartum psychiatric patients or normal parturient mothers are lacking (Brew & Seidenberg, 1950; Kline, 1955; Melges, 1968; Ostwald & Regan, 1957). While comparisons with controls are used on some measures, they are not used in examining personality traits or life history. It is therefore possible that many traits reported to be distinctive of postpartum psychiatric illness are present to a similar extent in the general psychiatric patient population (e.g., early object losses, poor or insufficient parental contact), and others may be present to a similar extent in the general female population (e.g., work outside the home, frigidity, menstrual difficulties). Anderson's (1933) study, one of the few efforts to test a psychoanalytic assumption by the use of a control group, found no significant differences in the prepsychotic sexual life of 50 postpartum psychiatric patients and 50 general psychiatric patients (in love affairs, married life, and sexual satisfaction); nor were there any differences in masturbation and other erotic phenomena during the illness. Frigidity, masturbation, eroticism, and homosexuality were not found to be distinctive or even common features of the postpartum group.

I would argue that the most profound source of error in these studies is not that of method but rather of basic assumptions. Nilsson and Almgren's (1970) study of a random sample of 152 parturient women found that a high number of psychiatric symptoms postpartum was correlated with a preference for masculine characteristics on the masculinity–femininity scale, low mother identification and high father identification, and a stated attitude that motherhood was not their primary aim; these characteristics are described as indicating a "basic poor adjustment to sexual and reproductive functions" arising from disturbance in gender role. While this study is well thought out methodologically, its interpretation of the data illustrates limitations found throughout the psychological postpartum literature: a failure to distinguish biological gender identity from culturally defined sex-role identity and biological aspects of mothering from the culturally defined mothering role; the use of polarized concepts of masculinity and femininity; and the implicit equation of acceptance of the culturally defined feminine role with psychological health.

Bem (Note 1) has defined gender identity as "a secure sense of one's maleness or femaleness" and "accepting as given the fact that one is either male or female in exactly the same sense that one accepts as given the fact that one is human" (p. 25). On the other hand sex-role identity as measured by psychological scales is degree of conformance to a constellation of traits and interests prevalent among individuals of one sex and infrequently found in the other. It has been traditionally believed that certain traits and interests are more common among one sex than the other because they are natural to that sex. But recent research on the role of socialization throughout childhood and adolescence in reinforcing behaviors considered appropriate to one's sex role and discouraging or punishing behaviors considered inappropriate has made clear the large extent to which sex-role identity is culturally acquired (Fauls &

188 E. M. Magnus

Smith, 1956; Kagan & Moss, 1962; Mussen, 1969; Schell & Silber, 1968; Bem, Note 2). Considering the all-pervasive influence of families, schools, the media, and other cultural institutions in teaching appropriate sex-role behavior, and the differences in the ways males and females are treated from early infancy, the belief that any traits are biologically inherent to the male or female personality is unjustified. Identification with the father (in the sense Nilsson and Almgren use it, stated resemblance to the father in traits and interests) may mean identification with the sex-role characteristics of the father; it does not necessarily mean identification with the father's gender. Similarly preference for masculine characteristics may mean preference for masculine sex-role characteristics without implying preference for a male gender identity.

The biological aspect of mothering is the fact that women are capable of bearing and nursing children; the mothering role, however, is culturally defined and varies not only from one society or group within a society to the next but also throughout history. Traditionally motherhood has been viewed as a woman's primary aim, the height of her creative potential, and the fulfillment of her deepest instinctive wish. Considering the social pressures on women to bear children, we cannot state with any certainty that the wish to bear children is instinctive; and considering the degree to which women have been discouraged in our society from having other primary aims and other outlets of creativity and self-expression, we cannot state that it is natural for motherhood to be the main focus of women's lives.

One reason that psychological scales of masculinity and femininity show a set of traits characteristic of males and an opposite, complementary set characteristic of females is that their construction essentially reflects the sex-role bias present in our society. These scales are set up with masculinity at one end and femininity at the other end of a single continuum; thus an individual can be masculine or feminine but not both. Further investigators use such scales to classify individuals as either sex typed or sex reversed but leave out those to whom neither of these labels applies. Certainly it is possible for individuals to exhibit both masculine and feminine traits depending on their appropriateness to a situation—to be both instrumental and expressive or both assertive and concerned for others. The fact that psychological androgyny cannot be measured on these scales illustrates their limited focus.

The search in the psychological literature for evidence of nonconformity to the feminine role (e.g., extended tomboy phase, a career, assertiveness) in postpartum psychiatric patients implies that those individuals who do not conform to the status quo of traditionally defined sex roles are psychologically disturbed, while those who are highly sex typed are the most healthy psychologically. Recent research, reviewed by Bem (Note 2), contradicts this view. For males high masculinity on sex-role inventories has been positively correlated with anxiety, guilt proneness, neuroticism, suspiciousness, low self-acceptance, and low self-assurance, while low masculinity has been correlated with warmth and emotional stability (Harford, Willis, & Deabler, 1967;

Mussen, 1962). For females high femininity has been associated with high anxiety, low self-esteem, and low social acceptance (Cosentino & Heilbrun, 1964; Gall, 1969; Gray, 1957; Sears, 1965; Webb, 1963). A lower degree of sex typing in both males and females also seems to be associated with higher intelligence and greater creativity. Women who do not conform to the traditional female role have been found by several studies to have a higher masculine orientation in interests and personality traits than other women, but this seems to be in addition to feminine traits and may result from a broader definition of the female role that includes both masculine and feminine traits (Heilbrun, 1968; Rand, 1968; Tyler, 1964). Bem's (1975) research suggests a similar pattern. In Tyler's study women with career interests showed higher self-acceptance, well-being, self-control, and tolerance than women with a homemaker orientation as rated on vocational interest tests.

AN ALTERNATIVE APPROACH

I stated earlier that the psychological literature on postpartum psychiatric illness is based on three assumptions: that postpartum psychiatric illness represents a conflict over mothering; that this conflict arises from rejection of or ambivalence towards femininity; and that these attitudes are a sign of psychological malfunctioning resulting from abnormal personality development. If we take femininity to mean sex role rather than gender identity, the assumption that rejection of or ambivalence toward femininity is a sign of psychological malfunctioning seems to be contradicted by recent research comparing individuals with a high and a low degree of sex typing. It *may* be true, however, that psychiatric disturbance postpartum in both its mild and severe forms is based on conflicts over mothering (i.e., the culturally defined mothering role) or that some conflicts over mothering arise from ambivalence toward or rejection of femininity (sex role).

A further exploration of these assumptions requires a closer examination of what aspects of mothering cause the most stress and why. Psychoanalytic theorists have seldom put this question to mothers themselves. Parlee (Note 3) has noted that studies of postpartum have so far failed to isolate predictor factors, psychological or physiological, of postpartum psychiatric illness or critical variables revealing significant differences in postpartum reactions. She suggests that this may be a failure to attend seriously to relatively unstructured firsthand accounts of the postpartum experience, leading to a use of categories of analysis so foreign to what is experienced as to seem completely irrelevant. My own review of the few available unstructured firsthand accounts and structured surveys of women's attitudes (Boston Women's Health Collective, 1976; Darmstadter, Lucatorto, Lupton, & Winnick, 1972; Dyer, 1963; Larsen, 1966) as well as of the occasional references to women's own descriptions in the medical and psychological literature (Gordon, Kapostins, & Gordon, 1965; Melges, 1968; Pitt, 1968) yields mention of several stresses frequently reported as experienced to varying degrees of intensity among both the general population of mothers and postpartum psychiatric patients. In order to discover what causes differences in the intensity of experiencing these stresses (and presumably in the intensity of experiencing emotional disturbance), I have further explored the possible sources of each stress.

Stresses of the Postpartum Period

Inadequacy of Caretaking

Melges (1968) reports that conflicting messages on how to care for the infant were a severe problem for one-fourth of the 100 psychiatric patients in his sample and a moderate difficulty for another 59.2%. Often the patient's mother, sisters, mother-in-law, and husband all offered conflicting and ambiguous advice. "The new mother was often reluctant to take any advice or give any hint of her inadequacy, for she felt that her conduct as a mother was a test of her worth and femininity" (p. 102). The infants' incapacity to give specific feedback and to signal for specific needs was a major difficulty for 6.8% of the patients and a moderate difficulty for another 50%. The babies' crying and frequent lack of response to the mothers' attempts to appease them made mothers feel inadequate and rejected. Melges quotes one mother: "When they cry, you don't know what they're crying for . . . you do everything under the sun you can think of to do, and they still cry . . . I get upset after a few minutes. . . . I feel that I am not being a good mother when I don't know what to do for him. . . . I feel stupid" (p. 102). In Darmstadter's (1972) collection of firsthand accounts of postpartum psychosis, one mother similarly reports, "If the baby didn't eat—I was nursing her—or cried a lot, I thought I was doing something wrong" (p. 13). Dyer's (1963) survey of 32 normal primiparous mothers reports that 58% mentioned feelings of inadequacy and uncertainty about being able to fill the mother role as one of the major stresses of the postpartum period. Pitt's (1968) study of postpartum depression mentions the prevalence of feelings of inadequacy and inability to cope with the baby, particularly in conjunction with a conviction that no other mothers had such feelings. This conviction is expressed by one of Darmstadter's (1972) informants, who says, "I saw myself as unique—none of my friends had had reactions like mine. For everyone else, baby care was normal, natural, easy, beautiful. Simplest thing in the world, just follow your instincts" (p. 12).

Estrangement from the Infant

Especially during the first month postpartum, babies show little social responsiveness (i.e., smiling, cooing, direct eye contact) (Robson & Moss, 1970). Melges (1968) reports that this made some mothers feel they were dealing with a dummy or a vegetable (p. 103). It was difficulty for them to provide the large amounts of care required when the infant gave them no positive reinforcement and in fact did not even seem to recognize them. This reaction is not peculiar to postpartum psychiatric patients. Robson and Moss's (1970) study of the development of maternal attachment among 54 primiparous mothers reports that maternal attachment developed slowly and did not become strong until about 3 months postpartum. The modal mother felt a lack of personal connection to her baby during the first 4–6 weeks of life, and some mothers even described their babies as dolls, dummies, or animals.

Guilt

Strongly related to feelings of estrangement from the infant are feelings of guilt. One of Darmstadter's (1972) informants says, "Constantly meeting the baby's needs, I resented being unable to meet my own. Because I was unable to sleep at first, I had time to think, fantasize my escape, and build up feelings of guilt over my inability to respond to the situation with unmitigated happiness and love" (p. 12). Pitt (1968) reports, "babies who would not sleep and kept crying were found hard to love, with consequent guilt and anxiety," and "guilt was mainly confined to self-reproach over not loving or caring enough for the baby" (p. 1327).

Entrapment

Melges (1968) reports that feelings of entrapment (in a marriage or in motherhood) were a major stress in 15.5% of his sample and a moderate stress for another 48.3%. He also reports that "the care of the infant interfered with the pursuit of a career more than some mothers had anticipated" and that "loss of freedom" was significant for several mothers (p. 104). Dyer's survey reports that 35% of the new mothers mentioned difficulty in adjusting to being tied down at home and to curtailing outside activities and interests. When all mothers were asked what problem they considered most severe, adjusting to being tied down or being restricted to the home was most frequently indicated. In the words of one of Darmstadter's (1972) informants, "I began to miss the social contact my previous job had provided.... The apartment became a prison" (p. 12). As illustrated by the previous quote of the woman who spent time fantasizing her escape, not only lack of love for the baby but also feelings of entrapment and resentment over entrapment can provoke guilt about one's "inability to respond to the situation with ummitigated happiness."

Worries about Responsibility

Another commonly mentioned stress is feelings of enormous responsibility in caring for a baby and consequent anxiety. Larsen's (1966) 130 respondents to her survey on stresses of the childbearing year reported worry over the baby as one of the major stresses of the first 3 postpartum months. One of Darmstadter's (1972) informants reports, "My euphoria from the actual birth continued until I actually began to care for our helpless babies. Suddenly I felt completely overwhelmed and started crying constantly. I was struck with the realization that I had become responsible for the well-being of another human being" (p. 13). Robson and Moss (1970) report that a majority of their sample of primiparous mothers felt that their babies were very fragile and expressed fears of harming them.

Exhaustion

Larsen's (1966) survey indicates that fatigue was one of the main stresses of the first 3 postpartum months. Related to it were difficulty with housework and routines and difficulty in adjusting to the needs of other children, the husband, and the baby all at once. As Pitt (1968) describes it, "Undue fatigue and ready exhaustion were frequent, so that mothers could barely deal with their babies, let alone look after the rest of the family and cope with housework and shopping" (p. 1237). Similarly Melges (1968) reports,

> Many patients felt overwhelmed by the demands placed upon them after the birth of the baby; not only did they have to care for the infant, but also they had to attend to their houses, meals, laundry, husbands, and interested guests and relatives. Moreover, if they had other children, the arrival of the infant often prompted regression and sibling rivalry in the older children, who then made even greater demands on the mother. A vicious circle frequently ensued, in which the mother's distress augmented the children's distress and vice versa. Some patients felt unduly stressed by having too many young children to care for at one time. (p. 103)

Such difficulties were reported as a major problem for 30% of Melges's sample and a moderate problem for 58%. Physical illness of baby or mother causes an even greater degree of exhaustion. Dyer's survey found that 87% of the primiparous mothers mentioned exhaustion and loss of sleep as a major difficulty in adjusting to the arrival of the infant; 35% mentioned inability to keep up with housework; and 67% mentioned feelings of neglecting their husbands.

Sources of Stress

While most mothers experience some of these feelings, they seldom become overwhelmed by them. For postpartum psychiatric patients on the other hand these feelings become so overwhelming that the mother panics, and fear and guilt become obsessional. To find out why some mothers experience these reactions far more severely than others, we must examine the sources of each stress, and the ways in which each stress can be intensified or relieved.

Characteristics of the Infant

Traditionally, research on early mother-infant interaction has focused on the ways that a mother affects her infant's behavior and personality. Only recently has there been a shift to research on how characteristics of the infant affect behaviors and emotions of the mother (Bell, 1971; Gewirtz & Boyd, 1976). Several studies have related basically demographic child variables (e.g., infant gender, age, and development level) to observed mental variables (e.g., maternal attention, speech, expressed feelings of attachment, caretaking behaviors); others have described individual differences in infant behaviors as independent variables affecting parent behavior (Beckwith, 1971; Ferguson, 1964; Lewis, 1972; Moss, 1967; Osofsky & Danzger, 1974; Robson & Moss, 1970; Snow, 1972; Thoman, Leiderman, & Olson, 1972; Vuorenkoski, Wasz-Hockert, Koivisto, & Lind, 1969; Wolff, 1969). Here we are concerned primarily with effects of infant characteristics on maternal attachment and on feelings of capability or inadequacy in caretaking.

Robson and Moss (1970) have conducted one of the few studies on the development and determinants of mothers' attachment to their infants (as opposed to the numerous studies on infants' attachment to their mothers). They interviewed 54 primiparous mothers during the last trimester of pregnancy and at approximately $3\frac{1}{2}$ months postpartum, covering such topics as course of and feelings about labor and delivery, concerns about and attitudes toward the infant, apprehensions about maternal functioning, and descriptions of the infant's behaviors. They found that in the immediate postpartum mothers' feelings about and descriptions of the infant tended to be vague. First real contact with the infant elicited no feelings at all in over one-third of the sample and positive, though usually mild and impersonal feelings (e.g., "I liked him," "I had a good feeling") in 59%. During the first 4-6 weeks postpartum the modal mother's affectionate feelings toward her infant continued to be impersonal and she continued to perceive the infant as an anonymous nonsocial object. Especially during the first 3 or 4 weeks mothers felt insecure about not being able to control their infants' behavior and not being able to communicate with them. Infant eye-to-eye contact and smiling do not appear until at least the third or fourth week, and this is the time when modal mothers stated that they first felt positive feelings or love for their babies. At first these feelings were brief and intermittent, but attachment gradually evolved from this time onward. Approximately half of the mother and infant behaviors reported by mothers as related to these early positive feelings were babies' responses—smiling, eye-to-eye contact, following with eyes. Another 20% were related to holding or feeding the infant.

Four to six weeks was a transitional period during which mothers began to feel more confident about their caretaking and perceive the infant as a person. During this period 72% of the instances of strong and clearly articulated feelings of attachment were again related to infant responsiveness (smiling, laughing, eye contact, following with eyes). At 7-9 weeks mothers began to feel that their infants recognized them as separate individuals and found this reassuring and gratifying. By the end of the third month, the modal mother was strongly attached to her baby, an attachment expressed most intensely by mothers' comments about leaving or losing their infants.

The strong relation of maternal attachment to infant responsiveness is further supported by the authors' examination of mothers whose attachment developed unusually early or unusually late (or not at all) and mothers whose feelings of attachment underwent an especially radical change during the first 3 months. Mothers who experienced early and intense attachment to their infants had either an extraordinarily high investment in having a baby or an infant with precocious social behavior (responsiveness). Mothers who experienced late attachment or none at all either did not want the infant to begin with or had babies with retarded social behavior or high crying and fussing and low consolability. The authors cite one case of a woman who felt immediate and intense attachment at the infant's birth yet later on, when noticing how unresponsive the baby was and how late in exhibiting smiling and eye contact, felt so estranged that she wanted to abandon the baby. The baby was subsequently diagnosed as brain damaged. Another mother wanted to give up her baby at 6 weeks because she felt no love for him. She felt intensely guilty and every day searched anxiously within herself for some trace of maternal feeling. When the infant finally began smiling and recognizing her she noticed a dramatic shift in her feelings toward him, and by the end of the third month found her son irresistible. As yet another piece of supporting evidence, the authors cite Fraiberg and Freedman's (1964) findings that mothers of blind babies have difficulty in forming maternal attachments.

Moss's (1967) study of infant sex, age, and state as determinants of mother-infant interaction showed that male babies slept less and cried more than females at both 3 weeks and 3 months. He found a lessened maternal response to male crying and fussing over time: while at 3 weeks there was a high correlation between infant irritability and maternal contact (feeding behaviors subtracted out) for females but none for males, at 3 months the correlation was somewhat lower but still significant for females, while significantly negative for males. In other words by 3 months mothers tended to spend less time with irritable male babies. The author explains the lessened response to male irritability by citing studies suggesting that males are more subject to inconsolable states in infancy. Mothers are probably more often negatively reinforced in their attempts to soothe males, and the negative reinforcements gradually makes them try to soothe males less.

Thus if a mother has a baby who is unusually irritable (high crying and fussing) and difficult to console or a baby who shows these behaviors temporarily because of physical illness, she may have special difficulties in becoming attached to the infant. Mothers of babies who are blind, brain damaged, or late developers in exhibiting social behaviors may also have special difficulties. These mothers may feel especially inadequate and unloving in relation to their infants. But even mothers of normally responsive babies may feel inadequate and unloving and experience guilt and depression because of what they assume to be maternal deficiencies if they believe erroneously that normal or good mothers do not have these problems. If a women believes that it is normal for mothers to feel intense, immediate, and unqualified attachment to their babies, her own lack of maternal feeling in the first postpartum months may frighten and depress her and make her feel guilty and ashamed. Similarly if she believes that normal mothers quickly and easily develop a rapport with their infants, intuitively sensing and satisfying their needs, her response to the early lack of communication with her infant will be one of bewilderment, fear, and inadequacy. An infant's high irritability, wakefulness, or physical illness may also contribute to extreme exhaustion in the mother.

Hospital Practices

In the 1960s several studies appeared in the field of animal ethology that dealt with the mother–neonate relationship for various mammalian species, among them cattle, sheep, goats, rats, and mice (see especially Klopfer, Adams, & Klopfer, 1964; Moore, 1968; Noirot, 1964; Rosenblatt, 1963). In general these studies found that if contact was delayed by separation of the animal mother from her infant for a period of time immediately or shortly after birth, she was likely to exhibit maladaptive maternal behavior when contact was resumed. Further it was found that some species separation of the mother from her young, even for an hour in some species, produced a disturbance in the mother–infant relationship that was often irreversible (Moore, 1968).

This research led some developmental psychologists to propose a similar "sensitive period" for human mothers, during which the amount and quality of mother–infant interaction might have a strong influence on subsequent maternal behavior (Barnett, Leiderman, Gorbstein, & Klaus, 1970; Klaus, Jerauld, Kreger, McAlpine, Steffa, & Kennell, 1972; Klaus & Kennell, 1970; Klaus, Kennell, Plumb, & Zuehlke, 1970). The existence and definition of such a period are still controversial. Richards (1971), for example, argues that evidence for humans points to a gradual period of time over which maternal attachment develops rather than a discrete sensitive period; this view is corroborated by the Robson and Moss (1970) study cited earlier. Still there is some evidence to suggest that the development of maternal attachment and caretaking ability might be facilitated by modifying certain hospital birth practices. Klaus et al. (1972) have suggested that the brief mother–infant separation imposed by hospitals in cases of normal full-term delivery may affect later maternal behavior. The usual contact that hospitals allow consists of a glimpse of the baby shortly after birth, brief contact and identification 6-12 hours later, and then visits for 20-30 minutes every 4 hours for bottle feeding. Klaus et al. allowed 14 primiparous mothers this usual hospital contact while allowing a second group of 14 mothers (matched for age, socioeconomic and marital status, race, premedication, sex of the infant, and days hospitalized) 16 hours of additional contact during the first 4 post-partum days. Maternal behavior was measured 28–32 days later during a standardized interview, an examination of the baby, and a filmed bottle feeding. Extended contact mothers were more reluctant to leave their infants with someone else, usually stood and watched during the examination, showed greater soothing behavior, and engaged in significantly more eye-to-eye contact and fondling.

Mothers of premature babies undergo a far more severe and lengthy separation from their infants, and it has been hypothesized that this separa-tion causes disturbances in later maternal attachment and caretaking. A study by Leifer, Leiderman, and Barnett (1970) compared two sets of mothers, those allowed physical contact with and some caretaking of their infants during the first 5 postpartum days and those who had only visual contact with their infants in the premature nursery and were unable to touch, smell, or hear them for the first 30–40 days. Observations of the mother and infant were made on the mother's fifth visit to her infant in the discharge nursery, in the home one week after discharge, and in the pediatric clinic one month after discharge. Mothers allowed early physical contact with their infants were more skillful in caretaking only during the first observation. Attachment behavior (looking at the infant, smiling at the infant, the closeness with which the infant is held, caressing the infant) of the nonseparated mothers was greater than that of the separated mothers at each of the three observations; it was significantly greater only at the third observation. Another study by Kennell, Gordon, and Klaus (1970) compared feeding behavior just before discharge and one month after discharge of two groups of mothers, one permitted physical contact within the first 5 days of life and the other separated from their infants with only visual contact for the first 20 days. At the predischarge feeding the mothers allowed early contact with their infants cuddled their babies more and held them more closely than did mothers who had been separated from their infants. At the feeding one month later the late-contact mothers held their babies differently, changed position less, burped less, and were not as skillful in feeding as mothers in the early contact group.

These studies suggest that early mother–infant interaction should be restricted as little as possible and that hospital practices should be modified to allow for the option of extended maternal contact with the infant during the first few postpartum days. Some hospitals now offer a rooming in arrange-ment, which imposes partial restriction of interaction and no caretaking during the first 24 hours (as in regular care) but full contact and caretaking during the rest of the hospital stay (Barnett et al., 1970). Barnett and associates are engaged in a study of the effects of maternal separation from premature infants and the safety of permitting mothers to enter the premature nursery and handle their infants. So far they have shown no increase in infection when mothers are permitted to visit and no disruption in the care of the infant.

Another hospital practice that may disrupt later maternal attachment and caretaking ability is the administration of anesthesia and analgesia to mothers during labor. Brackbill, Kane, and Manniello (1974) demonstrated that several items in Brazelton's Neonatal Behavioral Assessment Scale (e.g., lack of startles, consolability, cuddliness, ability to suck steadily and vigorously) were performed more capably by the babies whose mothers had received no premedication. Brackbill et al. speculated that drug effects on infant behavior might disrupt the initial mother–child relationship. This possibility has been more fully explored by Richards (1971), who argues that a central issue in the growth of the mother–infant relationship is the temporal phasing of each partner's behavior. Several infant behaviors (e.g., crying, sucking, and eye movements) have been found to show constant rhythmical properties that seem to be endogenously generated. In interacting with the infant a mother must adapt to these rhythms and phase her behavior to them. For example, in smiling and vocalizing to her infant a mother must reduce and restrain her behavior at certain intervals to give the infant time to respond. If instead she subjects the infant to an unphased barrage of stimulation, it begins to fuss and cry and turn away from the mother's face. In feeding, the mother must adapt to the infant's sucking pattern rather than repeatedly stimulating the baby to suck, a behavior that may actually inhibit sucking.

Several serially organized systems of infant behavior have been shown to be very sensitive to drugs given the mother during labor. Richards (1971) has found temporal disorganization in eye movements (8 or 9 days postpartum) and sucking patterns (10 days postpartum) of infants whose mothers were given meperidine in labor. For example, drugged infants were fed for shorter peiods, had the nipple in their mouths for a briefer time, and received more stimulations to suck from their mothers. He suggests that mothers of infants whose behavior shows disturbances of temporal organization may have difficulty in phasing their behavior with that of the infant and thus in developing a strong mother–infant tie.

Hospital practices concerning infant feeding may inhibit successful breast feeding, the attainment of which is regarded by some mothers as an important test of mothering ability. Newton (1955) has enumerated several practices that contribute to lactation failure. Prohibiting feeding until the day after delivery, limiting the number of feedings to five or six a day, and limiting each feeding to about 3–5 minutes all limit sucking to an amount far lower than that probably needed to establish an abundant milk supply in most women. Giving babies water or formula during the first 2 or 3 days and giving supplemental feeding by bottle may teach the baby to be indifferent to the breast later on. Finally limiting sucking and denying the mother peace and privacy during breast feedings may encourage the failure of the let-down reflex.

Hospital practices may intensify other postpartum stresses besides feelings of inadequacy in caretaking and estrangement from the infant. Such labor and delivery practices as episiotomy, unnecessary labor induction and Caesarian section, restrictions on food and drink during labor, double clamping of the umbilical cord, and overmedication during labor may all contribute to physical weakness, exhaustion, and discomfort in the early postpartum (see Chapter 8). Emotional aspects of the birth experience, such as lack of emotional support during labor and delivery, a dehumanizing hospital atmosphere, and only brief contact with the baby, may cause either a sense of unreality or detachment about the entire situation of having given birth or feelings of emotional shakiness and vulnerability. In fact the blues syndrome experienced by a majority of mothers in the immediate postpartum might well be caused not only by hormonal changes, as some researchers have suggested, but also by emotional aspects to hospital births.

Separating women from their babies because of severe mental disturbance postpartum may intensify many of the stresses these women already experience, particularly anxiety about the baby, feelings of inadequacy in caretaking, feelings of lack of personal connection with the baby, fears of harming it, and a sense of unreality about having given birth. Recently a few programs have experimented with allowing postpartum psychiatric patients to room in with their babies on the psychiatric ward; results have indicated a high success rate, with most mothers considering the baby's admission a primary factor in their recovery. One study indicated that these women had an improved degree of recovery, a lower relapse rate, and a higher confidence in their caretaking ability after discharge than did other postpartum psychiatric patients (Baker, 1961; Luepker, 1972).

Lack of Assistance and Support for Caretaking

The Gordons and their colleagues (Gordon, 1957; Gordon & Gordon, 1957, 1958, 1960; Gordon, Kapostins, & Gordon, 1965) constitute that small minority of researchers who have studied the role of environmental stresses in the development of postpartum emotional disturbances. They have demonstrated that postpartum psychiatric patients differ significantly from normal parturient mothers in having received less practical assistance and emotional support from husbands, friends, and relatives during the first postpartum weeks. Frequently their husbands are unavailable in the weeks after the baby's birth (Gordon, 1957; Gordon & Gordon, 1957). Another of their studies (Gordon & Gordon, 1958) compared the success of psychotherapy to that of therapy focused on pointing out social strains and helping the patient to do something about them. Socially oriented therapy resulted in greater success as measured by fewer sessions before remission, a lower number of patients who rejected therapy after one or two sessions, and a lower number of psychiatric hospitalizations.

Yet another study (Gordon et al., 1965) set up an experimental group of expectant mothers who received, in addition to standard antenatal classes, instruction emphasizing seven recommendations that mothers could follow to reduce the environmental stresses contingent on childbirth. These recommendations suggested holding to a minimum any major life changes (e.g., moving residence, husband's taking a new job) during the pregnancy and postpartum period and setting up a support network in advance by discussing plans, fears, hopes, and problems with husband, friends, and relatives and actively soliciting their assistance. The experimental group was found to take significantly more of the recommended steps than controls (given only standard antenatal classes), and members of the experimental group had significantly fewer emotional problems postpartum than did controls.

Melges (1968) corroborates the observation that postpartum psychiatric patients often receive little assistance from their husbands. He writes: "Some of the husbands remained surprisingly uninvolved in their wives' struggle with mothering. It was rare for 12.1% of the husbands to give reinforcement for their wives' mothering duties, and another 21.2% were moderately disengaged. Five husbands increased their outside activities, such as taking on extra jobs, writing a book, etc., in order to get away from the home" (p. 103). Pitt (1968) writes about depressed mothers that "negative feelings for the husband, regarded as unhelpful or unsympathetic, were admitted by just under one quarter of the group" (p. 1328).

This lack of assistance and support may have several causes. First the husband may feel that it is not his obligation to assist in any major way with the infant's physical care. As time-budget studies have indicated, men's contribution to primary childcare (direct interaction with children as opposed to activities during which the children are merely present) is small, and its largest component is playing with children rather than direct provision or care (see Pleck, in press). Second the husband may take on extra outside work because of the increased financial pressures caused by the child. Third, as Melges (1968) has pointed out, the new mother may feel reluctant or unjustified in asking others for support because she feels that the task is hers and enlisting others proves her inadequacy.

Belief on the part of either a new mother or her husband that infant care is primarily the mother's job may be based not only on the mother's having more time for her infant while the father works but also on the assumption that men are not biologically programmed to respond nurturantly to children. Evidence contradicting this assumption is reviewed by Pleck (in press). While it is sometimes thought that in the animal world the mother is universally the prime caregiver, there are in fact several species even among primates for which the reverse is true (e.g., the marmoset and the titi monkey) (Mitchell, 1969). Even in primate species in which adult males are typically hostile toward the young, such as the rhesus, males will develop maternal behavior if they are exposed to the young over a period of time (Mitchell, Redican, & Gomber, 1974; Redican & Mitchell, 1973). Further some recent research indicates that human fathers' attachment to their infants develops in ways quite similar to that of mothers. Parke and O'Leary (1976) observed mothers and fathers with their newborns, both together and separately, in a university hospital and a general metropolitan hospital sample. During the observation periods fathers were very active interactors with their infants and were just as nurturant as mothers. Fathers were actually more likely than mothers to hold and visually attend to the infant and to stimulate the child physically and verbally. The only behavior they exhibited less frequently than mothers was smiling. Fathers' interactions with their newborns did not depend on the mothers' presence, and there were no differences between fathers in the two hospital samples, which drew on very different socioeconomic groups. A study by Parke and Sawin (1976) comparing mothers and fathers in ability to feed infants found that fathers were just as sensitive as mothers in responding to the infants' cues.

Lack of practical assistance in childcare may contribute to several of the major stresses of the postpartum period, particularly exhaustion, feelings of entrapment, longing for the stimulation of work and outside contacts, feelings of inability to cope, and anxiety over one's large responsibilities. If a woman feels obligated to devote most of her time and energy to childcare even as the child grows older and if she feels reluctant or is financially unable to provide substitute care, the birth of a child may represent an exclusive commitment to mothering and a sacrifice of other major activities for several years to come. A few articles on postpartum disturbances have tangentially discussed the effects on mothers' psychological health of ending work outside the home in order to bear and rear a child. LeMaster's (1957) study of the effects on parents of the arrival of the first child noted that the eight mothers in his sample with professional training and extensive professional work experience suffered extensive or severe crisis in every case (ratings 4 or 5 on a 5-point scale, arrived at jointly by the interviewer and the parents). In contrast Dyer's (1963) restudy showed that although 62% of the wives in the sample had been employed before their children were born, only 12% expressed feelings of loss since quitting, and none expressed a desire to return to work. This study, however, does not distinguish professional work or other work to which women might be expected to have a high commitment and work taken out of necessity only. Clearly it is necessary to examine degree of women's attachment to their work and the significance they place on their work role in order to study effects of its loss. It is also necessary to examine the extent to which the loss is regarded as permanent and the extent to which women who have never worked but desire work regard childbearing as the closing off of opportunities to work, as suggested by Rubin's (1967) discussion of "grief work" in the postpartum period:

Among the mothers there was a progressive obliteration of former roles and former ideal images. Employment was a wistful wish of many of the women, but the wish moved from bereavement for an idealized career necessitated by a first or second child to a bereavement for the financial and interpersonal enrichments of a job, any job, with the third or higher ordinal child. . . . Each review progressed from "I am . . ." to "I was . . . " to "I used to be . . . " to "I did." Very few relinquished their former identities readily. (p. 244)

Thus a woman's responsibility to provide, alone, most of the care that infants require may have powerful effects on her life choices and satisfaction not only in the first few weeks or months postpartum but for several years to come. It is not surprising that women should be most intensely aware of the repercussions of their decision to have a child in the immediate postpartum, when their outside activities are most restricted.

Unplanned or Unwanted Pregnancy

Two studies by Nilsson and his colleagues (Nilsson & Almgren, 1970; Nilsson, Kaij, & Jacobson, 1967) suggest that unplanned and/or unwanted pregnancy has an influence on the development of psychiatric symptoms during pregnancy and postpartum. The 1967 study of a random sample of 861 childbearing women contacted by questionnaire 3, 6, 9, and 12 months postpartum yielded a nearly significant relationship between unplanned pregnancies and psychiatric symptoms both before and during pregnancy and a strong relationship between unplanned pregnancy and those subjects who reported more than eight psychiatric symptoms postpartum.

Nilsson and Almgren (1970) followed a representative sample of 152 women from late pregnancy through 6 months postpartum to measure attitudes toward the pregnancy and symptoms of emotional disturbance. The view that the majority of women will have accepted a pregnancy after only a few months was contradicted by this study's evidence that almost one-fourth (23%) of the women at 6 months postpartum (compared to 39% in the prenatal interview) showed a range of negative attitudes toward having a child, regarding the pregnancy as an unwelcome stress and handicap. Women who could not accept the pregnancy at either the prenatal or the 6-month postpartum examination reported psychiatric symptoms both during and after pregnancy to a considerably greater extent than others.

As Robson and Moss (1970) suggest, unwanted pregnancy may have an adverse effect on the development of maternal attachment. Further it probably accentuates the feelings of entrapment commonly described by women who experience emotional disturbance postpartum.

Internalized Cultural Attitudes about Mothering

A reading of the firsthand accounts and surveys of women's attitudes about postpartum difficulties suggests that most of the stresses women experience are intensified by belief in the ideology of motherhood described at the beginning of this chapter. Women who believe that their success in the tasks of mothering is a test of their femininity and basic worth will react to any difficulties of the postpartum period with far more anxiety and self-blame than women who do not have this orientation. If they believe that women should love their infants immediately and that feelings of irritation and resentment about the mothering role are not permissible, they may become anxious, guilty, and depressed if attachment develops slowly and mothering is not immediately rewarding. If they believe that women have instinctive capacities for caretaking, then their infants' crying, lack of responsiveness, lack of interest in breastfeeding, or lack of consolability may make them feel inadequate as mothers. The belief that they should naturally know what to do may also make them ashamed to ask others for advice. If they believe that it is their responsibility to provide almost all of the infants' care, they may feel unjustified in asking others, such as their husbands, to help. A belief that their responsibility extends to staying home with the children for the whole time that they are growing up may intensify feelings of entrapment and conflicts over working. Finally the belief that having a child should be their greatest fulfillment may make women feel guilty and confused when they have negative or ambivalent attitudes about the mothering role, when they are not happy enough in the postpartum period, or when they feel trapped and want other sources of fulfillment in their lives besides the bearing and rearing of children.

CONCLUSIONS

My review of the literature presenting women's own descriptions of the postpartum experience shows a widespread incidence of stresses of estrangement from the infant and consequent guilt, feelings of inadequacy in mothering, fatigue, anxiety over responsibilities, and feelings of entrapment among new mothers. I would argue that these stresses are common features of the postpartum experience and that they account for the common occurrence of major and minor emotional disturbances during this period. The interaction of both environmental and psychological factors accounts for the degree of intensity to which these stresses are experienced and the degree of emotional disturbance. While physiological changes common to all women postpartum, such as hormonal fluctuations and disruption of sleep patterns, may also contribute to stress, their coincidence with a time of numerous social changes makes their effects difficult to evaluate.

I contend that postpartum emotional disturbance does indeed represent a conflict over the (culturally defined) mothering role. It is not, however, a rejection of the mothering role, as so many psychological theorists have suggested. One finding clearly emerges from women's descriptions of the stresses they experience: these women do not take the mothering role lightly. Even when they do not love their infants, they want very badly to be able to love them—their estrangement from their infants cannot be justly called rejection. Even when they feel inadequate in taking care of their infants, they want very badly to be good mothers. Even when they long for the stimulation of outside contacts or some time for themselves, they do not ignore the needs of the infant; in fact the needs of the infant may be so paramount in their minds that any personal longings make them feel guilty. Their exhaustion arises not from unwillingness to give but from a crushing awareness of the needs of the baby, other children, and husband all at once and a willingness to give to all of them even when it is not humanly possible. If rejection of the mothering role were so marked, these women would not set such high standards for themselves in their conduct as mothers, and they would not feel so conscience stricken when they failed.

I would state rather that the conflict arises from *acceptance* of cultural expectations of the mothering role that contradict most women's actual feelings and experiences during the postpartum period. The greater the contradiction between cultural ideology and personal experience and feelings and the more women validate the ideology and invalidate their feelings, the greater the stress and consequent emotional disturbance.

Numerous circumstances of the postpartum period act on women to produce feelings that contradict the motherhood ideology. Attachment to the new baby develops slowly, as does caretaking ability. Adjustment to the infant's needs is a learning process, and in the beginning when the infant is often unresponsive to a mother's efforts to interact, please, or console it and in fact may not even seem to recognize her, she may have difficulty in feeling either loving or capable in relation to her infant. Care of the newborn is an exhausting task, especially if there are other children in the family. Usually the husband contributes little practical assistance and sometimes he may not even support his wife emotionally when she is anxious or confused. Because mothers bear most of the responsibility for their infants' care alone, the responsibility may seem frightening and overwhelming. Lack of assistance from others may leave many mothers confined to the home, with former activities, paid work, and social contacts restricted or cut out altogether. Finally some mothers may suffer under unusual circumstances that make postpartum adjustment especially difficult: unplanned pregnancy, a difficult financial situation, mental or physical abnormalities of the infant, physical illness of infant or mother, poor marital relationship, an especially alienating or frightening hospital experience, or childbirth outside of marriage.

Such circumstances alone may act on many women to produce fatigue, anxiety, and depression in the postpartum period. But they are especially likely to cause severe reactions in women who have set unrealistically high standards of mothering for themselves. The more women accept cultural expectations of the mothering role, the more likely they are to react with anxiety, guilt, feelings of inferiority, and depression when their experiences of the postpartum period do not fit with cultural expectations. Lowering the incidence of postpartum disturbances, then, requires two kinds of major changes: first, changes in cultural attitudes about the meaning of motherhood in women's lives to reflect more realistically women's actual feelings and experiences; and second, changes in the allocation of childcare responsibilities so that they no longer severely limit possibilities for other sources of fulfillment in women's lives.

REFERENCE NOTES

1. Bem, S. L. *Beyond androgyny: Some presumptuous prescriptions for a liberated sexual identity.* Unpublished manuscript, 1973.
2. Bem, S. L. *Psychology looks at sex roles: Where have all the androgynous people gone?* Paper presented at UCLA Symposium on Women, May 1972.
3. Parlee, M. B. *Psychological aspects of menstruation, childbirth, and menopause.* Unpublished manuscript, Harvard Medical School, 1973.

REFERENCES

Anderson, E. A study of the sexual life in psychoses associated with childbirth. *Journal of Mental Science,* 1933, *79,* 137–149.

Astrachan, J. Severe psychologic disorders of the puerperium. *Obstetrics and Gynecology,* 1965, *25,* 13–25.

Baker, A. A. Admitting schizophrenic mothers with their babies. *Lancet,* July 29, 1961, *2,* 237–239.

Ballachey, E., Campbell, D., Claffey, B., Escamilla, R. Footer, A. Hamilton, J., Harter, J., Litteral, J., Lyons, H., Overstreet, E., Poliak, P., Schaupp, K., Smith, G., & Voaris, A. Response of postpartum psychiatric symptoms to L-triiodothyronine. *Journal of Clinical and Experimental Psychopathology,* 1958, *19,* 1707.

Barnett, C. R., Leiderman, P. H., Grobstein, R., & Klaus, M. Neonatal separation: The maternal side of interactional deprivation. *Pediatrics,* 1970, *45,* 197–205.

Beckwith, L. Relationships between attributes of mothers and their infants' IQ scores. *Child Development,* 1971, *42,* 1083–1097.

Bell, R. Q. Stimulus control of parent or caretaker behavior by offspring. *Developmental Psychology,* 1971, *4,* 63–72.

Bem, S. L. Sex role adaptability: One consequence of psychological androgyny. *Journal of Personality and Social Psychology,* 1975, *31,* 634–643.

Billig, O., & Bradley, J. Combined shock and corpus luteum hormone therapy. *American Journal of Psychiatry,* 1946, *102,* 783–787.

Blumberg, A., & Billig, O. Hormonal influence upon "puerperal psychosis" and neurotic conditions. *Psychiatric Quarterly,* 1942, *16,* 454–462.

Boston Women's Health Collective. Postpartum blues: As natural as childbirth. In *Our bodies, ourselves: A book by and for women* (2nd ed.). New York: Simon and Schuster, 1975.

Bower, W., & Altschule, M. Use of progesterone in the treatment of postpartum psychoses. *New England Journal of Medicine,* 1956, *524,* 157–160.

Brackbill, Y., Kane, J., & Manniello, R. L. Obstetrical premedication and infant outcome. *American Journal of Obstetrics and Gynecology,* 1974, *118,* 377–384.

Brew, M., & Seidenberg, R. Psychotic reaction associated with pregnancy and childbirth. *Journal of Nervous and Mental Diseases,* 1950, *3,* 408–423.

Carlson, H. B. Characteristics of an acute confusional state in college students. *American Journal of Psychiatry*, 1958, *114*, 900.

Cosentino, F., & Heilbrun, A. B. Anxiety correlates of sex-role identity in college students. *Psychological Reports*, 1964, *14*, 729–730.

Danowski, T. S., Gow, R. C., Mateer, F. M., Everhart, W. C., Johnston, S. Y., & Greenman, J. H. Increases in serum thyroxin during uncomplicated pregnancy. *Proceedings of the Society of Experimental Biological Medicine*, 1950, *74*, 323–326.

Danowski, T. S., Hedenburg, S., & Greenman, J. The constancy of the serum precipitable or protein bound iodine in healthy adults. *Journal of Clinical Endocrinology*, 1949, *9*, 768–773.

Danowski, T. S., Huff, S. J., Mrvos, D., Wirth, P. George, R. S., & Mateer, F. M. Is pregnancy followed by relative hypothyroidism? *American Journal of Obstetrics and Gynecology*, 1953, *65*, 77–80.

Darmstadter, R., Lucatorto, K., Lupton, M. J., & Winnick, S. Childbirth and madness. *Women: A Journal of Liberation*, 1972, *3*(3), 11–16.

Davidson, J. R. T. Postpartum mood change in Jamaican women: A description and discussion of its significance. *British Journal of Psychiatry*, 1972, *121*, 659–663.

Deutsch, H. *Psychology of women.* New York: Grune & Stratton, 1945.

Dyer, Everett D. Parenthood as crisis: A re-study. *Journal of Marriage and the Family*, 1963, *25*, 196–201.

Fauls, L. B., & Smith, W. D. Sex-role learning of five-year-olds. *Journal of Genetic Psychology*, 1956, *89*, 105–117.

Ferguson, C. A. Baby talk in six languages. *American Anthropologist*, 1964, *66*(part 2), 103–114.

Fraiberg, S., & Freedman, D. A. Studies in the ego development of the congenitally blind child. In *The psychoanalytic study of the child* (Vol. 19). New York: International Universities Press, 1964.

Gall, M. D. The relationship between masculinity–femininity and manifest anxiety. *Journal of Clinical Psychology*, 1969, *25*, 294–295.

Gewirtz, J. L., & Boyd, E. F. Mother-infant interaction and its study. In H. W. Reese (Ed.), *Advances in child development and behavior* (Vol. 11). New York: Academic Press, 1976.

Goodrich, F. W., Jr. Psychosomatic aspects of obstetrics. *Psychosomatics*, 1961, *2*, 194.

Gordon, R. E. Emotional disorders of pregnancy and childbearing. *Journal of the Medical Society of New Jersey*, 1957, *54*, 16.

Gordon, R. E., & Gordon, K. K. Some social-psychiatric aspects of pregnancy and childbearing. *Journal of the Medical Society of New Jersey*, 1957, *54*, 569–572.

Gordon, R. E., & Gordon, K. K. Social factors in the prediction and treatment of emotional disorders of pregnancy. *American Journal of Obstetrics and Gynecology*, 1958, *77*, 1074.

Gordon, R. E., & Gordon, K. K. Social factors in the prevention of postpartum emotional difficulties. *Obstetrics and Gynecology*, 1960, *15*(4), 433.

Gordon, R. E., Kapostins, E. E., & Gordon, K. K. Factors in postpartum emotional adjustment. *Obstetrics and Gynecology*, 1965, *25*, 158.

Gray, S. W. Masculinity–femininity in relation to anxiety and social acceptance. *Child Development*, 1957, *28*, 203–214.

Gruenberg, E. The psychosomatics of the not-so-perfect fetal parasite. In A. Guttmacher & S. Richardson (Eds.), *Childbearing–Its social and psychological aspects*. Baltimore: Williams & Wilkins, 1967.

Hall, D. E., & Mohr, G. J. Prenatal attitudes of primiparae: A contribution to mental hygiene of pregnancy. *Mental Hygiene*, 1933, *17*, 226.

Hamburg, D. A., Moos, R. H., & Yalom, I. D. Studies of distress in the menstrual cycle and the postpartum period. In R. P. Michael (Ed.), *Endocrines and human behavior.* London: Oxford University Press, 1968.

Hamilton, A. H. *Postpartum psychiatric problems.* St. Louis: Mosby, 1962.

Harford, T. C., Willis, C. H., & Deabler, H. L. Personality correlates of masculinity-femininity. *Psychological Reports,* 1967, *21,* 881–884.

Heilbrun, A. B. Sex role, instrumental–expressive behavior, and psychopathology in females. *Journal of Abnormal Psychology,* 1968, *73,* 131–136.

Heiman, M. A psychoanalytic view of pregnancy. In J. Robinsky & A. Guttmacher (Eds.), *Medical surgical and gynecologic complications of pregnancy* (2nd ed.). Baltimore: Williams & Wilkins, 1965.

Hemphill, R. E. "Incidence and Nature of Puerperal Psychiatric Illness." *British Medical Journal,* 1952, *2,* 1232–1235.

Jacobson, L., Kaij, L., & Nilsson, A. Postpartum mental disorders in an unselected sample: Frequency of symptoms and predisposing factors. *British Medical Journal* 1965, *1,* 1640.

Jansson, B. Psychic insufficiencies associated with childbearing. *Acta Psychiatrica Scandinavica (Suppl.),* 1964, No. 172.

Jones, E. *Papers on psychoanalysis* (5th ed.). Baltimore: Williams & Wilkins, 1950. Ch. 21.

Jones, R. Puerperal insanity. *British Medical Journal,* 1902, *1,* 579–585.

Kagan, J., & Moss, H. A. *Birth to maturity: A study in psychological development.* New York: Wiley, 1962.

Kaij, L., & Nilsson, A. Emotional and psychotic illness following childbirth. In J. Howells (Ed.), *Modern perspectives in psycho-obstetrics.* Edinburgh: Oliver & Boyd, 1972.

Karacan, I., Heine, W., Agnew, H. W., Williams, R. L., Webb, W. B., & Ross, J. J. Characteristics of sleep patterns during late pregnancy and the postpartum periods. *American Journal of Obstetrics and Gynecology,* 1968, *101,* 570–576.

Karacan, I., & Williams, R. L. Current advances in theory and practice relating to postpartum syndromes. *Psychiatry in Medicine,* Oct. 1970, *1,* 307–328.

Karacan, I., Williams, R. L., Hursch, C. J., McCaulley, M., & Heine, M. W. Some implications of the sleep patterns of pregnancy for postpartum emotional disturbances. *British Journal of Psychiatry,* 1969, *115,* 929–935.

Kennell, J., Gordon, D., & Klaus, M. The effects of early mother–infant separation on later maternal performance. *Pediatric Research,* 1970.

Kilpatrick, E., and Tiebout, H. M. *American Journal of Psychiatry,* 1926, *83,* 145.

Klaus, M. H., Jerauld, R., Kreger, N. C., McAlpine, W., Steffa, M., & Kennell, J. H. Maternal attachment: Importance of the first postpartum days. *New England Journal of Medicine,* March 1972, *286*(9), 460–463.

Klaus, M. H., & Kennell, J. H. Mothers separated from their newborn infants. *Pediatric Clinics of North America,* Nov. 1970, *17*(4), 1015–1037.

Klaus, M., Kennell, J., Plumb, N., & Zuehlke, S. Human maternal behavior at first contact with her young. *Pediatrics,* 1970, *46,* 187.

Kline, C. L. Emotional illness associated with childbirth. *American Journal of Obstetrics and Gynecology,* 1955, *69,* 748–757.

Klopfer, P., Adams, D., & Klopfer, M. Maternal "imprinting" in goats. *Proceedings of the National Academy of Science,* 1964, *52,* 911.

Larsen, V. L. Stresses of the childbearing year. *American Journal of Public Health,* Jan. 1966, *56*(1), 32–36.

Leifer, A., Leiderman, P., & Barnett, C. Mother–infant separation: Effects on later maternal behavior. *Child Development,* 1970.

LeMasters, E. E. Parenthood as crisis. *Marriage and Family Living,* Nov. 1957, *19,* 352–355.

Lewis, M. State as an infant–environment interaction: An analysis of mother–infant interaction as a function of sex. *Merrill-Palmer Quarterly,* 1972, *18,* 95–121.

Luepker, E. T. Joint admission and evaluation of postpartum psychiatric patients and their infants. *Hospitals and Community Psychiatry*, 1972, *23*, 284–286.

Marcé, L. V. *Traité de la folie des femmes enceintes, des nouvelles accouchées, et des nourrices*. Paris: J. B. Baillière et Fils, 1858.

Meares, R., Grimwade, J., & Wood, C. A possible relationship between anxiety in pregnancy and puerperal depression. *Journal of Psychosomatic Research*, 1976, *20*, 605–610.

Melges, F. T. Postpartum psychiatric syndromes. *Psychosomatic Medicine*, 1968, *30*(1), 95–107.

Mitchell, G. Paternalistic behavior in primates. *Psychological Bulletin*, 1969, *71*, 399–417.

Mitchell, G., Redican, W., & Gomber, J. Lesson from a primate: Males can raise babies. *Psychology Today*, April 1974, pp. 23–28.

Moore, A. Effects of modified care in the sheep and goat. In G. Newton & S. Levine (Eds.), *Early experience and behavior*. Springfield, Ill.: Charles C Thomas, 1968.

Moss, H. A. Sex, age and state as determinants of mother–infant interaction. *Merrill-Palmer Quarterly*, 1967, *13*, 19–36.

Mussen, P. H. Long-term consequences of masculinity of interests in adolescence. *Journal of Consulting Psychology*, 1962, *26*, 435–440.

Mussen, P. H. Early sex-role development. In D. A. Goslin (Ed.), *Handbook of socialization theory and research*. Chicago: Rand McNally, 1969.

Newton, N. Women's feelings about breast feeding. In N. Newton (Ed.), *Maternal emotions*. New York: Hoeber, 1955.

Nilsson, A., & Almgren, P.-E. Paranatal emotional adjustment: A prospective investigation of 165 women. *Acta Psychiatrica Scandinavica* (Suppl.), 1970, No. 220, 1970.

Nilsson, A., Kaij, L., & Jacobson, L. Postpartum mental disorder in an unselected sample: The importance of the unplanned pregnancy. *Journal of Psychosomatic Research*, 1967, *10*, 341–347.

Noirot, E. Changes in responsiveness to young in the adult mouse: The effect of external stimuli. *Journal of Comparative Physiology and Psychology*, 1964, *57*, 97.

Osofsky, J. D., & Danzger, B. Relationships between neonatal characteristics and mother–infant interaction. *Developmental Psychology*, 1974, *10*, 124–130.

Ostwald, P., & Regan, P. Psychiatric disorders associated with childbirth. *Journal of Nervous and Mental Diseases*, 1957, *125*, 153–165.

Paffenbarger, R. The picture puzzle of the postpartum psychoses. *Journal of Chronic Diseases*, 1961, *13*, 161–173.

Paffenbarger, R. Epidemiological aspects of parapartum mental illness. *British Journal of Preventive Social Medicine*, 1964, *18*, 189–195.

Paige, K. The effects of oral contraceptives on affective fluctuations associated with the menstrual cycle. *Psychosomatic Medicine*, 1971, *33*, 515–537.

Paige, K. Women learn to sing the menstrual blues. *Psychology Today*, 1973, 7(4), 41–43.

Parke, R., & O'Leary, S. Father–mother–infant interaction in the newborn period: Some findings, some observations, some unresolved issues. In K. Riegel & J. Meacham (Eds.), *The developing individual in a changing world* (Vol. 2). The Hague: Mouton, 1976.

Parke, R., & Sawin, D. The father's role in infancy: A re-evaluation. *Family Coordinator*, 1976, *25*, 365–372.

Pitt, B. "Atypical" depression following childbirth. *British Journal of Psychiatry*, 1968, *114*, 1325–1335.

Pitt, B. "Maternity Blues." *British Journal of Psychiatry*, 1973, *122*, 431–433.

Pleck, J. Men's new roles in the family: Housework and child care. In Safilios-Rothschild (Ed.), *Family and sex roles*. In press.

Pleshette, N., Asch, S., & Chase, J. A study of anxieties during pregnancy, labor, the early and later puerperium. *Bulletin of the New York Academy of Medicine*, 1956, *268*, 1224–1228.

Rand, L., Masculinity or femininity? Differentiating career-oriented and homemaking-oriented college freshman women. *Journal of Counseling Psychology*, May 1968, *15*, 444–450.

Redican, W., & Mitchell, G. A longitudinal study of paternal behavior in adult male rhesus monkeys: I. Observations on the first dyad. *Developmental Psychology,* 1973, *8,* 135–136.

Richards, M. P. M. Social interaction in the first weeks of human life. *Psychiatria Neurologia Neurochirurgia,* 1971, *74,* 35–42.

Robin, A. A. The psychological changes of normal parturition. *Psychiatric Quarterly,* 1962, *36,* 129–150.

Robson, K. S., & Moss, H. A. Patterns and determinants of maternal attachment. *Journal of Pediatrics,* 1970, *77*(6), 976–985.

Rosenblatt, J. S., & Lehrman, D. S. Maternal behavior of the laboratory rat. In H. Rheingold (Ed.), *Maternal behavior in mammals.* New York: Wiley, 1963.

Rubin, R. Attainment of the maternal role: I. Processes. *Nursing Research,* Summer 1967, *16*(3), 237–245.

Schell, R. E., & Silber, J. W. Sex-role discrimination among young children. *Perceptual and Motor Skills,* 1968, *27,* 379–389.

Schmidt, H. The use of progesterone in the treatment of postpartum psychosis. *Journal of the American Medical Association,* 1943, *121,* 190–192.

Sears, R. R. Development of gender role. In F. A. Beach (Ed.), *Sex and behavior.* New York: Wiley, 1965.

Smalldon, J. L. A survey of mental illness associated with pregnancy and childbirth. *American Journal of Psychiatry,* 1940, *97,* 80–101.

Snow, C. Mothers' speech to children learning language. *Child Development,* 1972, *43,* 549–565.

Stevens, B. C. Psychoses associated with childbirth: A demographic survey since the development of community care. *Social Science and Medicine,* 1971, *5,* 527–543.

Strecker, E., & Ebaugh, F. Psychoses occurring during the puerperium. *Archives of Neurology and Psychiatry,* 1926, *15,* 239.

Thoman, E. B., Leiderman, P. H., & Olson, J. P. Neonate-mother interaction during breast-feeding. *Developmental Psychology,* 1972, *6,* 110–118.

Tucker, W. Progesterone treatment in postpartum schizo-affective reactions. *Journal of Neuropsychiatry,* 1962, *3,* 150–153.

Tyler, L. E. The antecedents of two varieties of vocational interests. *Genetic Psychology Monographs,* 1964, *70,* 177–227.

Vislie, H. Puerperal mental disorders. *Acta Psychiatrica Neurologica Scandinavica* (suppl.) no. 3, vol. 31, 1956.

Vuorenkoski, V., Wasz-Hockert, O., Koivisto, E., & Lind, J. The effect of cry stimulus on temperature of the lactating breast of primiparas. *Experientia,* 1969, *25,* 1286–1287.

Webb, A. P. Sex-role preferences and adjustment in early adolescents. *Child Development,* 1963, *34,* 609–618.

Wilson, J. E., Bargelow, P., Shipman, W. The prognosis of postpartum mental illness. *Comprehensive Psychiatry,* 1972, *13*(4), 305–316.

Wolff, P. The natural history of crying and other vocalizations in early infancy. In B. M. Foss (Ed.), *Determinants of infant behavior* (Vol. 4). London: Methuen, 1969.

Yalom, I. D., Lunde, D. T., Moos, R. H., & Hamburg, D. A. "Postpartum blues" syndrome: A description and related variables. *Archives of General Psychiatry,* Jan. 1968, *18,* 16–27.

Zilboorg, G. Post-partum schizophrenics. *Journal of Nervous and Mental Diseases,* 1928, *68,* 370–383. (a)

Zilboorg, G. Malignant psychoses related to childbirth. *American Journal of Obstetrics and Gynecology,* 1928, *15,* 145. (b)

Zilboorg, G. Depressive reactions related to parenthood. *American Journal of Psychiatry,* 1931, *10,* 926.

Zilboorg, G. The clinical issues of postpartum psychopathological reaction. *American Journal of Obstetrics and Gynecology,* 1957, *73,* 305–312.

10

Adult Life Cycles: Changing Roles and Changing Hormones

Malkah Notman
Harvard Medical School
Beth Israel Hospital, Boston

A psychiatrist working in the field of liaison between psychiatry and obstetrics and gynecology is constantly confronted by the interface between the biological and emotional, which creates the framework in which we live. This state is manifested as biological determinants of emotional responses or in reverse as physical expressions of emotional states. The mind–body dualism has been much discussed; current views emphasize the unitary quality of mind and body and the mutual influence of each upon the other (Nagler, 1967).

Nevertheless the human body and its state of maturity, level of function, and condition of health has a determining influence on development. Except for the adult stages described by Erikson, adult development has received little attention until the past few years. Recent work by Neugarten (1975), Levenson and Darrow (1974), Gould (1972), Barnett and Baruch (1978), and others has focused attention on the middle years as a time of development and change rather than a static period or one whose major dynamic is toward aging and death. This chapter will explore the impact of some of these changes on women's adult development.

There are some important differences in the adult development of men and women. Most work in psychology (Gould, 1972; Levenson & Darrow, 1974; Loevinger, 1976) has been based on a male model, in which development is seen as proceeding linearly through a series of stages. Barnett and Baruch (in press) point out that this is not as likely a pattern for women, for whom the resolution of issues of identity and autonomy may take place only partially in early adult years, are temporarily replaced by the developmental experiences of motherhood, and then returned to when children are grown. In addition Levenson, in his conceptualization of the life stages, observed that the role of work is of central importance in establishing a man's sense of self in the world. Although the importance of family relationships for the adult man is acknowledged, these relationships are not the organizing theme of his life. In his development separation from his family of origin is placed more centrally than the birth of his first child. While separation from her family of origin is also important for a woman, the birth of her first child is undoubtedly one of the most far-reaching developmental changes that can occur. Women's lives have been described as being closer to their bodies, that is, to biological variables and natural forces (Ortner, 1974; Parlee, Note 1). Their phases of life are marked by divisions that must take into account their reproductive functions. Thus biology, in particular fertility, may play a more central role in the phases of women's development.

In an attempt to attain a better understanding of the stages of midlife many authors have discussed the inappropriateness of developmental criteria based primarily on chronological age (Barnett & Baruch, 1978; Butter, 1963; McKinlay & Jefferys, 1974). Neugarten (1968), describing a sample studied over 10 years ago of "100 well-placed men and women," stresses characteristics of middle age relating to "a heightened sensitivity to one's position within a complex social environment" and the previous theme of "reassessment of the self" (p. 93). Chronological age was a less important marker than for young or old people. Women, but not men, in this group defined their age status "in terms of timing of events within the family cycle. For married women, middle age is closely tied to the launching of children into the adult world, and even unmarried career women often discuss middle age in terms of the family they might have had." The difference in the time perspective and the finite quality of time is a frequent theme of midlife (Levenson & Darrow, 1974; Feinbloom, Note 2). Awareness of the temporality of life is in fact an important characteristic of middle age. Thus for women this awareness is closely related to the issue of having children.

Giele (Note 3) stresses the importance of the social definition of a particular stage of life. She observes that as a country modernizes, for example, it tends to lengthen childhood and youth and refines stages into more precise time periods with special developmental tasks for separated age groups. She draws a parallel with the current elaboration of stages of adulthood and offers as explanation the extension of the life-span and changes in patterns of work and family life, with smaller families and a longer postparental period. All these help identify the middle years as a distinct phase of life.

Giele also emphasizes that the new concepts of adulthood involve a change in definitions of sex roles as well as age roles. "The very ideology of midlife development implies growth of the personality to encompass some characteristics that had stereotypically in the past been assigned to the opposite sex." Thus biology diminishes its influence on much of what had been held to be immutably biological characteristics. Individuals may also work out more flexible adaptations.

It is important to distinguish concerns about reproductive potential from the concept that fulfillment and self-realization for women is limited to childbearing or is dominated by children. In reality many women have not found their children or their role as mothers predominantly gratifying. They may be draining, stressful, and conflict producing. However the limited number of years during which pregnancy is possible makes the choice an issue that cannot be avoided. Developmental stages for women are thus produced by an interweaving of those experiences related to childbirth, parenting, and family development with those related to personal identity, separation and autonomy, and intellectual growth and relation to work.

However inappropriate it may be to consider women as defined by their biological destinies, there is nevertheless a clear reality to these concerns. For a woman life does take place within the limitations of a biological timetable that influences her options. Also important is her perception of these options. The pressure from prevailing medical and societal opinions about the optimal time for pregnancy may influence her decisions about work, her anxiety about establishing relationships, and her priorities and commitments toward both.

Although in adolescence both boys and girls reach sexual and reproductive maturity with dramatic endocrine and physical changes, the adult man does not experience any further biological phase in which his life options are as definitely changed as does the women at menopause. Nor does his body undergo as clear a change as provided for a woman by the cessation of the menses.

In another sense as well women are constantly confronted by their physical selves in their response to the hormonal changes of menstruation, pregnancy, childbirth, and menopause. The monthly variations in physical state, often with associated mood and behavior changes, have further emotional implications varying with the individual and her personal societal context. Although the hormonal and physical changes mark the major periods of her life, at the same time the characteristics and experiences of these periods may be less related to the actual biological changes than has been assumed.)

The decision to have or not to have children is central to childless women during the fertile period. The separation of the biological and social life cycles has meant that the time of childbearing corresponds less to the beginning and end of fertility than in the past. With the advent of reliable fertility control and the increasing availability of careers for women the birth rate has declined markedly. Women have been waiting to have children until their careers are established or have been contemplating not having children at all. As long as there is a fluid situation with the possibility of choice remaining, there is little possibility of a crisis arising. But at some point the fluidity of the choice decreases.

The importance of childbearing and menstruation to females suggests two periods during women's adult years that may have significant developmental implications: the 30-year-old midlife crisis and menopause. At 30 many women are trying to resolve their parenting and personal identity roles. For those with children this period may be a time to reconsider personal identity issues. For those without children the choice between remaining childless or having children may become central. Similar issues resurface at menopause. For purposes of this paper I will focus on the issues of resolving childbearing during the 30s and establishing a renewed personal identity at menopause.

AGE 30 CRISIS

The psychological differences between men and women as they enter midlife were ascribed by Freud (1933/1965) to differences in their natures. While making allowances for individual differences, Freud wrote, "a man of about thirty strikes us as a youthful, somewhat unformed individual, whom we expect to make powerful use of the possibilities for development opened up to him by analysis. A woman of the same age, however, often frightens us by her psychical rigidity and unchangeability." As Freud saw it a man's development in work and other areas of life was felt to be still open, whereas a woman at 30 was already entrenched in her role, usually having had a child, which closed off other possibilities for growth.

The 30th birthday is more crucial for women than for men because it symbolizes the loss of fertility as well as the loss of youth. The period of maximum fertility for women is from the early to mid-20s (Friedman, in press). Although there are individual differences, the age of 30 marks the start of an increasing irregularity of ovulatory cycles and a decrease in fertility. Improvement in general physical health has resulted in a diminished likelihood that an intercurrent illness or physical problem will affect women's physical health and thus their fertility. However, some gynecological risks such as endometriosis do increase with age, and there is greater possibility that an illness may develop as one grows older. Diminished fertility is thus dependent largely on these variables. Sontag (1972) has described the double standard of aging that penalizes women more than men. Since men's reproductive timetable is less rigid, the age of 30 does not have quite the same impact for them.

At about 30 many women feel that they will no longer have an uncomplicated choice about childbearing. Even those women who feel they are not interested in having children, become aware of the matter as a decision to be made as they approach 30. This may involve reworking an earlier decision, sometimes unconsciously. If they feel that the possibility of having children is remote because they are unmarried or because they are far from settling the underlying issues, there may be some depression and mourning for a part of themselves and for potential life plans that will never be realized. Other women feel anxiety that time is slipping away, and concerns that once seemed remote and postponable now become urgent. Some women come for help at this time for symptoms of depression or anxiety without awareness of the reasons. A birthday, the loss of a relationship, or a move in a career direction that is interpreted as an increased commitment to a childless state may bring on depression. A clinical example illustrates this point:

Ms. B, a young nurse, became depressed when given a responsible position in charge of a special ward, which she had previously wanted very much. She was angry at the physicians, who did not spend enough time there and who asked her to assume more responsibility and authority and involved her in the planning for the unit. This new position moved her up the career ladder, which she had also previously thought she wanted. She was puzzled about this reaction and sought consultation.

Recently she had ended a 5-year relationship with a man that had been close and warm, although not entirely satisfactory. He was clearly never going to marry her, and she had been disappointed and angry that the relationship was not getting anywhere, although at the same time she expressed ambivalence about marriage.

B's family background was a troubled one. Her relationships with her parents were difficult. Her father had been ill and disabled, always emotionally absent, and had died when she was in high school. Her mother, with whom she had often clashed, had been depressed and then alcoholic. One brother had dropped out of school; another younger brother was still at home. One sister had recurrent marital problems and was in the process of divorce. She herself had always been ambivalent about having children because of her own poor relationship with her mother and the constant turmoil in the family. She had been the family caretaker, an adaptation that had led her into nursing. There her intelligence and resourcefulness had resulted in her success and promotion. She had thought that was what she had wanted. Although she had felt convinced that she did not want children, with the disruption of a relationship she had not thought she really valued strongly, it seemed less likely that she would ever permit herself the opportunity to have children. At the time of her 30th birthday she found herself mourning the possibility that she felt she was losing. The responsibilities of the job seemed another step away from an alternate way of life.

Because of its implications for childbearing, reaching 30 often precipitates a reexamination of life plans among young professional women. Sometimes an "inadvertent" pregnancy results. After the disorganization and disruption of plans are settled, this may be accepted or even welcomed, since it may provide a resolution of the conflict that might have been difficult to arrive at deliberately. If the pregnancy produces more stress, the availability of abortion offers an opportunity to interrupt it and express the other side of her choice.

Childbearing at Midlife

A distinct trend toward older parenthood has been manifested in recent statistics (Prince, 1977), as well as a trend toward having a first child at an older age. The National Center for Health Statistics reported a 6% rise in first births during 1974 for women 25–39 at a time when first births on the average were increasing by only 1% and the national birth rate continued to decline.

Is there validity to the belief that a woman should have her first child by age 30? This view has been encouraged by physicians in the past, yet there is no objective reason to choose this point as the beginning of a higher risk period. Friedman (1978) states:

> While it is true that older women do not fare as well as their younger counterparts in pregnancy, the statistical data are too readily mis-interpreted; they refer to rates of complications in the population at large and cannot be applied thoughtlessly to the individual. Even cursory examination of such data quickly demonstrates that the older women who have difficulties in pregnancy are those with underlying or preexisting medical problems, particularly hypertension, kidney disorders or diabetes, all conditions which tend to make their appearance later in life. The healthy gravida who is free of such disorders need have no fear in this regard. Moreover, much of the remaining hazard of pregnancy in older women can be directly ascribed to frequently, closely-spaced pregnancies. This latter phenom-enon takes its toll without regard to age, although it stands to reason that women who have many babies are perforce older on average than those who do not; also they are more likely to manifest anemia, malnutrition and debilitation, thereby compounding whatever obstet-rical problem may arise. Whereas it is frequently stated that labor is longer and more difficult in older gravidas, careful study has failed to substantiate this. As to the fetus, the incidence of twinning increases with advancing age, especially with regard to development of double ovum or nonidentical twins, but the increase in frequency is relatively small.

Other Options at Midlife

The decision not to have a child as one enters the 30-year-old period can in a sense usher in middle age, since it constitutes a confrontation with options, choices, and awareness of the rest of one's life, thus reflecting important midlife issues. Even if a woman decides to have children under the pressure of this kind of examination of the future, the decision represents a process of anticipation and commitment different from the perspective of a young person who thinks of life as a long, possibly infinite, stretch into the future.

If a woman decides against parenting in her 30s, that decision is possibly not entirely established until some later time. However, increasing numbers of young women are making that decision permanent by seeking tubal ligation. The participants in a clinical study (Kaltreidar & Margolis, 1972) of young women who had made just such a decision were highly educated and gave well-articulated, internal psychological reasons for their decision. These women had histories of family disruption, fear of motherhood, and dislike of children. Short-term follow-ups of this group have indicated no regrets over their decision. Other short-term investigations (Campanella & Wolff, 1975; Kharaun & Vyas, 1975; Thompson & Band, 1968) have also found few regrets, although findings have been inconsistent across different clinical settings.

There are as yet no good long-term follow-up studies of women who have chosen sterilization at a young age. The data on the groups most vulnerable to menopausal depression suggest that those who decide against parenting work through the decision early and come to terms with it psychologically before their actual menopause. There are no data either concerning the impact of early sterilization on the emotional growth of women who thus close their options in at least one direction. Further research in this area should also include careful studies of the effects of hysterectomy and of the impact of surgical menopause.

MENOPAUSE

Turning to middle age we are brought to a consideration of the menopause, which is defined as the cessation of the menses for 1 year and thus is actually a retrospective diagnosis. A more appropriate term for this period is the *perimenopausal years.* During this time there is a gradual diminution of ovarian function and a gradual change in endocrine status (Perlmutter, 1978).

Menopause has been stereotyped as the dominant factor in the midlife phase for women. In clinical discussions of patients who present with depressive or other symptomatology, there is a tendency to focus automatically on the menstrual history as if it will explain the depression, irritability, or insomnia of the patient. Actually the relationships are neither inevitable nor clear (Bart & Grossman, 1976; McKinlay & Jefferys, 1974; Perlmutter, 1977, in press). Research in this area has been both sparse and poor. McKinlay and McKinlay (1973) in a review of the literature point to the lack of attention to menopause in the medical literature and are critical of the research that does exist. They cite methodological problems such as the failure to develop a consistent, objective definition of menopause and of the population at risk to menopausal symptoms. They offer further criticism of existing studies for relying on case histories, clinical impressions, or analyses of data from selected samples of women under the care of gynecologists or psychiatrists. The studies that are more reliable show that "psychosomatic and psychological complaints were not reported more frequently by so called 'menopausal' than by younger women" (McKinlay & McKinlay, 1973).

Although it is uterine function that is noted, it is actually the ovaries whose activity declines (Perlmutter, 1978). Normally levels of ovarian estrogens provide the signal for the hypothalamus, which in turn affects the pituitary production of gonadotropins, the follicle-stimulating hormone (FSH), and the luteinizing hormone (LH). This ovarian-hypothalamic-pituitary axis controls the menstrual cycles. When ovarian estrogen levels are high, the hypothalamic activity diminishes; when they are low, the hormones stimulate ovulation. As ovarian function fails, the hypothalamus continues to stimulate the pituitary to produce gonadotropins, which reach high levels. The ovary does not respond and there is a decrease in estrogen. Estradiol decreases by 90% or more and estrone by 70%. Some estrogen is produced from the steroids synthesized by the adrenal gland, which accounts for most of the estrogen that exists in the postmenopausal years. Some estrogen is produced by the stromal cells of the ovary.

What is the symptomatology directly attributable to the menopause? Here too endocrinological data and social-psychological data (Bart & Grossman, 1976; McKinlay & McKinlay, 1973; Neugarten, Wood, Kraines, & Loomis, 1968) indicate that many misconceptions have existed about the nature and extent of this. In a review of endocrinological data Perlmutter (1978) states, "There are multiple disorders that have been ascribed to the changing hormonal balance and are equated with menopause. In reality, not all the changes that are noted are due to hormonal imbalances, some are the consequences of aging and others have a basis in psychological factors and life patterns" (p. 323).

Vasomotor instability, manifested as hot flashes, flushes, episodes of perspiration, or attacks has been one of the consistent symptoms accompanying menopause. A hot flash or flush is a sensation of warmth pervading a part of the body and often accompanied by perspiration lasting a variable amount of time, usually several minutes. Perspiration may be severe, drenching the woman, and if it occurs at night contributes to the insomnia associated with menopause. This is present in a large number of women, up to 75% reporting some degree of symptoms. McKinlay and Jefferys (1974), in a review of symptoms of women aged 45-54 in the London area, found that hot flushes and night sweats are clearly associated with the onset of a natural menopause and that they occur in a majority of women. The other symptoms that were investigated, namely, headaches, dizzy spells, palpitations, sleeplessness, depressions, and weight increase, showed no direct relationship to the menopause but tended to occur together.

The length of time a woman experiences the hot flashes is also variable. They may originate several years before actual menopause and can be considered a sign of waning estrogen levels, reaching a peak at about the time of the actual cessation of the menses, and persisting as long as 5 years (Perlmutter, 1978; Reynolds, 1962).

The etiology of the hot flashes is unclear. Although there is general agreement that estrogen therapy will alleviate the symptom in most women, other disease processes in which estrogen levels are low (e.g., stress amenorrhea and anorexia nervosa) are not characterized by hot flashes (Perlmutter,

1978). Thus the etiology of the symptoms appears to be more complex than simple estrogen deficit. Psychological factors such as anger, anxiety, and excitement are considered important in precipitating flashes in susceptible women as are conditions giving rise to excess heat production or retention such as a warm environment, muscular work, or eating hot food (Reynolds, 1962). However, the symptoms may arise without any clear psychological or heat-stimulating mechanism.

Another group of changes that consistently accompany menopause are atrophic changes in skin, subcutaneous tissue, and mucosa. These occur as part of the aging process. The natural moisture of some tissues is lost, accentuating atrophic changes and resulting in dryness of skin and mucosa and altered vaginal secretions. This has some potential effect on susceptibility to infection and on sexual functioning, since vaginal lubrication may be slower to develop. This may create difficulties if the balance of sexual response is very sensitive for a couple. Local estrogen treatment can be highly effective if sexual problems result from changes in lubrication (Perlmutter, 1978). However, estrogen is absorbed via the vaginal mucosa and the same concerns that apply to treatment with oral estrogens may be relevant to this treatment as well.

Age at menopause varies from the late 30s to the middle or even late 50s. This variation supports the tendency to assign a variety of symptoms occurring during these years to a woman's menopausal status. In a study of age at menopause McKinlay, Jefferys, and Thompson (1972) found that "the median age at menopause in industrial societies now occurs at about 50 years of age and there is no firm evidence that this age has increased at least in the last century, nor any indication of any close relationships between the age at menopause and the age at menarche or socioeconomic status . . . There is some evidence that marital status and parity are related to the age at menopause, independently of each other" (p. 171).

Many other midlife symptoms have been attributed to menopause, and many menopausal symptoms have been attributed to estrogen deficiency or the hormonal changes. The range of symptomatology considered part of the menopausal syndrome has varied considerably. Insomnia, irritability, depression, diminished sexual interest, headaches, dizzy spells, and palpitations have been considered part of the menopausal period, but they do not occur consistently and in fact may be depressive symptoms or indications of anxiety (Barnett & Baruch, 1978; Perlmutter, 1978). Neugarten and her co-workers (Neugarten, 1975; Neugarten et al., 1968) studied 100 women aged 43-53, using menstrual histories as an index of menopausal status. They found "climacteric status to be unrelated to a wide array of personality measures." They also found "very few significant relationships between the severity of somatic and psychosomatic symptoms and these variables." Kraines (cited in Barnett & Baruch, 1978) found that menopausal status was not a contributing factor in self-evaluations of middle-aged women. She also found, as one might expect, that women who had previous low self-esteem and life satisfaction were likely to have difficulties with menopause. This leads to an understanding of menopause as one of the important experiences for women but best understood in the context of their entire lives and suggests that women's reactions to menopause may be consistent with their reactions to other reproductively based turning points.

In line with this interpretation, both Benedek (1950) and Deutsch (1945) concluded that a woman's reaction to menopause was similar to her reaction to puberty. Cross-cultural data (Barnett & Baruch, 1978) has provided support for this conclusion and has cast doubt on earlier notions that it is the woman with high-motherliness scores and those with heavy investment in childbearing and rearing who react most severely to menopause.

The current data is also contrary to the earlier ideas of Deutsch (1945) and Benedek (1950) that childless women would have the most intense reactions to menopause. Many of these women have had to come to terms with their childlessness earlier and have found other ways of organizing their lives. For some, childlessness reflects a choice based on ambivalence about motherhood, which is more readily expressed in contemporary society than was possible earlier and can be better implemented with effective contraception and abortion. For these women, then, menopause does not represent a crisis.

Reactions to menopause vary across social classes. Middle and upper-class women appear to find the cessation of childbearing more liberating than lower-class women, perhaps because more alternatives are open to them (Barnett & Baruch, 1978; Neugarten et al., 1968). In the relatively advantaged social class groups it is the younger women anticipating menopause who express the most concern. Postmenopausal women generally took a more positive view than the premenopausal women "with higher proportions agreeing that the menopause creates no major discontinuity in life and agreeing that except for the underlying biological changes, women have a relative degree of control over their symptoms and need not inevitably have difficulties." But, in general, menopausal status is not associated consistently with measurable anxiety in any group (McKinlay & Jefferys, 1974).

Alternative roles are also important determinants of menopausal reactions. Bart and Grossman (1976) stress that cultural factors play a role in determining the importance of menstruating, childrearing, and mothering in the self-esteem and status of women as well as determining their alternatives. A woman who has given all of her life to her children and then feels useless when they are gone is more likely to feel depressed.

Depression is one final symptom that has been linked with menopause. Depression does not appear as clearly associated with the endocrine changes as with the psychosocial variables that have been discussed. Weissman and Klerman (1977) review the evidence for the relationship of depression to female endocrine status and conclude that the pattern is inconsistent and, in particular, they believe that there is good statistical evidence that the menopause does not effect an increase in rates of depression. Other authors agree (Osofsky & Seidenberg, 1970; Winokur, 1973). They cite the lack of studies correlating clinical state with endocrine state that utilize modern endocrinological methods.

On the positive side there is a postmenopausal rise in energy and activity possibly deriving from the diminished time and energy needed in caring for children. This increase in psychic energy permits a developmental impetus for nonneurotic women whose lives offer them opportunities for growth (Benedek, 1950). Neugarten (1968, 1975) talks of the 40-60-year-old group recognizing that they are the powerful age group vis-à-vis other age groups. Reassessment of the self is the prevailing theme in her study. Whether women meet this challenge depends on many factors.

Family experiences are undoubtedly integral to the direction of the outcome. The midlife transition for men, often the husbands of menopausal women, brings new stresses. This period for men is often accompanied by sexual problems, sometimes leading to affairs, marital disruption, and the abandonment of women. Adolescent children may be sexually and aggressively provocative, challenging, or disappointing. Children leaving home for school or marriage change the family balance. This has been described generally as loss. However, some women view it as extension or expansion of parenting to include the wider interests and loci of their children. Far-flung needs of family members and expanded interests and activities lead to a different kind of parenting. Change and transition do cause stress and require new adaptations, sometimes accompanied by symptoms (Zilbach, Note 4).

Studies of marriage indicate that at least in some dimensions marital satisfaction increase as children leave the home. The empty nest syndrome does not appear to be universal. Some women experience this period as being restored to themselves and to their own development. Restored to themselves does not mean alone. Women depend much more on their relationships for their development—not only for their emotional comfort and security but also to express the acting-on-the-world component of their aggression (see Miller, 1976). The potential for autonomy, changes in relationships, and the development of their occupational skills, contacts, and self-image may start after childbearing is over.

At this time separation is an important developmental task, that is, the ability to separate from children as they move out of the family. These moves may revive earlier separations in the woman's own past and may be difficult if the earlier moves have remained unresolved (Zilbach, Note 4). Occasionally separation fails; children do not leave or they return (Foote, 1978). The woman may become depressed. The following two clinical examples illustrate the problems of the empty nest refilled.

Mrs. N is a 45-year-old married woman who would have been considered successful and fulfilled had her life been assessed 2 years before she sought help. She came from a poor southern town, with an extended family whose relationships were stable and members close. She met and married her husband there, then moved north in search of better opportunities for both of them. She had two daughters, 11 months apart, now in their mid-20s. When the children entered school she herself returned to school, went on to graduate training, and now works as a skilled accountant. Her husband also went into graduate school and is an engineer.

Although she has never liked New England and misses her family, her husband loves it and they have made an "adjustment." They moved to the suburbs, bought a large house, and from the very beginning raised their children to be achievers, which was very important to Mrs. N. The older daughter entered law school 2 years ago, the younger one was accepted to business school. Because they went to college locally, graduate school was the first departure from home.

After both children left, Mrs. N and her husband became closer. They started "dating" again. He was ordinarily not communicative and neither was she, but she made an effort to reach him and he responded. They resumed sexual relations and made plans to travel and remodel the house. Mrs. N was pleased with this but still uneasy about the new balance in the family. At the same time the girls began to have difficulty in school and became homesick. The eldest was at school on the West Coast. She gradually began to do less and less well academically. She was depressed, confused, and anxious about what might be going on at home. Her advisor suggested a year off and then another year. She had to return home until she felt able to study.

The younger daughter also began to have difficulty; she felt she did not really like business, dropped out of school, and shifted after a year to a primary teaching program and finally returned home, then became depressed. The dynamics of this development were not clear at first, but all experienced a sense of failure.

Relations between mother and daughters became tense. They argued about money, space, all household arrangements. She gave them a small allowance but felt they always seemed to want more than was available. She refused to let them return to their old rooms, stating that this would make them more dependent. Mrs. N became more and more depressed and anxious. She felt constantly intruded upon and frustrated not to be alone with her husband. She felt trapped; it seemed impossible to find a way out. She eventually asked the girls to sleep in the partially remodeled basement to establish some distance. The mutually hostile dependency seemed unresolvable. Her husband withdrew again. She finally sought a consultation.

Mrs. N described her depression as long standing, although previously less severe. She mentioned her sad feelings about her father, who had died of leukemia when she was in her early 20s. He had bought a farm and was a cattleman and became ill just when the farm began to make money. In spite of the geographical distance she had been close to him and had felt abandoned when he died. Her mother was living but had always been more remote. She had two sisters and two brothers. One brother, younger than she, was killed in an accident 10 years ago. Now she felt as if it were a recurrence of that earlier time; both deaths were reexperienced poignantly, and accompanying her anger at her daughters was a puzzling sense of loss.

She had never completely dealt with the earlier separations, namely the loss of her father and the death of her brother. She had attempted to become closer to her husband, perhaps to fulfill some of the longing for her father as well. Her daughters' leaving home for college was the fulfillment of her own ambitions and hopes for them. However, it was also experienced as abandonment, and she had subtly undermined their autonomous development. Their mutual attachment was strong; she encouraged their achievement yet all had difficulty with the separation. She felt vulnerable and deserted. When the dauthers returned she resented their presence yet could not let them go. Her husband's relative uninvolvement intensified the relationship among the women. Her own further growth was inhibited by the return of the children. Attempts to achieve some solution were frustrating, since the underlying problem was related to a lack of resolution of the original losses. None of the women were then able to develop without an eventually undermining conflict until further therapeutic work.

Mrs. N's dilemma seemed precipitated by the children's return, by the refilling of the menopausal empty nest. It could also have been labeled a depression, since she was experiencing her menopause. As with many midlife issues the return of her children actually confronted her with her unresolved past.

The second clinical example also illustrates a depression accompanying return of children. Mrs. R was the wife of a retired diplomat, who had taken a teaching post in the United States after many years of living abroad. She was almost 50 at that time. Her four children were born in various Asian countries. In the years abroad she functioned well in the American diplomatic and professional communities, which gave her status and support. She taught, she became interested in art, wrote, and even published.

Before leaving the last post she discovered her husband had had an affair some years ago and had contemplated another. A confrontation led to a greater communication and honesty and better sexual relations between them but also a residue of anger. She wanted to find some way of feeling less dependent on him. She decided to enter graduate school and was planning to start the following fall. Her own family had been American but had lived abroad in Asia. Her father had also been a government employee, and they lived in the East until she was an adolescent, when they returned to the United States because of World War II. She was educated in the U.S., then married a man whose work would take him abroad to a life that she realized she found comfortable and familiar. She had not really questioned her relative dependency or the limitations created by the social group in which she moved until her husband's affair.

By the time of their return to the United States her youngest child was in high school, the others in college. The pressures of finding a house, getting settled, then arranging for school took up much of her time and energy at first. Then in the summer before school began her three older children returned from college. One had graduated but had no clear plans and was groping for direction; a second found the family relocation confusing, decided to spend some time at home, and took a year out of college. The third one had been unhappy about his choice of school and was exploring a transfer. When it seemed that they would all remain the following year, she became depressed. She missed the social supports, servants, and automatic status of their life abroad and was angry with her husband for the rupture of their previous lifestyle, with its reminder of her happy childhood in a similar place. But beyond this was a conflict between the independence that she felt she wanted and her need to be an old-style mother, available to her children, in a way that was perhaps not appropriate to their present ages. The children were also working at restoring some aspects of the family life and coming to terms with life in the U.S. However, for Mrs. R some of her previous sense of security was no longer available, and her confidence in her husband and the network of social supports and household help were changed. She also felt unable to respond to demands that she perceived and perhaps projected. Thus she felt inadequate, guilty, and anxious.

The way toward the independence that Mrs. R wanted is not unconflicted for most women. Early socialization against assertiveness and current conflicts about aggression make for difficulties in new career adaptations where this behavior may be necessary (Nadelson, Notman, & Bennet, 1978). The return of children or the emergence of other new family demands may serve to prevent a woman from attempting to pursue new career goals, either because of a defensive withdrawal from an anxiety-producing new situation or because her conflict about roles prevents her from finding reasonable creative solutions to demands to which she previously responded alone.

These vignettes suggest the complexity of the issues. Had either of these women presented themselves to a gynecologist with less awareness of the psychological issues, their depression might have been diagnosed as related to their menopausal status and treated with estrogen.

Further research is needed about development in women in a variety of life circumstances, with fewer assumptions about the phases that they are experiencing, but at the same time with due attention to the implications of their reproductive life stage and its interplay with the other social factors operating in each individual woman's life space.

REFERENCE NOTES

1. Parlee, M. *Psychological aspects of menstruation, childbirth, and menopause: An overview with suggestions for further research.* Paper presented at conference on New Directions for Research on Women, Madison, Wisconsin, 1975.
2. Feinbloom, D. *The physician at mid-career*, AOA Lecture, Baylor Medical School, March 1976.
3. Giele, J. *Adulthood as transcendence of age and sex.* Paper prepared for the Conference on Love and Work in Adulthood, sponsored by the American Academy of Arts and Sciences, Stanford, California, May 6–7, 1977.
4. Zilbach, J. *Some family developmental considerations of midlife.* Paper presented at the American Psychiatric Association panel, "New Look at the Midlife Years," May 1975.

REFERENCES

Barnett, R., & Baruch, G. Women in the middle years: A critique of research and theory. *Psychology of Women Quarterly*, 1978, *3*(2).

Bart, P., & Grossman, M. Menopause. *Women and Health*, 1976, *1*, (3).

Benedek, T. Climacterium: A developmental phase. *Psychoanalytic Quarterly*, 1950, *19*(1), 1–27.

Butler, R. The facade of chronological age. *American Journal of Psychiatry*, 1963, *119*(8).

Campanella, R., & Wolff, J. R. Emotional reaction to sterilization. *Obstetrics and Gynecology*, 1975, *45*, 331–334.

Deutsch, H. *Psychology of women* (Vol. 2). New York: Grune & Stratton, 1945.

Foote, A. Kids who won't leave home. *The Atlantic*, March, 1978, p. 118.

Friedman, E. Pregnancy. In M. Notman & C. Nadelson (Eds.). *The woman as a patient.* New York: Plenum, 1978.

Freud, S. [*New introductory lectures in psychoanalysis*] (J. Strachey, Ed. and trans.). New York: Norton, 1965. (Originally published, 1933.)

Gould, R. The phases of adult life: A study in developmental psychology. *American Journal of Psychiatry*, 1972, *129*(5).

Kaltreider, N., & Margolis, A. Childless by choice: A clinical study. *American Journal of Psychiatry*, 1972, *134*(2).

Kharaun, A. B., & Vyas, A. A. Psychological complications in women undergoing voluntary sterilization by salpingectomy. *British Journal of Psychiatry*, 1975, *127*, 67–69.

Levenson, D., Darrow, C., Levenson, M., & McKee, B. The psychosocial development of men in early adulthood and the mid-life transition. In D. F. Rides, A. Thomas, & M. Rolf (Eds.), *Research in psychopathology* (Vol. 3). University of Minnesota Press, 1974.

Loevinger, J. *Ego development.* San Francisco: Jossey-Bass, 1976.

McKinlay, S., & Jefferys, M. The menopausal syndrome. *British Journal of Preventive and Social Medicine*, 1974, *28*(2).

McKinlay, S., Jefferys, M., & Thompson, B. An investigation of the age at menopause. *Journal of Biosocial Science*, 1972, *4*, 161–173.

McKinlay, S., & McKinlay, J. Selected studies on the menopause. *Journal of Biosocial Science*, 1973, *5*, 533–555. (Annotated bibliography).

Miller, J. *Towards a new psychology of women.* Boston: Beacon, 1976.

Nadelson, C., Notman, M., & Bennet, M. Success or failure: Therapeutic considerations. *American Journal of Psychiatry*, 1978, *135*, 1092–1097.

Nagler, S. The mind-body problem. In A. Friedman & H. Kaplan (Eds.), *The comprehensive textbook of psychiatry.* Baltimore: Williams & Wilkins, 1967.

Neugarten, B. The awareness of middle age. In B. Neugarten (Ed.), *Middle age and aging.* Chicago: University of Chicago Press, 1968.

Neugarten, B. Adult personality: Towards a psychology of the life cycle. In W. Sze (Ed.), *Human life cycle.* New York: Aronson, 1975.

Neugarten, B., Wood, V., Kraines, R., & Loomis, B. Women's attitudes toward menopause. In B. Neugarten (Ed.), *Middle age and aging.* Chicago: The University of Chicago Press, 1968.

Ortner, S. Is female to male as nature is to culture? In M. Rosaldo & L. Lamphere (Eds.), *Women, culture and society.* Stanford, Calif.: Stanford University Press, 1974.

Osofsky, H. J., & Seidenberg, R. Is female menopausal depression inevitable? *Obstetrics and Gynecology,* 1970, 611–615.

Perlmutter, J. *Temporary symptoms and permanent changes in the menopause.* L. Rose (Ed.). New York: Hawthorn Books, 1977.

Perlmutter, J. The menopause: A gynecologist's view. In M. Notman & C. Nadelson (Eds.), *The woman as a patient.* New York: Plenum Press, 1978.

Prince, J. *You're not too old to have a baby.* New York: Farrar, Straus, 1977, p. 6.

Reynolds, S. Physiological and psychogenic factors in the menopausal flush syndrome. In W. Kroger, (Ed.). *Psychosomatic obstetrics, gynecology, and endocrinology.* Springfield, Ill.: Charles C Thomas, 1962.

Rossi, A. Transition to parenthood. *Journal of Marriage and the Family,* 1968, *38*(1).

Sontag, S. The double standard of aging. *Saturday Review,* September 23, 1972, p. 29.

Thompson, B., & Baud, D. Follow-up of 186 sterilized women. *Lancet,* 1968, *I*, 1023–1027.

Weissman, M., & Klerman, G. Sex differences and the epidemiology of depression. *Archives of General Psychiatry,* 1977, *34*, 98–111.

Winokur, G. Depression in the menopause. *American Journal of Psychiatry,* 1973, *130*(1), 92.

Zilbach, J. Family development. In J. Marmor (Ed.), *Modern psychoanalysis.* New York: Basic Books, 1968.

IV

CYCLICITY
AND MENSTRUATION

11

Research on Menstrual-related Psychological Changes: Alternative Perspectives

Diane N. Ruble
Princeton University

Jeanne Brooks-Gunn
Educational Testing Service
Princeton, New Jersey

Anne Clarke
Princeton University

The menstrual cycle, although experienced by almost all women every month for over half of their lives, is not a well-understood phenomenon and has been subject to much misconception, myth, and taboo. As recently as 1970 a *New York Times* article quoted a physician and member of the Democratic Party Committee on National Priorities as saying, with reference to menstruation, "If you had an investment in a bank ... you wouldn't want the president of your bank making a loan under these raging hormonal influences at that particular period" ("Role of Women," 1970, p. 35). Some scientists hold similar views as illustrated by descriptions of cycle changes as "an inherent disability" (Abramson & Torghele, 1961, p. 233) and as "a curse" (Janowsky, Gorney, & Kelley, 1966, p. 242). These statements are representative of the negative views that many people, scientists and lay persons alike, hold concerning the menstrual cycle (Parlee, 1974).

Negative evaluations of menstruation have been made since the beginning of Western civilization (see Hillman, 1972). As late as 1951 it was written that "in various parts of Europe, it is still believed that if a woman in her courses enters a brewery, the beer will turn sour; if she touches beer, wine, vinegar or milk, it will go bad; if she makes jam, it will not keep ... " (Frazer, 1951,

Preparation of the manuscript and the research were supported by grants SOC-76 02137 and SOC-76 02179 from the National Science Foundation. We thank R. L. Doty and B. L. Jacobs for helpful comments on an earlier draft.

cited in Stephens, 1961, p. 393). Many euphemisms about menstruation still used today also imply a negative stereotype (Ernster, 1975).

Not only is the societal view of menstruation quite negative but it is also popularly believed that we know all the answers about menstrual-related symptoms, their causes, and cures. For example, the September 1976 issue of *Cosmopolitan* featured an article entitled "Premenstrual Tension." Its subheading read: "Are menstrual jitters and *pain* the blight of unliberated *hypochondriacs* or the result of real (hormonal!) changes? Herewith, the truth about monthly 'indisposition' plus coping advice. . . . " The article, under the guise of truth, goes on to list 11 symptoms that characterize the premenstrual syndrome, describes the hormone bases of such discomfort, and discusses ways to alleviate the problems (e.g., a diuretic and no-salt diet during the premenstrual week to get rid of excess water plus tranquilizers to calm nerves). In a similar vein one physician wrote in a popular article, "your brain becomes waterlogged too; theoretically, the brain swelling may cause nervousness, anxiety and depression" (Nolen, 1973, p. 12). The cultural view of menstruation is also reflected in magazine ads, which suggest that women must take medication to keep them normal.

In this chapter we argue that neither the nature of menstrual symptomatology nor its hormonal basis have yet attained the status of truth or scientific fact implied in popular writings. We are not denying that menstrual-related pain, for example, may exist for some women or that some symptoms may have a physiological basis. However, the nature of the evidence is such that the physiological links are still hypothetical and the extent of the premenstrual syndrome is still an open question. In the sections that follow we examine menstrual-cycle research from various perspectives, specifically focusing on the physiological and sociocultural bases of psychological changes and menstrual symptomatology. First, a brief description of the menstrual cycle and its hormonal correlates is presented. Second, the physiological basis of related psychological changes is evaluated. Finally the merits of considering such changes from a sociocultural perspective is considered. Some of our own research on menstrual-related expectations and attitudes is presented as evidence for the usefulness of a sociocultural approach.

MENSTRUAL CYCLE AND ITS CORRELATES

Menstrual Physiology

Menstruation, the sloughing off of nutrients and blood from the wall of the uterus, is only one event in a complex cycle that occurs, on an average, every 28-30 days in mature women. The cycle may be divided into four phases: (1) follicular, (2) luteal, (3) premenstrual, and (4) menstrual. In the preovulatory or follicular phase of the cycle the pituitary gland secretes the follicle-stimulating hormone (FSH), which stimulates several ovarian follicles (the sacs that contain the ova or egg) to increase in size. Soon after, the pituitary begins to produce luteinizing hormone (LH), and the follicles begin to secrete estrogen, which in turn acts to inhibit FSH. The end of the follicular phase is marked by ovulation, the release of the egg from the follicle into the fallopian tubes, where it begins its journey to the uterus. The collapsed follicle, called the corpus luteum, then begins to produce progesterone, beginning the postovulatory or luteal phase. If the ovum is not fertilized, the corpus luteum begins functional degeneration within about 8-10 days after ovulation, beginning the premenstrual phase. Menstrual flow appears to be triggered by the withdrawal of progesterone and, to a lesser extent, estrogen, which is produced in reduced amounts by the corpus luteum.

In brief the cycle is schematized as a follicular phase of 10-14 days, ovulation, luteal phase of about 8-10 days, a premenstrual phase of 4-6 days, and a menstrual phase of 3-7 days, which overlaps somewhat with the follicular phase (Segal, 1974; Turner & Bagnara, 1971). The most notable aspect for the purposes of this chapter is that estrogen peaks at ovulation, dips, and then rises again in the middle of the luteal phase, while progesterone rises only once, during the second half of the cycle. In addition levels of both hormones are low during the immediate premenstrual and menstrual phases.

This short description of the menstrual cycle is necessarily oversimplified. The interactions of the ovarian and pituitary hormones are extremely complex, and a great deal of controversy about these interactions exists in the neuroendocrinological literature. Only in the past decade have relatively accurate techniques for measuring hormone levels in the blood been developed. In the past they have been estimated from levels of metabolites in the urine using a wide variety of criteria. Furthermore the steroid hormones, progesterones, estrogens, and androgens, are chemically very similar, and all are synthesized by both men and women (Turner & Bagnara, 1971).

The separation of the menstrual cycle into discrete phases of specific lengths (± 2 days), although generally accepted, is also beginning to be questioned. For example, ovulation occurs in normal women anywhere from the 4th to the 26th day of the cycle and has been observed to occur every day of the cycle, including during menses. Also, the timing of ovulation seems to vary a great deal in individual women from month to month, as do hormone levels in a given phase and the lengths of the various phases (Parsons & Sommers, 1962; Snow , 1977). In addition numerous methods of determining cycle phase have been used, making comparisons difficult. Although hormonal assays are recognized as the most accurate way of determining cycle phase, basal body temperature, vaginal cytology, menstrual day (counting forward from the onset of menses), and reversed-cycle day (counting backward from the onset of menses) are all used. (James, 1971; Dan, Note 1)

Psychological Correlates of the Cycle

A number of investigations have examined the relationship between a woman's phase of cycle and various indices of behavioral and emotional change. In accord with popular beliefs described above many have found a relatively high incidence of negative symptoms and behaviors (e.g., irritability, headache, water retention, and accidents) to be associated with the menstrual and premenstrual phases and a relatively low incidence of negative symptoms and/or high incidence of positive effects (e.g., self-esteem) to be associated with midcycle. These studies have been the subject of several recent reviews and critiques (Paige, 1973a; Parlee, 1973) and are considered elsewhere in this volume; thus they will not be summarized here. However, it is worth noting that this kind of correlational research is continuing at a rapid pace. Studies within the last few years have reported cyclic changes in behaviors such as volunteering to be a subject in a study (Doty & Silverthorne, 1975), magnitude of figural aftereffects (Satinder & Mastronardi, 1974), decision to seek psychological services (Surrey, Scott, & Phillips, 1975), and a mother's response to illness in her child (Tuck, 1975). Affective changes (anxiety, depression, mood shifts) have also been observed in recent studies (Golub, 1976; May, 1976; Patkai, Johannson, & Post, 1974).

The question of how to interpret the above findings is often not explicitly considered. Because the research is correlational, both the directionality of cause and the possibility of other causal variables should be considered. Instead, however, many investigators appear to assume that the parallel between cyclic hormone changes and apparent cyclic psychological changes indicates that a physiological mechanism must be the causal agent. Thus it is worth considering the nature of the evidence concerning a physiological theory of menstrual distress and possible alternative interpretations of the data.

PHYSIOLOGICAL INTERPRETATIONS

One of the most striking aspects of menstrual cycle research is the proliferation of theories concerning physiological mechanisms that may underlie cyclic changes. Theories about premenstrual changes alone include increased monoamine oxidase (MAO) activity caused by decreased estrogen and progesterone levels during the premenstruum (Grant & Pryse-Davies, 1968), influence of progesterone on serotonin metabolism (Ladisich, 1977), upset of adrenal hormones because of low progesterone (Dalton, 1964, 1969), allergic insensitivity to estrogen or progesterone, sodium and water retention caused by high antidiuretic hormone, or increased permeability of the capillaries to protein (Tonks, 1968). Several other theories are mentioned in reviews of the physiological changes of menstruation (Smith, 1975; Southam & Gonzaga, 1965).

Investigations of Physiological Theories

A number of studies have provided correlational support for one or more of these theories. For example, Janowsky, Berens, and Davis (1973) found moderately high correlations among self-reports of negative affect, weight, and potassium–sodium ratios, with increases in all variables occurring during the luteal and premenstrual phases of the cycle. In another study, plasma dopamine beta-hydroxylase (DBH), an enzyme involved in chemical neuro-transmission, was shown to parallel the mood "surgency" over the cycle (Lamprecht, Matta, Little, & Zahn, 1974). However, several other recent studies have failed to find relationships between such physiological measures and indices of menstrual-related symptoms (Belmaker, Murphy, Wyatt, & Loriaux, 1974; Gilmer, Robinson, & Nies, 1971; Little & Zahn, 1974; Patkai et al., 1974).

The above studies and much of the recent research on physiological mechanisms emphasize the likely role of central nervous system (CNS) neurotransmitters in the etiology of cyclic changes. It is thus worth consider-ing briefly some of the difficulties involved in demonstrating a causal brain–behavior relationship of this sort. In an oversimplified form the hypoth-esis is that alterations in levels of estrogen and progesterone affect levels of *biogenic amines* (a general term referring in this case to neurotransmitters such as norepinephrine or dopamine) or related enzymes, which in turn cause menstrual-related symptoms. The neurotransmitters thought to be involved are concentrated in areas of the brain that mediate functions (such as arousal and appetite) that are impaired in affective disorders (Akiskal & McKinney, 1973). These aminergic hypotheses represent extensions of various theories of a physiological basis of affective disorders, such as depression (e.g., Akiskal & McKinney, 1973; Baldessarini, 1975; Bernard, 1975; Prange, Lipton, Nemer-off, & Wilson, 1977; Schildkraut, 1965). The possible role of biogenic amines and enzymes such as MAO in such disorders was initially inferred from pharmacological evidence linking, for example, administrations of reserpine (a known depletor of biogenic amines) to the onset of depression.

A large number of assumptions must be validated before behavior may be linked to brain processes. In order to illustrate the complexities involved we will briefly list some of the methodological and interpretive difficulties in these experiments. One primary problem relates to the significance of various measures of neurotransmitters. Only a small part of the total transmitter available is needed for adequate function, with the rest in storage pools (Baldessarini, 1975). Thus changes in brain amine levels, ratios, or even turnover rates may have little functional relationship to the behavior studied (Bernard, 1975). Furthermore it is not clear to what extent measures taken in the periphery (e.g., plasma or blood platelet levels) reflect levels of activities in the CNS. As an example of this problem, human platelet and brain MAOs are quite dissimilar with respect to some functions, such as oxidation of dopamine (Shaskan & Becker, 1975).

Second, it is difficult to demonstrate the assumed connection between the sex hormones estrogen and progesterone and the chemical under investigation. Although cyclic fluctuations have been observed in relevant enzyme levels, such as MAO and DBH (Belmaker et al., 1974; Lamprecht et al., 1974; Southgate, Grant, Pollard, Pryse-Davies, & Sandler, 1968), the direction of such changes is not always consistent across studies. In addition, since platelet life-span is about 10 days, studies employing platelet measures cannot easily correlate sex hormone levels with MAO or DBH changes (Belmaker et al., 1974; Redmond, Murphy, Baulu, Ziegler, & Lake, 1975).

The inconsistent findings, technical difficulties, and untested assumptions have led many reviewers of these theories to conclude their evaluations with considerable skepticism (Akiskal & McKinney, 1973; Baldessarini, 1975; Bernard, 1975; Parlee, 1973). The current status of this literature is aptly represented in the title of a recent National Institute of Drug Abuse monograph, "Aminergic Hypotheses of Behavior: Reality or Cliché?" (Bernard, 1975).

Interaction of Physiological and Psychological Changes

Even if psychological stress and physiological mechanisms can be clearly linked, the direction of the relationship still needs to be specified. Until recently physiological changes were assumed to result in behavioral changes, not the reverse. However, the relationship between physiology and behavior is probably reciprocal. A considerable amount of research has shown that behavioral states and changes, especially stress-related ones, can lead to physiological changes. First, either stress or a high level of aggressive activity can affect hormone levels (Gibbons, 1968; Levi, 1968; Rose, Bernstein, & Gordon, 1975), which in turn can have a major impact on other aspects of physiological functioning (Levine, 1971). For example, Gibbons (1968) found that an increase in adrenal activity frequently occurs when an individual is placed in either a disturbing or a novel situation. Second, physical symptoms and disease (such as ulcers and heart disease) have been shown to be related to stress-related factors or certain patterns of social behavior (e.g., Jenkins, 1971; Wolff, 1968).

The application of these results to the work on menstrual-related changes makes purely physiological interpretations difficult to accept. Thus a socially conditioned stressful reaction to the event of menstruation may affect behavior and physiology. For example, if menstruation is experienced as a stressful event, physical symptomatology may increase. There are several lines of indirect evidence to support this hypothesis. First, some physical symptoms associated with stress—headaches, cramps, and so forth—are very similar to the symptoms purportedly associated with menstruation, indicating that the premenstrual syndrome may, in part, reflect a psychological stress reaction to the approach or onset of bleeding. In addition there is some evidence of the direct influence of social environmental factors on the physiology of menstruation as seen in a stress-related delay of onset or amenorrhea (Paige, 1973a; Sherman, 1971).

Second, the results of a recent study (Paige, 1971) suggest that some aspects of menstrual-related distress, such as anxiety, may be a socially mediated response to the menstrual flow (and the inconvenience and possible embarrassment associated with it) rather than to underlying biochemical changes. Paige (1971) notes that menstrual flow is at best inconvenient and that having to be concerned with various hygienic tasks and the possibility of embarrassment could themselves result in irritability and anxiety. In addition she argues that such inconvenience and embarrassment would likely increase with intensity of menstrual flow. Accordingly Paige tested the hypothesis that menstrual-related distress is a socially mediated response to the menstrual flow rather than to underlying biochemical changes. She compared the levels of anxiety and hostility (determined from an analysis of unstructured verbal material) at four times during a cycle in women using two types of oral contraceptives and women not taking contraceptives. The results suggested that cyclic fluctuations in anxiety are related to the intensity of menstrual flow independent of the hormone fluctuations that would be predicted from the contraceptive group.

In short it is likely that behavior and physiology interact in a complex fashion, making interpretation of menstrual-related changes difficult. In order to explore the relationship adequately, more work linking behavioral states, physiology, and social factors such as stress and anxiety associated with the menstrual cycle is needed.

SOCIOCULTURAL VIEW OF MENSTRUATION

Measurement of Menstrual Symptomatology

All these difficulties (hormone measurement, interaction among systems, interpretation, etc.) serve to point out that many of the physiological mechanisms associated with menstruation are only very generally understood. A more basic problem is specifying and defining the phenomena that these theories are presumably explaining. That is, the nature and extent of menstrual-related changes have not yet been made clear. Although a vast number of studies purport to show cyclic fluctuations in physical discomfort, emotions, and behaviors, much of this work has methodological problems that make interpretation and generalization difficult (see reviews by Parlee, 1973, and Sherif, Chapter 12).

One major difficulty in clarifying the nature of the syndrome is the frequent failure to find cross-measure consistency. For example, a woman's daily self-reports often do not relate to her retrospective self-reports

(McCance, Luff, & Widdowson, 1937; May, 1976). In addition, according to a recent review (Sommer, 1973), most objective measures fail to show an impairment in performance associated with the menstrual cycle, even though many women believe that their performances are affected by their cycles. This apparent inconsistency reflects the difference between studies employing objective measures and studies employing various methods of self-report. The latter group shows far more significant findings suggesting that social-psychological factors may be important in interpreting cyclic fluctuations observed in this way. That is, women's self-reports of their somatic and psychological symptoms are susceptible to various kinds of biases. Since self-report measures provide the major data base for statements of the prevalence and extent of cyclic fluctuations (Moos, 1969b; Parlee, 1973), it is important to question the meaning of findings gathered in this way.

The most basic problem in studies employing self-report is that responses may simply reflect cultural beliefs concerning the phenomenon studied. Such self-report biases are particularly likely to occur when women are aware that the study is concerned with menstrual-related changes. For example, the woman may consciously or unconsciously try to respond in accordance with the researcher's hypotheses. In addition if a woman believes that women normally experience a variety of premenstrual symptoms, she may report such symptoms in part to make herself appear normal.

The meaning of self-report data may be questioned even if the woman is not aware of the nature of the study, since she is aware of her own cycle phase. For example, a woman may discount cramps or irritability that do not correspond to the premenstrual or menstrual phases and thus not report them. In addition she may perceive her own physical and psychological state more negatively when she is menstruating or believes she is premenstrual, and this negative self-perception may in turn affect responses of various sorts. Findings of a recent study are consistent with this idea (Beaumont, Richards, & Gelder, 1975). Self-reports of symptom changes by normally menstruating women were compared with those of women who had undergone simple hysterectomies with conservation of the ovaries (thus preserving a normal cyclical hormonal pattern but abolishing menstruation). The normal women's reports showed significant cyclic fluctuations with more negative affect and pain occurring menstrually and premenstrually than intermenstrually, while those of the hysterectomized women did not. Thus as the authors suggest, self-reported symptomatology may be highly dependent on women's awareness of their cycle phase (which allows for an association between symptoms and cycle phase). These findings, however, should be interpreted with caution, since the number of hysterectomized women was small ($n = 7$).

The biases associated with self-reports are further demonstrated in one of our recent studies (Ruble, 1977). This study tested the hypothesis that the reported relationship between cycle phase and mood is to some extent independent of underlying physiological states. Briefly, 44 undergraduate women were told that it was possible through new scientific techniques to predict the expected date of menstruation and that their menstrual period was due either in a week to 10 days or immediately. That is, the subjects were told that they were participating in contraception-related research in which a new technique for predicting the expected date of menstruation from an electroencephalogram (EEG) was being surveyed on young women, having been successfully tested with older women. Brief menstrual histories were obtained, and each subject was scheduled to be tested on the 6th or 7th day (as estimated from her menstrual history) before her next menses.

The research was conducted in the university infirmary in two connecting rooms. One experimenter took the temperature and blood pressure of the subject and explained the EEG procedure. She then attached the electrodes to the head and forehead of the subject with beautician's tape and proceeded to run the EEG machine. (However, the polygraph machine was not turned on and no EEG was actually taken.) She then informed the subject, according to the experimental group to which the subject had been randomly assigned, that (1) she was premenstrual and her period was due in 1 or 2 days (premenstrual group); or (2) she was intermenstrual and her period was not expected for a week to 10 days (intermenstrual group); or (3) she was given no information at all about the expected date of menstruation (control group). In other words some women believed they were premenstrual and some believed they were intermenstrual, though actually they were all in the 21st or 22nd day of their cycles. They were asked to rate by a second experimenter the extent to which they had experienced a set of presumably menstruation-related symptoms. It was predicted that premenstrual women would score higher on stereotypically premenstrual symptoms and moods than either intermenstrual women or women given no information. Since the women were assigned to premenstrual and intermenstrual groups on a random basis, such differences were unlikely to result from hormone levels or other physiological differences between the groups.

The results showed that mean ratings for all variables were higher for premenstrual than for intermenstrual groups and attained significance for three of the four variables that had shown the strongest associations with the premenstrual phase in earlier research: water retention, pain, and change in eating habits. Thus regardless of their actual phase of cycle or underlying physiological state women who believed that they were premenstrual reported a higher level of premenstrual symptoms than women who believed that they were intermenstrual. These data suggest a need to reexamine conclusions regarding women's experience of premenstruation based on self-report studies and regarding physiological interpretations of previous findings. (see Ruble & Brooks-Gunn, in press, for a more extensive review of self-report studies.)

Menstrual-related Expectations and Beliefs

The above observations question the extent to which women's self-reports represent in an externally valid way their experiences associated with the menstrual cycle. This conclusion, however, should not lead us to dismiss the importance of the belief system revealed on self-report scales as a psychological phenomenon itself worthy of study. Such beliefs may affect women's behaviors and self-evaluations. According to research and theory on social expectations, people tend to act in ways that conform to their own and other's expectations (Rosenthal & Jacobson, 1968). If applied to the menstrual cycle, these findings suggest that behavioral and affective changes associated with the menstrual cycle may be significantly affected by menstrual-related expectations in the same way that students' behavior is influenced by their own and their teachers' expectations. That is, the belief that women are moody, irritable, and tired premenstrually not only makes more likely the possibility that an individual woman will act in these ways but also probably affects her self-esteem, feelings of competency, and interactions with others. For example, if a woman believes her stamina in sports is inevitably affected negatively according to the phase of her cycle, then she may not participate or may not try as hard when she is menstrual or premenstrual. Such actions may in turn generate feelings of incompetency and frustration.

Although the effect of social expectations on menstrual-related behavior changes has not been directly tested, a few lines of research lend indirect support to this hypothesis. Paige (1973b) describes several social factors that seem to be related to menstrual distress. In a questionnaire study she related the degree of reported distress to religious affiliation, general illness behavior, social behavior associated with menstruation (e.g., sex taboo), and various socialization factors. One of the most interesting findings is that the relationship between reported distress and social factors varied across religious groups. Among women indicating a religious preference Jewish women who found coitus during menstruation embarrassing and unpleasant and attended to social and hygienic rituals during menstruation were those most likely to experience menstrual distress. Among Catholics women who had the most menstrual problems were those who had the most traditional views of femininity (e.g., beliefs that a woman's place is in the home). These findings are certainly inconsistent with hormonal explanations of menstrual distress (it is unlikely that traditional Jews and Catholics are hormonally different from less traditional Jews and Catholics), and it also suggests that an extremely complex set of sociocultural variables influences a woman's psychological response to her body.

Labeling and attribution processes may also affect the perceived link between mood states and the menstrual cycle. In a now classic study Schachter and Singer (1962) demonstrated that an individual will label physiological arousal for which there is no explanation in terms of the cognitions available. This principle may be applied to menstrual cycles in the following way. If a woman views her cycle as having particular effects on her moods, she may label any feeling state according to where she thinks she is in her cycle. That is, since women and men "know" that premenstrual women are often bitchy and irritable, when a woman acts in a negative way, she or others are likely to label this reaction as premenstrual tension and ignore other factors that may be influencing her mood. Support for this hypothesis is provided by a recent questionnaire study (Koeske & Koeske, 1975) in which college men and women were found to attribute negative moods primarily to premenstruation even when the environment was described as unpleasant. As the investigators point out, the acceptance of such a pattern might adversely affect women's self-esteem, predispose them to guilt, anxiety, and depression, and thus make action to alter upsetting situations more unlikely. Thus if a woman believes she is upset entirely because of her menstrual cycle, she will be less likely to take steps to change any external factors that may be contributing to her emotional state (Koeske & Koeske, 1975).

In our own research we have begun to assess the range of expectations and attitudes associated with menstruation. Very few previous studies have been explicitly concerned with such belief systems. Parlee (1974) asked men as well as women to complete the Moos (1968) Menstrual Distress Questionnaire (MDQ) according to what they think women in general experience (in contrast to asking women to rate actual personal experiences as Moos did). She found that men and women report very similar patterns of symptoms across menstrual cycle phases and that their patterns were similar to Moos's sample. Thus as Parlee argues, self-reports of menstrual symptoms may reflect social expectations of what is the normal menstrual experience and as such may be a biased representation.

Attitudes toward menstruation have been examined in a few studies, with most work being based on the assumption that menstruation is perceived negatively. For example, adolescent girls were found to rate menstruation unfavorably on a semantic differential (Haft, 1973) and to view menstruation as a "monthly reminder of cultural and biological restrictions" (Kovar, 1968, as cited in Haft, 1973). Similarly in other research women were found generally favorable toward the idea of eliminating the menses (Miller & Smith, 1975). However, findings of some studies suggest that at least some women believe menstruation has positive as well as negative aspects.

Thus our own research is aimed at providing a more systematic description of various kinds of expectations and attitudes that women express about their cycles. Although Parlee's (1974) findings suggest that menstrual-related cycle changes may result from stereotypic beliefs about such changes, there is no directly comparable work on the extent to which women have expectations for their own experiences rather than for women in general. It may be, for example, that women believe others are affected by their cycles but believe that they themselves are not. Thus in one study (Brooks, Ruble, & Clarke, 1977) college women were asked to respond to the MDQ as if they were intermenstrual or premenstrual to see whether their expectations for phase differences would parallel others' findings concerning both real and stereotypic phase differences. In addition this study explored the nature of women's attitudes toward menstruation by examining potentially important aspects of the cycle besides positive-negative evaluations, such as keeping in touch with one's body and styles of dealing with menstruation.

Participants in the study were 191 Princeton University female undergraduates, 41 of whom were taking oral contraceptives. Each woman completed a questionnaire comprised of three sections: (1) the MDQ, in which they were asked to rate a variety of symptoms *as if* they were premenstrual or intermenstrual; (2) 46 agree/disagree statements concerning attitudes toward menstruation; (3) questions concerning specific knowledge about menstruation, the effect of oral contraceptives on psychological and physiological symptoms, and their general psychological and physiological distress connected with menstruation.

The responses on the MDQ indicate that the women expected to experience more severe symptoms when they were premenstrual than when they were intermenstrual. The women's actual cycle phases and their use of oral contraceptives were not related to expected symptoms. The magnitude of the mean differences are very similar to the men and women in Parlee's study who responded for women in general and to the women in our other study who responded to the MDQ according to the cycle phase that they *thought* they were experiencing. Taken together these findings support suggestions that menstrual-related symptomatology may reflect stereotypic expectations (Parlee, 1974).

The attitude questionnaire yielded five different attitude dimensions using a factor analysis. These five were menstruation (1) as a psychologically and physically debilitating event, (2) as a positive event, (3) as a bothersome event, (4) as an event whose onset can be predicted and anticipated, and (5) as an event that does not and should not affect one's behavior. These five factors are presented in Table 1. The percentage of women indicating agreement with the ideas expressed in each factor is, respectively: 32%, 59%, 77%, 54%, and 12%.

The relationship of expectations and attitudes were also examined. Women who believed that menstruation was debilitating and could be

TABLE 1   Summary Statistics and Representative Items for the Five Dimensions from the Menstrual Attitude Questionnaire[a]

Dimension	Mean	SD	Agree (%)	Disagree (%)
Debilitating	3.39	1.09	32	68
Bothersome	4.18	1.26	59	41
Positive	4.64	1.09	77	23
Predicted and anticipated	3.79	1.16	54	46
Denial of effect	2.73	0.96	12	88

Note. From Brooks et al., 1977.
[a]$n = 191$.

predicted reported significantly higher symptom scores for premenstruation expectations on all eight MDQ factors than women who believed menstruation was less debilitating and predictable. Beliefs about menstruation as positive or as bothersome and denial of the effects of menstruation were not related to expected changes.

Our findings on attitude dimensions indicate that women may conceptualize the experience of menstruation along a number of dimensions, not just an evaluative one. In addition the findings suggest that menstruation is seen, in part, as a positive event and that most women in this college sample accept menstruation rather routinely and do not see it as overly disruptive (32% perceived it as slightly debilitating). In short the experience of menstruation as reported in the literature may have overemphasized the negative and debilitating aspects.

Development of Menstrual-related Expectations and Beliefs

The research reviewed above suggests that societal attitudes concerning menstruation are generally quite negative and that these attitudes may affect the experience of menstruation itself. Although such findings imply that research efforts should be directed toward understanding the development and socialization of these negative attitudes, only a few previous studies have examined this process (see Whisnant, Brett, & Zegans, 1975; Whisnant & Zegans, 1975). For example, Whisnant et al. (1975) examined the contents of the booklets used in health classes that are distributed by the personal products industry. Menstruation was characterized as a normal, natural part of life but at the same time was also characterized as an embarrassing event, a hygienic crisis, and a somewhat debilitating event.

We are currently exploring the development and socialization of such beliefs in adolescence (Clarke & Ruble, 1978; Ruble & Brooks, Note 2). In this research, symptom expectations were assessed using the MDQ. The samples consisted of 7th-8th-grade boys and pre- and postmenarcheal girls in the Clarke and Ruble study, and 5th-6th, 7th-8th, and 11th-12th-grade girls in the Ruble and Brooks study. They were asked to rate what girls in general experience during different cycle phases. In the Clarke and Ruble study the pre- and postmenarcheal girls and the same age boys all reported that girls in general experience more severe symptoms during the menstrual than the intermenstrual phase. Similar findings were reported in the Ruble and Brooks study, except that the young girls, those in the 5th–6th grades, reported less severe cycle phase differences for some of the major symptoms, such as premenstrual water retention. These findings suggest that social expectations concerning menstruation are learned at a young age and that a major component of a girls' self-reported experience is sociocultural. Boys, premenarcheal girls, and girls who were menstruating responded similarly and with the socially appropriate expectations. However, their expectations do develop with age, as the elementary school girls had not yet learned all the cultural expectations associated with menstruation. We are hopeful that information about how and when negative attitudes are formed may lead to the design of methods for minimizing their effects on girls and women.

In conclusion, although many assume that psychological changes associated with the menstrual cycle are physiologically caused, clear empirical support for this assumption is lacking. Furthermore because of biases in measures employed, it is still an open question as to which kinds of symptoms actually change over the cycle, what the level of magnitude of change is, and what proportion of women are affected. The research reviewed here suggests that a productive alternative approach to this area is to examine menstruation as a sociocultural phenomenon. This research shows that a wide range of societal attitudes about menstruation exists, that many of these attitudes are quite negative, and that these attitudes may affect the experience of menstruation itself.

REFERENCE NOTES

1. Dan, A. J. *Behavioral variability and the menstrual cycle.* Paper presented at the annual convention of the American Psychological Association, Washington, D.C., September 1976.
2. Ruble, D. N., & Brooks, J. *Adolescents' attitudes about menstruation.* Paper presented at the biennial meeting of the Society for Research in Child Development, New Orleans, March 1977.

REFERENCES

Abramson, M., & Torghele, J. R. Weight, temperature change, and psychosomatic symptomatology in relation to the menstrual cycle. *American Journal of Obstetrics and Gynecology,* 1961, *81,* 223–232.

Akiskal, H. S., & McKinney, W. T., Jr. Depressive disorders: Toward a unified hypothesis. *Science,* 1973, *182,* 20–29.

Baldessarini, R. J. The basis for amine hypotheses of affective disorders. *Archives of General Psychiatry,* 1975, *32,* 1087–1089.

Beaumont, P. J. U., Richards, D. H., & Gelder, M. G. A study of minor psychiatric and physical symptoms during the menstrual cycle. *British Journal of Psychiatry,* 1975, *126,* 431–434.

Belmaker, R. H., Murphy, D. L., Wyatt, R. J., & Loriaux, L. Human platelet monoamine oxidase changes during the menstrual cycle. *Archives of General Psychiatry,* 1974, *31,* 553–556.

Bernard, B. K. *Aminergic hypotheses of behavior: Reality or cliché?* Rockville, Md.: National Institute of Drug Abuse, 1975.

Brooks, J., Ruble, D. N., & Clarke, A. E. College women's attitudes and expectations concerning menstrual-related changes. *Psychosomatic Medicine,* 1977, *39*(5), 288–298.

Clarke, A. E., & Ruble, D. N. Young adolescents' beliefs concerning menstruation. *Child Development,* 1978, *49,* 231–234.

Dalton, K. *The premenstrual syndrome.* Springfield, Ill.: Thomas, 1964.

Dalton, K. *The menstrual cycle.* New York: Pantheon Books, 1969.

Doty, R. L., & Silverthorne, C. Influence of menstrual cycle on volunteering behavior. *Nature,* 1975, *254,* 139–140.

Ernster, V. L. American menstrual expressions. *Sex Roles: A Journal of Research,* 1975, *1,* 3–13.

Gibbons, J. L. The adrenal cortex and psychological distress. In R. P. Michael (Ed.), *Endocrinology and human behavior.* London: Oxford University Press, 1968.

Gilmer, N. J., Robinson, D. S., & Nies, A. Blood monoamine oxidase levels in pregnancy and during the menstrual cycle. *Journal of Psychosomatic Research,* 1971, *15,* 215–219.

Golub, S. The effect of premenstrual anxiety and depression on cognitive function. *Journal of Personality and Social Psychology,* 1976, *34,* 99–105.

Grant, C., & Pryse-Davies, J. Effects of oral contraceptives on depressive mood changes and on endometrial monoamine oxidase and phosphates. *British Medical Journal,* 1968, *28,* 777–780.

Haft, M. H. *An exploratory study of early adolescent girls: Body image, self-acceptance, acceptance of traditional female role, and response to menstruation.* Unpublished doctoral dissertation, Columbia University, 1973.

Hillman, J. *The myth of analysis: Three essays in archetypal psychology.* Evanston, Ill.: Northwestern University Press, 1972.

James, W. W. The distribution of coitus within the human intermenstruum. *Biosocial Sciences,* 1971, *3,* 159–171.

Janowsky, D. S., Berens, S. C., & Davis, J. M. Correlations between mood, weight and electrolytes during the menstrual cycle: A renin-angiotensin-aldosterone hypothesis of premenstrual tension. *Psychosomatic Medicine,* 1973, *35,* 143–154.

Janowsky, D. S., Gorney, R., & Kelley, B. "The curse": Vicissitudes and variations of the female fertility cycle: Part I. Psychiatric aspects. *Psychosomatics,* 1966, *7,* 242–247.

Jenkins, C. P. Psychological and social precursors of coronary disease: A review of recent findings. *New England Journal of Medicine,* 1971, *284,* 244–255; 307–317.

Koeske, R. K., & Koeske, G. F. An attributional approach to moods and the menstrual cycle. *Journal of Personality and Social Psychology,* 1975, *31,* 474–478.

Ladisich, W. Influence of progesterone on serotonin metabolism: A possible causal factor in mood changes, *Psychoneuroendocrinology,* 1977, *2,* 257–266.

Lamprecht, F., Matta, R. J., Little, B., & Zahn, T. P. Plasma dopamine-beta-hydroxylase (DBH) activity during the menstrual cycle. *Psychosomatic Medicine,* 1974, *36,* 304–310.

Levi, L. Sympatho-adrenomedullary and related reactions during experimentally induced emotional stress. In R. P. Michael (Ed.), *Endocrinology and human behavior.* London: Oxford University Press, 1968.

Levine, S. Stress and behavior. *Scientific American,* 1971, *224,* 26–31.

Levitt, E. E., & Lubin, B. Some personality factors associated with menstrual complaints and menstrual attitudes. *Journal of Psychosomatic Research,* 1967, *11,* 267–270.

Little, B., & Zahn, T. Changes in mood and autonomic functioning during the menstrual cycle. *Psychophysiology,* 1974, *11,* 579–590.

McCance, R. A., Luff, M. C., & Widdowson, E. E. Physical and emotional periodicity in women. *Journal of Hygiene,* 1937, *37,* 571–605.

May, R. Mood shifts and the menstrual cycle. *Journal of Psychosomatic Research,* 1976, *20,* 125–130.

Miller, W. B., & Smith, P. J. Elimination of the menses: Psychosocial aspects. *Journal of Psychiatric Research,* 1975, *12,* 153–166.

Moos, R. H. The development of a menstrual distress questionnaire. *Psychosomatic Medicine,* 1968, *30,* 853–867.

Moos, R. H. Assessment of psychological concomitants of oral contraceptives. In H. A.

Salhanick et al. (Eds.), *Metabolic effects of gonadal hormones and contraceptive steroids.* New York: Plenum Press, 1969. (a)

Moos, R. H. A typology of menstrual cycle symptoms. *American Journal of Obstetrics and Gynecology,* 1969, *103,* 390–402. (b)

Nolen, W. A. What men don't understand about premenstrual tension. *McCalls,* 1973, *100,* 12; 15.

Paige, K. E. Effects of oral contraceptives on affective fluctuations associated with the menstrual cycle. *Psychosomatic Medicine,* 1971, *33,* 515–537.

Paige, K. E. Women learn to sing the menstrual blues. *Psychology Today,* 1973, *7,* 4–46.

Paige, K. E. "The curse." Possible antecedents of menstrual distress. In A. A. Harrison (Ed.), *Explorations in psychology.* Belmont, CA: Brooks/Cole, 1973. (a)

Paige, K. E. Women learn to sing the menstrual blues. *Psychology Today,* 1973, *7,*4–46. (b)

Parlee, M. B. The premenstrual syndrome. *Psychological Bulletin,* 1973, *80,* 454–465.

Parlee, M. B. Stereotypic beliefs about menstruation: A methodological note on the Moos menstrual distress questionnaire and some new data. *Psychosomatic Medicine,* 1974, *36,* 229–240.

Parsons, L., & Sommers, S. C. *Gynecology.* Philadelphia: Saunders, 1962.

Patkai, P., Johannson, G., & Post, B. Mood, alertness and sympathetic–adrenal medullary activity during the menstrual cycle. *Psychosomatic Medicine,* 1974, *36,* 229–240.

Prange, A. J., Lipton, M. A., Nemeroff, C. B., & Wilson, I. C. The role of hormones in depression. *Life Sciences,* 1977, *20,* 1305–1318.

Redmond, D. E., Murphy, D. L., Baulu, J., Ziegler, M. G., & Lake, C. R. Menstrual cycle and ovarian hormone effects on plasma and platelet monoamine-oxidase (MAO) and plasma dopamine-beta-hydroxylase (DBH) activities in the rhesus monkey. *Psychosomatic Medicine,* 1975, *37,* 417–428.

Role of women sparks debate by congresswoman and doctor. *New York Times,* July 26, 1970, p. 35.

Rose, R. M., Bernstein, I. S., & Gordon, T. P. Consequences of social conflict on plasma testosterone levels in rhesus monkeys. *Psychosomatic Medicine,* 1975, *37,* 50–61.

Rosenthal, R., & Jacobson, L. Teacher expectations for the disadvantaged. *Scientific American,* 1968, *218,* 19–23.

Ruble, D. N. Premenstrual symptoms: A reinterpretation. *Science,* 1977, *197,* 291–292.

Ruble, D. N., & Brooks-Gunn, J. *The menstrual cycle: A case study in a social cognition analysis of perceptions of symptoms.* In press.

Satinder, K. P., & Mastronardi, L. Sex differences in figural after-effects as a function of the phase of the menstrual cycle. *Psychologia,* 1974, *17,* 1–5.

Schachter, S., & Singer, J. E. Cognitive, social and physiological determinants of emotional state. *Psychological Review,* 1962, *69,* 379–399.

Schildkraut, J. J. The catecholamine hypothesis of affective disorders: A review of supporting evidence. *American Journal of Psychiatry,* 1965, *122,* 509–522.

Segal, S. J. The physiology of human reproduction. *Scientific American,* 1974, *231,* 52–79.

Shaskan, E. G., & Becker, R. E. Blood platelet monoamine oxidase activity in anergic schizophrenics. In B. K. Bernard (Ed.), *Aminergic hypotheses of behavior: Reality or cliché?* Rockville, Md.: National Institute of Drug Abuse, 1975.

Sherman, J. A. *On the psychology of women: A survey of empirical studies.* Springfield, Ill.: Thomas, 1971.

Smith, S. L. Mood and the menstrual cycle. In E. J. Sachar (Ed.), *Topics in psychoendocrinology.* New York: Grune & Stratton, 1975.

Snowden, R. The statistical analysis of menstrual bleeding patterns. *Journal of Biosocial Science,* 1977, *9,* 107–120.

Sommer, B. The effect of menstruation on cognitive and perceptual–motor behavior: A review. *Psychosomatic Medicine,* 1973, *33,* 411–428.

Southam, H. L., & Gonzaga, F. P. Systemic changes during the menstrual cycle. *American Journal of Obstetrics and Gynecology,* 1965, *91,* 142–165.

Southgate, J., Grant, E. C. G., Pollard, W., Pryse-Davies, J., & Sandler, M. Cyclical variations in endometrial monoamine oxidase: Correlation of histochemical and quantitative biochemical assays. *Biochemical Pharmacology,* 1968, *17,* 721–726.

Stephens, W. A cross-cultural study of menstrual taboos. *Genetic Psychology Monographs,* 1961, *64,* 385–416.

Surrey, J. L., Scott, L., & Phillips, E. L. Menstrual cycle and the decision to seek psychological services. *Perceptual and Motor Skills,* 1975, *40,* 886.

Tonks, L. M. Premenstrual tension. *British Journal of Hospital Medicine,* 1968, 282–286.

Tuck, R. The relationship between a mother's menstrual status and her response to illness in her child. *Psychosomatic Medicine,* 1975, *37,* 388–394.

Turner, C. D., & Bagnara, J. T. *General endocrinology* (5th ed.). Philadelphia: Saunders, 1971.

Whisnant, L., Brett, E., & Zegans, L. Implicit messages concerning menstruation in commercial educational material. *American Journal of Psychiatry,* 1975, *132*(8), 815–820.

Whisnant, L., & Zegans, L. A study of attitudes toward menarche in white middle-class American adolescent girls. *American Journal of Psychiatry,* 1975, *132*(8), 809–814.

Wolff, H. *Stress and disease.* New York: Thomas, 1968.

12

A Social Psychological Perspective on the Menstrual Cycle

Carolyn Wood Sherif

The Pennsylvania State University

Legend gave us the tale of Lizzie Borden of Fall River who, it is chanted, "gave her father forty whacks"—or was it twenty? In fact, Lizzie Borden's father and stepmother died by axe. But did you know that Lizzie was menstruating at the time?

I read this unsung detail in a review of *The Curse: A Cultural History of Menstruation* by Delaney, Lupton, and Toth in *Newsweek* (September 13, 1976, p. 82). Suddenly the biopsychology of the legendary crime was clear: Long detesting her father and stepmother, Lizzie's hormonal balance was out of whack, plunging her into dark moods, deranging her thought processes, and lowering her intermenstrual threshold for environmental stress. Or was she already so stressed by her parents that menstrual flow was prematurely induced, hence secondary in the sequence of events that both started with and ended the father and mother?

Both chains of reasoning appear in the literature on the biopsychology of menstruation. Unfortunately neither explains the deaths of the Bordens. The reason is simple: we do not know who killed them. Lizzie was acquitted, in part owing to the discovery that some of the stains on her garments were menstrual blood.

Do you feel tricked by the legend into believing that Lizzie's menstruation explains the murders? Or do you feel tricked by me into wasting your time on events whose circumstances are unknown and whose relationship to

For generosity in sharing references and resources I am particularly indebted to Dr. Dorothy Harris of The Pennsylvania State University, who lent her copy of the Jacobi monograph among other useful resources; Dr. Mary Parlee of Barnard College for her own work as well as others; Linda Wilcoxon, Susan Schrader, Susan Light, Basam Abed, and A. R. Palwal. A small grant from the research office, College of the Liberal Arts, The Pennsylvania State University, in support of research by Wilcoxon, Schrader, and Sherif (1976), is gratefully acknowledged. That research, which originated as a project in a course on psychology of women in the Department of Psychology, was awarded the first annual prize for student research from the Association for Women in Psychology.

Lizzie's menstruation and actions is a mystery? In either case you are sharing my own reactions to much of the research literature on psychological phenomena associated with women's cyclicity.

THE REQUIREMENTS OF A SOCIAL PSYCHOLOGICAL PERSPECTIVE

In summarizing and criticizing the research literature I develop a thesis that is simple and hardly revolutionary: The *psychology* of the menstrual cycle must be predicated upon the documented experiences and actions of women living in social circumstances that are understood at least as well as the hormonal and other physiological changes occurring during the cycle. The social psychological perspective that I adopt does not minimize the importance of the physiological cycling or its associated biochemical processes nor of exploring other little studied or as yet unknown cyclicities as a comparative guide. It does insist that psychological correlates of such physiological alterations are meaningless unless related to their social context. If that statement seems at all radical to you, consider for a moment that the experiential and behavioral correlates of food ingestion, digestion, metabolism, and elimination are equally meaningless unless linked to a social context—even in accounting for what, if anything, is eaten, what kinds of food, how much, when, where, and how. Such linkage is essential if one wishes to deal with the emotions aroused, the moods changed, the cognitions evoked, and the actions associated with each phase of that cycle.

Sparked by the modern women's movement, the greatly increased interest among women in their bodies, bodily control, their health, and physiological functioning is both necessary and beneficial. However, it would be genuine irony if this interest were to stimulate nothing more than preoccupation with the fine details of physiology. The primary reasons that experiential and behavioral correlates of the cycle are at issue are social, including at least three closely related social phenomena: (1) Power-related allegations that women are unfit physically, emotionally, or cognitively for socially significant responsibilities during the paramenstruum, including alleged incapacitation as parents owing to "impaired judgment and mental dullness" (Dalton, 1966); (2) countercharges by feminists, sometimes accompanied by data, some of which have been collected in the hope of refuting the allegations; (3) reactions by women indicating that they regard the menstrual flow as a considerably greater inconvenience than other bodily functions and, by an unknown proportion of women, that their discomfiture is considerable or great.

All these issues are social and psychological phenomena that no amount of physiological research can clarify, except possibly some of the more disturbing physical symptoms. Reviewing history has not made me sanguine about the effectiveness of a physiologically oriented psychology in refuting power-motivated myths. On the contrary it is my contention that psychologists interested in the menstrual cycle will have to spend more time and effort studying women's social context than most psychologists, including the social brand, have been willing to invest previously. By the social context I mean not only the cultural beliefs, ritual, and technology associated with the menstrual cycle itself but also those social practices related to a woman's health and physical activity that affect her bodily self-image, those relationships with significant other persons that convey to her who and what she is in their eyes, and the rounds of activities that she engages in as a participating member in some part of a society, in some capacities, with some social standing.

In making a case for revision of theoretical and research models to include the social context explicitly, I start with a brief review of the morass in which we find ourselves, considering its historical antecedents. That review leads to a critical account of research strategies and findings on mood and cognitive and behavioral correlates of the menstrual cycle, including my own research.

SCIENCE, POLITICS, AND THEORIES OF CAUSATION

The morass in which we find ourselves reflects a theoretical schism that began in the last century with the development of the biological and social sciences. The schism is between biological determinism on the one hand and sociocultural determinism on the other.

Few today would argue against dealing with physiological facts in terms of physiological concepts or social facts in terms of concepts developed for the study of social organization, cultural value systems, and so on. But a great many people will argue about the best way to explain individual feelings, thoughts, and actions when these are clearly related both to physiology and to culture as the menstrual cycle is. As Parlee (1977) has emphasized, the literature on human reproductive processes, including the menstrual cycle, typically reflects an assumptive model that assigns cause to physiological variables, with psychological and social phenomena being interpreted as effects. This causal model is a brand of biological or physiological determinism.

The most extreme physiological determinism foresees the ultimate explanation of psychological or social phenomena as when they can be reduced to physiological or biochemical events (cf. Jessor, 1958; Sarup, 1975; Schneirla, 1951; Sherif & Sherif, 1953). This is reductionism.

Needless to say the sophisticated reductionist obscures the linear causal assumption in the model by granting some impact to sociocultural factors and to what are called mediations of obdurate psyches, especially those of women; but these are merely complications. In fact one can entertain reductionist assumptions while retaining employment as a social scientist. The writings of anthropologists like Tiger and Fox (1971) are examples. They attempted no less a feat than explaining the historical differentiation of social sex roles on the basis of gene-controlled hormonal differences so powerful that societies can violate them only at the cost of the mental anguish of both sexes, social conflict, and the ultimate return to what are seen as natural roles anyway. Fortunately several women anthropologists and psychologists have exposed the political implications of such theories as well as their selectively chosen or inaccurate data base (see Friedl, 1975; Martin & Voorhies, 1975; Mednick, 1975).

Social psychologists are more often accused, at times correctly, of assuming the opposite pole of cultural determinism. Stemming from the considerable impact of Emile Durkheim in the development of the social sciences, cultural determinism in its simplest form argues that physiological differences between the sexes are both smaller and less significant than a biological determinist would have us think. More important, they are universal, whereas historical and anthropological data show striking variations between societies and groups within them in the following important respects: division of labor as well as other relationships between the sexes; practices and beliefs associated with sexual maturation, including menstruation, sexual intercourse, conception, childbirth, kinship, residence, and responsibilities in childcare. Since such variations cannot be explained in terms of physiological or biological concepts, the cultural determinist contends that the cultural environment must be regarded as the significant determinant of behaviors distinguishing the sexes (cf. Friedl, 1975, pp. 3-4). A concrete example is the explanation of a woman's experiences and actions during the menstrual cycle solely in terms of cultural beliefs about the cycle, woman's sex role in the society, and so forth. In light of our own society's practices and beliefs about menstruation, it is very easy for a woman to adopt the view of cultural determinism.

Many psychologists prefer to pretend that the schism between biological determinism and cultural determinism does not exist or that its resolution lies in pragmatic choice of convenient concepts and research strategies from each. Unfortunately, however, the choices that a researcher makes do shape how the problem of study is defined; they do affect what is to be included and excluded in the research and how the included variables are defined and studied. These are merely the first lessons from the "sociology of knowledge" as applied to problems of researcher bias (e.g., Maccoby & Jacklin, 1974; Rosenthal & Rosnow, 1969; Sherif, C. W., 1976, Chapter 6; Sherif, M., 1936, 1966; Shields, 1975a).

Issues of researcher bias are particularly sensitive when the problems to be studied are believed to pertain singularly to one sex or one part of the population. A hundred years ago the difficulties were elucidated by Dr. Mary Putnam Jacobi, Professor of Materia Medica at the Women's Medical College of New York, in her remarkable 232-page dissertation that received the 1876

Boylston Prize from the Medical Committee appointed by the President and Fellows of Harvard University. Jacobi responded to the second of two questions posed by the committee a year earlier, namely: Do women require mental and bodily rest during menstruation and to what extent? Jacobi (1877) began with this observation: "An inquiry into the limits of activity and attainments that may be imposed by sex is very frequently carried on in the same spirit as that which hastens to ascribe to permanent differences in race all the peculiarities of a class, and this because the sex that is supposed to be limiting in its nature, is nearly always different from that of the person conducting the inquiry" (pp. 1-2).

Jacobi (1877) was laboring against a form of reductionism that regarded menstruation as illness and attributed "the majority of all cases of disease in the female sex" to the menstrual period. She regarded such reductionism on a par with Hahneman's theory that traced both insanity and consumption to "suppression of scabies" (p. 16). In short she saw reductionism as applied to women as parallel to the unscientific theoretical bias of the treatment of diseases more prevalent among the poor.

Today the sensitive issues of researcher bias in studies of cyclicity tend to hinge upon researcher's sex or sociopolitical attitudes about feminism. We need not assume self-interested motives in order to criticize bias implicit in biological or cultural determinism, however. On the contrary the causal model adopted by a researcher may simply reflect what he or she learned in graduate school as the correct or scientific way to study the menstrual cycle. For whatever reason a commitment to one pole or the other does affect what is studied, how the study is conducted, and therefore of what the research findings consist. And such commitment does have political implications in the sense that it leads to definite viewpoints on the use and maintenance of political power.

I am reminded of Maccoby and Jacklin's (1974) complaint in their valuable review of research on early sex differences that the research designs and choice of variables in the literature almost forced them into the stance of a "trait psychologist" in reviewing it. They were forced to operate within these confines by the way most researchers had defined the problem, by the variables studied, and, especially, by what was left out. Being a trait psychologist does influence the substance of research and so does physiological reductionism.

By the same token cultural determinism may be criticized for bias when cross-cultural data are selectively cited, out of context, to suggest that physiological processes are merely culturally dependent variables. For example, one may applaud emphasis on the importance of cultural beliefs and practices for individual experiences as well as the suggestion that some of our own beliefs are harmful or ridiculous. But cultural determinism is implied if one assumes a one-to-one correspondence between "relaxed" cultural beliefs and personal experience, particularly without regard to other aspects of the social context. For example, in order to assess the report that women of the Bolivian Siriono deliver their own babies publicly with little fuss or bother (cf. Mead & Newton, 1967; Rossi, Note 1), one needs to know that sexual beliefs were relaxed among the Siriono because they were secondary to pressing problems created by a persistently inadequate food supply in a tropical climate preventing food storage (Holmberg, 1946). Food, not sex, was central to the Siriono's cultural life, even to occasions for sexuality. The Siriono would leave behind a woman too ill or decrepit to travel together with the others in search of food. In such societies, where men and women hunt and forage together, menstrual taboos are often minimal or absent (Friedl, 1975; pp. 29-30).

MISSING LINKS IN THE REDUCTIONISTIC CHAIN: FROM HORMONES TO BEHAVIOR

Before World War I, research was available on the menstrual cycle that should have made physiological reductionism an untenable position. Jacobi (1877) had assembled histories, theories, statistics on women working, background and interview data on 268 women, a performance experiment on 19 women, and physiological measures over 1-3 months. Despite the fact that her 268 cases included some very unhealthy women by today's standards, 54% reported no or trifling discomforts associated with the cycle. Their case histories enabled her to point to the importance of good health from childhood, greater physical activity (as indicated by a mean walking capacity of 5 miles), "mental education," "steadiness of occupation," and "marriage at a suitable time" (p. 58).

Despite the demurrals of her supervisor, E. L. Thorndike (one of psychology's notable reductionists), Leta Stetter Hollingworth had completed her doctoral dissertation in 1914 showing no menstrually related performance decrements on several perceptual-motor and mental ability tasks. She had tested six women daily for 3 months using two males as controls and had also followed the progress of three of the women in learning to type (Shields, 1975b). Research using a variety of tasks has supported Hollingworth's findings of no significant changes in performance associated with phase of the menstrual cycle (Golub, 1976; Sommer, 1973).

Neither these nor other researches relating performance to the menstrual cycle-phase phenomena slowed the progress of reductionism. The continued elaboration of research designs stripped more information from the data base in the interests of more precise measurement of selected variables—all in the name of science.

As Ruble, Brooks-Gunn, and Clarke (Chapter 11) indicate, the interrelationships in the endocrine system and the details of the physiological process are not completely understood, as indicated by competing theories, particularly at the biochemical level of analysis. Very likely we are in for a period of research in which a few physiological measurements suggested by one or the other rival theories are correlated with equally truncated indicators of experiential and behavioral phenomena. Such a course is reasonable if a psychologist really believes that the basic causes are on the physiological level. I would urge, however, that we follow the causal chain a bit further to see where it leads.

We find, first of all, from D. B. Kelley (1976) of the Rockefeller University's Animal Behavior Laboratory that the "meanings" of the few reported "correlations between endocrine states and human behavior" have not been determined. Also undetermined is the "applicability to human beings of principles derived from research on other animals" (p. 881). Recalling the lack of evidence for significant changes in women's performance on a variety of motor and cognitive tasks during the cycle, we may well wonder what all the fuss is about. However, we have forgotten the ingenuity of true reductionists.

The next link in the chain grew from a combination of the great popularity of psychodynamic theories of personality and psychopathology in this country and women's complaints of their unhappiness, which Betty Friedan (1963) called the "illness that has no name." Thus the next link in the causal chain became mood states and emotional arousal, one of the most difficult and poorly conceptualized areas in all of psychology. Moods and emotions cannot be observed directly but have to be inferred from overt actions, verbal reports, or from several physiological measurements with poorly understood relationships to one another. Thus an invaluable *hidden* link was added. The hormonal and physiological changes during the menstrual cycle directly affected a woman's moods and emotions, which of course directly produced evil thoughts, confusion, and clouded judgment. Never mind that the alleged despairing moods and confused cognitions were not revealed in studies of performance! Their failure to be manifest in the behaviors of some women in performance situations merely revealed overcompensation, a term lifted from the psychodynamic theories fathered by Freud. If women's performance is not debilitated by menstruation, let us define debilitation in terms of moods.

By 1969 Moos referred to over 150 symptoms reported at one or another phase of the menstrual cycle, some bodily changes but most of them labels for mood states or emotional changes. Most referred to the premenstrual and menstrual phase in negative terms (see Parlee, 1973; Sommer, 1973). Researchers were hard at work attempting to document the phenomena, with varying degrees of success. I would like to emphasize that the findings in that literature are by no means as unequivocal or as easily interpreted as some references to it imply. For example, findings on premenstrual and menstrual phases frequently report negative moods, but sometimes they do not (e.g., Gottschalk, Kaplan, Glesser, & Winget, 1962). And nowhere could I find support for the contention that premenstrual symptoms increase with age and with childbearing (cf. Golub, 1976), except in Dalton's reports (1964) in England of the early 1960s, which is exactly the period of the "housewives' discontent" that made Friedan's *Feminine Mystique* a best seller. (Dalton herself reported contradictory data in a later article, 1966.) In this context let us recall that cultural or religious attitudes as well as traditional-versus-modern views of the sexes do correlate with differences in self-reported symptoms (e.g., Beck, 1971; Gough, 1975; Paige, 1973).

What of the intermenstruum? Research literature on moods and emotional states between menstruation and premenstruum is confused. A few studies suggest positive moods and elated emotional states at midcycle; however, that evidence is slim and contradictory (cf. Wilcoxon, Schrader, & Sherif, 1976). Sherman (1971) even suggests "psychological disturbance" at midcycle, based on research on suicide attempts (p. 131), and probably with tongue in cheek. A recent report indicated that women's activity levels are highest during the follicular phase rather than the ovulatory phase (Dan, Note 2). And James's (1971) reanalysis of older data along with new data casts doubt on the alleged increase in copulation at midcycle. The doubts about what happens between menstrual periods (that is, most of the time) are astounding.

Much criticism of research on moods and physical symptoms during the cycle has focused on the use of self-report instruments, which as Ruble et al. comment in Chapter 11, have well-known shortcomings. However, as they note, it is significant that some women report themselves unhappy with their bodies or states of mind during the cycle, whether at the time or retrospectively. In order to determine what difference such reports make in women's lives, I believe we have to go outside the framework set by the reductionist model altogether, collecting different kinds of data. Otherwise we are caught in the unanswerable question of whether particular women really, truly feel as they say they do or in the hopeless search for absolutely valid methods to tap their experiences.

For example, it is suggested that a projective technique, placing a woman in an unstructured situation then asking her to free associate or tell of a dramatic moment (e.g., Ivey & Bardwick, 1968), is a better key to true feelings. Such a suggestion perpetuates another psychoanalytic myth. No test can guarantee an uninterrupted chain from hormones to the content of what a woman says. The unstructured task or situation certainly requires that she herself structure it. However, an ambiguous task or situation is also precisely the kind in which a person is most amenable to being influenced by social cues or suggestions for the ways that she or he does decide to structure it (Sherif & Sherif, 1969, Chapter 4). Thus in unstructured tasks a woman's knowledge that the research concerns the menstrual cycle is even more consequential, channeling the way that she structures the situation.

A METHODOLOGICAL INVESTIGATION OF MOOD AND ACTIVITY CHANGES

The methodological shortcomings in the great bulk of research using self-report measures recently led Wilcoxon, Schrader, and me (1976) to investigate self-reports of physical symptoms and moods during the cycle, including information on what women were doing day-to-day during the cycle. Several shortcomings in previous research were minimized in the following ways:

1. To minimize awareness of the research purposes, volunteers were recruited for a study of body awareness, receiving research credit in introductory psychology with $10 payment and an interview–discussion offered for 35 days of participation.
2. To reduce the biases of retrospective reporting, reports were completed and mailed daily to the researchers.
3. As bases for comparison within the same population data were obtained from equal numbers of women taking combination oral contraceptives, women not taking oral contraceptives, and men enrolled in the same classes.
4. All items on the research materials were equally applicable to both sexes except one item, among many others regarding the body, on the onset and cessation of menstrual flow.
5. An expanded version of the Green–Nowlis Mood Adjective Checklist, previously factor analyzed for data obtained from the same population, provided a check on responses to similar factors on the disguised Moos Menstrual Distress Questionnaire and, equally as important, provided a context for pleasant mood and emotional states to be reported.
6. Separate daily self-reports were obtained on the day's activities that the person regarded as pleasant or stressful events. We regarded these data as equal with others, not as contaminating events (cf. Ivey & Bardwick, 1968). (The stressful events inventory had been constructed previously on the basis of judgments from the same population and ranged over the possibilities in students' lives. The pleasant activity schedules were individually constructed on the basis of each individual's own prior ratings of the pleasantness and frequency of occurrence of 320 possible pleasant activities).

We checked the authenticity of the disguised study purpose at its close through the subjects' probability ratings that each of several possible hypotheses about moods, activities, stress, body awareness, and biorhythms must be under study. About 28% of the subjects, including one-fifth of the males, rated the hypothesis concerning biorhythms, including the menstrual cycle, as highly probable. However, all but two of these individuals rated the probability of other alternative hypotheses as high or higher than that of biorhythms. Thus, excepting these two cases, we can claim moderate success in making the menstrual cycle less salient in subjects' expectations than most reported research, in which the researcher's interest is scarcely disguised at all. Of course such unobtrusiveness on our part did nothing to eliminate the effects of the woman's own beliefs about herself as a menstruating person, which other research indicates are related to the predominant stereotypes in the culture (cf. Parlee, 1974; Ruble et al., Chapter 11).

We first analyzed the large quantity of data on 13 self-report scales obtained from four separate instruments across the 5 weeks of the study, without regard to when anyone was menstruating. These initial analyses of variance on repeated measures were undertaken for two reasons.

1. We were concerned that daily reports over so many weeks might lead to increasingly casual or sparse reporting. Thus it was with some relief that we found a significant linear trend for only two variables: pain and water retention, as assessed by subscales in the Menstrual Distress Questionnaire. Our relief is explained by the fact that the frequencies of premenstrual and menstrual days reported by women in the entire sample also revealed a linear trend, including twice as many such days in the first week as the last week. As we shall see, reports on these two physical symptom scales were also most clearly and unequivocally associated with one's sex and phase of cycle. I will not engage in speculation, which is tempting, about the overabundance of premenstrual and menstruating women willing to commit themselves as volunteer subjects for a few credits and dollars. I shall later attack the logic of research that, like Dalton's, attempts to make such giant backward leaps across the chain of physiological reductionism.

2. Having included both pleasant and stressful activities in the data pool, we were particularly eager to check the validity of the self-reports. While the 5 weeks of study gave no clear criteria for checking pleasant events and indeed no significant differences between weeks were found, it did contain a natural check on stressful events. Our study started during the midterm examination period and ended a day or two before final examinations. We were pleased, therefore, that the week-by-week analysis on the stressful events showed a significant quadratic trend with peaks of reported stress at the beginning and at the end of the study period.

All subsequent data analyses were performed on repeated measures divided into premenstrual, menstrual, and intermenstrual phases according to the women's reports on the onset and cessation of menstrual flow. (The 4 days preceding the onset were designated as premenstrual and those starting with cessation and ending with the premenstruum were designated intermenstrual days.) For each male participant one of the 35 days was randomly assigned as a first premenstrual day, with the 5 days following the 4-day premenstruum being compared to women's menstrual days and all others being compared to intermenstrual days.

The first striking finding in the analyses of variance on 13 variables according to cycle phase for women on the pill, women not on the pill, and men was that the largest proportion of variance in every analysis was associated with individual differences. Of course, this is not the sort of outcome that scientific research concerned with regularities according to sex and cycle phase takes great joy in reporting. I emphasize it to show how fragile the alleged determinants of sex, pill taking, and cycle phase really are. This outcome translates into the conclusion that differences between individuals and in their ups-and-downs from day to day are more closely associated with causes that we did not study than with their allegedly all-powerful determinants. If nothing else, this finding suggests that our research designs need to be enlarged in scope.

The next striking outcome concerns the lack of statistically significant differences between the men, women on the pill, and women not on the pill on several variables. There were no significant differences of any kind on two mood factors called *concentration* and *fatigue-energy* (Mood Adjective Checklist). On the Moos Menstrual Distress questionnaire there were similarly no main effects associated with sex or sample either on the related subscale called *impaired concentration* or on those subscales most obviously designed to assess the dark outlooks attributed to the paramenstruum in the literature, namely Moos's *negative affect* and the Mood Adjective Checklist factors called *anxiety* and *happy versus sad.* (As I shall note, each of these latter factors did show significant interaction effects associated with the phase of the cycle and the sample considered.) It is surely significant to pause over the fact that over a 35-day period men's variations in reporting such moods and difficulties in concentrating are comparable to those reported by women.

Similarly there were no main effects over the 35-day period showing differences in men's and women's reports of the frequency or intensity of stressful events. This is among the reasons why the concept and measurement of stress will have to be specified a great deal more than it is currently if stress is introduced as a research variable.

A third overall finding should be noted. There were some significant main effects showing differences between the sexes. The most enigmatic of these are all pleasant in affective tone. Overall, males reported significantly fewer pleasant activities than females not taking the pill, who in turn reported significantly more pleasant activities than females who did take the pill. The males also reported significantly lower positive mood and emotional states than either sample of females (e.g., the *arousal* subscale on the Moos questionnaire and the closely related *surgency* subscale on the mood checklists). Both of the subscales were designed to reflect feelings of well being, bursts of energy or excitement, and positive emotions. I wonder whether the men really did not experience them or did not think them worth reporting. Of course, we shall never know, since self-report data alone can never address such questions.

The other significant differences according to sex were those related to the physical symptoms most frequently associated with premenstrual and menstrual phases, namely water retention (e.g., weight gain, swelling, skin disorders, or painful breasts) and pain (e.g., headache, cramps, backaches). The level of reports on the water retention cluster was higher for women at all phases of the cycle than for men, and those levels increased significantly premenstrually and menstrually for women on the pill and not on the pill. The phase of cycle by sample interaction was also significant for reports on pain symptoms by women as compared to men, the only significant follow-up comparison being that between the intermenstrual and premenstrual phases for women not on the pill, suggesting that some relief of such symptoms is associated with pill taking. Again, however, the general levels of reported pain symptoms by women were consistently higher than those reported by men across the cycles. Men also reported significantly fewer changes in their behavior from day to day than women not taking the pill, who in turn reported fewer behavioral changes than women taking the pill. Such changes included, for example, lowered school performance, taking naps or staying in bed, staying at home or avoiding social activities. In view of the sex differences and differences between women in these reports, it is important to note that there was no significant association between reported changes in behavior by women and phase of their cycles.

Those mood measures that were significantly associated with women's phase of the cycle, even though overall comparisons by sex were not significant, all pertained to similar and negative experiences. These scales assessed negative affect, anxiety, happy versus sad feelings, and impaired concentration. Reports of stressful events were also cycle related. The pattern of the means for all five was similar across cycles: negative affect increased significantly for women but not for men from the intermenstrual to the premenstrual phase. However, there was a significant decrease with onset of menstrual flow for women on the pill but not for women who did not take the pill. Again let me emphasize that these cycle changes occurred within an overall framework in which the three samples (men and the two women samples) did not differ significantly for the entire period.

Two questions are provoked by these outcomes, neither of which can be answered fully by the data alone that we collected. The first concerns the allegedly linear relationship between hormonal changes and mood changes. Our pertinent data concern the variances of those self-report measures that were significantly cycle related. On the two bodily symptom factors (water retention and pain) we found increased variances for the women but not the men at the premenstrual and menstrual phases. These increases in variance suggest that if hormonal and other physiological changes are directly related to bodily symptoms, their effects are strikingly different from one woman to the next. Even more impressive, however, was a consistent pattern across all reports on psychological changes that were cycle related. Consistently both samples of women revealed significant and huge increases in variance in the latter, which, despite the alleged sturdiness of the analysis of variance model, cannot be ignored.

On every measure the increase in variance premenstrually was greater for women on the pill than women not on the pill. Conceivably this contrast could reflect highly differential reactions to sudden cessation of the pill's hormone content. However, it is not at all clear why, if that were so, it would be reflected most in reports of psychological changes rather than bodily changes. Whatever these patterns of increased variance associated with the premenstrual period may mean, they certainly suggest a more complex model than one positing linear causation from hormonal levels to bad moods. If the women's reactions to the arrival of the premenstrual period were diverse, which they were, they also clearly included a number that were highly negative. Of course this finding also suggests that we may have to revise our models for statistical analysis, since the central tendency in a dispersion with enormous variation may be no more than a fiction. The proper comparison may be on an individual basis with magnitude of change the more meaningful measure. Moos (1977) has recently stressed the importance of analyzing individual patterns of variation as well.

The second question arising from our findings concerns the strength of associations between self-reports on affectivity and mental concentration, on one hand, and reports of activities that were stressful or pleasant, on the other, as these relate to the phases of the cycle. It is not possible to address this question definitively in a research design using correlated measures. However, we did have one indication of validity for the stressful events reports, which had also revealed a significant interaction associated with phase of cycle. Consequently we performed two elaborate analyses of covariance on each of the mood measures and physical symptoms, following explicitly conservative rules. According to this analysis we could conclude that the physical symptoms (pain and water retention) were more closely associated with cycle phase than with reported environmental stress or pleasant events. On the other hand the four measures of negative affect or mental states (negative affect, impaired concentration, happy–sad, anxiety) each had significantly greater association with reported stress than with cycle phase, when the association between stress and cycle phase was controlled statistically. Similarly, pleasant activities were more closely associated with two mood factors than phase of cycle, namely, happy–sad and anxiety–dysphoria. These outcomes permit no causal conclusions, except to weaken a simple physiological reductionism. They do suggest the great importance of research that gets outside of the reductionist model to see what women are doing and how their interpretations of those activities are related to their appraisals of self. After all it is one's self that feels happy or sad, anxious or blue, or that finds difficulty in concentrating.

We may find, as Golub (1976) recently reported, that significantly higher scores by premenstrual than intermenstrual women on self-report instruments bear no significant relationship to other behaviors, in her case to performance on 13 cognitive tasks ranging in difficulty from simple to extremely difficult. This outcome was obtained despite the fact that the tasks were selected as "vulnerable to changes in affect."

Both in Golub's study of married, parous middle-class women and in ours on healthy college students the significant differences reported are actually small in magnitude. For example, within a possible range from 8 to 40, the means of the Moos negative affect subscale in our research differed only from a low mean of 12 to a high of less than 16. Similarly Golub's differences between intermenstrual and premenstrual women were dwarfed by those with psychiatric patients or students tested after a stressful movie. Under such circumstances it is probably specious, as Golub suggests, to theorize that premenstrual women are overcompensating or trying harder when they perform equally as well as intermenstrual women. On the other hand women reporting high levels of symptomatology may, as Rodin (1976) has shown, perform better when they attribute their anxiety in a test situation to the menstrual phase. She suggests that accuracy in self-attribution promotes behavioral stability.

Clearly then the answer to our concerns about self-reports need not be a wild goose chase for measures of internal states that really tell it like it is. Self-reports on almost any psychological phenomena become valuable only when carefully evaluated and related to other measures and to significant activities. If one finds that the various measures converge to clarify both experience and behavioral episodes, we know far more than if we would rely only on self-reports or ignore them. This conclusion applies in a great many areas of psychology, notably in the study of social attitudes (see Sherif, C. W., 1976, Chapters 9–10). On the other hand, if we find various measures of the same phenomenon or measures of different phenomena that should be related pointing toward different or contradictory conclusions, then it is time to stop measuring for awhile. Either our measures are unreliable or we do not understand the phenomena well enough to measure them. Maybe we need to learn more by observing or by talking with women in order to ascertain whether we understand the related phenomena sufficiently. (Koeske, Note 3, has come to a similar conclusion.) We might consider the wisdom of allowing women to report feelings, thoughts, and physical sensations other than those suggested by the "raging hormone" theorists.

As Parlee (1974) and Ruble et al. (Chapter 11) have noted, the fact that women may report their experiences in terms reflecting cultural stereotypes makes them no less interesting or significant. Certainly we would not discard self-report data on love, sexual desire, love of nature, religious experience, or devotion to country on such grounds. We would simply want more information about how such reports relate to the ways that individuals live their lives in order to understand how such sentiments pertain to their dealings with self and others, if indeed they do.

Finally, let me suggest that completely discrediting self-report data would be a cruel irony for those women, probably few in number, who regularly endure moderate or severe discomfort, prolonged or copious bleeding. Too frequently such women have been told by physicians either to grin and bear it, that they are neurotic, that "it's in your head" (meaning "your hormones are raging"), or they are given pills designed to kill pain, tranquilize, or prevent ovulation, which at least some regard as the cause of menstrual discomforts (Thomas, in press). Discarding what such a woman says on the grounds that she mimics the cultural stereotypes would be cultural determinism in the raw. A strict cultural determinism has nothing to say about such a woman or for that matter about the individual who experiences very little change during the cycle in a society that says that she should.

Within a framework that accommodates both the cultural stereotypes and physiological processes, the further study of attributional process and its behavioral outcomes, along lines suggested by Rodin's (1976) research and that of Ruble et al. (Chapter 11) take on particular importance. Koeske (Note 3) suggests that attention to variations in both physiological state and beliefs may clarify the significance of self-attributions.

ON JUMPING BACKWARD
FROM EFFECT TO CAUSE

Consider for a moment the significance of the fact that we really do not know much about the etiology or distribution of menstrually related discomfort or emotional arousal in the population. Into this sea of ignorance come researchers who seek out cases of criminal acts, accidents, suicides, hospital visits, and other infrequent events, then ask those involved to recall when they last menstruated (Dalton, 1959, 1960, 1964, 1966, 1968, 1970). Assuming that such women are equally likely to menstruate at any time during a 28-day period, Dalton has reported higher frequencies of self-reported premenstrual or menstruating women among such unusual cases than expected by chance.

Parlee (in press) has given an excellent critique of the Dalton research, concentrating on the curious logic that attributes causality to the paramenstruum whether the event is one over which the woman has some control (e.g., in committing a crime) or whether the event is controlled by others (e.g., a scheduled examination or being a bystander at an accident). As an equally tenable hypothesis given the sparse information available Parlee suggested that antecedent events or the events themselves are stressful ones that can affect the timing of the menstrual phases.

In fact Dalton's research estimating statistical probabilities of unusual events associated with women's paramenstruum has been received less critically than it would have been if it had concerned, for example, the association between such events and the use of a popular drug, such as alcohol or marijuana. On the latter topics no one would rely (as Dalton did) on the individuals' retrospective reports. Dalton also excluded women who had not menstruated within the previous 28 days, although individual cycles do vary.

Dalton's statistical analysis includes several errors, such as the following: Using a sample of 65 mothers, Dalton (1966) tested the hypothesis that the probability of mothers' visits to a physician for a child's harmless cold would be higher during their paramenstruum. The diagnosis of harmless was made by a single physician. During 8 months the physician recorded 91 episodes of harmless colds. Dalton classified the children into four samples that were not mutually exclusive (under 2 years of age, only child, symptoms less than 24 hours, mother under 30 years of age). She used the figure 28.5% as the chance probability in any one of these overlapping groups that a mother would be premenstrual or menstruating. Finding that 49 of the 91 episodes involved paramenstrual mothers, she presented a chi-square test on this proportion (54%) against an expected frequency of 28.5%. Then she presented separate tests for each of the overlapping subgroups. All were statistically significant (1 df). She concluded that "the mother's well-being is affected during the paramenstruum" and "the child responds by similar feelings of ill health." But the statistical tests are on frequencies of visits, 26 of which must have involved the same women more than once. The latter is interesting, but the statistical tests are classic cases of the misuse of the chi-square statistic, artificially inflated through repeated cases and arbitrary expected frequencies. As for the child's feelings of ill health, we have to rely on the physician's diagnosis.

The great difficulty in research on unusual actions or events of the kind presented by Dalton is that of determining what the chance probability of finding women in the premenstrual or menstrual phase would be. Dalton assumes that since all women menstruate the probability of finding a woman in the paramenstrual phase is equal on any given day. However, the probability that a woman will engage in crime, have an accident, attempt suicide, or take a child to the hospital is not equal on any given day. These are infrequent events not equally likely to occur to any woman or to occur on any day. Dalton's selection of cases raised their probabilities to 1.00. If life insurance companies calculated risks on this basis, they would have to charge such exorbitant rates that no one would buy insurance.

The research literature is full of a similar misuse of statistics in studying highly selected samples. For example, the astounding finding that juvenile delinquents are more likely than an unselected sample of nondelinquent peers to have mesomorphic body builds is enough to make one hope for an ectomorph child—unless one knows that mesomorphy is the most desirable body type among adolescent boys, including high school athletes, and that most juvenile delinquents are in the companionship of peers when they commit crimes (Sherif & Sherif, 1964). Recently a large team of researchers (Witkin et al., 1976) exposed the fallacy of estimating probabilities from selected populations by studying the incidence of XYY chromosome combinations in a population nearly as complete as possible of men in Copenhagen at least 26 years old and at least 184 centimeters tall. They went to all this trouble because of reports that men convicted of violent crime ($p = 1.00$) included an unusually high frequency of men with XYY chromosomes. Using public documents and chromosomal assays from the men, they compared XY,

XXY, and XYY males in several respects, finding, for example, that the tested intelligence of both unusual chromosome combinations tended to be lower. However, their data did not support the earlier reports of an unusual frequency of XYY men among a sample of men convicted for violent crimes. On the contrary they reported "no evidence . . . that men with either of these sex chromosomal complements are especially aggressive" (Witkin et al., 1976), p. 354).

Such a study design and careful research methodology might serve as a good model for anyone who wants to assess the probabilities that crimes, accidents, suicide attempts, or hospital visits by women are associated with the paramenstruum. One would want to compare the rate of paramenstrual women for all women committing crimes during a given period with the rate for all women not committing crimes during the same periods. Until then it is my fervent hope that Dalton's research and other selected comparisons of unusual acts will die the quiet death they deserve. Let us remember Dalton instead for her mission to convince fellow physicians not to dismiss women's problems as neurosis.

TOWARD A SOCIAL PSYCHOLOGY
OF WOMEN'S CYCLICITY

At the outset I declared that an adequate account of women's cyclicity would have to be based on the documented experiences and actions of women in their social contexts, these contexts being as well understood and as explicitly included in the causal model as the physiological changes during the cycle. Let me say now that there are cases of menstrual discomfort and excessive flow that have physical and physiological origins and hence can be corrected only when the social context includes enlightened medical practice. What I shall say, which I believe applies quite broadly with those exceptions, pertains to what needs to be studied in the social context in order that its junctures in women's lives can be understood.

We need to understand the system of organizing social life, work, play, leisure, relations with parents and peers, school, and political activities that makes both women and men regard a woman's body as somewhat mysterious, its cyclicity so secret and private, yet the critical focus of her self-system. This occurs in a society in which a woman's body is valued more and is more the measure of her individual worth than what the woman can do, including the bearing of children. From an early age the female body in this society is a measure of worth in her own eyes and in the eyes of others in ways quite different from that of a male.

One of the few studies to inquire into cycle-related variations in reported moods in context of lifestyle organization was performed by Alice Rossi and Peter Rossi (Chapter 13). They found that the reported moods of males were enhanced on weekends, especially those relevant to bodily feelings and sexual arousal. They used a regression analysis to examine the reports by women to control statistically for the fact that women are at different points in their cycles on weekends. They found that weekends also enhanced women's moods, both experiential ones and reported bodily states, especially if a woman was either menstruating or ovulating at the time. Since the physiological status of ovulating and menstruating women differs, it is particularly interesting that elevated positive moods greeted the weekends of both. One wonders what the women had been doing during the week and what they planned to do on the weekend.

Most of the recent research that has sought to clarify cycle-related phenomena relative to the culture has focused upon causal beliefs. Certainly it is revealing to know that these beliefs differ according to ethnic subgroups, religions, social classes, and sociopolitical stands that pertain to feminism. It is important to understand that bad sorts of experiences and behaviors are more readily attributed to biology than to social circumstances in our society (Koeske, 1976) and that accurate attributions of causality enable the individual to behave more consistently over time (Rodin, 1976). I trust and hope that we shall see more research focused on cultural beliefs and attribution processes.

However, I should like to point to the limitations of exclusive concern with belief systems. The limitations become clear when we inquire into issues concerning their change. To suggest that the change in such beliefs and attributions is a simple affair or will occur simply through the dissemination of enlightened information is to fly in the face of the one clear conclusion that emerges from the confused research literature on attitudinal and belief changes. This conclusion is: Given that no simultaneous changes are occurring in the ways that people live their lives, those attitudes and beliefs that are *most* resistant to change are those most closely connected with the person's self-defining attitudes (cf. Sherif, Sherif, & Nebergall, 1965; Sherif, C. W., 1976). The research literature also suggests that changes in attitudes and beliefs are more likely to occur when the new information or attributions are not too strikingly discrepant from those the person already holds. Further the literature does suggest that individuals confronted with prolonged and intense contradictions pertaining to their self-identities are more likely to be influenced by new discrepant information pertaining to self (Sherif, C. W., 1976, Chapters 11-13). I think you might agree that these generalizations suggest that the most effective impact of new or enlightened beliefs about the menstrual cycle is likely to be found among well-educated, enlightened women and those already on their way to substantial changes in self-conceptions.

Recognition of the importance but the limitations of exclusive focus on belief systems sends us elsewhere in the search for other variables that should be included in our models. One obvious set pertains to the girl's or woman's actual role relationships with significant others in her daily activities. In my opinion this set of variables is crucial in understanding the self-system. For emphasis it sometimes helps to step outside of our contemporary culture. I will illustrate my point first with role relations between the genders differing strikingly from our own. In one of the most sexually divided societies I have read about, the Kaffir Aryans of Afghanistan (Palwal, 1972), the work and lives of men and women are segregated in all important phases of life. The men tend herds in the mountains while women cultivate the fields. During menstruation, women are segregated in a secluded dwelling, which interestingly enough contains one of the more important goddesses of the culture. Contact with men is forbidden, the penalty being a curse upon the man. Observing women in the environs of the hut, the anthropologist saw men who approached threatened with sticks and words, and the men retreated. In a similar vein an elderly woman of Polish peasant extraction who had spent her adult life on a midwestern farm once told me that the menstrual period was a blessing in her farm days on two counts. First, it relieved her periodically from arduous work in the fields, and second, it was intermittent relief from the otherwise regular sexual ardors of her husband. In both cases I am struck by the temporary power that menstruation gave to women to control something about their lives. For a few days the powerless had some power.

In short I believe that we need research into the menstrual cycle or its phases and the meanings that a woman places upon them relative to various significant activities and role relationships. I have heard college students freely admit that at some time or other they had used premenstrual tension or the menstrual flow as reasons to be excused from physical education classes, an outing that was not welcome, an unpleasant date, or an examination. The point to be emphasized is that these reasons were wholly acceptable to those who received them.

At least by the menarche a girl knows that her body is something special but that men are considerably more "equal" than she. This implicit knowledge underlies the wish by a large number of girls to be male at one time or another and the memories of around 40% of college women of being or being regarded as tomboys during childhood (e.g., Cooper, 1974). Her cyclicity has actually started well before menarche, although she probably does not know it, and no one to my knowledge has studied its possible effects. But the breast buds, pubic hair, and growth that ordinarily precede the first menstrual period are clear signs that she is becoming a woman. We already know that the way she interprets her growth to maturity, its timing and pace, are notably related to how her peers as well as older persons size it up (Clausen, 1975). While those girls who are totally surprised, hence shocked, by the onset of menstruation are probably fewer than the 15–20% estimated 20 years ago, the incorporation of the event into one's self-identity is poorly understood. The cultural practices and even the advertising tell us that it is a secret event to be kept private or whispered to best friends, to be referred to as the curse or self-indexed as "on the rag"—an archaicism if there ever was one—and that all efforts should be made to avoid odors (by filling the air with perfumes), to avoid spots on clothing, and to be sure to be prepared.

Remember that this is the period in girls' lives when sexual activity, future occupation, and future self are all converging. The older adolescent literature tells us that this is the time of greatest preoccupation with popularity and dates, the greatest conservatism about being a woman or man (cf. Bernard, 1975; Farley, 1970), and the time when the vast majority of girls narrow their future occupational choices to housewife and mother or one of the traditionally female occupations. The older literature on measures of physical skills and strength also showed during these years a decline so marked as to suggest incipient aging (Horrocks, 1969) for girls but not for boys.

Of course all of this is changing a little thanks to both the necessities of life and the women's movement. We should be studying those changes, for the study of change is often the best way to understand a phenomenon. For example, the research literature clearly shows that age of menarche, which now averages about 12.6 years in the United States, has been markedly affected by nutritional and health standards. Does anyone know anything definite about the menstrual cycle as it relates to regular nutritional intake or expenditure of physical energy? With more young women becoming active in sports, hiking, backpacking, and so forth it is worth our while to inquire.

The data available on active women seem to reflect both the beneficial effects of exercise and the possibility that the self-systems of active women incorporate the experiences of menstruation in ways quite different from those less active. For example, Erdelyi (1961) reported that 42–48% of women athletes studied in a variety of sports achieved at their average levels during menstruation and some 15% showed improvement, with the remainder, less than half, showing some performance decrement from their average. However, performance changes varied from sport to sport, decrements being more frequent in tennis and rowing, while improved performance was found more often in ball games, swimming, gymnastics, track and field events. Remember that when these data were collected the amateur woman athlete was often confined to her own social circle by the adamant peer norms that dubbed such activities as unfeminine.

When we consider superior women athletes, some astounding results are available. Zacharieva (1973) reported that of 1,540 Olympic women athletes, 76% considered their performance to be independent of their menstrual cycle. In fact, women have won gold medals and established new world records while menstruating (Thomas, in press; Foreman, Note 4). Of course these are unusual women in many ways, but I would suggest that their self-definitions as women are as relevant to their views on menstruation as their biochemistry. It even seems possible that their regular training may affect their biochemistry, as well as self-definitions. Zacharieva (1973) reported that the only reports of menstrual difficulties, especially amenorrhea, occurred among the most highly trained women and was probably related to excessive practice schedules. (In inquiring about this matter of a colleague, Dorothy Harris, in physical education, I discovered that there is little research on what is considered optimal and excessive practice or their effects. I would take it that these data suggest actual physical stress.)

In closing let me refer briefly to the variable that showed up in our research and that Parlee has proposed as quite important in understanding reactions during the menstrual cycle, namely psychological stress. In my opinion the search for what is considered stressful in women's lives and how that stress is met (e.g., as a painful burden or as a challenge) is going to send us exactly in the directions I propose. Stress is defined as oppressive and burdensome when seen as oppressive and burdensome to one's self. When related to positive goals the challenge is one to be met, thereby affirming oneself. What constitutes a woman's self is not defined solely by the biological facts of being woman, including the integral and normal cyclicity that marks her months for three or four decades. It is defined over the years in relation to significant other (reference) persons and groups, to activities that she engages in, to the worth attributed to her and to her activities, to her position relative to others, to what she hopes for in the future. Within this context it will also be more meaningful to inquire about anxieties related to having or not having children, as these relate to the cycle. (Incidental findings in our research indicate that the anxiety about pregnancy is not absent even for women on the pill.) We also need life cycle research in such a context.

If, as Florence Denmark and co-workers (Denmark, Kerenyi, & Murgatroyd, Note 5) demonstrated, it is possible for women who suffer severe symptoms at menstruation to learn to raise or lower their uterine temperatures through biofeedback thereby relieving their symptoms, it should be possible for the vast bulk of women to integrate the experiences of menstruation into a self-system that makes them glad to be women. I believe that this is one important goal in the centuries-long struggle for women's equality in society, and I do not believe that we can understand women's cyclicity without understanding that struggle. However, I do not intend to imply, in a paraphrase of Gordon Childe's title, that "woman makes herself." On the contrary, as Martha Mednick (1976) put it, any causal model that leaves out those with sufficient power to reward or punish our efforts "ultimately places the total responsibility for change in the wrong place—on the victim" (p. 28). There can be little doubt that reductionist accounts of the menstrual cycle and of related social psychological phenomena have been used to victimize women.

REFERENCE NOTES

1. Rossi, A. S. *A biosocial perspective on parenting.* Mimeographed manuscript, University of Massachusetts, Amherst, 1976.
2. Dan, A. J. *Behavioral variability and the menstrual cycle.* Paper presented to panel "Beyond the Menstrual Cycle" at the annual convention of the American Psychological Association, Chicago, Illinois, August 1976.
3. Koeske, R. K. D. *Theoretical perspective on menstrual cycle research: The relevance*

of attributional approaches. Paper presented to conference on the menstrual cycle, University of Illinois College of Nursing, Chicago, Illinois, June 27–28, 1977.

4. Foreman, K. *What research says about the female athlete.* Mimeographed manuscript, Seattle Pacific College, March 19, 1972.

5. Denmark, F. L., Kerenyi, T., & Murgatroyd, D. *Effects of autogenic and temperature-feedback training in dysmenorrhea and other menstrual discomfort.* Paper presented to panel "Beyond the Menstrual Cycle" at the annual convention of the American Psychological Association, Chicago, Illinois, August 1976.

6. Mednick, M. T. S., *On the psychology of women.* Paper presented to the New York Academy of Sciences, 1976.

REFERENCES

Beck, A. Chronological fluctuations of six premenstrual tension variables and their relation to traditional–modern sex role stereotypes. *Dissertation Abstracts International,* 1971, *31,* 8-B, 4980.

Bernard, J. Adolescence and socialization for motherhood. In S. E. Dragastin & G. H. Elder, Jr. (Eds.), *Adolescence in the life cycle: Psychological change and social context.* Washington: Hemisphere, 1975, 127–254.

Clausen, J. A. The social meaning of differential physical and sexual maturation. In S. E. Dragastin & G. H. Elder, Jr. (Eds.), *Adolescence in the life cycle: Psychological change and social context.* Washington: Hemisphere, 1975, 25–48.

Cooper, P. E. *Tomboyism as an aspect of female sex-role development.* Unpublished master's thesis, Pennsylvania State University, 1974.

Dalton, K. Menstruation and acute psychiatric illness. *British Medical Journal,* 1959, 148–149.

Dalton, K. Menstruation and accidents. *British Medical Journal,* 1960, *2,* 1425–1426.

Dalton, K. *The premenstrual syndrome.* Springfield, Ill.: Thomas, 1964.

Dalton, K. The influence of mother's menstruation on her child. *Proceedings of the Royal Society of Medicine,* 1966, *59,* 1014–1016.

Dalton, K. Menstruation and examinations. *Lancet,* 1968, *2,* 1386–1388.

Dalton, K. Children's hospital admissions and mother's menstruation. *British Medical Journal,* 1970, *2,* 27–28.

Erdelyi, G. J. Women in athletics. In *Proceedings: Second National Conference on the Medical Aspects of Sports.* Chicago: American Medical Association, 1961.

Farley, J. T. T. *Women on the march against the rebirth of feminism in an academic community.* Doctoral dissertation, Cornell University, Ithaca, New York, 1970.

Friedan, B. *The feminine mystique.* New York: Dell, 1963.

Friedl, E. *Women and men. An anthropologist's view.* New York: Holt, Rinehart and Winston. Basic Anthropology Unit, 1975.

Golub, S. The effect of premenstrual anxiety and depression on cognitive function. *Journal of Personality and Social Psychology,* 1976, *34,* 99–104.

Gottschalk, L. A., Kaplan, S. M., Glesser, G. C., & Winget, C. M. Variations in magnitude of emotions: A method applied to anxiety and hostility during phases of the menstrual cycle. *Psychosomatic Medicine,* 1962, *24,* 300–311.

Gough, H. Personality factors related to reported severity of menstrual distress. *Journal of Abnormal Psychology,* 1975, *84,* 59–65.

Holmberg, A. R. *The Siriono. A study of the effect of hunger frustration on the culture of a semi-nomadic Bolivian Indian society.* Doctoral dissertation, Yale University, 1946.

Horrocks, J. *The psychology of adolescence.* Boston: Houghton Mifflin, 1969.

Ivey, M. E., & Bardwick, J. M. Patterns of affective fluctuation in the menstrual cycle. *Psychosomatic Medicine*, 1968, *30*, 336–345.

Jacobi, M. P. *The question of rest for women during menstruation.* New York: Putnam, 1877.

James, W. H. The distribution of coitus within the human intermenstruum. *Journal of Biosocial Science*, 1971, *3*, 159–171.

Jessor, R. The problem of reductionism in psychology. *Psychological Review*, 1958, *65*, 170–178.

Kelley, D. B. Psychoendocrinology. *Science*, 1976, *193*, 881.

Koeske, R. K. D. Premenstrual emotionality: Is biology destiny? *Women and Health*, 1976, *1*, 11–14.

Maccoby, E. E., & Jacklin, C. N. *The psychology of sex differences.* Palo Alto, Calif.: Stanford University Press, 1974.

Martin, M. K., & Voorhies, B. *Female of the species.* New York: Columbia University Press, 1975.

Mead, M., & Newton, N. Cultural patterning in perinatal behavior. In S. A. Richardson & A. F. Guttmacher (Eds.), *Childbearing: Its social and psychological aspects.* Baltimore: Williams & Wilkins, 1967.

Mednick, M. T. S. Social change and sex-role inertia: The case of the kibbutz. In M. T. S. Mednick, S. S. Tangri, & L. W. Hoffman (Eds.), *Women and achievement.* Washington: Hemisphere, 1975.

Moos, R. H. Typology of menstrual cycle symptoms. *American Journal of Obstetrics and Gynecology*, 1969, *103*, 390–402.

Moos, R. H. *Menstrual distress questionnaire manual* (mimeographed). Stanford, Calif.: Stanford Social Ecology Laboratory, 1977.

Paige, K. E. Effects of oral contraceptives on affective fluctuations associated with the menstrual cycle. *Psychosomatic Medicine*, 1971, *33*, 515–537.

Paige, K. E. Women learn to sing the menstrual blues. *Psychology Today*, 1973, *4*, 41–46.

Palwal, A. R. *The Mother Goddess in Kafiristan.* Unpublished master's thesis, Louisiana State University, Baton Rouge, December 1972.

Parlee, M. B. The premenstrual syndrome. *Psychological Bulletin*, 1973, *80*, 454–465.

Parlee, M. B. Stereotypic beliefs about menstruation: A methodological note on the Moos Menstrual Distress Questionnaire and some new data. *Psychosomatic Medicine*, 1974, *36*, 229–240.

Parlee, M. B. Woman's body/woman's mind. In J. L. Laws, & P. Schwartz (Eds.), *Sociological perspectives on female sexuality.* Hinsdale, Ill.: Dryden, 1977.

Parlee, M. B. Menstruation and crime, accidents, and acute psychiatric illness: A reinterpretation of Dalton's data. In Press.

Rodin, J. Menstruation, reattribution and competence. *Journal of Personality and Social Psychology*, 1976, *33*, 345–353.

Rosenthal, R., & Rosnow, R. *Artifact in behavioral research.* New York: Academic Press, 1969.

Sarup, G. Levels of analysis in social psychology and related social sciences. *Human Relations*, 1975, *28*, 755–769.

Schneirla, T. C. The "levels" concept in the study of social organization in animals. In J. H. Rohrer, & M. Sherif (Eds.), *Social psychology at the crossroads.* New York: Harper & Row, 1951.

Sherif, C. W. *Orientation in social psychology.* New York: Harper & Row, 1976.

Sherif, C. W., Sherif, M., & Nebergall, R. E. *Attitude and attitude change.* Philadelphia: Saunders, 1965.

Sherif, M. *The psychology of social norms.* New York: Harper & Row, 1936.

Sherif, M. *Social interaction: Process and products.* Chicago: Aldine, 1966.

Sherif, M., & Sherif, C. W. *Groups in harmony and tension.* New York: Harper & Row, 1953, Chapters 1, 4.

Sherif, M., & Sherif, C. W. *Reference groups.* New York: Harper & Row, 1964.

Sherif, M., & Sherif, C. W. *Social psychology.* New York: Harper & Row, 1969.

Sherman, J. A. *On the psychology of woman. A survey of empirical studies.* Springfield, Ill.: Thomas, 1971.

Shields, S. A. Functionalism, Darwinism, and the psychology of women: A study in social myth. *American Psychologist,* 1975, *30,* 739–754. (a)

Shields, S. A. Ms. Pilgrim's Progress: The contributions of Leta Stetter Hollingworth to the psychology of women. *American Psychologist,* 1975, *30,* 852–857. (b)

Sommer, B. The effect of menstruation on cognitive and perceptual-motor behavior: A review. *Psychosomatic Medicine,* 1973, *35,* 515–534.

Thomas, C. L. Special problems of the female athlete. In A. J. Ryan & F. A. Allman (Eds.), *Sports Medicine,* in press.

Tiger, L., & Fox, R. *The imperial animal.* New York: Holt, Rinehart and Winston, 1971.

Wilcoxon, L. A., Schrader, S. L., & Sherif, C. W. Daily self-reports on activities, life events, moods and somatic changes during the menstrual cycle. *Psychosomatic Medicine,* 1976, *38*(6), 399–417.

Witkin, H. A., Mednick, S. A., Schulsinger, F., Bakkestrom, E., Christiansen, K. O., Goodenough, D. R., Hirschhorn, K., Lundsteen, C., Owen, D. R., Philip, J., Rubin, D. B., & Stocking, M. Criminality in XYY and XXY men. *Science,* 1976, *193,* 547–555.

Zacharieva, E. Comparative studies on the progress of certain physiological functions of female Olympic athletes. In O. Grupe, D. Kurz, & J. M. Teipel, (Eds.), *Sport in the modern world: Changes and problems.* Heidelberg: Springer-Verlag, 1973, p. 231.

13

Body Time and Social Time: Mood Patterns by Menstrual Cycle Phase and Day of Week

Alice S. Rossi
University of Massachusetts, Amherst

Peter E. Rossi
University of Chicago

INTRODUCTION

The research reported in this chapter focuses on two time dimensions that potentially structure human affect and behavior, one rooted in biology, the other in social organization. The biological time dimension is the female menstrual cycle, and the social time dimension is the 7-day calendar week, while the research question is the extent to which these two variables affect mood and sexual behavior independently and in interaction with each other. Here we will report results only for moods; the analysis of sexual behavior in relation to menstrual cycle and social week will be published separately.

Research on the correlates of the menstrual cycle has a long and diverse history, but the focus on moods in relation to the menstrual cycle can be traced to the stimulus of Benedek and Rubenstein's 1939 papers (1939a, 1939b). By comparison research on the effect of social time on human affect and behavior is sparse, despite the notable example in sociology of Durkheim's (1897/1951) early work on the relation between day of week and season of

This article first appeared in *Social Science Research,* 1977, *6,* 273–308. Copyright © 1977 by Academic Press, Inc. Reprinted with permission.

Two funding sources contributed to the support of the research reported in this paper, with awards to the senior author: the Ford Foundation under a Faculty Research Fellowship (1976) and the University of Massachusetts under a Biomedical Sciences Support Grant, RR07048 (1975–1976). The authors thank Karen Garrett for literature review, Elizabeth Gelineau for data coding, and Robert M. Lazarsfeld for assistance in the computer analysis of individual variation in mood cycling. We also thank Richard Berk for his comments on the issue of hypothesis testing and external–internal validity, and we thank Richard Berk and Peter H. Rossi for their comments on an earlier draft.

year and suicide rates. This imbalance in the social science literature has contributed to the notion that human periodicity is unique to the female. Whether there is mood cycling rooted in body processes in the human male is an open question, but one of the advantages of a research design that includes both body and social time is the legitimation for obtaining data from male as well as female subjects.

Most studies of menstrual mood cycling have been of two design types, retrospective and prospective. Retrospective studies typically use symptom lists in which subjects are asked to rate from memory each of three phases (menstruation, the week before menstruating, and the remainder of the cycle) of their most recent and their worst menstrual cycle (Moos, 1968, 1969b). By relying on recall and one contact per subject, such studies readily obtain reasonably large samples. Studies with a prospective design involve laboratory testing or subjective reports at specified points during the cycle. While they avoid the recall problem, prospective studies have tended to be very small in sample size and noncomparable in terms of the specific days or phases of the cycle on which ratings were obtained, as shown in the section on phase definition below.

The general profile of mood patterning that has been found across numerous diverse studies involves the presence at ovulation of feelings of elation and activity, while depression, irritability, and tension mark the premenstrual phase. (Four useful reviews of these studies are McCauley & Ehrhardt, 1976; Parlee, 1973; Persky, 1974; Sutherland & Stewart, 1965.) Thus Ivey and Bardwick (1968) report an ovulatory anxiety level significantly lower than that during the premenstrual phase. Hamburg, Moos, and Yalom (1968) report a rise in feelings of pleasantness, activation, and sexual arousal at midcycle, with decreases during the premenstrual and menstrual phases. Other researchers (Luschen & Pierce, 1972; Michael & Zumpe, 1970; Udry & Morris, 1968; Udry, Morris, & Waller, 1973) have reported that sexual arousability peaks in the midcycle. Diamond, Diamond, and Mast (1972) report a peaking of visual sensitivity as well as sexual arousal during ovulation, linking this to other reports that auditory and olfactory sensitivity increase, and pain sensitivity decreases during the ovulatory phase. They suggest, "these sensory changes could result in a higher incidence of coitus at ovulation time because of the combined effect of greater sensitivity to arousing stimuli and decreased sensitivity to pain" (p. 174). McCauley and Ehrhardt (1976) point to the inconsistency in this area but suggest that this does not indicate a lack of hormonal effect but the inadequacy of current knowledge. No known research has traced mood shifts consistently throughout the cycle on a large sample of menstrual days in a prospective design as the study reported here has done.

Very few studies have attempted to investigate individual variation in the extent to which moods are structured by the menstrual cycle. An exception is the report that women who showed rapid clearing of progesterone in the premenstrual phase had fewer complaints of premenstrual and menstrual symptomatology (Hamburg et al., 1968). Other researchers have explored the effect of oral contraceptives on mood (Augur, 1967; Kane, Daly, Ewing, & Keeler, 1967; Moos, 1969a; Paige, 1971), personality factors in relation to menstrual complaints (Beck, 1971; Levitt & Lubin, 1967) or the synchronizing influence of proximity to other menstruating women (McClintock, 1971). Such research, however, tends to focus on one phase of the menstrual cycle rather than to explore the determinants of individual variation in the overall menstrual cycle mood pattern. Recent publications begin to reflect the ability to directly assay hormones of specific kinds and to explore the correlates of individual variation in hormonal levels or hormonal ratios. Daitzman (1976) has shown, for example, that men who score high on a feminism scale have lower androgen and higher estrogen secretion levels as well as being smaller in stature, lighter in weight, and having less body hair.

Most menstrual studies have been correlational in method and unidirectional in causal interpretation. The assumption is that if mood patterning is shown across the phases of the cycle, it is attributable to known endocrine fluctuation in estrogen and progesterone secretion levels. The present study did not obtain direct measures of hormonal secretion levels, but it does explore social and psychological characteristics that differentiate between women whose moods are strongly related to the menstrual cycle and those whose moods appear not to be related to the cycle. It will remain for future research to gather direct measurement of hormonal levels, subjective mood ratings, and social psychological characteristics for the same sample of subjects.

RESEARCH DESIGN

The research used volunteer subjects who filled out daily rating slips for 40 days, recording their moods of the preceding 24 hours on four different mood measures (described below), the kinds of sex activity, if any, they experienced that day, and whether orgasm was attained. Each subject was given a rating sheet with instructions, questions, and their response codes and a packet of 40 rating slips. They were asked to do the rating task at the same time each day and under no circumstance to fill out a slip retrospectively; if a day was missed they were to leave the slip blank. They were instructed to begin the task by entering their personal code numbers and the calendar dates beginning with the first-rated day on the consecutive slips in their packets. Women subjects were asked to circle the calendar date on whatever day they began to menstruate during the rating period. They were also requested to return the rating slip packets at the end of 40 days even if they did not complete the whole series.

In the week following the rating period, subjects filled out a questionnaire that covered personal and social characteristics; sex experience; contraceptive practice; future plans for education, marriage, and parenthood; and additional information on their menstrual cycles (i.e., the specific date the last period began before the 40-day rating period and the most recent period onset if another began after the rating period but before they filled out the questionnaire). When linked to the circled date of menstrual period onset on the rating slips, this information provided the necessary data to estimate ovulation date and to classify the rated days on a standardized 28-day cycle code (described below).

The design was pretested with a small sample of 20 subjects; partial data analysis and interviews with 10 of the subjects led to a revision of both the mood measures and the questionnaire for the final samples.

Sample Characteristics

Subjects in this study were undergraduate students in the greater Baltimore area; 67 were women, 15 were men. The women subjects were predominantly from a residential woman's college (50 subjects), supplemented by 17 women from a local public college who commuted to school from their parental homes. The men students either attended the public college (7 men) or were friends of women subjects from a local private university (8 men). Sixty subjects participated in the study during the period from mid-September to mid-November 1973; 22 in the period from mid-March to early-May 1974. (These time periods are each longer than 40 days since not all subjects began the rating period on the same calendar date.)

The modal subject was a 19-year-old woman sophomore from a middle-class family, currently living in a college dormitory and enrolled in a full academic program. Two subjects were under 18 years of age and seven were over 21, so fully 90% of the subjects were between 18 and 20. Almost all subjects were conscientious in filling out the daily rating slips. Perfect response would have yielded 3,280 rating slips (82 subjects × 40 days). In fact rating slips containing at least one piece of information totaled 3,183, although on any given rating dimension the total dropped to an average of roughly 2,890 slips. Of the 82 subjects 72 filled out all 40 rating slips; 5 completed 39 slips, 2 completed 34, and only 3 completed fewer than 20 each. Women were slightly more conscientious in the rating task than men: 67 women turned in 2,645 rating slips for an average of 39.4 per subject, while the 15 men turned in 538 rating slips for an average of 35.8 per subject.

Women subjects were classified by their profiles of sexual activity and contraceptive usage. Virgins were empirically defined on the basis of self-reports that they had never experienced coitus.[1] The remaining women were

---

[1] Virginity is an increasingly archaic category, not only because sexual experience among young women has increased, but because the category does not exclude heterosexual activity to orgasm other than through coitus. Indeed, Sorenson's study

subdivided into those who had taken contraceptive pills during the rating period and those who had not. Among the latter the majority reported using some form of contraception if they were sexually active (although 20% of the sexually active women had used no contraception during the rating period). Of the women 36% were technically virgins; 40% were sexually active nonpilltakers; and 24% were sexually active pilltakers (15% on combination pills, 9% on sequential pills).

Menstrual Cycle Phase Definition

No commonly agreed upon definition of menstrual cycle phase has yet emerged in research on menstrual cycles, no doubt reflecting the wide range of substantive interest researchers bring to the topic. Those with concern for clinical and medical aspects of the menstrual cycle have focused on the premenstrual and menstrual phases. Physiological and endocrinological researchers have shown more detailed concern for specific days and a more refined specification of phases within the cycle. The early Benedek and Rubenstein (1939a, 1939b) work on menstrual cycle and mood contributed to a concentration on the ovulatory phase and the days before and just after the onset of menstruation. It is probably fair to say that both behavioral science and medical research have focused more on menstruation than on the full menstrual cycle of which it is only a small part. A contributing factor to the focus on menstruation is the greater ease of doing research on this phase. It is easier to request that a subject stop by for testing on the second or third day of her period than to request such contact on an estimated ovulatory day or the day following an elevation in body temperature. It is also easier to ask retrospective questions about her last menstrual period or the 4 days before her period than it is to inquire about a nonspecific, intermenstrual period of the month. Prospective studies, following a daily or periodic rating or testing design, have tended to be very small in sample size and diverse in both phase definition and mode of analysis. With small Ns the temptation is great to combine days into phases to increase sample size, but this makes it difficult then to compare results across studies.

Of the dozens of studies in this area 26 studies in which the days of the cycle were explicitly defined were examined more closely for phase definition. A few studies divide the cycle into arbitrary equal units or percentiles; for example, Dalton (1959) and Liskey (1972) used seven 4-day units of a standardized 28-day cycle; Hamburg et al. (1968) used eight percentile units with a finer specification in the latter half of the cycle because their interest was in the premenstruum. Of the 26 studies 5 used four phases, 9 used three,

---

(1973) of sex activity among 13- to 19-year-old adolescents reports higher orgasm rates for female virgins (through mutual masturbation and cunnilingus) than for coitally experienced females.

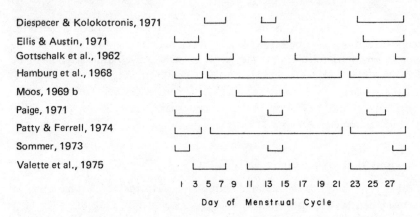

FIGURE 1 Examples of day–phase definitions in nine menstrual cycle studies using
three phases. Lines enclosed by bars are specific days used to define each phase in the
studies cited.

6 used two, and 3 concentrated on one phase. But which specific days of the
28-day cycle were combined to define a phase showed considerable variation
even within the set of researches that deal with the same number of phases.
Figure 1 illustrates this with the 9 studies that used a three-phase definition.
Not only does a given phase vary in number of days but the specific days in
the cycle themselves vary among the 9 studies.

On the other hand it is clear that 8 of these 9 three-phase studies
attempted to cover the same three phases, that is, the premenstrual, menstrual, and ovulatory phases of the menstrual cycle. Our original analysis plan
was to follow this tradition by using a three-phase cycle, each 7 days in
length, thus discarding data from rating days that fell outside the 21-day,
three-phase classification. A large phase definition was used in order to
examine moods on days presumably free of the specific hormonal–physiological events of a phase. For example, with a 7-day (M1–M7) definition for
menstrual phase, presumably M6 and M7 for most women are nonmenstrual
days. So too a 7-day band around the midpoint in the cycle means the first
and the last few days of the midcycle phase are either clearly pre- or
postovulatory for most women. These "extra" days, in other words, were
designed to provide an anchor against which to examine moods characteristic
of the three phases of special interest to the study—the premenstrual,
menstrual, and ovulatory phases. The preliminary results, however, suggested
mood patterns unique to the luteal phase and far less consistent mood profiles
in the premenstrual and menstrual phases than expected. Consequently the
menstrual cycle code was redesigned to the full five-phase code used in this
report.

Assuming a 28-day menstrual cycle, the final code used in this study was
as follows:

Phase	Length in number of days	Specific days in phase	Hormonal–physiological events
Menstrual	4	D1–4	Low estrogen and progesterone; varying quantity of menstrual flow, heavier D2–3; drop in water retention; possible backache, headache, cramps
Follicular	7	D5–11	Estrogen secretion rise; low progesterone
Ovulatory	5	D12–16	Estrogen peak, drop, secondary surge; progesterone secretion from corpus luteum
Luteal	8	D17–24	High estrogen and progesterone; decline toward end of phase
Premenstrual	4	D25–28	Rapid decline in estrogen and progesterone; possible water retention, breast swelling, weight gain, skin eruption

The major difference between this phase classification of the menstrual cycle and that used in most other studies of menstrual mood cyclicity is the explicit attention given to the follicular and the luteal phases. In retrospect it is surprising that the luteal phase of the cycle has not received more research attention than it has, since its unique feature is the elevation of progesterone levels, which conceivably have as much impact on mood as the estrogen rise during the ovulatory phase or the physiological discomfort surrounding menstruation.

Of course many women have cycles either shorter or longer than 28 days. The sample has a mean cycle length of 29.4 days, a median of 28.4 days. One subject (2%) had a cycle shorter than 23 days, nine subjects (14%) had cycles longer than 33 days. The procedure followed in defining the phases for each subject was as follows: given the length of the cycle during or overlapping the rating period, a midpoint was taken to anchor probable date of ovulation, with a band of 2 days before and 2 days after the midpoint for a 5-day ovulatory phase. Menstrual and premenstrual phases were readily calculated forward and backward from the first day of period onset. For a 28-day cycle the 7 days between the menstrual phase and the ovulatory phase were coded as the follicular phase, and the 8 days between ovulation and the premenstrual phase were coded as the luteal phase.

In cases of short cycles (less than 28 days) additional *uncoded* days were inserted between the follicular and ovulatory phases and between the ovulatory and the luteal phases. For cycles in excess of 28 days the necessary number of days were dropped from the rating slip sequence. Table 1 demonstrates the procedure with the examples of 24- and 32-day cycles. In cases of odd-number length cycles, an extra day was dropped or added uncoded between the ovulatory and luteal phases. By this procedure, regard-

TABLE 1   Menstrual Phase Code for 28, 24, and 32-Day Cycles

Cycle (days)	Menstrual	Follicular	Ovulatory	Luteal	Premenstrual
28	1 2 3 4	5 6 7 8 9 10 11	12 13 14 15 16	17 18 19 20 21 22 23 24	25 26 27 28
24	1 2 3 4	5 6 7 8 9 0 0	10 11 12 13 14	0 0 15 16 17 18 19 20	21 22 23 24
32	1 2 3 4	5 6 7 8 9 10 11	14 15 16 17 18	21 22 23 24 25 26 27 28	29 30 31 32

Note. A standard 28-day cycle was created in the following way: for women with cycles shorter than 28 days, days were inserted but left uncoded (e.g., days coded 0 in 24-day cycle). For women whose cycles were longer than 28 days, days were dropped from the sequence (e.g., days 12, 13, 19, and 20 for 32-day cycle).

less of actual cycle length, all subjects were treated as if they had 28-day cycles. With a 40-day rating period, some subjects with short menstrual cycles actually rated close to two full cycles, while subjects with very long cycles did not rate full ones. Of the 67 women subjects, 2 were amenorrheic and hence their ratings could not be utilized in the mood X menstrual phase analysis. As a consequence of short cycles producing both uncoded days and more than one cycle and of long-cycle coding, which dropped days, there is a range in the number of ratings that constitute the base N for analysis by specific menstrual cycle day, from a high of 89 ratings for D1 to a low of 32 for D18, with a mean per day of 78 ratings.

Mood Measures

Items were designed to cover four dimensions of daily moods. The most global rating was the first item on the rating sheet: "By and large, how would you rate your *mood* over the past twenty-four hours?" Response categories and marginal frequencies (in parentheses) for the total sample of days were: in very good spirits (24%), in rather good spirits (55%), in rather poor spirits (17%), and in very poor spirits (4%). The variable is labeled *poor spirits*.

The second mood measure taps changeability of moods during the preceding day, with an item that read "How *changeable* or *stable* has your mood been over the past twenty-four hours?" Response categories and frequencies for the total day sample were: very changeable (9%), somewhat changeable (35%), quite stable (39%), and very stable (17%). The variable is labeled *mood stability*. It was expected that changeable daily moods might peak in the premenstrual and menstrual phases of the cycle.

The third mood measure was an effort to tap preference for solitary as opposed to interpersonal social time, by means of a question that read "If you had two or three hours today to spend *just as you like,* which of the following would you prefer?" Response categories and frequencies were: alone in some solitary activity, for example, read, listen to music, walk, daydream

(29%); with one close friend of my own sex (11%); with one close friend of the opposite sex (43%); or with a group of friends doing something together that we all like (17%). It was expected that solitary preference might be associated with physical discomfort in the menstrual phase or generally negative moods stemming from personal or academic difficulties, and that preference for heterosexual or group contact might peak in the ovulatory phase of the cycle. It was also expected that sociability would peak on the weekend and solitary preferences during weekdays. The variable is labeled *group preference.* This is the least satisfactory of the four mood measures since there is no simple progression from solitary to social in the response categories; it is not clear that preference for group activities is any more social than preference for contact with one close friend.

The fourth measure, and the one relied upon most heavily in the analysis, consisted of a list of 16 *mood adjectives.* Subjects were requested to "record the number(s) on your daily slip if any of the following particularly describes how you felt today. Record as many as apply." The 16 adjectives were selected with two dimensions of mood in mind. One was to distinguish between positive and negative moods, on the assumption confirmed by Bradburn's (1969) research that an overall state of happiness tends to be a balance between positive and negative experience and feeling rather than the mere absence of negative factors. In other words people with high subjective ratings of happiness are not those who are undergoing no difficulties in life and only pleasure and success; rather, the happiest people were those with an increment of positive over negative feelings and experience. In the literature on menstrually linked moods there is an implicit assumption, with no empirical base to support it, that discomfort, pain, and depression associated with premenstrual and menstrual phases of many women necessarily means women do not also feel happy and loving. This assumption was not made in this study, and consequently 8 positive and 8 negative adjectives were included for rating each day. The data therefore permit an independent investigation of the mood curve on both positive and negative dimensions for all days of the cycle. It will be seen that a particular phase of the cycle may have significant elevations of positive moods with no significant decrease in negative moods.

The second dimension of mood was to differentiate between body-linked and psychological moods, so that each set of 8 positive or negative adjectives could be further subdivided into potentially 2 body and 2 psychological subscores (e.g., *healthy* as a positive item with somatic reference, *happy* as a positive item with social and psychological reference; or *sick* as a negative body item but *depressed* as a negative psychological item). The interest here was to explore, for example, to what extent menstrual phase moods were heavily body linked and ovulatory phase moods psychological in nature.

The use of 16 mood adjectives represents a compromise between the desire for as detailed a set of data as possible and concern that lengthy lists would reduce the willingness of subjects to persist through the 40-day rating period. The list was revised from a 10-item list used in the pretest samples on the basis of an analysis of item intercorrelations and interviews with pretest subjects. The items sick and crampy were substituted for clumsy and bloated; healthy and unhappy were added to provide appropriate contrasts to sick and happy; and subjects' recommendations led to the addition of *loving*, nervous, depressed, and tired.

The incidence level of the mood adjectives across the 40 rating days projects a basically positive frame of mind and mood: more positive adjectives are recorded than negative, with the balance between them strongly tipped to the positive. One-half of the days rated by subjects recorded more positive than negative moods, compared to about one-third more negative than positive moods. Very few moods are reported for more than one-half of the days, a useful reminder that moods are more variable and situational than constant. Even an individual who is generally a loving person or generally a depressed person has many days on which they do not view themselves that way.

Table 2 shows the detailed intercorrelations among all 16 mood adjectives. The results provide confidence in the construction of the two total scores based on all 8 positive and all 8 negative items, since all the correlations are positive and statistically significant within the negative and

TABLE 2 Intercorrelations of Mood Adjectives

| | Negative adjectives | | | | | | | |
	Depressed	Unhappy	Angry	Sick	Achy	Crampy	Tired	Nervous
Depressed	–	.51	.30	.24	.21	.19	.23	.26
Unhappy		–	.32	.28	.19	.11	.21	.25
Angry			–	.15	.13	.15	.17	.19
Sick				–	.33	.29	.20	.09
Achy					–	.34	.23	.13
Crampy						–	.15	.09
Tired							–	.21
Nervous								–
Happy								
Friendly								
Loving								
Energetic								
Healthy								
Sexy								
Mentally alert								
Calm								

Note. Items enclosed by the dashed lines are the total negative and total positive scores, respectively. Items enclosed by solid lines are subscores: psychological negative, body negative, psychological positive, and body positive subscores, respectively. Base: Total day sample, 2,887

positive clusters (triangles marked off by dashed lines in Table 2); in no instance do any of the 64 negative-positive pairs show a positive sign, and many are not significant. Almost all correlations in excess of .05 are significant statistically, though of little substantive interest.

In constructing the subscores that differentiate between body and psychological factors, two criteria were used: (1) that the items have construct validity and (2) that all items comprising a score show correlations of .25 or better. Thus while *tired* would seem to be a valid candidate for a body negative subscore, its correlation with *achy, sick,* and *crampy* all fall below .25, perhaps reflecting the fact that most subjects filled out the rating slips just before bedtime. Note that only one of the nine correlations between somatic and psychological subscore items in the negative cluster exceeds .25, while seven of the nine do so in the positive cluster. Hence the distinction between body and psychological is a more arbitrary matter in the positive than in the negative subscores.

There is some evidence in the data that women draw a sharper distinction between body and psychological factors in their negative moods than men do. When the item intercorrelations are examined separately by sex, the average correlation among the nine negative body-psychological pairs is .32 for men and only .17 for women. A specific example can be seen in the correlation

Positive adjectives							
Happy	Friendly	Loving	Energetic	Healthy	Sexy	Alert	Calm
−.25	−.23	−.12	−.20	−.21	−.12	−.15	−.15
−.20	−.20	−.02	−.17	−.17	−.06	−.12	−.15
−.11	−.11	−.05	−.04	−.04	−.08	−.03	−.08
−.16	−.13	−.07	−.16	−.19	−.06	−.13	−.08
−.13	−.09	−.05	−.14	−.14	−.02	−.09	−.06
−.12	−.11	−.05	−.11	−.11	−.04	−.08	−.05
−.14	−.12	−.07	−.18	−.20	−.07	−.10	−.06
−.11	−.08	−.02	−.04	−.10	−.00	−.03	−.14
−	.42	.35	.37	.30	.26	.24	.19
	−	.25	.33	.32	.25	.25	.17
		−	.21	.17	.48	.19	.19
			−	.33	.25	.34	.11
				−	.25	.28	.23
					−	.22	.12
						−	.21
							−

days. All correlation coefficients in the positive and negative mood clusters are significant at the .001 level.

between angry and sick: for women this is a weak .13, while for men it is .34. Furthermore, when the 16 mood adjectives are correlated with the global mood measure (poor spirits) and examined separately for men and women, there are just three items on which men show higher correlations with the global measure than women do. The three items are sick, achy, and crampy; for men they relate to poor spirits with correlations of .37, .39, and .35, respectively, while for women the comparable correlations are .26, .21, and .18. By contrast 11 of the 16 correlations between mood adjectives and the global mood rating were higher for women than for men. For men, being sick, achy, and crampy contributes almost as much to being in poor spirits as being depressed or unhappy, while for women these physical factors are less than half as powerful in relation to general mood state as psychological factors (e.g., depressed correlates .49, achy .21 to poor spirits among women, but .46 and .39 for men).

Why such gender differences occur may be rooted in both the experience of and the predictability of menstrual cycle fluctuations. Even a 19-year-old woman has already lived through approximately 100 menstrual cycles since menarche, a base in experience for both tolerating some physical discomfort and for knowing its predictable basis in normal body functioning. As a consequence women may be better able to tolerate moderate physical discomfort, menstrual and nonmenstrual in origin, without letting such discomfort spill over into psychological distress. Lacking both predictability and repeated experience, men by contrast may react more globally when ill, feeling not just sick but angry and depressed as well. Differences in physical energy level may also contribute to greater stress for men than women when illness requires rest and a slackened pace of activity.

It is also instructive to examine more closely the incidence of items that have been stereotypically associated with the female menstrual cycle, sick, achy, and crampy. Such items often appear on symptom lists and as a result tend to be associated only with the menstrual cycle. Yet the incidence level of such items shows that men report feeling achy, sick, and crampy as often as women do (data not shown). Clearly respiratory infection and digestive upset are tapped when sick, achy, and crampy are reported, not merely menstrual discomfort. Since women are exposed to such risk of respiratory or digestive infection as well as men but may have menstrually linked discomfort in addition, one might have predicted that the incidence level for such somatic negative factors would be higher for women than men. That is not the case in these data. By far the largest gender difference is in the incidence level of sexy moods; young adult males exceeded females in the proportion of days they were sexually aroused (36 vs. 23%).

Since the mood adjective scores are more similar to the mood measures used in previous studies of menstrual mood cycling, the analysis to follow leans heavily on the *total negative* and *total positive* mood measures, the subscores derived from each, and the composite score that shows the balance

TABLE 3 Intercorrelations of General Mood Measures

	Poor spirits	Total positive	Total negative	Positive–negative balance	Mood stability	Group preference
Poor spirits	–	−.58	.51	−.67	−.34	−.26
Total positive		–	−.33	.85	.30	.27
Total negative			–	−.77	−.33	−.18
Positive–negative balance				–	.38	.28
Mood stability					–	.09
Group preference						–

Note. Base: Total day sample, 2,887 days.

between positive and negative moods, called *positive–negative balance.* Hence it is of considerable importance to establish how these adjective-based measures relate to the other mood measures. Table 3 indicates high correlations between the global mood rating and the three measures derived from the mood adjectives (a range from .51 to .67). The group preference measure and the mood stability measure both show predictable and meaningful signs but generally lower correlations with the global rating and adjective scores. Subjects who judge themselves to be in very good spirits tend to report their moods with positive adjectives with an overall balance strongly tipped to the positive, to report stability of mood during the day, and to show preference for sociability. Those in poor spirits are more changeable, tending to prefer social withdrawal into solitary activities and to report more negative than positive mood adjectives.

Mood stability relates to the other mood measures more strongly for men than for women. As the initiators of social events to a greater extent than women, young men may be able to structure their days in a way that makes them "more of a piece" and consistent with their basic mood of the day than women can. On the other hand the correlation between negative and positive mood scores are more strongly negative among women (−.37) than among men (−.18), suggesting greater independence of black and rosy moods among men than women. With the data available it is not possible to tell whether differences in current life situations may contribute to these mood pattern differences between the male and female subjects.

MENSTRUAL MOOD CYCLING

The basic unit in the analysis is the day, each day classified in terms of the two independent variables, day of the calendar week and day of the menstrual cycle. The dependent variables are the daily mood measures described in the preceding section. Eight mood measures were primarily used:

poor spirits, total positive, total negative, positive–negative balance, and the four subscores that differentiate body from psychological components of the negative and positive scores. We posit that the mood adjective scores can be modeled by the following linear equation:

$$MM_{1...8} = a + B_1 MCDAY_{01} + \cdots B_{28} MCDAY_{28} + \epsilon \qquad (1)$$

MM are the eight mood measures, $MCDAY_{01...28}$ are the dummy variables for the 28 days (value of 1 if that day is rated) in the standardized menstrual cycle code, and ϵ is a random disturbance (error) term.[2] Mood measures recorded on menstrual days not included in the menstrual phase code fall into the intercept term and are the standard of reference in statistical tests on the coefficients.

Equation (1) is the embodiment of a hypothesis concerning the mood patterns of menstruating women in the sample of women we have drawn from the population of menstruating females. It is a simple additive model; for example, the predicted mean mood score for women on the first day of menstruation is simply $a + B_1$. The B coefficients measure the difference in the mean mood scores between particular days of the menstrual cycle and the class of days that fall into the intercept term. This approach is mathematically identical to an analysis of variance model; each of the menstrual cycle days may be thought of as hormonal "treatments." The advantage of the regression approach is that the mean differences are computed and can be plotted to form some crude approximation to the function that describes mood patterns (this is known as spline analysis in econometrics). In addition the choice of the first day of menstruation as the first coefficient in the plots is admittedly an arbitrary one, since the menstrual mood pattern forms a continuous loop from one menstrual phase through to the next.

A comparison of the ratings early in the rating period with those done late in the rating period and of the fall samples compared to the spring sample suggested the presence of an additional long-term trend of a seasonal nature in the dependent variables. At least one element in this long-term trend is related to the social and personal change in experience and mood that takes place between the fall and spring of an academic year. Comparison of the fall with the spring samples revealed a sharp increase in psychological positive moods (42% in fall to 62% in spring) and body positive moods (20% in fall to 39% in spring). Going along with this were several other trends in the sample: the women subjects themselves assessed their moods in the spring rating period to

[2] The regression model actually estimated and reported in this section included six dummy variables for each day of the week. In the next section the coefficients of these variables are discussed in detail. Dummy variables were included for each day Tuesday through Sunday, while rating days that fell on Monday are included in the intercept term. It should be borne in mind in this section that the coefficients that suggest significant mood patterns by menstrual phase day are independent of any day-of-week effect.

be better than usual three times more often than did the fall sample (20% in spring vs. 6% in fall); the proportion reporting high contact with male friends doubled by spring (53% in spring vs. 24% in fall); and the proportion of rated days that involved some sex activity was higher in the spring than the fall sample.

Thus there is evidence that secular trends may have impact on mood patterns as well as hormonal flow. Statistically these trends will manifest themselves as correlated disturbance terms (ϵ) of different time lags. An important assumption in the classical linear regression model is that the disturbance terms of different time lags be uncorrelated, and initial examination of the data showed the presence of first-order autoregressive residuals. Ordinary least squares would not be the most efficient estimation procedure as a result. Consequently a two-stage procedure was applied to the regression equations to correct for the presence of first-order autocorrelation, using the Durbin–Watson statistic to estimate ρ, the coefficient of autocorrelation, on the assumption that only residuals one time period apart (one day in this case) are correlated.[3]

Application of statistical hypothesis testing to the regression model in Equation (1) requires that several theoretical and mathematical assumptions be made. First, the tests are constructed to determine whether the estimated mood cycles could have been the result of random fluctuations (noise) and not systematic variation. We do not employ the statistical tests to address the questions associated with inference about the larger population of all menstruating women. Second, the distribution of the mood measures ($MM_{1...8}$) is not continuous and is truncated; in most of the test statistics used it is assumed that the mood measures have a well-defined continuous probability density function. The extent to which violation of the assumptions about the distribution of the mood measures will bias the values of test statistics is not easily evaluated. Further as our approach addresses a null hypothesis about a particular ordering of the signs and magnitude of the estimated coefficients, patterns of significance are the key to evaluating this hypothesis.

The regression analysis therefore involved 28 time coefficients in each equation, on eight dependent mood measures for all female days and then separately for the three subgroups of pilltaking, nonpilltaking, and virgin women. This section will concentrate on the menstrual cycle day effects, graphing the B coefficients to show the increments or deficits contributed by each menstrual cycle day. The independent effects of day of week will be reported separately in the section to follow. Only results on the total negative

---

[3] See Kmenta (1971, pp. 287–289) for a discussion of estimation procedures. If positive autocorrelation is present, the sampling variances of the parameter estimators will be underestimated by the least squares procedure, with the result that the F statistics on the uncorrected regression coefficients are larger than the corrected. All tables and figures report regression coefficients computed with this correction of autocorrelation.

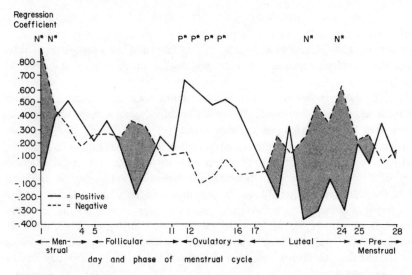

FIGURE 2   Coefficients in multiple regression analysis of effects of day–phase of menstrual cycle on positive and negative moods. Shaded area indicates extent to which negative coefficient exceeds positive coefficient. Intercept for total positive is 1.409, for total negative 1.100. Asterisks denote days on which regression coefficients are significantly different from zero at the .05 level or better, N* pertaining to negative moods, P* to positive moods.

and total positive mood measures and their subscores will be reported, since they represent the best substantive indication of the underlying hormonal shifts during the course of the menstrual cycle. (Results are similar when the global rating is used as the dependent variable.)

Figure 2 provides the best single overview of the results of the regression analysis, graphing the shift in magnitude of the regression coefficients for both the total negative and total positive mood measures in relation to the menstrual cycle. Consistent with the results of other studies, the ovulatory phase of the cycle emerges as uniquely characterized by an elevation of positive moods and a slight depression of negative moods; all four of the statistically significant coefficients on the positive mood measure fall in the ovulatory phase (Days 12, 13, 14, and 15).

Each of the least squares estimators of the coefficients of the menstrual day dummies can be shown to equal the difference in mean response between the days that fall into the intercept term and the day of the cycle that a particular dummy variable represents. To conclude that a regression coefficient is significantly different from zero is also to conclude that the mean responses of the two categories of menstrual cycle days are not equal. By changing the coding of the menstrual cycle days (specifically which days are left uncoded and fall into the intercept term), one can change which of the MCDAY dummies have coefficients significantly different from zero. It is important to note the pattern of signs of coefficients and the clusters of significant coefficients. For example, the coding could be changed so that the mean response recorded on the intercept days was higher than in the coding system used here; in this case a number of coefficients close to and below zero would become significant. However, the patterns of significance would also confirm the *same* structuring of moods by menstrual activity as observed above.

In light of the fact that much previous literature either uses a combined premenstruum and menstrual phase code or a very long menstrual phase without a specification of day, it is important to note that these data show

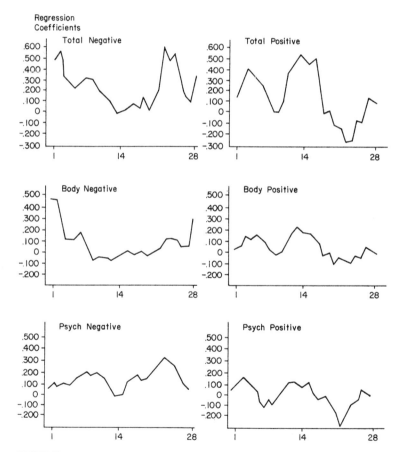

FIGURE 3   Moving average of regression coefficients in analysis of effects of days of menstrual cycle on moods. The top two graphs show coefficient averages for total negative and positive scores; the two bottom graphs at left show body-versus-psychological negative coefficients; the two bottom graphs at right show body-versus-psychological positive coefficients.

only 2 days with significantly elevated negative coefficients (Days 1 and 2 in Figure 2). If anything, the premenstrual phase shows slightly larger coefficients on the positive than the negative mood measures. Third, and of special interest since it is a phase almost totally neglected in previous work on mood and menstrual cycles, is the profile of the luteal phase: as indicated by the magnitude of the shaded area (measuring the extent to which negative coefficients exceed positive coefficients) and the presence of two strongly significant coefficients (Days 22 and 24), the key characteristic of the luteal phase is an elevation of negative moods and a depression of positive moods, exactly the reverse of the profile shown for the ovulatory phase.

The data permit a closer specification of these results through the four subscores that differentiate between body and psychological dimensions of the positive and negative moods. In Figure 3 a 3-day moving average of the regression coefficients is charted. The graphs on the negative mood coefficients (the left column of Figure 3) clearly show that the negative moods associated with the menstrual phase are essentially somatic in character, while the negative moods elevated during the luteal phase are of a psychological nature. The counterpart for positive moods shows less contrast between body and psychological components: there is a clear peaking of somatically based good feelings in the ovulatory phase as well as a slight elevation at the end of the menstrual phase, while during the luteal phase there is a significant tendency for positive psychological factors to be depressed (Day 22).

The results are also interesting from the perspective of Bradburn's (1969) balance theory of psychological well-being. Only in the luteal phase is there both a significant elevation of negative moods and a significant depression of positive moods. By contrast the significant peaking of negative moods in the menstrual phase is not matched by a significant depression of positive moods, nor is the elevation of significant positive moods in the ovulatory phase matched by a significant decline in negative moods. In neither of the latter two instances do the coefficients even dip to negative signs; only in the luteal phase is this the case.

A useful alternative way to describe these results on moods as a function of menstrual cycle phase is to fit curves to the daily ratings through the use of polynomials. Polynomials of the following form were fitted to the data:

$$M = a + B_1 \text{MCDAY}^1 + B_2 \text{MCDAY}^2 + \cdots B_5 \text{MCDAY}^5$$

where M equals the dependent mood variables.[4] Figure 4 shows the polynomial curve fitted to the menstrual cycle with the positive–negative balance

---

[4] Several assumptions were made in fitting polynomials to these data: (1) that the menstrual day code can be thought of as a continuous variable (i.e., that it is plausible to conceive of mood ratings collected for menstrual 1.5, for example); and (2) that all the relevant features of mood-rating patterns can be captured by a continuous function (there is

Estimated Value for

Mood Variable

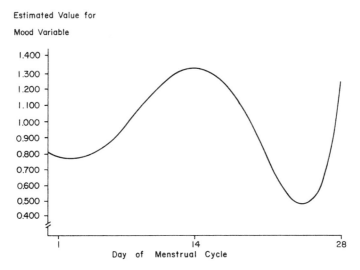

FIGURE 4   Plot of positive–negative menstrual cycle mood balance polynomial. As Y' (mood variable) values increase, balance is toward more positive moods. Day 14 is the estimated ovulatory midpoint of the menstrual cycle.

code as the data for estimating the values of the mood variable. As with the regression coefficients in Figure 3 the polynomial curve shows a slow ascent to an ovulatory peak followed by a rapid drop in the positive balance during the luteal phase.

If it is the case that the naturally increasing levels of estrogen secretion during the follicular and ovulatory phases and the unique presence of progesterone during the luteal phase account for the menstrually linked mood patterns, then it should follow that pilltaking women do not show these significant shifts of mood, except possibly for the menstrual phase peaking of body negative moods. Table 4 summarizes the results of 12 separate regression analyses (four mood measures X three sex–contraceptive types) on this test. It is readily seen in Table 4 that the analysis confirms the test: there are no days on which the regression coefficients are significantly different from zero in either the ovulatory or luteal phase for pilltakers, while the profile of positive

---

a smooth change from, say, the luteal mood profile to the menstrual mood profile rather than merely clusters of mood ratings). It should be noted that the fitting of curves to the day ratings through the use of polynomials is merely a method of describing mood patterns and does not prove that in the population of all menstruating females such a pattern is responsible for the generation of mood-rating patterns. Further a polynomial of only five terms was chosen because, for theoretical reasons, only three inflection points (places where the concavity of the curve changes) could be justified. We suspect that (from the regression analysis) there are local maximums at ovulation and in the premenstrual phase and local minimums in the menstrual and the luteal phases (for positive mood scores). The second derivative of a fifth-degree polynomial has at most three roots.

TABLE 4 Days of Menstrual Cycle with Statistically Significant Regression Coefficients by Sex Activity–Contraceptive Type

Sex activity–contraceptive type	Mood measure	Day and phase of menstrual cycle				
		Menstrual	Follicular	Ovulatory	Luteal	Premenstrual
Pilltaker	Body negative	D1				
	Psychological negative					
	Body positive		D5			
	Psychological positive					
Nonpilltaker, sexually active	Body negative	D1, D2	D5			
	Psychological negative				D22, D23	
	Body positive			D13, D14		
	Psychological positive			D14	D22 (neg)	
Virgins	Body negative	D1, D2, D3				
	Psychological negative				D23, D24	
	Body positive			D12, D14		
	Psychological positive				D22 (neg)	
Total number significant coefficients		6	2	5	6	0

Note. Entries in the body of the table are the specific days on which regression coefficients are significantly different from zero at the .05 level or better.

288

peaking during ovulation and negative peaking in the luteal phase is sustained among nonpilltakers and virgins. (This is similar to Augur's, 1967, finding that mood variation is significant for nonusers but not for users of oral contraception.)

The reader may note that pilltaking women show a significant coefficient on Day 5 on the body positive score. While only a speculation, other analysis suggests a possible explanation: pilltakers are far more likely to engage in sexual activity during the menstrual phase than other women, although they show a lower orgasm rate during this phase than any other. It may be that lack of orgasm and some physical menstrual discomfort pave the way for a contrasting positive response once the menstrual period ends and sexual experience becomes generally more positive once again. Unfortunately we did not ask how long the menstrual period lasted, so it remains a speculation whether a greater number of significant body negative mood coefficients for virgins and nonpilltakers than pilltakers is related to variation in menstrual duration.

SOCIAL WEEK AND MOOD PATTERNS

Although work, school, and family life are organized around the 7-day week, this time variable has received very little research attention. We commonly assume Mondays are a low point and Saturdays a high point of the week, but there is little empirical evidence to support such views. Our research suggests the peaking of positive affect takes place on Fridays, and the low point is reached on Tuesdays (see Figure 5). The data also suggest that men's moods are more strongly structured by social week than women's, perhaps precisely because women's moods are also affected by menstrual cycle phase.

Other analyses (not shown) suggest that the component of positive moods among men that varies by day of week is somatic rather than psychological:

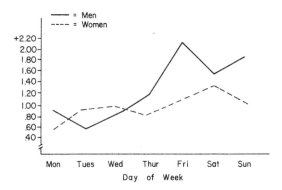

FIGURE 5 Gender differences in mean ratings of positive–negative mood balance by day of week. As Y' values increase, balance is toward more positive moods.

feeling healthy, energetic, and, in particular, sexy, is strongly linked to day of week for men (Friday and Saturday) but much less so for women. Though less than in the past, it is probably still the case that men are initiators of social contact more often than women, so that mood and experience are perhaps more apt to mesh for men, adding to the pattern shown in our data.

Since the timing of the menstrual cycle is unrelated to a calendar week, it requires more complex procedures to test whether women's moods are affected by the day of the week, independent of any menstrual cycle effect upon mood. To assess the impact of the social week on mood patterns, six additional dummy variables that represent each day of the week were added to the basic model in Equation (1).

$$MM_{1...8} = a + B_1 MCDAY_{01} + \cdots + B_{28} MCDAY_{28} +$$
$$B_{29} WEEKDAY_{02} + \cdots + B_{34} WEEKDAY_{07} + \epsilon \quad (2)$$

$WEEKDAY_{02}$ through $WEEKDAY_{07}$ are the dummy variables that take on a value of 1 if the mood-rating day falls on Tuesday through Friday (rating days on Monday fall into the intercept term) and ϕ otherwise.

Figure 6 shows significant elevations of positive moods and depression of negative moods on the weekend, a pattern that holds among women for both body and psychological positive moods, as seen in the bottom two graphs. It is also the case (data not shown) that all three sex activity–contraceptive types show the same mood patterning by social week. Unlike in the menstrual cycle mood analysis, pilltakers show the same tendency as other women for a peaking of positive moods on the weekend.

INTERACTION EFFECTS: SOCIAL WEEK AND MENSTRUAL MONTH EFFECTS ON MOOD

Having seen that positive moods are associated with the ovulatory phase of the menstrual cycle and with Friday through Sunday of the social week, the question arises whether these two time cycles have a reinforcing effect when synchronized. Are moods significantly more positive during ovulation when that phase coincides with the weekend, or are moods more negative when the menstrual period takes place on weekdays? These questions can be explored by adding interaction terms to the basic regression model in Equation (2). In this procedure 10 interaction terms were added to the 34-variable regression equation, by collapsing the social week into a weekday-versus-weekend dichotomy and the 28-day menstrual cycle into five phases (2 × 5):

$$MM_{1...8} = a + B_1 MCDAY_{01} + \cdots + B_{28} MCDAY_{28} + B_{29} WEEKDAY_{02}$$
$$+ \cdots + B_{34} WEEKDAY_{07} + B_{35} INTER_{01} + \cdots + B_{44} INTER_{10} + \epsilon \quad (3)$$

Regression
Coefficients

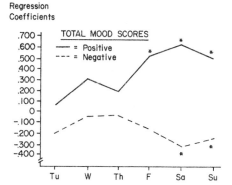

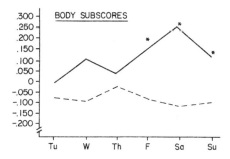

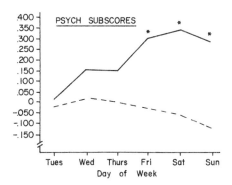

FIGURE 6 Regression coefficients on effects
of day of week on positive and negative moods.
Days on which coefficients are significantly
different from zero at .01 level or better are
shown by asterisks. Intercept values are 1.41
for total positive, 1.10 for total negative, .422
for body positive, .272 for body negative, .804
for psychological positive and .357 for
psychological negative.

INTER$_{01}$ $\cdots$ INTER$_{10}$ are the products of phase dummy variables and the weekday–weekend dummy variable that take on a value of 1 on the weekdays and 0 on the weekend. That is, INTER$_{01}$ equals PHASE$_1$ times WEEKDAY where PHASE$_1$ is a dummy variable that takes on a value of 1 if the rating day is one of the 4 days defined as the menstrual phase and 0 otherwise, and WEEKDAY is the weekday–weekend dummy variable. The interaction terms measure the added effect of the simultaneous intermeshing of hormonal and social events on mood ratings. For example, if a woman starts menstruating on Tuesday, her predicted mean response would equal B_1 (first day of menstruation) $+ B_{29}$ (social week variable) $+ B_{35}$ (interaction term).

The question then becomes whether over and above the contribution of any specific menstrual cycle day or day of the week, the fact that a phase of the menstrual cycle takes place on the weekend or a weekday contributes in any way to the mood levels shown. More specifically is the increment in positive moods during the ovulatory phase significantly higher when ovulation takes place on the weekend than when it occurs on weekdays? Table 5 gives an overview of the results. Social week has no significant effect on negative moods of any kind during any phase of the menstrual cycle. There are significant differences in positive moods in both the menstrual and ovulatory phases of the cycle, but only psychological moods, not those rooted in somatic factors.

If menstruation or ovulation takes place on a weekend there is a significant increment in positive mood scores, while there is a depression of such positive affect if these two phases of the cycle take place during the week. Viewing the social week variable as an index to changes in social activities, these results suggest that social circumstances can affect moods linked to menstruation and ovulation but not those linked to the luteal phase. Similarly social circumstances may affect moods of a psychological nature,

TABLE 5 T Statistics on Interaction Effect Variable Coefficients of Social Week and Menstrual Cycle on Moods

Mood measure	Menstrual cycle phase				
	Menstrual	Follicular	Ovulatory	Luteal	Premenstrual
Positive moods					
Total	1.941*	1.183	1.940*	1.417	.240
Body	.181	.126	.128	.158	.062
Psychological	1.815*	.201	1.663*	1.506	.153
Negative moods					
Total	.029	.044	.093	.020	.144
Body	.104	.070	.069	.049	.130
Psychological	.023	.122	.013	.139	.145

*Regression coefficients are significantly different from zero at the .05 level or better.

while body-linked moods seem more resistant to such social effects. It may be more difficult, in other words, to reduce pain and sadness or to increase health than it is to increase happiness or pleasure.

INDIVIDUAL VARIATION IN MENSTRUAL MOOD CYCLING

Thus far we have established that a general tendency exists for moods to be structured by both menstrual cycle and social week. An equally important issue is the question of variation around this general tendency. On clinical grounds we know that dysmenorrhea involves elevated negative mood ratings during the premenstrual and menstrual phases of the cycle for some women. Pilltaking women who do not ovulate may be spared the progesterone-induced negative moods associated with the luteal phase. Women with demanding study schedules at school, responsibilities for their families, or high motivation in their work may minimize completely or simply not experience any menstrually linked cycle of moods. Clearly there are numerous out-of-the-ordinary events in life that have powerful impact on moods independent of weekly or monthly cycles: travel plans, job success or failure, or a death in the family to cite only a few.

On the other hand some 70% of the subjects in our study reported that their general mood during the rating period was the same as usual, suggesting that whatever mood cycle they showed in the particular 40 days they rated might be found in any other 40-day period during the year. It seems a legitimate question, then, to explore individual variation among the women subjects in the extent to which their moods are structured by their menstrual cycles.

This analysis of individual variation is more illustrative than definitive for several reasons. For one, the analysis involves a shift from the day as the unit of analysis to the individual, thus sharply reducing the numerical base from 2,000-odd days to 67 women. Second, the questionnaire administered at the end of the rating period was not constructed with the analysis of individual variation in mood cycling clearly in focus, and hence the items available are not as solid as one might wish. Third, it is not a simple matter to devise an adequate measure of individual variation in menstrual mood cycling, in particular what criterion to use against which to measure individual variation. In light of these reservations but in the hope that the results stimulate better approaches in the future some detail will be given on the construction of the dependent variable of individual variation and the personal characteristics used as predictor variables to explain that variation.

MEASUREMENT OF INDIVIDUAL VARIATION IN MOOD CYCLING

Since the mood cycle that emerged in the regression analysis was a relatively weak if systematic one, the use of any measure of general tendency drawn from the empirical data is a poor standard against which to classify individuals by degree of fit to the pattern of menstrual mood cycling.[5] It therefore seemed desirable to devise a theoretical model of a very strong menstrually linked mood profile and to measure individual women by the extent to which their daily mood ratings over the 28-day cycle approximated this arbitrary standard. In order to root such a model in an empirical base we used the moving average of regression coefficients for the total positive and total negative mood measures. A curve was fitted to these coefficients, smoothing them out and exaggerating the menstrual mood pattern and superimposing a zero-to-eight metric on the curve. The curve was then adjusted to yield theoretical rating scores in whole or half integers for each of the 28 days in the cycle. Figure 7 shows the fitted curve compared to the regression coefficient 3-day averages, with the theoretical metric scores for each of the 28 days for the two mood ratings used. (Specific score values are shown in the hope that others will attempt replication using the same model of analysis.)

The next step involved the computation of the correlations between these theoretical scores and the actual daily rating scores for each individual subject. The correlations yield a dependent variable that ranks the subjects by the extent to which their mood scores during the rating period approximate the theoretical model. Hence the higher the correlation, the closer the individual subject shows a mood cycle strongly related to the menstrual cycle. The actual size of the correlations produced by this procedure has no special meaning of course, since our theoretical standard intentionally exaggerated the mood cycle curves. The correlations are only useful to *rank* subjects by the degree to which their mood pattern approximates the theoretical standard.

Predictor Variables

This analysis was guided by only a very general hypothesis concerning the characteristics that might predispose to moods being patterned by the menstrual cycle: that women whose moods are strongly related to the menstrual cycle might tend to be highly accepting of their femaleness, take pleasure in body functions unique to their sex, be physically healthy, and

---

[5] In a preliminary analysis we used the mean daily mood rating for the whole sample against which to assess the fit of individual women, by computing the correlations between individual daily ratings and the sample mean rating for each of the 28 days of the cycle for each subject. But since the group means show a moderate profile of menstrual mood cycling, a high correlation did not identify women with very strong mood cycles. In fact individuals with low correlations to the group means can include two opposite types of women: those with very strong menstrually linked mood profiles and women whose moods are relatively stable throughout the cycle. High correlations, in other words, were indexes of moderate rather than strong menstrual mood cycling, with the result that many cross-tabulations using this measure yielded curvilinear relationships between predictor variables and the dependent measurement of individual variation.

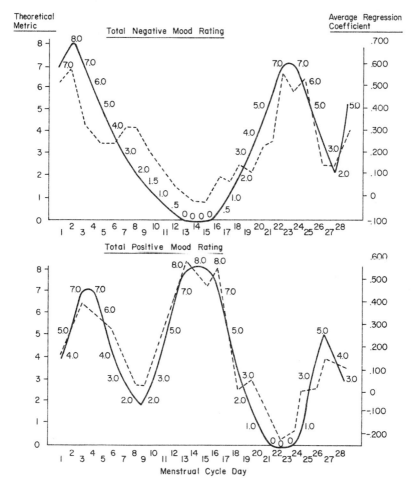

FIGURE 7 Theoretical metric for negative and positive mood ratings for individual variation analysis and average regression coefficient by menstrual cycle day. (——) Theoretical curve, with 0–8 metric as shown at the left; (– – –) moving average regression coefficients.

have life expectations of a relatively traditional variety concerning marriage and maternity. This profile assumes some sensitivity to body cues coupled with acceptance of physiological changes associated with the female reproductive cycle.

This idea had its origins in a lively debate with premed women students concerning the topic of menstruation and mood cycling, in the course of which preliminary findings from the pretest sample were presented. The women students were sharply polarized in their response to these ideas: one group took considerable pleasure in the idea of a close connection between mood and body function and the idea of a mood cycle suggested to them a positive image of earth tides and seasonal change, the body rooted in nature and the mind closely in tune with the body. The other group strongly rejected this notion, insisted the findings were probably spurious, drew a sharp body-mind distinction, and considered any suggestion of menstrually linked mood patterns merely a residue of female stereotypes in the culture. When the discussion shifted from the abstract to the personal, it turned out women of both views had personal expectations to marry but were divided on whether they wished to have children; those who liked the idea of cycle-linked mood patterns expected to have children, while those who rejected the idea planned no children. Echoes of this pattern will be seen in the results of the analysis of individual variation in menstrual mood cycling below.

Three primary types of predictor variables were selected to tap this general hypothesis concerning the determinants of menstrual mood cycling. The first type is most directly related to the general hypothesis: items that asked about anticipated importance of marriage and of parenthood in the life of the subject. Since the social route to future marriage and maternity is current heterosexual contact and responsiveness, the second type of predictor variable concerns amount of current male contact, amount of sexual activity, and orgasm rate. Sex activity taps intimate social relationships during the rating period, and orgasm rate is assumed to tap being in tune with and accepting one's body. The only item available relevant to future maternity was a question asking subjects how they react when they see a small baby. The third type of variable consists of two indexes of personal characteristics drawn from a battery of self-rating items: one such index, labeled simply *charm*, taps heterosexual attraction and social ambition, while the second index, labeled *strength*, taps physical health and athletic ability as well as social assertiveness.

Six of the eight predictor variables are from the questionnaires administered at the end of the rating period, while two (sex activity and orgasm rate) were aggregated over the total rating period from daily reports on whether any sexual activity and orgasm took place during the preceding 24 hours.

A more detailed specification of the eight predictor variables follows:

1. *Future salience of marriage and maternity.* The question read: "How important is it to you (a) to marry? and (b) to have at least one child?"

2. *Current activity and responsiveness relevant to future marriage and maternity.* Contact with men was measured by a direct question on frequency of association, which read: "During the 40-day rating period, how often did you spend time socially with friends of the opposite sex?"

The measure of sex activity is based on daily reports of specified types of activity on the rating slips: masturbation, coital sex, and any other kind of noncoital sex activity like fellatio or cunnilingus. In addition subjects recorded whether orgasm was experienced in relation to any of these sexual activities. The indexes of sex activity and orgasm rate are proportional to the number of rated days, since not all 40 days were rated by all subjects.

The *baby responsiveness* variable stems from the question: "Which of the following best describes your reaction when you see a small baby," with response categories ranging from "I want to hold the baby" to "no particular reaction; I prefer older children."

3. *Personal characteristics.* The questionnaire contained 11 items on which subjects rated themselves in one of four response categories from "not at all" to "extremely" characteristic of themselves. The self-ratings were intercorrelated to identify those that formed meaningful clusters for index construction, with an index criterion that all items be significantly correlated with all other items and not more than one correlation in the cluster fall below the .01 level of significance. (Disappointingly, the matrix did not warrant the construction of an index on intellectual assertiveness using the items *Competitive, intellectually aggressive, introspective,* and *ambitious,* since only two of the six correlations among these items even reached the .05 level of significance.) The strength index consists of *athletic, physically strong, sociable,* and *socially aggressive.* Together they suggest physical strength and social assertiveness with an emphasis on "doing." The charm index consists of the items *sensual, attractive to the opposite sex, attracted by the opposite sex,* and *ambitious.* Here the items suggest femininity and traditional social ambition through heterosexual success.

Table 6 shows the intercorrelations among the eight predictor variables. While some of the correlations are predictable, several patterns shown in the matrix were not. To begin with, the correlations suggest a cohesive cluster in which current contact with men and sex activity are related to the felt importance of marriage and maternity in the future. There is clearly a heavy loading of traditional social expectations and anticipation of conventional roles as wives and mothers here, with the route to that future through social and sexual association with men during the college years. The personal characteristics of attractiveness, ambition, and sensuality (caught in the charm index) facilitate the social path to eventual adult status as married women with a family.

More surprising are the patterns that involve orgasm rate and the strength

TABLE 6 Intercorrelations of Predictor Variables for Analysis of Individual Variation in Menstrual Mood Cycling

	Maternity	Marriage	Men	Sex	Charm	Baby	Orgasm	Strength
Maternity	—	.69	.52	.26	.20	.31	−.15	.05
Marriage		—	.50	.34	.23	.32	.00	.01
Men			—	.50	.30	.30	−.10	.10
Sex				—	.45	.07	.21	.01
Charm					—	−.13	.34	.26
Baby						—	−.19	.04
Orgasm							—	.06
Strength								—

index. Sex activity and orgasm rate are only moderately correlated (.21), and orgasm rate does not relate to male contact and future roles the way sex activity level does. Orgasm rate and male contact are in fact somewhat negatively related (−.10), perhaps because many women experience orgasm in stable ongoing relationships rather than in casual ones, and our measure of male contact gives high scores to both women who see the same man very frequently and women who see several men during the course of a week. But while sex activity level is associated with marriage (.34) and maternity importance (.26), orgasm rate is not (.00 with marriage, −.15 with maternity). Consistent with this is the negative correlation between orgasm rate and current responsiveness to the sight of a small baby (−.19), suggesting that those who are attuned to their own body responses are less turned outward to respond to others—men, babies, or expectations for adult roles as wives and mothers. That the charm index is more strongly correlated with orgasm rate (.34) than any other variable may reflect the focus on the self in the charm items on sensuality and social ambition.

The strength index is the most independent of the eight predictor variables, showing only a moderate correlation with one variable, charm, in part because of the shared component in both indexes of a general quality of sociability. On the other hand the fact that the strength index shows no relationship to future family-role importance, current male contact, or sexuality suggests that the sociability tapped by the strength index may involve relations with women rather than men.

Multiple Regression Analysis

Table 7 provides the highlights of the multiple regression analysis of individual variation in the degree to which moods are patterned by the menstrual cycle. To begin with (not shown in table) there is a positive correlation between individual variation in positive and negative moods (+.28), indicating that women whose positive moods tend toward the theoretical model of strong menstrual mood cycling also tend to show a similar relationship between negative moods and menstrual mood cycling. The first two columns of Table 7 show the correlations of the eight predictor variables to individual variation in positive and negative menstrual mood cycling. None of the correlations concerning negative mood variation are large (high), and among the positive mood correlations only the top three show correlations of .20 or above. Women with high male contact who consider marriage and maternity important to their future lives tend to show positive mood patterning by menstrual cycle phase.

When all eight predictor variables enter the regression equation, once again none of the eight variables show any significant coefficients in predicting negative mood patterning. On the other hand four of the eight variables contribute to individual variation in positive mood patterning. The two

TABLE 7   Multiple Regression Analysis of Individual Variation in Menstrual
Mood Cycling: Negative and Positive Moods

Predictor variable	Pearson correlation coefficients		Regression coefficients		T value	
	Positive moods	Negative moods	Positive moods*	Negative moods**	Positive moods	Negative moods
Maternity	.28	−.02	.310	−.117	1.653	−.565
Marriage	.21	.05	−.017	.082	−.092	.402
Men	.20	.03	.105	.061	.607	.317
Strength	.16	.01	.238	.003	1.754	.018
Baby	.15	.12	.026	.154	.185	.971
Orgasm	.15	.12	.323	.152	2.224	.947
Sex	.13	−.02	.092	−.109	.567	−.607
Charm	−.05	.04	−.347	.044	−2.117	.245

$^{*}R^2 = .222$; multiple $R = .471$.
$^{**}R^2 = .05$; multiple $R = .223$.

strongest predictors (T values of 2 or more) are orgasm rate and the charm index: *high* orgasm rates but *low* charm scores contribute to moods patterned by the menstrual cycle. More moderate in their contribution to individual variation in mood cycling (T values below 2 but more than 1.5) are the strength index and parenthood importance: *high* strength scores and *high* parenthood importance contribute to menstrual mood cycling. Apart from these four factors neither sex activity level, marriage importance, male contact, or baby responsiveness contribute anything significant to menstrual cycle patterning of positive moods.

The overall profile that emerges from this analysis of the women whose moods are responsive to the menstrual cycle is of physically active, strong, socially assertive, orgasmic women for whom the maternal role is important but who tend to be neither strongly attracted to men nor socially ambitious. If it is appropriate to interpret the lack of relationship between the strength index and such heterosexually loaded items as male contact, sex activity, and marriage importance as an indication that high strength women are socially oriented to women rather than to men, then these results suggest that women whose moods are patterned to the menstrual cycle have a dual orientation toward both women and children rather than toward men. The importance of maternity coupled with high orgasm rates suggest a particular sensitivity to their own body processes, especially those involving the genital–reproductive system. Some indirect but independent corroboration of this pattern is in the finding (to be reported elsewhere) that sex activity level has little or no relationship to menstrual phase, while orgasm rate drops during the menstrual phase and is elevated during the ovulatory phase. Orgasm is a more direct indicator of an individual's own responsiveness than sex activity per se, since the latter is interpersonal and therefore includes the desires of a partner and not merely the self.

None of the regression models are very powerful in explaining individual variation in menstrual mood cycling. Clearly no factors that predict negative mood patterns were identified. It may be that somatic factors are of great importance here, so that an index of menstrual phase discomfort might be a meaningful predictor variable that this study did not have. The fact that one of the peaks of negative moods is in the early menstrual phase suggests the role of body factors with direct impact on mood, independent of any personality characteristic or social activity of women. But while there may be a more direct relationship between hormonal–somatic factors and negative moods, positive moods may relate to hormonal changes during the cycle largely through the intermediary of social and personal characteristics and activities. Indeed one way of viewing the lack of predictive power of male contact and sexual activity is that they reflect male interest and initiative rather than women's, and therefore contact with men and sex activity cannot reflect any constitutional, cycle-linked predisposition on the part of the women toward seeing men and engaging in sexual activities.

We hope that future research will attempt a replication of this analysis of individual variation, using predictor variables of a more sophisticated sort. It would be important, for example, to more directly tap the factor of sensitivity to body cues, not merely those of genital and reproductive relevance but others as well. A battery that included such things as advance awareness of a cold coming on; awareness through body cues of when ovulation is taking place; awareness of breast swelling and weight gain during the premenstrual phase; and the extent to which psychological stress takes physical form in headaches, muscular tension, appetite change, or insomnia would be a useful general measure to illuminate variation among women in mood patterning. So too a measure of the relative weight of pleasure derived from physical contact as distinct from social contact with young children or an assessment of orgasmic pleasure through masturbation compared to coitus or cunnilingus would be useful. It would also be important to tap directly attitudes toward menstruation, the relative balance attributed to physiological compared to cultural factors in gender differences, the level of study and work aspirations, the demands of the current daily schedule, and preference for female as opposed to male companionship. It would also be important to study individual variation in mood cycles among older married women rather than the young unmarried, for married women would be in relationships in which their own predispositions play a greater role and opportunity for sexual contact is more constant from day to day.

But above all there is a great need for a better discrimination between marriage and maternity importance to women by specifying dimensions of both roles rather than relying on the kind of global status ratings used in this as in so many sociological investigations of family life. Indeed the most intriguing of the regression analysis results is precisely the suggestion that there are subtle but profound differences in women's orientation to men, sex, and marriage on the one hand and their orientation to women, maternity, and their own orgasmic pleasure on the other. Social customs have for so long made marriage a precondition for socially approved maternity in human societies that we may not have seen the levels at which there is a physiological and social difference between them. That positive moods are menstrually linked where orgasm, maternity importance, and sociable association with other women are concerned means outgoing, friendly moods during the ovulatory cycle, whose roots may be deep in human evolutionary history. To those who view the mother–infant bond as the most critical of all human bonds for human survival (Rossi, 1977) there is a suggestion in these data of a triad centered on woman as mother, other women, and the young that is reminiscent of the stress on the "uterine kin group" in current primatology.

Much of evolutionary theory about human origins has been strongly dominated by the stress on the importance of male bonding, male dominance and strength, and male initiative in procreation. A counter view has recently been published (Tanner & Zihlman, 1976) that stresses the sexual initiative of the female, the importance of female work in food gathering and infant care, the cooperative nature of female relationships, and the procreative selection by females of which males will transmit their genes to the next generation.

SUMMARY

The study explored mood patterning by two time dimensions, body time as indexed by the female menstrual cycle and social time as indexed by the calendar week. The central research question was the extent to which these two time dimensions affect mood and sexual behavior. Data consisted of daily mood ratings obtained from 82 subjects over a 40-day period, yielding a day-sample of mood ratings of approximately 3,200 cases.

Consistent with results from smaller scaled studies with less rigorous statistical analysis, the study found an elevation of positive moods in the ovulatory phase of the menstrual cycle and of negative moods in the early part of the menstrual phase. Unlike previous studies there was no significant elevation of negative moods in the premenstrual phase but a significant elevation of negative moods and decrease in positive moods in the luteal phase. Indirect support for the specifically hormonal contribution to these mood curves was given by the finding that menstrual mood patterning is not present among pilltaking women who have no endogenous ebb and flow of estrogen and no progesterone peaking in the luteal phase, while virgins and nonpilltaking sexually active women show the predicted menstrual mood pattern.

Moods were significantly related to the calendar week among male subjects, but since the menstrual cycle is not related to the social week, the independent effect of social week on moods among women is seen only through regression analysis, which permits an examination of social week effects independent of menstrual cycle effects. Psychological and body positive moods are associated with weekends among women, while men's mood enhancement on weekends is more limited to body factors, primarily sexual arousal.

An analysis of the interaction between body and social time found no significant effects of social week on negative moods, while psychological positive moods showed a strong interaction with social week in the menstrual and ovulatory phases: menstruation or ovulation on weekends significantly enhanced psychological positive moods.

An analysis of individual variation in menstrual cycle mood patterns suggests that women whose moods are responsive to the menstrual cycle are physically active, socially assertive, sexually orgasmic women for whom the maternal role is important but who tend to be neither strongly attracted to men nor socially ambitious.

Although tentative at this juncture, there is a suggestion in these data that negative body factors may have a direct impact on mood relatively impervious to the influence of social activities, while positive moods are related to hormonal changes through the intermediary of social and personal characteristics and activities.

REFERENCES

Augur, J. A. R. A psychophysiological study of the normal menstrual cycle and of some possible effects of oral contraceptives. *Dissertation Abstracts,* 1967, *28,* 3070–3071B.

Beck, A. C. Chronological fluctuations of six premenstrual tension variables and their relation to traditional–modern sex role stereotypes. *Dissertation Abstracts International,* 1971, *31*(8-B), 4980.

Benedek, T., & Rubenstein, B. B. The correlations between ovarian activity and psychodynamic processes: I. The ovulative phase. *Psychosomatic Medicine,* 1939, *1,* 245–270. (a)

Benedek, T., & Rubenstein, B. B. The correlations between ovarian activity and psychodynamic processes: II. The menstrual phase. *Psychosomatic Medicine,* 1939, *1,* 461–485. (b)

Bradburn, N. *The structure of psychological well-being.* Chicago: Aldine, 1969.

Daitzman, R. J. *Personality correlates of androgens and estrogens.* Unpublished doctoral dissertation, University of Delaware, 1976.

Dalton, K. Menstruation and acute psychiatric illness. *British Medical Journal,* 1959, *1,* 148–149.

Diamond, A., Diamond, A. L., & Mast, M. Visual sensitivity and sexual arousal levels during the menstrual cycle. *Journal of Nervous and Mental Disease,* 1972, *155*(3), 170–176.

Diespecker, D. D., & Kolokotronis, E. Vibrotactile learning and the menstrual cycle. *Perceptual and Motor Skills,* 1971, *33*(1), 233–234.

Durkheim, E. *Suicide: A study in sociology.* Glencoe, Ill.: Free Press, 1951. (Originally published, 1897.)

Ellis, D. P., & Austin, P. Menstruation and aggressive behavior in a correction center for women. *Journal of Criminal Law, Criminology & Police Science*, 1971, *62*(3), 388–395.

Gottschalk, L. A., Kaplan, S. M., Gleser, G. C., & Winget, C. M. Variations in magnitude of emotions: A method applied to anxiety and hostility during phases of the menstrual cycle. *Psychosomatic Medicine*, 1962, *24*, 300–311.

Hamburg, D., Moos, R. H., & Yalom, I. D. Studies of distress in the menstrual cycle and the postpartum period. In R. P. Michael (Ed.), *Endocrinology and human behavior*. London: Oxford University Press, 1968.

Ivey, M., & Bardwick, J. Patterns of affective fluctuation in the menstrual cycle. *Psychosomatic Medicine*, 1968, *30*, 336–345.

Kane, F., Daly, R., Ewing, J., & Keeler, M. Mood and behavioural changes with progestational agents. *British Journal of Psychiatry*, 1967, *113*, 265–268.

Kmenta, J. *Elements of econometrics*. New York: Macmillan, 1971.

Levitt, E., & Lubin, B. Some personality factors associated with menstrual complaints and menstrual attitude. *Journal of Psychosomatic Research*, 1967, *11*, 267–270.

Liskey, N. E. Accidents—rhythmic threat to females. *Accident Analysis & Prevention*, 1972, *4*(1), 1–11.

Luschen, M. E., & Pierce, D. M. Effect of the menstrual cycle on mood and sexual arousability. *Journal of Sex Research*, 1972, *8*, 41–47.

McCauley, E., & Ehrhardt, A. A. Female sexual response: Hormonal and behavioral interactions. *Primary Care*, 1976, *3*, 455–476.

McClintock, M. K. Menstrual synchrony and suppression. *Nature*, 1971, *229*, 244–245.

Michael, R. P., & Zumpe, D. Rhythmic changes in the copulatory frequency of rhesus monkeys (Macaca Mulatta) in relation to the menstrual cycle and a comparison with the human cycle. *Journal of Reproduction and Fertility*, 1970, *21*, 199–201.

Moos, R. H. The development of a menstrual distress questionnaire. *Psychosomatic Medicine*, 1968, *30*, 853–867.

Moos, R. H. Assessment of psychological concomitants of oral contraceptives. In H. A. Salhanick, D. M. Kipnis, & R. L. Vande Wiele (Eds.), *Metabolic effects of gonadal hormones and contraceptive steroids*. New York: Plenum Press, 1969. (a)

Moos, R. H. Typology of menstrual cycle symptoms. *American Journal of Obstetrics and Gynecology*, 1969, *103*, 390–402. (b)

Paige, K. E. Effects of oral contraceptives on affective fluctuations associated with the menstrual cycle. *Psychosomatic Medicine*, 1971, *33*, 515–537.

Parlee, M. B. The premenstrual syndrome. *Psychological Bulletin*, 1973, *80*(6), 454–465.

Patty, R. A., & Ferrell, M. M. A preliminary note on the motive to avoid success and the menstrual cycle. *Journal of Psychology*, 1974, *86*, 173–177.

Persky, H. Reproductive hormones, moods and the menstrual cycle. In R. C. Friedman, R. M. Richart, & R. O. Vande Wiele (Eds.), *Sex differences in behavior*. New York: Wiley, 1974.

Rossi, A. S. A biosocial perspective on parenting. *Daedalus*, 1977, *106*(2), 1–31.

Sommer, B. The effect of menstruation on cognitive and perceptual–motor behavior: A review. *Psychosomatic Medicine*, 1973, *35*(6), 515–534.

Sorensen, P. *Adolescent sexuality in contemporary America*. New York: World, 1973.

Sutherland, H., & Stewart, I. A critical analysis of the premenstrual syndrome. *Lancet*, 1965, *1*, 1180–1193.

Tanner, N., & Zihlman, A. Women in evolution: Innovation and selection in human origins. *Signs: Journal of Women in Culture and Society*, 1976, *1*(3), 585–608.

Udry, J. R., & Morris, N. M. Distribution of coitus in the menstrual cycle. *Nature*, 1968, *220*, 593–596.

Udry, J. B., Morrison, N. M., & Waller, L. Effect of contraceptive pills on sexual activity in the luteal phase of the human menstrual cycle. *Archives of Sexual Behavior*, 1973, *2*(3), 205–214.

Valette, A., Seradour, B., & Boyer, J. Plasma testosterone levels during the menstrual cycle. *Journal of Clinical Endocrinology and Metabolism*, 1974, *40*(1), 160–161.

Author Index

Subject Index